ABOUT THE AUTHOR

Shirley Camper Soman has been a longtime writer of popular material about children and families. Formerly the child-care columnist for *Redbook* and editor of *My Baby,* she is the author of *How to Get Along with Your Child* and *Let's Stop Destroying Our Children.* A social worker, she was for seven years family life consultant for The Family Service Association of America. She has lectured widely to parents and professional groups, chaired a number of conferences and committees—including the first National Child Advocacy Symposium—and has taught courses on child advocacy and children's rights.

Preparing for Your New Baby

PREPARING FOR YOUR NEW BABY

Shirley Camper Soman, ACSW

A DELTA BOOK

A DELTA BOOK
Published by Dell Publishing Co., Inc.
1 Dag Hammarskjold Plaza, New York, New York 10017

LIBRARY OF CONGRESS CATALOGING IN PUBLICATION DATA

Soman, Shirley Camper.
  Preparing for your new baby.

  "A Delta book."
  Includes index.
    1. Pregnancy. 2. Prenatal care. 3. Childbirth.
4. Infants—Care and hygiene. I. Title.
RG525.S64   618.2'4   81-22049
ISBN: 0-440-56136-1   AACR2

To all of my nieces and nephews, Marjorie Mann and Franklin Mann; David, Jonathan, Douglas, and Matthew Silverstein; and Eric, Sarah, and Abigail Mann, for all of the help they have given to me through the years in broadening my education about children.

And,

To my own children now adult, Fred and Francie, from whom as babies and growing children I received many of the most joyous, most ecstatic moments of my life.

And,

To the newest enchanting addition to my family, Alexandra Kathryn Levin, a Thanksgiving (1981) arrival.

Acknowledgments

This book was made possible only through the tremendously helpful creative abilities in both editing and writing of Marjorie P. K. Weiser and Judith Hendra. Both served as very capable editorial associates at different time periods.

My gratitude should also be expressed to The John Hancock Mutual Life Insurance Company for the use of some edited material from my publication "You and Your Baby," published by the company for a number of years.

My great thanks is also extended to the American Hospital Association for the valuable use of its study of hospital practices.

David and Lee Stewart, founders of the National Association of Parents and Professionals for Safe Alternatives in Childbirth and the publishers of a directory of such services, as well as *21st Century Obstetrics, Now!* and many other important volumes, have my enormous gratitude for their ready agreement to my use of material from these publications far beyond fair use. I also must thank them for opening my eyes and teaching me a new world about having a baby.

There are many, many other individuals and organizations who should be singled out for special thanks—beyond whatever credit line they may receive in the book itself. Some of these are:

. . . Ruth Lubic and the Maternity Center Association of New York for the use of their materials and pictures, and just for being there

. . . Doris Haire, and the National Foundation of Maternal and Child Health, for the tremendous amount of worldwide information I received from her, and for her long and continuing fight for better birth practices

. . . Eunice K. M. (Kitty) Ernst, C.N.M., M.P.H., and the founder of the Alternative Birth Center in Reading, Pennsylvania, as well as others, for both information and materials

. . . Lloyd deMause, the pioneering founder of the Psychohistory Press, The Journal of Psychohistory, and the International Psychohistory Association, and the author-editor of *The History of Childhood*, for his ready loan of historical pictures and materials, and most especially for helping to provide me with much more historical understanding than I believed possible

. . . Dan Kaufman for his wonderful home birth photographs

. . . The once-flourishing and always vitally important United States Children's Bureau for its magnificent publications, some of which are adapted on these pages and some directly quoted

. . . Robert B. O'Connell, who will be embarrassed by any attention paid to him since he has been an information official with the United States Department of Health and Human Services (I cannot fail to acknowledge his wonderful help from that wonderful department.)

. . . The National Institute of Mental Health for its research and materials

. . . The March of Dimes Birth Defects Foundation, and particularly their science writer, Dick Leavitt, who checked the genetic and birth defect material

. . . My friend, scientist Dr. Bob Dummel, a biochemist who gave me an overall science check

. . . The National Association of Science Writers which has helped me become much more knowledgeable about science and science journalism than I have been in the past

. . . Rockefeller University and Eugene and Estelle Kone who have also helped me become far more knowledgeable about health and science

. . . The New York Academy of Science for its incredible series of significant lectures, conferences, and tapes on science and health issues

. . . The still-magnificent New York Public Library

. . . The helpful United States Census Bureau and particularly two of its recently retired employees, Beulah Land and renowned statistician Dr. Paul Glick

. . . The Doubleday bookstores for staying open so late at night

. . . WCBS, WINS, WNYC, and WMCA, all New York radio stations with a great deal of feature news in the health areas

. . . The National Institute of Child Health and Development for supporting the basic research of Dr. James Prescott

. . . Barbara Sappinslee, a writer, who contributed some significant material for several sections

. . . My editors at Dell Publishing Company, Cara Erickson and, most especially, my continuing editor, Cynthia Vartan, for their uncanny ability to take a huge and unwieldy manuscript and shape it into a book

Beyond all of these, I am quite certain that there are many, many other helpful people and groups whom I have not acknowledged here or in the pages of this book. Since I am a person who believes very strongly in credit where credit is due, please forgive any unfortunate forgetfulness or oversight on my part. Also, if I inadvertently have stepped on someone's toes or turf, I do hope that that someone will also forgive and forget.

My purpose has been to inform and enlighten, and to help bring back the fun and joy that having a baby meant to me.

Oh, yes—last but more important than all other grateful acknowledgments are these:

To my late husband, Robert O. Soman, for asking me to do this book.

To my former husband and the father of my children for giving me the benefits of having two children.

Contents

What Is Happening to Your Baby-to-Be

FIRST MONTH

For the first seven weeks of life there is a precise daily developmental sequence, *an agenda of development*.

During the first 30 to 35 hours after a sperm penetrates an egg, these parent cells merge and become one—smaller than this period. This is fertilization.

The new cell develops two new nuclei, and the cell divides in two. (Each nucleus contains at least 15,000 genes, the vehicles that carry the hereditary material.)

A few hours later each of the two cells splits in two. This division continues as the cluster of cells (the blastocyst) moves down the fallopian tube, a journey of three days.

About a week after fertilization the dividing egg attaches itself to the lining of the womb (the uterus). This is the zygote.

During the second week hundreds of cells form and an embryonic shield develops. The placenta and umbilical cord are created together with their circulation.

During the third week there is an almost recognizable living being—an embryo—with a beating heart, a brain with two lobes, a spinal cord, a curved but straight body rather than a sphere. By the end of this week a basic circulatory system exists in this new being.

The fourth week brings about the traces of all internal body organs such as the kidneys, the digestive tract, and the liver. Rudimentary eyes and ears are formed.

The whole embryo is now ¼ to ½ inch long; its size has increased 10,000 times.

SECOND MONTH

Arms, shoulders, legs, hands, fingers, and toes begin to appear. Other facial features start to form—the eyes, the ears, the upper jaw and nose.

The embryo develops a face along with lips, tongue, and teeth buds.

On the same day that the rudimentary nose forms a tip and two air passages, the ears' internal hearing apparatus is almost complete, and the eyelids begin to form.

The internal organs start to work; the stomach produces digestive juices.

The beginning of this process changes the embryo to a fetus which is what it is called at the end of the ninth week.

Muscular reflexes occur, the fingers, thumbs, and even fingerprints appear toward the end of the month.

A complete skeleton made from cartilage exists in the sixth week, and toward the end of the month bone cells start to form.

The embryo now looks like a baby.

The head is quite large compared to the body.

The embryo weighs ¹/₃₀ of an ounce, and is one inch long.

THIRD MONTH

The external sexual organs are formed, so that male or female can be distinguished. Further, the fetus's reproductive organs carry sperm and egg cells.

Fingers and toes are almost complete. Fingernails begin to appear as do lifelong footprints and handprints.

The digestive tract grows, and the internal organs begin to shift into their permanent positions.

The vocal cords are formed, the taste buds appear, and the lips are completed.

All sorts of body functions show up in the third month: frowning, swallowing, kicking, urinating, sucking, head turning, plus wrist and thumb moving. Facial expressions are present and resemble those of adults.

The eyelids close over the eyes during the ninth week, for the first time, and stay closed until the sixth month.

By the end of this month every organ and part that the baby-to-be will have is present, although immature or nonfunctioning.

At the end of three months the fetus is 3 inches long and weighs less than an ounce.

FOURTH MONTH

Hair begins to grow, and eyebrows and eyelashes are present.

Hiccups occur; thumb sucking may start.

A stethoscope can pick up the fetal heartbeat.

The amniotic fluid in which the fetus lies has been gradually increasing, and by the end of the month it is more than one quart.

The skin is wrinkled, and red and thin. The blood vessels of the head and body are easily visible.

X rays reveal the skeleton of the body at this time.

The features of the face become clearer; the fetus looks more human.

The fetus becomes almost the same size as the placenta in this month. The placenta provides all nourishment to the fetus. It is the source of respiration and excretion. Its vessels, uncovered, resemble intertwining, intricate trees. *It is a prenatal tree of life.*

At the end of this month, the fetus is between 6 to 10 inches long and weighs between 6 to 8 ounces.

FIFTH MONTH

Fetal movements are felt by the mother. This is called quickening. (Some feel quickening at the end of the fourth month.)

The heartbeat is much stronger and may be heard with an ear to the mother's abdomen.

A white waxy substance—the vernix—covers the skin. (It gives protection to the skin in the liquid environment.) Fine downy hair—lanugo—appears on the body, even on the palms of the hands.

There is a grasp reflex which is a strong grip.

The fetus can hear sounds and is capable of being startled.

Fat is now being deposited under the skin, and iron is beginning to be stored. Fingernails start to harden.

The fetus sleeps and wakes in a regular pattern. Turning and moving—even head over heels—is frequent. The fetus finds a favorite position for most of the time. This is sometimes called a lie.

SIXTH MONTH

Buds, enamel, and dentine for the teeth begin to develop.

The fetus opens and shuts the eyelids during this month.

Breathing outside the womb can be sustained by the fetus for 24 hours if a premature birth occurs. But most babies born at this time do not survive.

The umbilical cord grows to its full length.

Fat continues to be deposited.

The brain is now well developed, but not entirely functional.

The fetus makes respiratory movements, stretches arms and legs, becomes quite a thumb sucker.

The baby is 12 to 15 inches long and weighs over 2 pounds.

SEVENTH MONTH

The male testes begin to descend into the scrotum.

The downy hair is shed from the body, usually.

Bumps on the mother's abdomen are clearly visible as the baby shifts a tiny fist or foot or moves the head.

The baby shifts around in response to pressure on the abdomen.

Fingernails reach fingertips.

Resistance to infection is still low and the fetus is too weak to nurse. But premature birth at this point gives the infant a far better chance to survive.

Body length is 16 inches, and the baby weighs about 3½ pounds.

EIGHTH MONTH

The skin is now smooth, and the baby is round, since fat deposits have continued.

Various necessary nutrients—iron, nitrogen, calcium, phosphorus—continue to be stored in large quantities.

The baby is wakeful for definite periods of time.

The baby is more than 90 percent likely to live if born now.

The infant now settles into a snug-fitting position, usually head down. (A feet-first position occurs with about 10 percent of the babies.) The baby moves from side to side rather than in somersault fashion.

The baby now measures about 18 inches in length and weighs 5½ pounds.

NINTH MONTH

Antibodies and gamma globulin in the blood of the "infant" equals the mother's during this month.

At any one time the baby's blood would measure only ½ pint—although hundreds of pints are pumped each day.

The smooth skin looks polished and is still covered with vernix.

The lanugo—or hair—may only be present on the shoulders and arms.

The baby's eyes are usually slate colored (no one can tell the final color at this point), and the scalp hair is dark. Some babies have hair as long or longer than one inch.

The week before birth no weight is gained.

The circumference of the baby's head equals that of the shoulders (thirteen inches) on the average.

The baby about to be born is around 20 inches long and weighs 7 pounds 6 ounces on the average.

What Is Happening to You

FIRST MONTH (0–4 weeks)

You miss your next menstrual period.

You may be nauseous in the morning, and tired often.

Your breasts swell, become more sensitive, and your nipples become broader.

Your ankles may swell.

Your uterus begins to soften and becomes spherical. It weighs two ounces and is three inches long.

Your pregnancy can last usually anywhere from 240 to 300 days, with the average being 266 days.

There will be bladder pressure, and quite possibly constipation.

SECOND MONTH (4–8 weeks)

You are likely to want to nap a lot. Fatigue is very common.

You may lose a little weight during this month.

Nausea, or "morning sickness," varies considerably from woman to woman, but if you experience it, it will occur, perhaps with vomiting, during the first 12 weeks. About half of all women have nausea.

The reasons for nausea are thought to be either emotional factors or due to changes in glucose metabolism and hormonal balance.

You will find a greater and more frequent need to urinate, because of increased pressure on your bladder.

Your uterus lengthens by another inch to 4 inches, and continues to change in shape and consistency.

THIRD MONTH (8–12 weeks)

Your breasts will become firmer and larger, and may be very tender.

Later in the month the area surrounding the nipples (the areola) will darken. The nipples may feel tingling or throbbing.

You may continue to feel drowsy and tired—but this tends to disappear at the end of this month.

The blood supply increases, the heart pumps harder, the pulse rate increases, the veins of the breasts may be very visible at this time.

At the end of the month the first enlargement of your stomach may become noticeable.

Just above the pelvic bone, you may feel a small lump—your uterus. It has now become 7 ounces in weight.

FOURTH MONTH (12–16 weeks)

By the sixteenth week, the phenomenon known as quickening usually occurs. This can feel like a butterfly fluttering, or there can be a stronger sensation of the feeling of life.

You're probably not nauseous anymore, and the pressure on your bladder is less.

A secondary areola—brownish spots on the skin surrounding the areola—may appear.

Vaginal discharge is increased; the very acid nature of the secretions is a deterrent to infections.

The uterus, by this time, weighs around 18 ounces. The placenta weighs 6 ounces.

Your average weight gain by now will be about 2 pounds per month, or eight pounds.

FIFTH MONTH (16–20 weeks)

About this time your "baby" begins to "show." Your uterus has expanded upward to your navel (about the twentieth week), and your abdomen reveals the result.

With the stretching of your skin you may feel itchiness. Also, stretch marks—known as striae—may appear. These are faint pink lines which will fade to tiny white marks after the baby is born. You may get darkening of the skin on your face.

Shortness of breath may occur, as well as some gum or nose bleeding. Backaches are likely.

Your energy level is likely to increase during these middle months.

Your breasts probably will not grow further until later in the pregnancy.

SIXTH MONTH (20–24 weeks)

The navel has stretched flat, and is now beginning to stick out because the uterus has continued to enlarge upward beyond it.

You will feel the fetus kicking, poking, and moving around in the temporary home of your body.

Dizziness and fainting is fairly common as a result of a drop in blood pressure which has resulted from the enlarged uterus's pressure on the major blood vessels.

Leg cramps may occur, suddenly and painfully, because of the uterus's pressure on the nerves going to the legs.

At this time you may be 10 to 12 pounds heavier.

The condition of both your skin and hair may improve.

SEVENTH MONTH (24–28 weeks)

There is a shift in the center of gravity which affects your posture, and can cause muscle cramps.

Sleeplessness may become common during these last months. A comfortable position can be hard to find.

As the uterus continues to push upward and crowd the lungs, you may feel somewhat short of breath.

Varicose veins are also common. The vein is stretched and enlarged which in turn thins out the vein wall. Hemorrhoids are varicose veins of the rectum.

Your average weight gain now totals about 20 pounds.

EIGHTH MONTH (28–32 weeks)

You are clearly "with child" by now—even to the unobservant. Your stomach, at times, seems to be all of you. You may or may not carry mostly in front and may carry high or low.

You may start to feel some mild contractions known as the Braxton Hicks.

You can see baby-style protrusions in your belly—an elbow, a knee, a foot—as your infant-to-be moves strongly around.

You may experience indigestion and even severe heartburn, because of the uterus pushing upward to meet the digestive system. Constipation may be a problem.

Edema—or puffiness of the ankles and hands—may become very marked.

The pelvic joints are softening to allow for the expanding weight of the fetus.

NINTH MONTH (32–36 weeks)

The uterus is now fully stretched out to its greatest height.

In many cases lightening occurs. This is a drop in the "baby's" position. Also, you will breathe a lot easier!

You may feel as though you are constantly needing to urinate, because of increased pressure on the bladder.

During these weeks you're likely to experience some bursts of energy—particularly during the few days before birth.

The cervix has flattened out and thinned.

Braxton-Hicks contractions are more frequent.

You are now about 24 to 28 pounds heavier.

The baby-to-be does not move much, owing to its snug position.

Most women deliver within a ten-day period of the due date, although some women can be several weeks "late."

Your Waiting–for–Baby Timetable

FIRST MONTH

1. Wonder . . . notice signs . . . relax.
2. Confirm pregnancy.
3. Celebrate . . . be joyous . . . but *give up* smoking, liquor, drugs.
4. Inquire about doctors, nurse/midwives, natural childbirth, husband-coached childbirth, courses.

SECOND MONTH

1. Get to the library or bookstore.
2. Talk to friends and family.
3. Decide on method of childbirth.
4. Interview doctors, midwives; visit hospitals, clinics, birthing centers, classes, and courses. Choose.
5. Get your first prenatal examination.

THIRD MONTH

1. Begin to estimate expenses; check your insurance and other money sources.
2. Start to make lists of needed maternity items, baby equipment, and clothing.
3. Start prenatal and baby courses.
4. Borrow, buy or make maternity wardrobe.
5. Examine your living space and arrangements.

FOURTH MONTH

1. Start to fix up your home *or*
2. Look for another place to live, if desirable.
3. Begin any long-term project for special items for the baby (knitting, carpentry, or whatever).
4. Figure out who is available to help out: make inquiries and arrangements.
5. Notify employers, parents and/or friends—anyone who may need to plan ahead.

FIFTH MONTH

1. Take an education-for-parenting course, and/or join or start a parents' group.
2. Borrow or buy or make layette and basic baby equipment.
3. Have discussions about feelings and caring and what you would do if . . . (to help you learn your reactions in advance and to help you cope with problems).
4. Take a vacation together.

SIXTH MONTH

1. Look into diaper services or other arrangements.
2. Start an exercise course, if you have not already.
3. Buy or make a special baby-arrival gift, just for your husband or wife.
4. Plan the birth day and the subsequent four weeks very carefully. (Stock up on needed supplies, check medicine chest, plan menus, figure out clean-ups, and who does what.)

SEVENTH MONTH

1. Inquire about pediatricians, general practitioners, well-baby clinics, emergency services. Interview several doctors and/or visit clinics.
2. Decide on names.
3. Talk to parents, in-laws, and other relatives on what they expect to do or not do.
4. Visit friends with babies. Watch.

EIGHTH MONTH

1. Choose your baby's doctor or clinic. Make or buy birth-announcement cards and address them.
2. Cook up a storm and pack several favorite meals in freezer containers.
3. Do a last check on how baby-crawler-toddler-proofed your home really is.
4. Pack two suitcases if you are to go to the hospital or birth center. *And/or,* if yours will be a home birth, make sure your supplies are all on hand.

NINTH MONTH

1. Get camera and film, tape recorder, and extra tapes ready, with labels, boxes, photo albums, and ready pens for marking.
2. Practice your breathing.
3. Relax. Rest. Dream.
4. Write a letter to your very own baby-to-come.

*Childbirth compels me because it is a living process,
and as such it teaches me about movement, change and
about continually facing fear and the unknown. It has
added to my life by teaching me about ritual and things
outside my control. . . . Childbirth teaches me about
the way life really is, which is movement and process
and continual growth.*

SUZANNE ARMS

Introduction

To have a baby is the most intensely personal and private event in anyone's life. Yet the giving of life is, in the largest sense, the event most involved with everyone else's life. The individual history of each of us is partly replicated in each childbirth, in each baby. More, the history of the human race—its physiology, its anthropology, its development—is a microcosm within that continuum of cells, zygote, embryo, fetus, baby, child, and adult. A raindrop contains the basic secrets of life. A baby contains that plus the secrets of poetry, of philosophy, of theology, of art, of emotion, of intelligence.

History—does it really matter to your baby's birth? Actually, history probably matters more than any single aspect of life—other than the sheer biology involved—to the process of growing and having a baby. Individual *and* group *and* human history.

The birth of that tiny, new human through the centuries has been the province of each of us—and of everyone we know. We were all born. We all had mothers and fathers who gave us life. We all were babies and children. We all have memories and emotions concerning our births, our families, our growing.

Each time a baby is born, all of the history of childbearing is repeated in that one birth. The relationship of mother to *her* mother, the far closer feeling that is engendered. The feelings of love and concern *and* ambivalence between father and mother about parenthood. The feelings between man and woman about each other in their new roles. The sense of seeking for family and ancestry and rootedness for the baby. The sense of total newness along with the sense of the ancient. Through time, history *is* repetitive—but birth is also unique to each person, as each participates in the extraordinary process of making his or her own history. There is a continuum, a chain—yet each birth is different. Each pregnancy, each baby is like every other—but each is unique.

This paradox is perhaps part of the mystery of creation—a creation celebrated and explored, probed and ritualized through the centuries, and still today, by poets and artists, scientists and philosophers, theologians and just plain parents. The birth of a baby has had vast effects upon and implications for every field of human endeavor.

And that baby, that new human alone, may have the capacity, the potentiality to be anyone. You or me. Pericles or Attila. Leonardo or Caesar. Jane Addams or Lucretia Borgia. Gandhi or Stalin. With all of the possibilities for good or ill, or any mix thereof, that a human being is heir to.

When I read about some incredibly brutal action one of us has committed, my mind automatically pictures a baby. That person *was* a baby once—a quizzical, searching, soft piece of humanity, all innocence and unknowingness. What went wrong?

Or when I meet someone who has spent a lifetime trying to alleviate the suffering of other people, or creating works of incredible beauty, I again picture a baby seeking and finding, joyful and developing. What went right?

Some of what happened—right or wrong—seems to be involved with the actual growing and birthing of a baby, as well as the very earliest care of that infant. Some of what happened involves our history, the history of our changing psychology, our changing conceptions of birth and babyhood. And some of what happened to any of us is intimately involved with our governments and our society. Some bureaucrat in Washington, for example, can with one decision change your baby's life totally. Remember thalidomide?

For these reasons this book—a labor of love for me—contains material not usually included in books about having a baby. Historical references, for one thing. Although the historical quotes are essentially lighthearted, it is important to know something about baby making of times past. The book covers a wide spectrum of issues because I believe that it is vital for parents-to-be to know. To learn as much as possible about the entire process of life giving, about the history and the psychohistory, about the anatomy and psychology, about the ways of other cultures and the impact of society upon young families.

The book demonstrates this author's belief that having a baby is a totality. At the end, which is a beginning, at the baby's birth, you experience a total, a whole, made up of all the pieces and parts of living and growing a new being. And for parents-on-the-way, if possible, there should be total involvement, total knowledge, total caring, total understanding. So that the totality of your new family will be perceived and appreciated for what it is—a miracle.

Of course, it is not possible to know and be and do all things. But in the attempt to learn everything, there will be a stretching of the mind, of the perceptions, perhaps of the feelings—along with the stretching of the body and way of life.

For while having a baby is individual, just you and the baby—it is also you and the baby and all of humanity. And perhaps the most wondrous aspect of this process is its place in human experience.

Part One

ON YOUR WAY TO A BABY

*The most important task anyone can ever undertake is
the making of a human being. Hence, no one should
ever undertake parenthood unless they are fully
equipped to meet all the challenges and assume all the
responsibilities which that very onerous but enormously
gratifying task involves. Genitorship should not be
mistaken for parenthood. Anyone can become a genitor
in a matter of a few minutes, but parenthood is an art,
the most important of all the arts and professions, and
the most rewarding. The essence of good parenthood is
in the communication of love to the child, the love that
has a creative quality and a discipline that nothing else
can equal.*

DR. ASHLEY MONTAGU

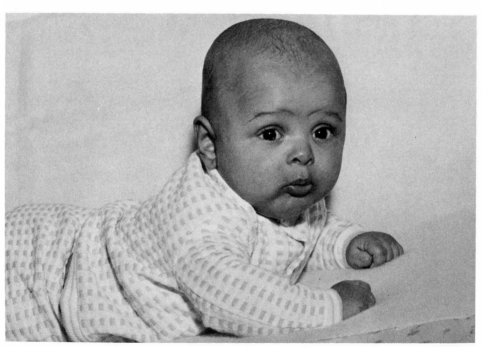

DHEW

All About Babies

Take the average baby. That baby won't be yours. Yours will seem far from average—cuter, livelier, stronger, more intelligent. But let's take the average anyhow, just as a starting point. What is this baby like—this tiny average—during those first weeks in the world?

First of all, this "average" baby weighs about seven pounds plus at birth, and gains about four to seven ounces a week. (He or she will lose in the hospital, however.) This baby is between eighteen and twenty-one inches long, with skin as soft as silk, and eyes of blue (which may change color later on). The baby's hair—if there is any at all—is flyaway fuzz. The baby's legs and arms seem rubbery. The baby has a soft spot at the top of the head, and no teeth—the first one comes at about five to seven months.

What does this baby do—this little average? He or she cries, naturally—this is the only way a baby can signal. And the nature of the cry often changes with different circumstances. The baby sucks. The baby waves arms and legs all around haphazardly—and sometimes accidentally scratches that tiny baby body with those tiny baby nails. The baby sleeps. Usually for a good part of the night, and two naps a day. But the baby also stays awake, sometimes when you least want a wakeful infant on your hands.

Average or not, the baby burps—and, alas, spits up. (They all do.) Wetting diapers is a frequent baby activity!

The baby's eyes follow a bright light. And at four weeks, they follow a moving object. Usually she or he makes burbling noises. But at other times just listens. The baby's facial expressions change from satisfaction to curiosity to disgust. He or she makes a fist and holds on to a small something tightly. The baby rolls a little—sometimes *over*—even in the early weeks. He or she lifts that little head and turns it when lying on that round belly. This baby, any baby, seems to be afraid of two things—a falling sensation and loud noises.

Sometimes the baby smiles. Doctors will tell you that new babies who smile before they are a month or two old are merely reacting to gas bubbles which distort their lips. But no parent believes a word of this. Every parent's baby smiles. Also, we are told, this just-born cannot recognize individual people. But no new parent believes this either. You'll be convinced that *your* baby sees *you*. And now scientists agree.

What can't this average baby do? He or she can't talk or chew, walk or sit. The baby can't reach out for something. The baby can't hold his or her back up straight. And that little average infant can't play in the usual sense because he or she can't control the body's muscles. Or time or withhold bodily functions for the same reason. Essentially, the average baby, your baby, any baby can't control anything about his or her body or environment. Despite all a new baby *can* do, an infant is pretty helpless. No baby would survive without considerable care.

As a result, what your baby needs from you is—almost everything. Certainly, everything that governs health and safety, growth and development, future abilities. What does this include? Food, cleanliness, warmth; the conditions that ensure sleep and rest, the safety and security of whatever place your baby is in—crib, tub, carriage, or your arms; communication with the world outside of your baby's body and toes (which are discovered at an early age); and finally, your baby needs you for a sense of well-being, of physical and emotional satisfaction.

This is a large order for new, inexperienced parents. You were free as a bird and now you are tied to a creature who relies on you almost completely for the very breath of life. But consider the tremendous joys and compensations you will have: the fun your very own child will bring you because your baby *is* yours and young and unconcerned with the world's cares; the sense of achievement you will feel when you understand what your baby *can't* do and *can* do—and as a result find better ways to care for and enjoy this growing infant; your own firm position in the world of parents and families; your baby's first mighty grin at *you* and your baby's many momentous discoveries, and how fresh your own view of the world will be when you see it through a baby's eyes; and the continuous, ever-present fact that this new human being brings more than the presence of a new baby—your baby's very existence establishes *a new family*.

How It All Begins

THE BEAUTY AND
THE MYSTERY

Love is basic to babies. To making them. To growing them. To birthing them. True, there are babies conceived and born without love. And some babies can grow and develop with a very inadequate semblance of love. But the most beautiful fact about most babies, and the most mysterious, is the love that they represent and engender. Most diagrams and texts about life's beginnings are mechanical, dry facts added to facts. They cannot adequately evoke the beauty, the wonder, the mystery, indeed the marvelous fact of Nature's love that goes into the making of a new human life, a new intelligence. Look with me for a moment at the wondrous facts themselves.

One of the greatest mysteries of life is the coming together of sperm and egg that takes place at the brief time period when one egg is ready to be penetrated. This is a mystery in itself, such a short time is the egg fertile. Then consider the role of the sperm—millions upon millions of those microscopic long-tailed swimming fertilizers which make their way up the long cervical canal in perhaps the most incredible migration in nature. Somehow only one of those millions will reach the fertile egg in the uterus. And mystery of mysteries, that infinitesimal projectile of sperm will penetrate the wall of the egg. Then suddenly a new life begins.

DIVIDING AND GROWING

Next the sperm and the egg fuse together to form one cell. Then the miracle of cell di-

vision occurs. From that one cell two are formed (thirty hours later), then four, then eight, then sixteen—each cell dividing and enlarging the whole.

Soon this still-microscopic being becomes implanted in the wall of the uterus. The placenta—a whole cosmos of nourishment—forms.

The umbilical cord, the lifeline between this still-extraordinary, tiny new being and the mother's body, develops. This cord contains three blood vessels that carry food into the fetus and remove waste from the fetus and placenta.

Just consider for a moment the remarkable events that have occurred up to now.

The love that has brought a brief time of man and woman joined; the few moments in the 43,200 minutes of a given month that one egg is ready to be fertilized by one sperm; the one-in-millions sperm (sometimes as many as 350 million!) that will succeed in reaching that egg; the new cell that then begins to divide, to find its own place and food. Remarkable? Surely as dramatic and astonishing as any miracle of any age. The frequency of its occurrence can only increase our wonder, for then—

THE DRAMA AND THE UNIQUENESS

—the drama and the miracle continue to build, since the being who is now forming is quite unique, like but unlike any other on the face of the earth. This not-yet-baby carries within its tiny not-yet-formed body every characteristic for an individual human life, from eyelash length and color to toe size and shape to style of temperament and potential for brilliance. Here within those new dividing cells are the almost never-to-be-duplicated fingerprints of a new individual, the voice that belongs to only one person, the kind of walk, the lift of brow, the tilt of head, the never-duplicated totality of each human being. All within that tiny and growing speck of living transistor.

This tiny being, at seven weeks of age, shapes a head and body and grows buds for arms and legs. There are indentations for eye sockets, a spot for a mouth, a beginning of inside parts and pieces. It-he-she rests in a warm, comfortable, enveloping fluid and yet "breathes" through the umbilical cord. The fluid cushions movements and insulates against noise, and the growing baby-to-be rocks and sways gently within.

THE CHANGES

As the time passes, a complex chain of events is set in motion. The mother-to-be changes. Her breasts are preparing to carry a milk supply; her internal and external organs begin to stretch and compress; her emotions are heightened. The fetus within

her begins more closely to resemble a baby; in a matter of months it will be an actual *human* being capable of living in our air, in our environment.

The drama builds as the "baby's" body becomes better prepared for our life. And then, about nine months after that act of physical joining, of expressed love between a mother- and father-to-be—the entire sequence of events comes to a crescendo in the climax of birth.

A miracle, repeated over and over, millions and millions of times through the centuries, and *many thousands of times on that special day—your baby's day*. A miracle of every kind of love, of human experience repeated and repeated . . .

And still a miracle of the unique, of the never-to-be-repeated in your lives and in your newborn's life.

For the most incredible aspect of the entire drama of baby making is that quality of sharing in a miracle with everyone else who has been born or who has become a parent—an experience which is nonetheless yours alone, your personal miracle of life and love for another being.

How It Used to Be

The time of the month at which conception takes place is considered . . . to have an influence upon the sex of the offspring. If conception takes place soon after the cessation of menstruation, the child is more liable to be a girl, while if it takes place just before a menstrual period the child is liable to be a boy.*

Edith B. Lowry, M.D., *Your Baby*, 1915

*These notions are, of course, completely false. Conception can take place *only* at the time of ovulation.

A Pinch for the Testicle and *Voilà!* A Boy

Everywhere, it seems, boys are the preferred sex . . .

In parts of Austria, some peasants believe that a year with a good nut harvest will also yield an abundance of boys. To help things along, midwives frequently bury the afterbirth under a nut tree—thus supposedly making sure that the next child will be a boy. In parts of Czechoslovakia, the bride lets a

small boy step on her hands, while in southern Yugoslavia the couple takes a boy to bed with them on their wedding night, again in the effort to beget a son.

In many of the Slavic countries, the wife is directed to pinch her husband's right testicle during intercourse. In the Italian province of Modena, the husband bites his wife's right ear. And in the backwoods of Pennsylvania some men still hang their pants on the right side of the bed if they want a boy, on the left side if they want a girl. (David M.

Rorvik and Landrum B. Shettles, M.D., *Your Baby's Sex: Now You Can Choose*, 1970)

Boy or Girl?—Food Can Tell

The food you eat can be stressful, too, if you are getting a poor balance of acid and alkaline foods. Inasmuch as such substances as caffeine, potassium iodide, baking soda, and vinegar can have an impact on sex ratios, we believe that diet should not be entirely overlooked. (Consider, too, the reports we cite showing that women exposed to LSD almost always give birth to females.) What we take into our bodies *can* have an effect on the sex of our offspring. Our knowledge in this area is rudimentary (the nutritional sciences in general are still very young), but it appears that a "safe" diet is one in which a *majority* of your foods are alkaline. This is true for *both* men *and* women whether you are interested in conceiving boys or girls. Never let the acids in your diet predominate, even if you are trying for a girl. If you are trying for a boy, however, you may safely and beneficially increase your relative intake of alkaline foods, if you like. (David M. Rorvik and Landrum B. Shettles, M.D., *Choose Your Baby's Sex*, 1977)

Author's Note: Popular opinion suggests that providing an acid environment may help produce a female child. Last year, when friends of mine were determined to conceive a girl, the wife used a vinegar douche to provide an acid environment. It worked!

How It Used to Be

All recent authorities agree that conception is more assured when the two individuals who cooperate in it participate at the same time in the transports of which it is the fruit. The disposition of the woman at the time of conception has much power in the formation of the foetus, both in modifying its physical constitution and in determining the character and temperament of its mind.

> George H. Napheys, M.D., *The Physical Life of Women: Advice to the Maiden, Wife and Mother*, 1889

FERTILITY BY THE NUMBERS

A woman will release between 300 and 400 ova during her reproductive lifetime.

A man will release hundreds of millions of living sperm in a single ejaculation—about three milliliters or ³/₅ teaspoon of fluid.

There are more than 350,000,000 spermatozoa in a cubic centimeter of semen. But only one sperm is necessary to fertilize an egg.

When a baby girl is born, her ovaries contain about 2 million egg follicles, each of which might become an ovum. But most of them disappear, until only about 300,000 remain at puberty—still many more than will be needed.

A mature ovum measures $1/175$ of an inch in diameter and weighs about $1/20$ of a millionth of an ounce.

A sperm measures about $1/500$ of an inch in length.

An egg is 90,000 times as large overall as a sperm.

In nonpregnant women the uterus is only 6½ to 8 centimeters—about 2½ to 3 inches—long.

The fallopian tubes are about 4½ inches long.

Sperm swim together in formation for a distance of about 6 to 7 inches in order for one of them to cause impregnation. The journey can take anywhere from 5 minutes to 2 hours. Most swim at the rate of an inch in 20 minutes.

The egg's journey down the fallopian tube and into the uterus—about 4½ inches—takes about 3 days!

In 9 months a fertilized egg grows from that one cell (of sperm and egg) to about the 5 trillion of a newborn human baby.

HOW WE HAVE LEARNED ABOUT CONCEPTION

In 1677 the Dutch scientist Anton van Leeuwenhoek became the first person to see a live sperm cell in a drop of semen under the microscope.

In 1827 a mammalian egg cell (from the ovary of a dog) was seen through a microscope for the first time by the Estonian biologist Karl Ernst von Baer.

Later in the nineteenth century the cell, the basic structural unit or "building block" of life, was discovered by two German scientists, Matthias Schleiden and Theodor Schwann, and it was recognized that the egg and sperm were cells.

In 1930 a mature human egg cell was observed leaving an ovary.

In 1944 the combining of egg and sperm was observed.

In the 1950s the changes that take place during the first week following conception were first accurately described.

In the 1960s the ways in which our cells develop according to the unique heredity of each individual began to be understood.

In 1978 the first "test tube" baby was born in England. The egg was fertilized outside of the mother's body, and then inserted back in the uterus where it continued to grow.

YOUR UNBORN "BABY" DEVELOPS

At the place in the wall of the uterus where the fertilized egg has become attached, an organ called a *placenta* begins to grow, and will take three months to be fully formed. The placenta is disk-shaped, slightly raised, and covered by a transparent membrane. It generally measures 7 inches across and 1 inch thick, and weighs about 1½ pounds. Blood from the mother and from the "baby" (now called the *fetus*) circulate through it.

Blood from the fetus flows in and out through two arteries and a vein, encased in the *umbilical cord*, which attaches to the surface of the placenta at one end and to the "baby's" navel at the other. The waste products of the fetus are carried through the arteries of the umbilical cord into the placenta, where they are exchanged for oxygen and nutrients from the mother. The vein in the cord carries these materials back to the "baby." The basic purpose of the placenta is to make this interchange possible. The placenta emerges from the mother's body after the baby is born. You have probably heard it referred to as the "afterbirth."

During the first week of life within the uterus, your future baby is a group of tiny cells, the blastocyst. The enlarging cluster of cells is at first called a *zygote*, then an *embryo*, then a *fetus*.

About two weeks after conception an embryo is still barely large enough to be seen with the naked eye. The place where a head and brain will later develop is growing very fast, however, and there are little indentations where the eyes will be.

At the end of four weeks your "baby" is still only about a quarter of an inch long. This is a particularly important time because now the internal organs—heart, liver, digestive system, brain, and lungs—are beginning to form. The heart begins to beat, although no one will be able to hear it for many weeks. This is when you are probably beginning to think that you may be pregnant.

At five weeks the embryo is the shape of a tiny quarter-moon. The backbone has started to form. Most of the bone in the body is first laid down in the form of cartilage, the flexible semibony material which adults still have in the nose and ears. The head is growing much faster than the rest of the body and will keep on doing so until after the baby is born. Tiny limb buds appear, the beginnings of arms and legs. At six weeks the baby-to-be is almost half an inch long. The four limb-buds have started to grow into arms and legs.

By the seventh week ears and eyelids are

forming and the internal organs are moving into place. The embryo is now floating in a sac of fluid that is sometimes called the "bag of waters" or the amniotic sac. If you are wondering why the embryo doesn't drown, there is a simple answer: it cannot because it does not use lungs to get oxygen until the baby comes out into the air at birth. The embryo gets all the oxygen needed from your blood. The fluid evenly warms and also acts as a shock absorber to protect it from any jolts or bumps caused by your own activity.

After the eighth week the embryo is called a fetus. *In the third month* of pregnancy, it is about two and a half inches long and weighs about an ounce. The "mother's" abdomen is beginning to enlarge. The "baby's" fingers and toes are usually well formed by the fourth month and tiny nails begin to show. The back is still curved like a bow, but the head is straightening up. A little hair, usually dark, is starting to grow on the scalp and teeth are forming, deep in the gums. In both sexes the external sex organs have now appeared. *At sixteen weeks* the fetus is 4 to 5 inches long and weighs about 4 ounces. The muscles are active and you may feel their contractions.

Sometimes during *the fifth month* the doctor may hear the first faint fetal heartbeat through the stethoscope. You will probably notice light fluttering movements as the fetus stretches its arms and legs. These movements begin about five calendar months before the expected time of birth, so it is well to make a note of the date. *At twenty weeks* the "baby" is about 8 inches long and ten and a half ounces in weight. Now the pregnancy really begins to show.

From this time on, the mother's abdomen will get bigger quite rapidly. *By the sixth month* the "baby's" movements are real thumps. You may at times be able to see them. Sometimes the fetus lies on one side, sometimes on the other, sometimes with head down, sometimes with it up. At *about seven months* along the baby-to-be will probably assume one position and keep it until after birth. At times you may not feel the "baby" at all. "Babies" have periods of waking and sleeping before they are born, just as they do afterward.

During the last two or three months of uterine life, a "baby" grows "tall" very fast, and gets his or her body fat. This fatty tissue stores energy and helps regulate body temperature. *From the sixth month on* until shortly before birth, he or she is covered with downy fuzz. A soft creamy substance called vernix begins to form on the body. By that time the unborn infant has gained about half of his or her birth weight.

During the eighth and ninth months the "baby" becomes more and more like the typical full-term child. The cartilages of nose and ears develop. The nails, still paper thin, grow beyond the tips of fingers and toes. The bones of the skull become harder and more closely knit. The hair on the head grows longer. The eyes, like the eyes of all newborn babies, are slate-blue. You will not be able to tell, when the baby is born, what color the eyes will be later on.

How It Used to Be

The influence of the health, occupations, desires and thoughts of the expectant mother upon her unborn child cannot be overestimated. At what period the greatest influence is exerted can only be a matter of conjecture. Some who have given this matter considerable thought have decided that during the first three months of the embryo the laws for physical perfection are especially in force. The second three months of the unborn child are considered by some to be the period during which the mental capacity of the child is influenced; therefore during this period the mother should be moderately active intellectually.

The last three months have been considered to be the moral prenatal period.

Edith B. Lowry, M.D., *Your Baby*, 1915

The First Generation

We are the first generation to be able to have a clear picture of the course of our development from a single cell to an individual, active and responsive to our environment long before birth. We are also the first to know the full history of our earliest hours and days. (Geraldine Lux Flanagan, *The First Nine Months of Life*, 1962)

First Steps, First Tests

WHEN WILL THE BABY ARRIVE?

Conception can only occur for about twelve hours following ovulation. Usually the exact day of ovulation cannot be determined. Therefore, it is customary to use the first day of the last menstrual period as a guide to the birth date.

How long your pregnancy will last is difficult to pinpoint: the duration changes for different women, or even for different pregnancies in the same woman. But here is the "formula."

For those women whose menstrual cycle is two or more days longer or shorter than the usual 28 days, or for those who menstruate irregularly, this method of figuring birth date will not be accurate. Then, too, sometimes the beginning of pregnancy has gone by unnoticed. In all of these cases the doctor can determine the approximate delivery date from the first movement of the "baby." Your happy fetus usually moves around near the end of the fourth month, and this movement indicates that there are five more months to go. It should be possible to determine the approximate week or two (not a particular day) during which the baby can be expected. You might figure an average of 266 days or 38 weeks.

One piece of important advice: Don't try to hurry your baby's arrival by running, jumping, engaging in hard physical work, or using a physic. Such an attempt may well harm you or the baby.

◇ ◇ ◇

Pregnancy Is Not Illness

Prenatal care is a form of preventive medicine, for when we are pregnant we are not sick. Our goal in seeing our doctor is to prevent sickness. (Boston Women's Health Book Collective, *Our Bodies, Ourselves*, 1971)

◇ ◇ ◇

HOW TO FIGURE YOUR BABY'S ARRIVAL DATE

Example:

First day of the last menstrual period
February 12
_____

Minus 3 months (count backward)
November 12
_____

Plus 7 days = delivery date
November 19
_____

Your own delivery date:

First day of the last menstrual period
_____

Minus 3 months (count backward)
_____

Plus 7 days = delivery date
_____

WHY EARLY MEDICAL CARE IS ESSENTIAL

It is very important that you receive early medical attention. You will find material on choosing a doctor or other birth attendant and on selecting a hospital or other place of birth in Part Three. In the meantime here are some of the reasons why you should consult a doctor quickly:

• You and your doctor or midwife or clinic will be better able to determine the date of the baby's arrival fairly accurately if you still remember the dates of your last menstrual period.
• You'll have enough time to establish a good working relationship with your doctor, midwife or clinic—or to look around for another one if necessary.
• Mothers who do *not* get prenatal care have a greater chance of having babies with severe medical problems. The chances of a premature birth, a malnourished or diseased infant, or a stillbirth are all greater if there is no care before the baby is born.

For instance, you may without knowing it have a venereal disease that could harm your baby. Such diseases in a woman usually do not have obvious symptoms. To find VD, tests are needed. Once identified and treated, VD can be cured and the unborn "baby" will be fine. But untreated, syphilis may cause several kinds of birth defects or a stillbirth; untreated, gonorrhea may cause blindness in the baby.

Early checking is vital. In the very earliest weeks, the developing "baby" may be injured by radiation, drugs, certain illnesses of the mother, or other factors.

Checked, tested, instructed, and possibly treated, you can relax and enjoy your pregnancy with the happy knowledge that you are giving the best possible physical start in life to your baby-to-be.

YOU CAN (ALMOST) HAVE THE BABY YOU WANT

Healthy. Intelligent. Active. Good-natured. All of these are the qualities we all want in our new baby. And now we're almost there. Such qualities can *almost* be planned for.

They are *almost* predictable.

Experience and science have brought us to the state of knowledge that may produce a far better generation than ours. Certainly, we are close to that capability. How can we tell? Let's look at the major areas that affect the kind of baby you will have.

YOUR NUTRITION

It is now a collection of scientific facts that your own good nutrition has a direct effect upon your baby's weight, health, and potential brain power. How well or poorly nourished you were before pregnancy, even how well nourished your mother was, can make a large difference.

Even the nausea that occurs in every fourth woman is in an overwhelming number of cases (80 percent) the result of a lack of vitamin B_6, according to renowned authority Dr. Lendon H. Smith.

Adequate nutrition also affects the intelligence of children. One double-blind study of retarded children showed a 10- or 20-point increase in the IQs of many after some months of a simple vitamin program.

YOUR EXERCISE

It is now well recognized, if not yet scientifically proven, that certain kinds of exercise during pregnancy can help make the delivery far easier—thereby avoiding problems that can affect the baby's health and well-being. Exercise in your earlier years makes a healthier you; therefore your baby's housing and ease of passage may be much better. You may not be able to stretch bones to accommodate a too-large head, but exercise can certainly help increase the stretch of the muscles, and the nerves, and the tissues. It also can ease the stressful sensations of birth in many instances.

YOUR SENSE OF WELL-BEING

Physical condition affects attitude very directly, as do many other factors. Your good health is primary, but, with or without that, the ability to "engineer" one's own attitudes and, in effect, one's own sense of well-being is almost attainable. Group support *and* approval is a major factor, as is that of one other well-loved person—husband, mother, father. Happiness during pregnancy—or its converse—can make a significant difference in the personality of your baby, in my opinion. The lovely sounds of music and the beauty of art were recommendations of old. They should be prescribed currently.

THE GENES

Not yet there, but close, is the ability to splice into a mammalian cell a single healthy gene which could overcome or replace a defective one. The tremendous technological advance of identifying and using recombinant DNA will, according to scientists, lead to the prevention of genetic defects. In a way, we *are* "cleaning up" our genes, so to speak, with the major advances of genetic counseling, early abortion, artificial insemination, and, potentially, of test-tube babies. However, when genetic engineering is really in full stride, we will be able to have babies without the major gene curses of our time.

THE ENVIRONMENT

No baby will need suffer from the genetic defects and other problems engendered by an unsafe and polluted environment. We know enough now, and have the ability, to prevent most of the large-scale or even individual disasters that face young couples. There is still *much* to learn—like how to ensure that PCBs and pesticides are not in mother's milk, and what to do with the nuclear waste we have collected, plus the nuclear bomb test materials (like strontium 90) which are still polluting the atmosphere, without pregnant parents and unborn babies being adversely affected. But we already largely can protect ourselves and our babies-to-be-born on an individual basis. And if our society made a *big* commitment and a large scientific push . . .

More, we certainly know enough to provide decent housing and decent living conditions for *every* baby-to-be. We *have* the resources. All we need do is define "decent" for our own children and work for it.

YOUR KNOWLEDGE OF
PREGNANCY AND CHILDBIRTH

If you learn enough early on, your choices will be informed and geared toward the best results for your baby. You will ensure your own nutrition and exercise, your own environmental controls (as much as possible). And, you will avoid all drugs before and

during, and instruct your doctor or other care-giver to do so, except in life-threatening situations. You will inspect America's way of birth with a careful eye and learn how to protect yourself and your baby-to-be.

YOUR KNOWLEDGE OF
BABIES AND BABY CARE

The key factor from earliest moments on (after physical/mental health and brain cells) is your own responsiveness. All else fades into the background if you can respond to your baby, and express it, in growth-enhancing ways. Even physical handicaps and insufficient intelligence and bad environmental conditions are usually less significant than your very own reactions, and your way of showing them, to your very own baby. *Love* can bring you a healthy, bright, happy baby—almost always. Love and knowledge are the two most important values for the best baby-growing. They are both intangibles, whose effects are clear and visible, even in a foggy atmosphere.

Be your own birth politician.

POSTSCRIPT

I believe that with my present knowledge, it would be possible for me to select a dozen couples and predict which ones are most likely to have the brightest babies. More, I think I could "engineer" a large number of gifted babies in a group of pre-pregnancy couples—if I were able to instruct them on how to manage *The Baby Year!*

Anyone for genius?

THE FIRST VISIT

After you know you're pregnant, you may go to your own private doctor or to a doctor who specializes in pregnancy and delivery, an obstetrician. Or you may first visit a clinic, a women's service, a nurse-midwife, or an obstetrical team. But wherever you go and whomever you see, the first medical examination in pregnancy is the same. If any area is left out in your own examination, *ask why*. If necessary, speak up, or go elsewhere.

Here is what *should* be included:

A thorough medical history (your menstrual history and record of previous pregnancies, miscarriages, abortions and births; chronic or major illnesses or operations; recent inoculations and any medications taken either recently or regularly)

A family medical history (information on the gynecological and obstetric history of your mother and perhaps other women relatives—aunts and grandmothers)

A complete physical examination (height, weight, blood pressure, breathing, heart)

Blood tests (to determine your blood type and whether you are Rh-negative, and to test for anemia, rubella, and venereal disease)

Urinalysis (to test for diabetes, kidney function, and infection of the urinary tract)

Breast examination

Internal examination (of the vaginal canal, cervix and uterus, including "Pap" smear to test for cervical cancer)

Almost always the first medical examination of pregnancy will confirm what you already know. But in a very small number of cases—fewer than five percent—the indications may be inconclusive. It may be too early in the pregnancy for the signals to show up clearly. Just waiting a week or two will bring the answer.

But because some symptoms of pregnancy could also be caused by other conditions, a laboratory test might be needed. In such cases prompt and accurate diagnosis is essential for the woman's health. Perhaps two percent of the time, the doctor may decide that a chemical diagnosis is called for.

These standard tests are routine precautions, designed to guard your health and that of your baby. They can pinpoint in advance potential problems of infection or disease; and early detection of any condition ensures plenty of time for treatment.

So if it seems that an awful lot of testing is being done, don't worry—you probably don't have anemia, rubella, diabetes, or whatever. But it's best to know for sure. If you're not certain whether a specific test has been done, be sure to ask.

You may not be asked much about your working conditions or home environment, but these can be vital. Describe your job and what you do right away. Volunteer all the information you can think of, since chemicals in your job or home surroundings may have a negative effect upon your "baby."

THE INTERNAL EXAMINATION

Perhaps your insides have never been inspected before. You may be shy or uncomfortable or afraid—you don't know what to expect. Well, here's a detail-by-detail description.

You'll be shown into a small room with an examining table, a scale, one or two chairs, possibly a sink. You'll need to undress completely. The laboratory gown you'll put on ties in the back. You may want to wear your shoes on your bare feet.

A nurse or an aide in a doctor's office will probably bring in your chart, take your weight, height, and perhaps blood pressure. Then you'll ascend the examining table, which is covered by a sterile pad or sheet.

You may have to wait until the doctor or nurse-midwife comes in. Then you'll lie down on the table with your knees up and spread apart. Your feet will rest in supports (stirrups) at either side of the table. When you are in this strange position, your reproductive system is easier to examine. It's hard sometimes not to tense up at first—but the more you can relax, the better.

While you are lying down, the doctor puts a metal instrument called a *speculum* into your vagina. The instrument spreads the walls of the vagina apart so your cervix and uterus can be seen. The speculum may feel cold or tight and uncomfortable, but it's not painful. With the speculum in place, the Pap test for cancer can be done. The doctor lightly scrapes the cervix wall to remove some cells, which are then placed on a slide and sent to a laboratory. In a few days you'll receive a card or note from the laboratory saying that all is well. A test for gonorrhea is made at this time, too.

After the speculum is withdrawn, the doctor or nurse-midwife will need to examine you with his or her fingers covered by a sterile glove. The doctor will be able to feel that your uterus is soft and beginning to enlarge, even in the first month of pregnancy.

Your breasts will be examined while you're lying down, and again when you're sitting up. If you don't already know how, ask to be shown how to examine your breasts yourself.

If your doctor is a man, you may feel uncomfortable about such intimate proceedings. Knowing what to expect should help. But you should also know that you have every right to have another woman present with you in the examining room. Ask in advance if a nurse will be with you, or if you can bring a friend or relative. Many women do this. It is your legal right to do so—and if your doctor is not cooperative, you will not want to continue seeing him—since consideration of your feelings at this time is important. In any case, this procedure will become *very* familiar through the next months. And you should continue to have internal examinations periodically throughout your life, to make sure that your pelvic organs remain healthy.

How It Used to Be

The medical profession claimed that a doctor who could not practice "by the sense of touch alone" was incompetent in midwifery, and American textbooks on midwifery, drawing from French originals, obligingly illustrated that point by showing drawings of the doctor on one knee before his standing patient, feeling under her long skirts, with his eyes averted and staring abstractedly into the distance.

Richard W. Wertz and Dorothy C. Wertz,
Lying-In: A History of Childbirth in America, 1977

Genetics

WHAT IS GENETICS?

Genetics, according to *Tabor's Cyclopedic Medical Dictionary* (1977), is: (1) The science that accounts for natural differences and resemblances among organisms related by descent and (2) The study of heredity and its variations.

Genetics is the study of how physical traits are inherited or passed on, in the genes, from parents to their children.

The process by which we inherit some of our traits is absolutely astounding. There is a universal code for all forms of life—from one-celled bacteria to fruit flies, sharks, mice, and people. Deoxyribonucleic acid, or DNA, the substance in which the basic information of life is coded, is an extremely long, thin molecule—long, threadlike strands of many hundreds of genes linked together—occupying so little space that the genetic information of the world's population today would easily fit into the tip of a teaspoon. DNA carries the information from one generation to the next. It also works on a daily basis within your own body for each new cell that replaces an old one. DNA actually directs the machinery for carrying on thousands of complex chemical processes.

Chromosomes are composed of about one-third DNA and about two-thirds protein. Every normal human cell (with the exception of the normal red blood cell) carries 46 chromosomes, which go together in pairs. Each of these chromosomes can be visualized as a string of beads, with each bead representing linked genes. One chromosome of each pair is derived from the maternal egg cell and one from the sperm cell.

Only in the past decade have we known that the forty-six human chromosomes form 23 pairs. Of the 23 paired chromosomes in any cell, 22 are not related to the sex of the individual and are called autosomes. In addition, there is a pair of sex chromosomes, X and Y chromosomes, which determine the sex of an individual. For a female these are both X. For a male, this pair is made up of an X and a Y. The female egg contains only the X chromosome and the sperm will have either an X or a Y. It is, therefore, the father who determines the sex of the child.

All of any baby's physical characteristics are transmitted at the time of conception by the genes and their chromosomes. Each child receives 23 unpaired chromosomes from each parent. We call this inheritance.

Some traits determined or influenced by genes are eye color, hair color, skin color, curly or straight hair, size and shape of nose, height, body build—characteristics of appearance.

Some inherited traits involve body functions—whether a person will be nearsighted, what blood type he or she will have, or whether she or he will have, or is likely to develop, certain diseases.

Inherited diseases may be relatively minor, or they may be serious. They may be unfamiliar, or very well known indeed. But there are scores of defects so rare that their names are unknown to most people; yet babies born with them cannot survive for long. And then again some inherited diseases may not show up in the new person until middle age or later.

Almost every pregnant woman worries a little that her unborn baby might be born with some kind of birth defect. Fortunately for you and other worriers most babies are born without significant defects. But if you have cause to worry, there is encouraging news! For many genetic defects, it is now possible to test prospective parents, *even before pregnancy*, to see whether they are carriers of more than 60 genetic disorders. Other tests can be done after pregnancy begins to determine whether the baby within is developing normally.

Those parents-to-be who believe they may be at risk *should* consult a genetic counselor.

THE SCIENTIFIC FACTS ON HOW BIRTH DEFECTS BEGIN

The number of genetic defects is uncertain, because researchers keep discovering others. Most defects are determined by only one, or perhaps a few, of the huge number of genes in the human body.

Genetic disease and defects fall into three categories. These are (1) an abnormality in the chromosomes, (2) a single gene defect, and (3) a combination of one or more gene defects, or interaction of such defect(s) with environmental factors.

A chromosome abnormality can occur because there is a missing chromosome or some form of damage or split in a chromosome. Or it can refer to the existence of an extra chromosome or extra part of one. For example, in Down's syndrome (mongolism) the individual nearly always has 47 chromosomes instead of 46. The extra chromosome is believed to originate from incomplete separation of the chromosomes during the formation of the egg or sperm cells. Many miscarriages are caused by chromosomal abnormalities. Because each chromosome carries hundreds of genes, a chromosome abnormality interferes with a large area of the infant's development. Fortunately, because chromosomes are so large (by comparison with genes, that is), abnormalities can be quickly detected under the microscope following amniocentesis.

Single gene defects occur in about two percent of all live births, and fall into several areas. These are *dominant, recessive,* and *sex-linked gene defects.* If a particular gene carries a defect, it may be a dominant gene—in which case it can override the gene from the other parent. Therefore, the child can inherit the defect from just one parent. But should the defective gene happen to be recessive, the child will only inherit the ailment or abnormality if the other parent also transmits this gene. In other words, how the genes from one parent combine with the genes from the other parent determines whether the defect shows up or not.

The difference between dominant and recessive genes can easily be seen in the (textbook) case of a brown-eyed man who marries a blue-eyed woman. Of their family of four children, according to the Mendelian law of inheritance, three are likely to be brown-eyed and one may have blue eyes. The genes that pass on brown eyes are dominant. However, there is no way of knowing—until children are born—whether a brown-eyed man may also carry the recessive blue-eyed gene. The same situation may pertain to two blue-eyed parents who have a brown-eyed child—a rare occurrence.

There is one chance in four that a child will inherit a defect that is recessive from two parents who are carriers. On the other hand, there is also one chance in four that the unborn infant will be totally free of it. That leaves two chances in four for the unborn baby to be a carrier; that is, to inherit one gene for the defect, as his/her father and mother did.

Actually, all of us carry defects, but we may be carriers without having the defect ourselves. Or the defect may never happen to show up. No one really knows how many genetic defects are recessive, dominant, or sex-linked. Dr. Victor McKusick's *Catalog of Mendelian Inheritance in Man* (1978) lists 736 quite certain (plus 753 less certain) autosomal dominant traits, 521 (plus 596) autosomal recessive traits, and 107 (plus 98) X-linked ones. Many inherited traits are simple nondefective characteristics like being able to roll the tongue or move the earlobe attachment. Scientific estimates are that the majority of these traits of inheritance are *not* for genetic defects.

Examples of recessive gene defects are: sickle-cell anemia, Tay-Sachs disease, and cystic fibrosis.

Sex-linked defects occur only on the X chromosome, because the Y chromosome seems to lack all genes, except those that determine male sexuality. All men and no women have the Y chromosome. Fathers never transmit these particular diseases to their sons, as a result. However, any daughter of an affected man will be a carrier; any daughter of a carrier woman has a fifty-fifty chance of being a carrier; any son of an affected woman also has a fifty-fifty chance of being affected. If a woman has one X chromosome containing the defective gene and if her other X chromosome is normal, she will usually not have the defect herself, but she will be a carrier. If, however, a man inherits a defective gene on his single X chromosome, he will have the defect because there is no other X chromosome to counterbalance the defective one. Hemophilia is the most famous of the sex-linked inherited diseases. Color blindness and one form of muscular dystrophy are also X-chromosome defects.

The third category of genetic defects is made up of those caused by unpredictable combinations of genes from both parents together with environmental influences. In this category are cleft lip and/or palate, clubfoot, spina bifida, and many other defects which involve a malformation.

There is another category of birth defects recognized more and more today. These are caused by something adverse that happens while the "baby" is growing inside the mother. It has been estimated that *only 25 percent of birth defects are inherited.* But environmental defects—those caused by something that affects the baby in utero—are in the majority. Drugs, radiation, infections, smoking, drinking alcohol, even drinking excessive amounts of coffee or tea or cola are among those elements currently believed responsible for the vast majority of birth defects.

By a special microscopic procedure, karyotyping, the chromosomes of the parents can be studied to find out whether or not they are carriers of a specific ailment. The chromosomes of unborn babies can be studied, through a special test called amniocentesis, to tell whether they have inherited the defect. It takes about three weeks for the results of this test to be determined. Through karyotyping the sex of the unborn can be determined, too.

Another new procedure, ultrasound or sound-wave scanning, can detect abnormal growth of a baby in utero. If, for example, you had German measles early in your pregnancy, your doctor may recommend sonar scanning to determine whether the fetus is continuing to develop normally. Such scan-

ning will reveal gross physical defects. German measles (rubella) is one of the leading causes of birth defects; it can be prevented through the use of the vaccine for immunization.

GENETIC COUNSELING: HOW DOES IT WORK?

Genetic counseling, a relatively new specialty, is provided by physicians and other professionals with specialized training in genetics. If you have some risks in your background, your doctor or hospital will refer you to a genetic counseling service—either before or after you become pregnant. Or you can contact the organizations yourself. Costs may be covered by medical insurance. If necessary, fees can be adjusted according to your ability to pay.

When you phone for an appointment, the procedure will be explained and you will be asked to bring complete family medical records with you. Collect what you can, write down what you remember.

At your meeting the counselor will ask numerous questions and draw up a detailed medical genealogy chart, called a pedigree. This will be kept in the strictest confidence. If you already have a child with a genetic ailment, the child will be given a thorough examination.

The counselor will consult with other specialists. They will decide if there is enough evidence to make a diagnosis or if more tests should be done. The results of examinations and tests could take from two to six weeks.

After all the evidence is in, the counselor will tell the parents-to-be what the chances are of a specific problem occurring in their child-to-be. But for many or most genetic problems, diagnosis of the unborn is still not possible. Every situation is individual. Genetic counseling is a new and growing field, and every case brings new information.

Some expectant parents are told that their baby-to-come has one chance in four of being born with a particular defect. Turn it around now—and that child has *three chances in four* of *not* having a genetic defect. On this basis the "parents" may well decide to see what nature brings, hoping that any defect will be mild, or that surgery or some other treatment will improve their future child's condition. Some problems can be helped by surgery and other techniques today, even before birth! Or the couple may choose to interrupt the pregnancy. They still may have several options for the future: trying again, sterilization, artificial insemination, foster parenting, adoption. The counselor will discuss every option with them, but the choice is always for those who would be parents. There is a *new* hope on the horizon: the replacement of a defective gene, which has been done successfully in mice.

For more information about birth defects and their prevention, and for a guide to genetic counseling services in your locality, or for referral to local testing centers, write to: March of Dimes Birth Defects Foundation, 1275 Mamaroneck Avenue, White Plains, New York 10605; or National Genetics Foundation, Inc., 555 West 57th Street, New York, New York 10019

A Genetic Checklist

This list is reprinted in part from *Is My Baby All Right?* by Dr. Virginia Apgar and Joan Beck (1972):
1. An individual, or couple, who thinks that a close relative has a disorder which might be hereditary should take advantage of genetic counseling.
2. The ideal age for a woman to have children is between 20 and 35. If possible, it is best not to begin having babies before the age of 18 and to complete childbearing before age 40.
3. A man should beget his children before he reaches the age of 45.
4. There should be an interval of at least two years between the end of one pregnancy and the beginning of another.
5. With every subsequent child, beginning with the third, there is increasing hazard of stillbirth, congenital malformation and prematurity.
6. When a couple plans to conceive a child, intercourse should take place at intervals of no more than 24 hours for several days just preceding and during the estimated time of ovulation.*

USE GENETIC SCREENING WHEN—

Women are 35 years or older. Of babies born to women under 30, only 1 in 3,000 has Down's syndrome; after age 30 (to 35), the increase in risk is sharp—1 in 600; if the mother is 35 to 39, 1 baby in 280 is afflicted; if the mother is 40 to 44, it is 1 baby in 80. There is also more risk when fathers are older. Age may not be the reason; increased exposure to radiation over time is thought by some researchers to be one possible cause.

There is a family history or another child with genetic problems.

Previous pregnancies ended in miscarriage or stillbirth. A leading cause of miscarriages is chromosomal abnormality, and so three or more miscarriages or unexplained stillbirths are considered to be an indication for genetic/chromosomal evaluation to see whether such a problem is to blame.

There is hyperthyroidism, diabetes, or any other metabolic disease in either parent, or a family history of such disease.

You are a member of certain ethnic groups whose genetic ailments can now be screened. Greeks and Italians may have a rare form of anemia, thalassemia; eastern European Jews may have Tay-Sachs, a rare metabolic disease; blacks may have sickle-cell anemia.

Parents are close relatives, such as first cousins (statistically, they have an above-average chance of having a baby with a recessive disorder).

AMNIOCENTESIS: WHAT IT IS, HOW IT'S DONE, WHAT IT SHOWS

Amniocentesis (AM-nee-oh-cen-TEE-sis) is a long word for an incredible procedure. A small amount of amniotic fluid (the liquid environment of the baby-to-be) is removed from the uterus by a needle through the mother's abdomen during the fourth month of pregnancy. This fluid contains cells from the unborn baby. These can be examined

*Points 4 and 6 are borne out by a higher statistical incidence of pregnancy and birth problems among women who do not follow these guidelines.

biochemically and microscopically for abnormalities of development. Cell examination may reveal genetic defects such as chromosomal disorders (Down's syndrome, or mongolism) and metabolic diseases (such as Tay-Sachs). Amniocentesis can also indicate the sex of the unborn "baby"!

A local anesthetic is applied to a small area of the mother's abdomen. The very thin hollow needle is introduced slowly. About one third of an ounce of amniotic fluid is taken up through the needle.

Amniocentesis should be done early in the second trimester, preferably at the fourteenth week of pregnancy. This allows for early diagnosis and other examination if necessary.

The latest large-scale study, done by a group of researchers from the University of California, San Francisco, involved 3,000 high-risk women between 1970 and 1978. The great majority of the women went to the special clinic there because they were over 35. One hundred thirteen fetuses were found to have defects—ranging from Down's syndrome to Tay-Sachs disease. But the very great majority of this group found that they were carrying normal babies.

The researchers concluded that amniocentesis was "safe, reliable, and extremely accurate" and foresaw that the test would be a boon to families who, without it, might not even take a chance on having a child because of a serious family history of defects.

There are some words of caution on this test, however. Of fourteen mistakes made in diagnosis, some were cases of mistaken sex identity. Of the misdiagnoses, six seriously affected the outcome of the pregnancies involved and two women decided on abortions that proved unnecessary, due to diagnostic errors. The researchers also felt that amniocentesis may have slightly increased the rate of spontaneous abortion for the women involved.

This study should give us some cause for reflection—and perhaps for pause. But there clearly will be no room for pausing in high-risk situations if doctors get worried about lawsuits. And recently there have been two cases brought as a single suit in New York by high-risk women whose doctors had *not* advised them about amniocentesis. The court ruled that doctors must advise women at risk that amniocentesis is available, or they will be open to lawsuits. This type of action may cause doctors to perform amniocentesis on larger numbers of women than necessary.

In a survey of a small group of high-risk patients in Birmingham, Alabama, the women polled said they had found the test to be very reassuring and would recommend it to other women. If you are in a high-risk category, you will certainly want to consider it. However, a small risk of misdiagnosis or damage does seem to exist, and of course at this point it is impossible to estimate any long-term effects on babies, although none has been found to date.

Some important new work is being done at Stanford University that may eventually make amniocentesis obsolete. Researchers have found that cells from the fetus can be detected in the mother's blood by the twelfth week of pregnancy. This has raised all kinds of fascinating questions about why they are there, but more practically, the discovery is considered to be the first step toward devising a simple blood test for all pregnant women to detect chromosome abnormalities. This is probably some years away yet.

ULTRASONIC SCANNING, OR SONOGRAPHY

Imagine a kind of sonar that looks inside of you and projects onto a televisionlike screen a picture of your unborn baby. Sounds like sci-fi, doesn't it? But that is sonography, or ultrasonic scanning—reported to be one of the easiest diagnostic tools to use.

Sonography is based upon the fact that sound travels in waves. High-frequency, or ultrasound, waves, so high-pitched that they cannot be detected by human ears, are beamed at the abdomen of a pregnant woman, and echoes bounce back from the bones and soft organs of her body and her "baby's." A sophisticated piece of equipment produces the ultrasound waves, directing them at various angles across the mother's body; then it receives the sound waves as they are echoed back, converting them into a printout that appears as a shadowy image on a screen, where it can even be seen by the mother. This information is interpreted by specially trained physicians, who can make out the form of the fetus and observe the development of its nervous system, brain, heart, and other internal organs.

Sonography, too, is controversial. Those

who question its use are concerned about its safety—especially over a span of years. We really do not know what eventual effects it could have. For this reason it should not be used lightly or routinely—despite its obvious wonders.

BOY OR GIRL?

Many parents-to-be have desired an amniocentesis test only because they wanted to learn the sex of their baby-to-be. They know that the procedure is not performed for that reason, so they devise another basis for the request, one more acceptable to the medical profession. After amniocentesis, some of these parents-to-be have considered—or have undergone—an abortion based upon the feeling that the baby would be the "wrong" sex. There are many people who still prefer boys to girls. And if such sex selection became the wave of the future, this would have extraordinary effects.

We are, in fact, on the threshold of newer, simpler techniques to find out, along with other information, the sex of a baby. We may not be too far away from actually engineering the sex of a baby in advance. Dr. Ronald Ericsson in Sausalito, California, has been successful in producing 13 boys out of a small experimental sample of 17 babies who were artificially inseminated. This changed the usual fifty-fifty ratio dramatically.

Dr. Benjamin Spock was recently quoted as saying that he couldn't "imagine any prospective parent rejecting a child because of its sex." Unfortunately, Dr. Spock is being unrealistic. A 1970 Princeton University survey of 6,000 women found that almost half of them not only would use a sex selection technique—but would prefer more boys to girls in a three-child family, and definitely wanted a boy as a firstborn. And these were *women* who preferred boy children! As far as I know, no one has yet surveyed men, but the likelihood is that even more men would prefer sons to daughters.

Particular ethnic groups place more value on sons than daughters. If sex selection becomes simple and available to all in the future, we might have a society skewed out of balance by male Orientals, for example—or by young parents who believe that all of life can be engineered just as miraculously as the sex of their baby.

There can be serious consequences for babies now—if parents strongly prefer one sex to the other, and consider the "wrong" sex almost as a defect. This attitude, even when unexpressed, can have a direct impact. If your sex preference feelings are strong, it is important *to talk* them out with some understanding counselor *before* your baby arrives. Doing so will lessen the strength of your feeling, and can only benefit your baby if he is a he when you want a she, or vice versa.

Amniocentesis: Possible Problems

This year [1977] marks the 10th anniversary of this medical procedure (amniocentesis) called "revolutionary" by *The New York Times*. Joining this revolution, neonatologists and obstetricians have recommended diagnostic amniocenteses for all pregnant women over the age of 35.

It has now become clear that the placenta is frequently damaged by the needle and the resulting feto-maternal hemorrhage must increase the risk of Rh (rhesus) sensitization. . . .

Clearly, the dangers of amniocentesis demand evaluation before its use becomes common practice. Needle puncture of the fetus during second trimester amniocentesis is a hazard of unknown magnitude. Since this complication may be more frequent than has been previously believed, there is the possibility that damage to the fetus may occur. (Frederic M. Ettner, M.D., "Hospital Obstetrics: Do the Benefits Outweigh the Risks?" *21st Century Obstetrics, Now!*, 1977)

No One is to Blame

It is believed that all people carry from eight to ten defective genes which are not harmful to the individual. However, when two individuals mate and are carrying the same defective gene pair(s), they have a 25% risk of having a baby with a serious genetic defect. If each parent gives the same defective gene, there is no normal gene to compensate for the abnormal gene. . . .

Some disorders can be inherited directly from one parent. These disorders are caused by a single affected gene. If the parent has the disorder, there is a 50% chance that it will be passed on to each child. (San Diego

Regional Center for the Developmentally Disabled, *Facts About Birth Defects*, 1978)

Diagnosis

Currently, about 100 different genetic disorders can be diagnosed prenatally, including some of the most common and more serious—all the major chromosomal abnormalities, about 70 biochemical disorders in which body chemicals that are missing or that accumulate in excess impair the baby's development, and structural defects of the brain and spinal column. (Jane E. Brody, "Personal Health," *The New York Times*, 1977)

How It Used to Be

The evils of a too-rapid succession of pregnancies are likewise conspicuous in the children. There is no more frequent cause, says Dr. Hillier—whose authority in such matters none will dispute—of rickets than this.* Puny, sickly, short-lived offspring follows over-production. Worse than this, the carefully compiled statistics of Scotland show that such children are peculiarly liable to idiocy.

> George H. Napheys, M.D., *The Physical Life of Women: Advice to the Maiden, Wife and Mother*, 1889

*There *is* evidence of more mental retardation in large families whose babies are born quite close together.

Part Two

ADJUSTING TO PREGNANT PARENTHOOD

Family life is the enriching ingredient in our daily lives. The sense of sharing, loving, learning together is what the word family means. Success in isolation is empty. Sharing it with one's family and loved ones makes it doubly meaningful. The family is a beautiful idea.

ELI WALLACH

Daniel Kaufman

All About You

FOR MOTHERS-TO-BE

In times gone by, the fashion in pregnancy was secrecy. Everything about pregnancy and childbirth was hidden under a heavy veil of mystery. Women often spent the duration in social and emotional isolation, with little knowledge about their condition.

Today we all want to know. And knowing often guides us toward one line of action or another. The choices are many, and those you make now during pregnancy and after the baby comes will be so much the better if you are informed and knowledgeable. Just one example: If you know what rooming-in is all about, you may decide on it for yourself, only to find that the nearest hospital doesn't provide for rooming-in—but another nearby hospital does.

One of your primary sources of information can be a good prenatal course. The sooner both of you take one, the better.

Before your baby is born, the most important thing about him or her is *you*. Because your baby's body is sustained by yours, because your baby's growth is affected by what happens to you during the waiting months, you need to know how best to take care of yourself. You need to know for yourself, too. Who wants flat feet, bothersome teeth, an aching back, and sagging spirits, either before or after a baby arrives?

By the time you know for certain that your baby is on the way, your body has already given you some signs. Your menstrual periods have stopped. Your ankles may have swollen. Your breasts and nipples may have begun to feel tight or itchy. You are a little more tired than usual. And you may feel woozy or nauseous in the morning.

You have consulted a doctor, and he or she confirms your suspicions. You and your husband have begun to make plans.

The first change may concern some of your usual activities. You should consult your doctor about continuing very active exercise—horseback riding, skiing, cycling, tennis. Unless your doctor advises against it, you can keep on working without any problems. But try to arrange time so that you can get a little more rest than usual.

It's quite essential now to consider what you eat. A good diet is vital (and if you don't know what a good diet requires, find out! See page 42). Drink a quart of milk daily. Or if you dislike milk, cook with it, and eat dairy products such as cheese and yogurt. If too much weight gain should be avoided, drink skim milk. Drink water. Avoid alcohol (bad for babies), fatty foods, fried foods, and highly seasoned or spiced foods (not good for you and hard to digest). The quality of your meals affects your baby's future health.

Don't take drugs unless they are truly essential, and check the literature carefully about any drug you are advised to take.

Another thing you should do early in the game is to see your dentist. Getting your teeth cleaned and cavities filled early can save you a good deal of trouble later. "One baby—one tooth" was the common experience of women before the advent of modern dentistry. This is seldom the case anymore, but your body's chemistry and metabolism will change and these changes can bring about more cavities and other problems.

How much sleep will you really need? More than you usually get, in the early months. Toward the end of your pregnancy you may find yourself sleepier than usual—or sleepless. Nighttime baby-kicking will assure you that your unborn night owl is fine—but your sleep won't be! So start to take a daytime nap—a useful habit after your baby arrives.

Your skin needs some extra care, too. Regular rubbing with Nivea cream or a good cold cream over your enlarging midsection will keep the skin smoother, and prevent some of that tight feeling. Rubbing your nipples with lanolin is often recommended, too. But a better way to toughen them up (and they will need it for nursing) is to spend a few minutes every day pulling at them with a Turkish towel.

Take very good care of your hair while you're waiting. Brush, brush, and brush it—because sometimes hair starts to fall out during and right after pregnancy. Good nutrition tends to prevent this, too.

Showers are better than baths for maneuverability. (Be sure to get a slip-proof rubber mat for your bathtub or shower.) When you start to get very heavy, take your shower when someone else can help you in and out. A fall at this time can spoil a lot for you.

The same applies to getting around. Avoid, as much as possible, bending, kneeling, carrying, stooping, and getting up on top of stepstools. Becoming dizzy in such a situation and losing your balance can result in a miscarriage or a premature birth. Of course, you'll have to clean your house and fix it up. But most of this can be done with other methods—and you don't have to be the one to take chances now.

You will probably want to start to shop for maternity clothes fairly early on (in the third or fourth month). Buy less rather than more of them. No one ever wears them after the baby comes—and you'll want to freshen your wardrobe with some new things for the second pregnancy anyway. Good bras which support without binding are essential. A nonbinding girdle with good back support helps backaches. Low- or medium-heeled shoes will keep you steadier on your feet, and balance your unbalancing weight. Also recommended: support hose for daily wear to help prevent varicose veins.

The most important thing during your wait will be your state of mind. Keep on doing whatever you're used to, with just a few limitations. You can certainly work and drive, cook and clean, take walks and exercise. (Even if you're not planning on prepared childbirth, exercise is useful. And after the baby comes, regular daily exercises are essential for recovering your flat stomach.)

Most of all, don't worry about the future. Problems are bound to arise—that's what happens in life—but worrying in advance won't help you solve them. On the contrary—a relaxed attitude toward life and whatever it brings will help you think on your feet and *cope*. In the meantime expect to enjoy almost everything about having a baby. It *is* all it's cracked up to be.

Another Reason for Women's Liberation!

Let us explore in detail the problem of living with pregnant women. Let's face a fact: they're nuttier than a fruitcake! But we love them and they're here to stay, so let's learn to live with them. (Robert A. Bradley, M.D., *Husband-Coached Childbirth*, 1974)

How It Used to Be

Young men of high attainment and noble purposes, there is still something for you to do, to transmit the best to your progeny. Make the noblest in you still nobler, root out the weeds, attain greater heights every year, seek nobler companionship among books and men, choose for your mate the woman whose desires and ambitions are like your own, and your children will be a blessing to you and the world, and may well "rise up to call you blessed."

Mrs. Emma F. Angell Drake, M.D., *What a Young Wife Ought to Know*, 1901

DO:

Enjoy lovemaking.

Stay at your job until the day the baby comes—if you want to.

Travel—with your doctor's okay, and perhaps the name of a source of emergency medical care at your destination.

Dance all night—well, you probably won't feel like very active dancing in the ninth month.

Exercise regularly—if you don't usually, now *is* the time to start. (But do begin slowly, build up gradually.)

Take baths or showers, hot or cold.

Drive your car—but not for hours on end.

Walk a lot—but if your feet start to ache, take the bus.

Jog—at an easy, steady clip.

Swim—but save the high diving until after the baby comes.

Play tennis—go easy on the lobs, though!

Play golf—but watch out for the club in the last months.

Get your teeth filled as necessary.

DON'T:

Ski. Ethel Kennedy did, but I wouldn't. Why take such an unnecessary risk?

Learn a new rigorous sport without your doctor's okay.

Engage in weight-carrying sports (for example, backpacking).

Enter competitions (yes, some women have done it; but why should *you* have to worry about any possible aftereffects?).

Start *any* exercise program without checking with your doctor first; there may be special circumstances which would indicate *no* swimming or golf or whatever.

Allow X rays, unless essential.

FOR FATHERS-TO-BE

In the past, almost all books and articles about having a baby were addressed to women. Almost everyone focused on the mother-to-be and the physical fact of the baby growing inside and emerging from the woman's body. Many men felt like a useless appendage—not at all necessary or even important to the final outcome.

Ah, but things and thinking are a-changing! Researchers are now finding that men *are* integral to the process of growing a whole new human being. Not that a child will *not* be a worthwhile human without a father's presence and attention before and after birth. Many babies who have come into the world without knowing their fathers become accomplished, remarkable men and women. But it *is* harder to find satisfaction in life, to become giving and loving *without* a sense of male love and protection and appreciation from conception on. This, of course, will sound wrong to some feminists. But my life experience, the reading and interviewing I've done, and the studies and case histories I've read, have convinced me that good fathering is almost as vital to the human offspring as mothering. And this holds true for the human fetus as well.

The first and most obvious reason, which is just beginning to emerge from the research, is that well-loved mothers are more likely to have healthier, more responsive babies. The chain of giving seems to have endless links, even to the placenta.

Then, after birth, a father's presence makes so much more possible for a child. In addition to the two extra hands (always valuable!), there is a sense of maleness, of sex identity that he inescapably brings. A father is not a "mother's helper"; he is a parent who is fathering.

There are, of course, enormous individual differences and no one should try to fit into a mold which will be uncomfortable. A man whose business life is filled with high-level pressures which leave him tired but exhilarated may not be capable of turning himself into a student of baby bathing. And there's no need for finger pointing or mea culpas if the father-to-be in your family is indeed absorbed in career areas rather than in the primary care of a baby.

Fathering has degrees and levels and nuances. My grandfathers didn't even see their children for several years of infancy and early childhood—and then were so busy working to live that little attention was possible. My father never bathed a baby or gave any primary care, and continued the pattern of long hours and hard work. But he did spend his little spare time playing with his babies, and a lot more with his grandchildren. My children's father and my nephew, on the other hand, played and fed and bathed and learned a lot about babies. None of these men of my family were in the labor or delivery rooms—or in the bedroom (since home births were involved) when the babies were born.

Today the men of my son's and daughter's generation are frequently far more involved in the experience of having a baby than any of the men of my family ever were. Men are preparing for fatherhood. They're in the labor and delivery rooms. They're helping to deliver their own children. And they are giving basic care in every way they can. All this in addition to the assumption of the traditional father's role of working and earning a livelihood. This trend has become a movement: a strong current carrying a whole generation with it. When we read that David Eisenhower was present and assisted in his first child's delivery, we know that the trend is respectable and established.

The existence of this movement—much greater involvement of men in fatherhood—makes life for fathers both easier and harder. It's easier to share, to know, to be human, rather than Olympian. But it's much harder to be and do all things. Often the narrow, limited, more defined pathway is less complicated. Not as rich a way of life, not as emotionally rewarding—but straight and simple.

Whichever the way for you, you do have free choice—unless your job or location prevents it. But if you do choose less involvement, you don't have to feel like a pariah.

Everything is not for everyone! You can stay out of the delivery room without being a traitor to "the movement" or to your wife and baby. You can be a great father, and never bathe or dress your infant. Fathering comes in many styles—but its one essential ingredient is loving, and loving doesn't mean always doing everything. Loving is not diapering; it *is* accepting, enjoying, giving to and giving up for someone else's welfare.

Even if you are basically traditional in your thinking about pregnancy, childbirth, and child care, you may still be able to try something different.

With that thought in mind, I have listed on these pages numerous things fathers can do during the pregnancy, childbirth, and early infancy of their child. You may decide to choose one or none, or all of these things to do. But whatever your decision, you will at least know your alternatives.

CHOICES AND OPTIONS:
A WAITING LIST FOR FATHERS

Think about fatherhood. Be excited. Enjoy the prospect of becoming a *family*!

Talk with your wife. Listen to her. Calm any worries she has; share your own with her. Show her all the love you feel for her. Be patient if she has changes of mood.

Go to the library and bookstores for materials about having a baby. (Look at all the references in this book.)

Learn about the physiology and psychology of pregnancy. Update your understanding of infant care, the psychology of relationships, the pressures present at periods of strong change in our lives.

Talk to other men about fathering. And if men you know find it hard to talk about feelings and experiences, start a fathers' discussion group in your own community.

Check into their credentials and visit doctors, hospitals, birthing centers, nurses, midwives.

Participate in the Lamaze, Bradley, or other preparation-for-childbirth courses.

Decide upon the extent of your participation in the actual birth process.

Decide with your wife about the options of hospital, home, or birthing-center birth.

Plan (with your wife) the money situation for the year and a half ahead. Do budgets, and schedule purchases and expenses.

Investigate the insurance situation for both you and your wife. Also, consider starting a fund for your child.

List items which you can make or fix up for the baby.

Give your wife thoughtful little gifts or notes during pregnancy.

Go out with your wife more than usual now.

Help your wife decide to nurse.

Make baby announcement cards.

Get cameras and tape recorder (buy, borrow, or rent) and learn how to use them to record your baby's first days.

Help other children in your family understand what is going on, and what will be happening.

Go new-home shopping or . . .

Plan space situations in your existing home.

Install locks on cabinets.

Get or make good storage for delicate equipment.

Investigate safety, utility, and price of products to be bought or made for your child.

Look into community and other services in your area for new parents and new babies.

Put all your (and your wife's) legal and financial documents in shape. A new baby changes things and makes responsibilities more significant.

Keep family ties strong by planning get-togethers and events with relatives.

Start a family history or record book for a later gift to your child.

Help your wife decide what to do about her job and career.

Keep up your sex life, as long as you're both comfortable: if your wife's *not* comfortable, either help her—or be patient.

Retrain yourself for parenting. Try on-the-job training by spending time with other young families. Work on your own problem areas. Go to workshops and seminars for parents. Visit friends with babies.

Learn everything you can about complications and variations so that you will be well-informed if last-minute decisions must be made.

Plan transportation to hospital/birthing center or ways to transport people to your home.

Decide on how much you can help (and when) in direct baby care later on. Make out a tentative schedule of sharing with your wife, or of relieving her.

Help your wife past the blues or anything else bothering her after the baby comes.

Do exercises with her to encourage her to get back in shape.

Love both your wife and baby—they're part of you!

FOR BOTH OF YOU

ATTITUDES, FEELINGS, MARRIAGE
RELATIONSHIPS, AND ALL THOSE
UNSEEN THINGS THAT INFLUENCE
YOUR BABY'S FUTURE

What will *your* baby be like? All babies are born with certain characteristics, but they do differ from each other no matter how alike they may seem in a hospital nursery. Some babies are fussy. Some are smilers from the first. Some are very active; others are placid. Personality traits and behavior characteristics seem to be inborn just as they are among kittens and other infant creatures.

Nonetheless, newborn infants are somewhat like a clean slate upon which you and other artists will be drawing a huge mural. What your baby brings along in inherited and basic characteristics is not yet completely within your control. More directly under your influence is the development of those traits and characteristics: your influence *and* that of others as well. The fact is, the total environment influences your baby. And there are many elements in all of us which develop only with care, or in its absence. Babies and children are notorious imitators of what they see, hear, and feel around them. According to practically all the child development and child care specialists, the factors which seem to have an enormous influence are the basic attitudes and feelings of those closest to the baby. This would seem to put a very heavy burden on young, inexperienced new parents. And indeed it does. What I hope to do in this book is help you—*both* of your baby's parents—to recognize that responsibility and fulfill it, as well as to lighten its awesomeness.

First of all, it is true. Your attitudes do count. What you think about your baby, what you do with your baby, right from the first minutes, can make a difference. A very large difference. Will you make mistakes? Yes—many. Everyone does. Will your feelings be harmful to your baby? Yes—sometimes. It's only natural. There are no absolutely perfect parents. Still, there is so much room for plain "humanness" in everybody's parenthood that there is no reason for anybody to be afraid. By "humanness" I mean everything that goes into being human, the negative as well as the positive, including a large dose of inadequacy, errors, misdirections, old conceptions, negative attitudes, bad feelings. But . . .

If there is a reasonable balance and your feelings are more good than bad, more loving than hating, more giving than taking, your baby will show almost immediately a certain responsiveness and contentedness a good part of the time. So much so, that you will be able to recognize the baby as a "happy baby."

Very often young parents do not quite realize how impressionable babies are. Something as personal and private as your marriage or your relationship with your spouse, or even with your parents, can make a difference between a happy child and an unhappy one. The ways in which you feel loved directly influence the ways that you can love.

When a new baby is born, it's important for both partners in a marriage to give to each other emotionally as much as possible, before and after the baby comes. Sometimes this will be very hard; sometimes it may even seem completely unreal. Here you are thrown into a different circumstance of life than you have ever known before, responsible for the well-being of a very small dependent creature, and expected to be all-loving and all-giving to your spouse. No new parent will be happy and loving constantly. The object here is to try. Not for perfection because you won't reach that, but for understanding of each other's needs, for tolerance of each other's quirks, and for patience.

This is not to say that each of you, partic-ularly the new mother, should not be your own person, an individual with specific needs and wants and desires yourself. Indeed, you cannot be otherwise. But unfortunately, mothers have traditionally been expected to be martyrs to their families, sometimes to the detriment of their own self-image. This kind of personality situation is as bad for a baby born into today's world as is that of the mother who is so self-centered that she constantly puts herself before her husband and baby. There must be a balance that combines a secure sense of self-identity with the ability to comprehend the needs of the other parent.

A balance means a father's involvement. It benefits every member of the family. Babies and children whose perspective and care is only that of the mother may grow up with a more limited personality development than children who have the benefits of a father's active participation. (*This does not mean they will:* there is just more possibility.)

The father's life, too, is enriched by the new closeness to his children's development. But if a new father feels burdened by this more active role, it is up to the wife to try to make the adjustment easier through understanding.

Without question, new-baby time is one of adjustment. The ability to adjust, as individuals and as a couple, is a crucial social skill which becomes ever more important throughout married life. This is a paradox: one would think the greatest adjustment in a marriage would come at the beginning. But when there were just two of you, marriage was a continuation of courtship. When a new baby expands your family, your relationship to each other is bound to change. And as your child grows, and goes into different stages of development, and as other children are born, your relationships are bound to change even more. Therefore, adjustment must be continual throughout marriage—indeed, throughout life. Time and situations do not stand still for any of us.

THINKING AHEAD TO . . .
MOTHERHOOD, FATHERHOOD,
PARENTING

To keep both your burdens and your frictions to a minimum after the baby's birth, *plan ahead*, and *talk it over together*. Such planning can ease the problem times when they come, and talking together can help each of you to know what the other expects. Plans should be flexible. Even if they don't exactly fit every situation, they will prepare you to cope with whatever lies ahead.

Both of you may be incredibly tired. Tiredness often results from the emotional demands of giving up some of yourself to another human being—who must have *you* to live. But even if its cause is largely emotional, the actual fatigue is physical and must be recognized as something to take into account in making all plans for care of the baby. Don't expect yourselves to be superhuman. Instead, expect both of you to have more than ordinary needs, problems, and desires surrounding the new baby.

One of the huge areas of difficulty that occurs in the relationship between parents after the baby comes is the expectation level of one in terms of the other. Sometimes there is a feeling that it is going to make all the difference in the world if something *is* or *is not* done. A lowered expectation level on the part of both of you can help enormously toward a good adjustment.

A good time to figure out who will do what and when is before a baby is born. For instance, if both of you will be working full time, sharing the evening and weekend tasks and chores probably will be fairly automatic, unless you plan differently. If the new mother is going to stay home at least for the first months, and the new father is going to work outside the home, then her share of those activities with and around the baby is automatically going to be considerably more than his. However, she may expect that as soon as the father comes in from work, he will take over the baby completely. He may feel differently since he is contributing a large share to the family by providing the wherewithal for that family to function.

Still and all, any new father, however tired he may be after work, probably would want to spend some time caring for the baby, especially on weekends. If your plan now is to separate your time and your chores, even though it may not quite work out that way after the baby comes, such a plan could make a large difference in not leaving everything to chance.

There are many potential problem areas that you can project. For instance, if the baby is wakeful at night—as many babies are—decide in advance on an arrangement that will ease the situation for both of you. One night one of you takes the swing shift, and

the next time that your baby wakes, the other one takes over.

Your plans ahead should include some of the areas you can share together. One is bathtime, for bathing baby can be either a single or a joint activity. Then, if either of you is too tired or busy, it is understood that the other will take over at that point.

A time for play, a specific playtime beyond the regular play-as-you-go-along kind of care, can be set aside if you plan in advance.

In planning, consider also the atmosphere of your home—what it is and what you expect it to become. For instance, are you going to be worried about noise when the baby is sleeping? Or do you want to have the kind of household where people come and go casually, as usual? This area can create considerable conflict if one new parent feels differently from the other. (As far as the baby goes, it probably doesn't make too much difference for most infants whether there is absolute silence or reasonable hustle and bustle—provided there is some unanimity and harmony concerning his or her place and role after birth.) Of course, if either of you is addicted to high-volume rock, it would be preferable to get cured immediately—or to wear earphones, or to move your listening or performing completely outside the home. You don't want your baby to suffer severe hearing loss.

There are other areas not often found in the baby books which do make a difference and do have effects upon relationships within the baby's family.

Here, to set your thinking going, is a long list of questions about such matters:

Are you going to pick up the baby every time he/she cries? Is there going to be an investigation into what is the matter? Or will you let the baby "cry it out" unless it's a scheduled feeding or changing time?

Will the visit to the pediatrician automatically call for the presence of both parents in the mind of the baby's mother but not in the mind of the baby's father?

Does father-to-be expect you two to have quiet candlelit dinners alone after the baby goes to sleep—while mother-to-be expects to have baby present at the table during the parents' meal? This, incidentally, can get to be more of a problem after the child gets to high-chair age and older and his/her bedtime gets to be later.

Does either of you expect a weekly visit to your parents or from them, while the other expects much less involvement, or much more?

Does either of you expect that the baby's mother is going to continue working while the other one does not expect any such thing?

Is one of you thinking about home-mades and built-ins and hand-me-downs for the baby's furniture, equipment, toys, clothes—while the other one is looking forward to spanking-new items?

Does either of you expect to have a considerable amount of privacy and time to oneself, while the other believes that the arrival of the baby will make it mandatory for both of you to give up time alone?

How is the laundry going to be taken care of? Who is going to do it and when? A decision in advance can make this chore fairly automatic.

Is the television set going to be part of your family's life from the moment that your baby is born, or is it going to be phased out or toned down during the child's early years?

Are you going to attempt to cover the baby's every moment with either of your physical presences or with that of another adult? Or are you going to rely on teen-age, and perhaps even quite young, baby-sitters? Or are you planning not to use a baby-sitter because a stranger's presence might make you nervous?

Do you expect to travel with the baby everywhere you go, whether on a short visit to the neighbor's or a long trip across many states?

Are you the type not to worry about your child's safety or health while your spouse is likely to be a tiger in guarding your new addition from every prick, scratch, or fall?

Is your religious training such that you would expect your child to become a part of family or church services quite early on?

When and how do both of you feel about breast feeding versus bottle feeding, toilet training, sleeplessness, discipline, redoing your home, putting away or not using some of your prized possessions?

How do you both feel about money and expenses—current money and current expenses versus savings for the future?

Is either of you expecting to have a very heavy social life regardless of your new addition, while the other one has no such expectations?

The reason for all these questions is because knowledge of your own and each other's attitudes will affect your future. Your expectations and decisions are sure to have direct consequences upon your new child. Often you may not even be aware of such an effect. You may not see that a continuous disagreement or dissatisfaction with your husband or wife over the time of the dinner hour or over the question of vacation-now-worry-later is germane to your baby's well-being. But even the tiniest infant can be extraordinarily sensitive to the general atmosphere in the home, to the sounds of stress, the silence of anger, the tension of arms that move too sharply, the preoccupation of an adult in something other than who is in his or her arms.

Tiny tots and small children are not able to verbalize feelings. But if there is conflict in the home atmosphere, they pick it up—believe me, they pick it up. Then, your own feelings and attitudes become part of a circular effect—part of how you react to your child and how that child reacts to you.

Naturally, you can't anticipate during pregnancy how you will react to *all* these situations later on. And what may become problematic for one couple may be easy as pie for another. These queries are intended to set you thinking and—more important—talking it over. In many (but not all) instances, *what* you decide isn't nearly so important as *how* you arrive at that decision. If you can talk together, anticipate problems realistically (instead of imagining that love will carry you through), and learn each other's points of view in advance, you'll be well on the way to dealing effectively with situations as they arise.

The mother-to-be should realize that:

You may be tired after the baby is born, for physiological reasons alone. You may not be back to yourself for many months.

You will be doing new things, learning new daily and weekly routines. You will not have as much time to yourself or for your husband.

Therefore, plans for the immediate weeks or even first few months after the baby is born should be kept easy and flexible. Do not set up a tight schedule of Things That Must Get Done.

If you have been used to an active professional and/or social life, plan ahead for ways to keep in touch with colleagues and friends: frequent phone calls, occasional lunches or visits.

You may have been warned against postpartum depression—a persistent case of the "blues" that some women experience after their babies are born. Postpartum depression is relatively common but it is usually not necessary. And a husband can get it, too. There are ways to predict whether you are more or less likely to develop such a problem—and there are ways to reduce the possibilities of the risks. (See page 276.)

After the baby is born, you may occasionally feel overly burdened. Every parent feels this way sometimes—especially when the baby is wakeful, fretful, or ill, which is bound to happen. It helps to realize right from the start that all new parents are inexperienced, that being a mother/father is an on-the-job learning process and that there are ways to alleviate such feelings.

You'll be giving up some things—especially time—that are important to you. There will be days when there really are too many demands being made on you. At such times you may want to be taken care of and pampered. Don't be a martyr and go through an evening grim with exhaustion. But try not to take it out on your husband. Say what's on your mind, postpone dinner, take a rest. Try alternate rest shifts until you both feel refreshed. The important point here is for each parent to be considerate of the other.

The man of your household will be making a major adjustment, too. He is not used to sharing you, your time and attention. He is not used to being awakened at 2:00 A.M. or 6:00 A.M. He is not accustomed to changing diapers. Probably he is not used to being the sole earner and having complete financial responsibility for three people—if indeed he is. This is all as new an experience for him as it is for you. He needs your affec-

tion and understanding just as much as you need his.

The father-to-be should realize that:

Being a father does not end with conception or delivery and does not start again when the "kid" is old enough for electric trains. Being a father is a continuum, just as being a mother is. Your *active* involvement with your child starts at birth. Helping out with the baby's care is good for your baby, good for your wife, and good for *you.*

The baby's mother needs more rest during pregnancy and when the baby arrives. She is not being a spoilsport or overly demanding if she says she is tired—she really is. And the more help and assistance you can provide, the more rapidly she will be able to recover her strength and energy.

Finances and financial planning should be shared with your wife, especially if she is no longer working. There will inevitably be greater expenses. And realize that all parents have problems managing finances when their families are expanding, and particularly during inflationary times. Don't compare yourself to others—you never know what really goes on in someone else's household.

You and your wife will probably not be able to go out together as often as you used to. Baby-sitters cost money, and so do evenings out. But you don't have to eliminate them entirely. You can do yourself and your family a special service by planning special evenings out at realistic intervals. Plan evening or day trips where you can take the baby—hiking, dinner with friends, drive-in movies. Have your friends over to your home regularly. And each of you needs some time alone out of the house—for shopping, taking courses, card playing, dinner with a friend, golf, bowling, whatever. Make room for your night out, and for your nights in. Also, when your baby develops a more or less regular pattern, plan a romantic evening at home for just the two of you—in between feedings, of course.

The care of a baby is time consuming. Your wife will not have as much time for you. And if you truly intend to father, you will not have as much free time as you used to. Obviously, you're going to be jealous of the baby. But your wife still loves you, even if she may no longer be able to pay as much attention to you. You may not be able to do so either, and you still love your wife.

You now have two people who want your love and affection. Try to show how much you love them both—often—in little ways and words. If you have been brought up not to express too much affection, as many men have, you'll never have a better reason to change the pattern. Go at it gradually. Try touching more; try a few phrases of appreciation; try funny sounds of caring.

Don't let yourself get overwhelmed by responsibility. If you consider yourself the head of the household, remember that fathers have been heads of households psychologically and economically for thousands of years. You are not a pioneer. You've got the same pleasures and problems, senses and situations, as countless others. There are also other ways to be a husband and father. You can be cohead, or sharer, or partner in the household, or at least you can think of yourself in this light—and that alone can relieve the sense of too much responsibility. In any case, do relax—and enjoy!

Quality Counts

My wife, Helen, and I have eight children and eleven grandchildren. Like so many other union members, our struggle to organize the United Farm Workers has very much been a family affair. One of my burdens has been the need to spend so much time away from home. Therefore, the time I do spend with my family has come to be very important. Sometimes one hour spent really concentrating on your kids and their needs is worth days or weeks spent hanging around them. (Cesar E. Chavez)

How It Used to Be

Take child care . . . Male physiology and psychology aren't geared to it. Not that there's anything wrong with a father occasionally giving a baby a bottle, if the situation requires it or he enjoys it. What's wrong is thinking that it adds to his parenthood. When a man tries to be a "better" father by acting like a mother, he is not only less fulfilled as a father, but as a man, too. A father's relationship with his youngsters can't be built mainly around child-caring experiences. If it is, he's a substitute mother—not a father!

Similarly, under this "petticoat rule," if a tired father is bludgeoned into serving as a kitchen aide and handyman, it doesn't enrich his fatherhood either. Actually, a wife who shifts her unpleasant household chores to her husband is downgrading her own activities in her children's eyes.

Dr. Bruno Bettelheim, "Fathers Shouldn't Be Mothers!" *This Week Magazine*, April 20, 1958

Today's View

While there is hardly a coherent body of research about men and children, studies done so far are highly provocative. In a Cincinnati hospital, for example, when fathers and mothers were given an equal chance to hold their babies in the first few days after birth, fathers were more likely than mothers to hold and visually attend to their infants. At a time when such studies are rare, some researchers make it sound as if they have discovered a new creature—it doesn't lactate and it doesn't have a uterus, but it shows a surprisingly warm response to its offspring! (James A. Levine, *Who Will Raise the Children?*, 1976)

◇ ◇ ◇

Four *keys* to a better life with baby:

Talk it over together.
Plan ahead.
But stay flexible.
Laugh a lot.

Personal qualities that aid in developing a better life with baby:

Patience
Flexibility
Adaptability
Understanding
Being a good listener
Ability to organize your time
A constructive approach to differences
Tolerance of such differences
Liking to solve problems
Being able to speak up
Ability to enjoy and to laugh

EXPECTATIONS AND WORKING ON THEM

One of the most anxiety-producing areas between couples can be a wife's belief that her husband should be more than he is or a husband's belief that his wife should be more than she is. This critical dissatisfaction with the other can become a crack in the marriage. It often appears early on and frequently centers on issues of child care.

The reason we sometimes expect the love-of-our-life—or at least the person with whom we have the intimate relationship of sharing parenthood—to be so much better than he or she is goes back to the most important and certainly the most intimate of our own early relationships—with our own parents. If you are very unhappy about aspects of your relationship with one or both of your parents, watch your own expectation level, your own critical level about your wife or husband.

You can often do something about it. It is quite possible to tone down your discontent by learning to accept another person's inadequacies, weaknesses, or simple differences of opinion.

Of course, one cannot and should not accept behavior that is obviously and directly harmful. Giving in to destructive behavior can present a danger far greater than lack of tolerance.

What are such behaviors? Clearly, such extremes as physical abuse, flagrant dishonesty, any behavior-altering addictions, consistent lack of responsibility for child or family, or a constant stream of criticism. All of these are so destructive to a relationship that you *must* not tolerate them—for the sake of the other person as well as for yourself.

If reasonable discussion of the problem does not produce improvement, professional help is needed. If the person behaving destructively will not go for such help, the person who has to live with and struggle against it should. It is possible to learn a more effective way to deal with these, and other, personality problems. In any case, living daily with such destructive behavior can be depressing and debilitating, and professional assistance can help make life worth living again.

Short of such extremes, however, it becomes a baby-and-child-care factor of pri-

---

How It Used to Be

If you demand much of a husband, he has a right to demand just as much from you.

Mrs. Mary Wood-Allen, M.D., *What a
Young Woman Ought to Know*, 1913

mary importance to learn to accept your baby's father or mother. Acceptance does *not* mean being a doormat, a victim, or a passive acceptor of whatever unfair, inequitable, or unreasonable behavior your spouse may choose to foist upon you. Speaking up may clear an air too heavily laden with emotional pollutants, and actually bring about a change for the better. Growth and self-development often come through a nondestructive but objective view that others have of us.

Look at yourself clearly, if you can. Are you hell-bent on being in control of your spouse or your child? Or can you let them be as they are, without feeling enormous disappointment or discontent? An accepting attitude speaks volumes for infants, babies, and all small-size people. It also reflects on what is done with and about your child. If it is possible for you to accept the flaws and flummery of your spouse, it will be easier to accept the flaws and flummery of your baby.

Flaws? *Your* baby? Yes, flaws.

Every baby has flaws. (There is no such thing as a perfect baby, although a lot of them come quite close!) And being able to accept and love a whole child, warts and all, may be directly related to your way of accepting the other intimate persons in your life.

GRANDPARENTS: ANTICIPATING PLEASURES AND PROBLEMS

Grandparents can be a delight. My own grandmother seemed a paragon of virtue to me—handing out nickels for ice cream, providing extra love and wonderful tea-in-a-glass (with homemade jam in it), joking and laughing a lot and always being fair—without directing anyone's behavior and feelings. My father carried on the tradition of great affection and givingness without criticism or reproach: providing an endless supply of nickels for my toddler son's jukebox joys, lots of happy gifts, helpful regular letters, and plenty of fun and stability. These members of my family and many other grandparents I've known have been very supportive to their grandchildren *and* to their grown children—without being controlling or demanding.

But sometimes some grandparents are so thrilled and delighted with the birth that they tend to take over, to direct and to guide too much, indeed even to supply too much of the basics, a responsibility which should belong largely to the parents. One grandmother I know provided meals for her daughter's family from the birth of the first baby on. The son-in-law and children took to regarding her as the source of sustenance, thereby shutting out the mother of the house and making her react intensely against even the best of recipes and meals. One grandfather was such an educator that he set up learning programs for his grandson from infancy on, eventually causing the growing boy to believe his parents were rather unintelligent.

Some grandparents tend to be distant and cold, not at all involved, not willing to be of much help. Either kind of grandparents may also be far too critical—particularly of a new mother.

Any of these extremes can put pressure on the relationship between the parents and can create more difficulties for the baby.

What can you *do* about grandparents? Involve them, if you can. Even if you're worried about encroachments and takeovers. Involve them as much as you can, but if there's a problem, do let them know that you—the parents-to-be—are going to be in charge of your own child and your own decisions. Try your best *not* to shift a grandparent up, over, and out. Your child—and you—need them if they're halfway nice, halfway helpful.

Discuss together, you the new parents-to-be, how you both view your own and each other's parents. Talk over what you will expect, and what they might expect. Talk to the prospective grandparents, too, about the role they see for themselves. They may well be delighted to plan with you.

In anticipating the reactions of your parents and in-laws, give them the benefit of the doubt. Grandparents nowadays are young, active, and busy people. They often know how important it is for you to lead your own life and raise your own baby—and even to make your own mistakes and learn from them. But they also know, from firsthand experience, the pressures and responsibilities faced by new parents. Don't anticipate grandparent problems—unless you already have parent or in-law problems that give you a good indication of what's to come. But do take another look at these grandparents-to-be; they may be capable of giving you the counsel that can come only with experience. Their experience, too, can be useful to you, if only to help you understand your husband or wife.

Encourage grandparents to give their best. Find the things that they can do best for you and your baby. Emphasize your need for independence only if it becomes necessary. Show your maturity in how you handle *them* as well as your baby: then even the most doting grandparents will have confidence in your ability to survive parenthood, as they did.

(Although I've specified grandparents in this discussion, the same applies to other relatives with whom you are closely involved—the baby's aunts and uncles, perhaps, or your own aunts and uncles.)

The Pride of Parents

When I look at my parents, I think, "That's the thing they should be most proud of—the fact that all their children really care for one another, and are really there for each other, in times of need." (Lola Redford)

Caring for Two Bodies

THE BASIC DOS AND DON'TS OF PREGNANCY

DO:

Be happy. Keep your spirits up. The downs will be there anyhow—the awkwardness, the discomforts, the worries or fears. So your emotional job is to look at these downs squarely—without letting them get *you* down. Think happy. Think new life. Think pleasant ideas. Play music. Dance. (Yes, you can.) Enjoy.

Take care of your body. Eat carefully and well. (Read on for some pregnancy diets and menus.) Sleep enough—take naps, if possible, at least on weekends.

Make time for extra activities—for exercising, for walks, for reading, for courses, for shopping, for visits to the doctor or clinic or midwife, for planning and preparing your life-to-be. But keep a calm, steady pace.

Talk to each other, for you are both your baby's parents. Share concerns, worries, pleasures, little kicks, and much anticipation.

Do listen to suggestions, advice—if it's constructive. Let others share your joy.

Love. Relax. Be optimistic.

DON'T:

Don't listen to doomsayers, complainers, antibaby comments. You can find the facts—the pros and the cons—by reading and taking courses. But you surely *don't* need a negative view of parenthood and having a baby. Avoid people who tell you unpleasant stories about pregnancy, childbirth, or babies.

Don't insult your body. Give up smoking. In 1978–79 we found out so much more about the consequences of smoking during pregnancy, that *not* smoking is almost mandatory. The same is true of alcohol. Avoid it. And certainly—*don't* take mind-altering drugs.

Don't get frantically busy or try to cram all the new things to do into an already too-crammed life. Don't panic—things *will* get done if you plan ahead.

Don't shut out your baby's other parent because you (the mother) are preoccupied with your changing body or because you (the father) are worried about providing for another family member.

Don't live in an enclosed little capsule keeping the rest of the world away.

Don't hate. Don't tighten up. Don't expect problems.

How It Used to Be

Pregnant women have an instinctive desire to lie abed late, which, like the other promptings of nature during this period, should not be disregarded. No night-watching ought ever to be undertaken during pregnancy. Feather beds should be avoided. The heat which they maintain about the body is inconvenient and dangerous, predisposing to flooding and exhausting perspirations. The hair or sponge mattress is to be preferred.

George H. Napheys, M.D., *The Physical Life of Women: Advice to the Maiden, Wife and Mother*, 1889

How It Used to Be

The expectant mother should give her child all possible advantages of a good mental impression, and, during its prenatal life, the mother should think nothing but loving and wholesome thoughts. She should train her mind in habits that she wishes to impress upon the child. She should cultivate habits of system, she should cultivate a correct taste and ear for music. Her surroundings should be artistic but simple. She should live as close to Nature as possible.

Edith B. Lowry, M.D., *Your Baby*, 1915

HEALTH HABITS

Your body provides the life-support system for your baby for the first nine months of his/her life. For this reason alone your "housing" should have top-notch care! But there is another reason for taking good care of your body—you. This is the only body you've got, the only one you'll ever have.

Good care of your body and your baby's during pregnancy is not that much different from good care at any time. Basic hygiene, quality nutrition, adequate rest and exercise—that's almost all there is to it.

Unfortunately, many young women are neglectful of themselves, assuming that there will always be time to tone up muscles or eat balanced meals. But this isn't true. You can't completely make up for the loss of body condition caused by even a few months of neglect.

Your entire being consists of interdependent systems, every one of which must be in top working order for maximum health—*for you and your baby*. If you are in good shape, you will be less affected by the extra strains on your body resulting from pregnancy and delivery.

If you have neglected yourself until now, do consider the ways in which you can improve your physical condition and the consequent care of your baby *before* your infant is born. And let the suggestions on this and the following pages help you both during and after your pregnancy. Better health for both of you is in your power today.

IF YOU EXPERIENCE:

Morning sickness. Keep a tin of plain salt crackers or soda biscuits on your night table. Eat one or two first thing in the morning, while still in a reclining position, before getting out of bed.

In the morning gradually assume a sitting position. Stand up slowly.

Eat two small meals (no sweet snacks) instead of one regular meal. Breakfast might be tea and toast, followed by juice and cereal or one egg an hour or two later. Try several combinations and see what works best for you. Many women find that morning coffee can cause additional nausea.

Acid indigestion. Eat a light evening meal.

Avoid overeating at any meal.

Avoid spicy, greasy foods.

Drink one-half cup milk before every meal.

Take antacids (or other medication) *only* if your doctor says it is vital. And avoid *any* drugs if you can.

Varicose veins, Swollen ankles, Lower-back pain. These are all essentially the same problems: extra weight and poor circulation, which in turn affects the blood vessels and the nerve endings of the pelvic region and legs. Do all the following things:

Use only support hose or support pantyhose. Put them on the first thing in the morning, after getting out of bed. Be sure they are the right size for your current dimensions.

When you must sit for long periods, try to put your feet up. Use a footrest, the rung of your chair, or a bar at the back of your desk. If nothing else is available, stack up phone directories, dictionaries, or newspapers (secure these into a neat bundle with masking tape) and place this makeshift footrest under your desk.

When you lie down, put a pillow beneath your legs and feet.

Do exercises that stretch the leg muscles and keep them limber. Wave a leg in circles in the air; try to touch your toes. Move your feet in circles, toes up, then toes down. You should feel the muscle underneath your knee pulling, and your lower back unkinking. For immediate relief, do these for a few minutes every now and then, instead of or in addition to longer stretches of exercise once a day.

Sleep the same way your unborn baby does, on your side, curled up in the fetal position. It's good for your back, and probably more comfortable than any other position as your abdomen enlarges.

Wear a maternity girdle for support. Make sure it fits properly and is not binding or constricting anywhere. (They have come back into fashion these days.)

Sleepiness during the day. At home lie down whenever you feel tired. Don't try to keep going. A ten-minute rest every hour or two, or a half-hour nap twice a day, should keep your energy levels moderate.

At work try to arrange your activities so you can take an occasional break. Perhaps you can take a half hour for lunch instead of an hour, and use the extra time for conveniently spaced rest breaks. Eat lunch at your desk occasionally; don't buck the noonday crowds or tire yourself out by trying to run errands during lunch hour. Talk to your supervisor or co-workers to see how you can reschedule your on-the-job time to get needed rest.

Sleeplessness at night. Lie in bed in a relaxed position, eyes closed, and breathe deeply and rhythmically.

Try sequential relaxation: first your feet,

How It Used to Be

An old-fashioned remedy for this condition [morning sickness] is pop-corn. This may be eaten (without butter) at various times during the day and usually can be retained when other food cannot. Pop-corn tea also may be taken. A hot water bag or a mustard plaster to the abdomen sometimes relieves.

A hot bath, by drawing the blood away from the brain, often will be beneficial [for sleeplessness]. . . . Keep the mind free from the cares of the day. If they will intrude, crowd them out by repeating some soothing sentence as "There is no reason why I should not sleep, therefore I shall sleep. My body is relaxed, my mind is at peace, sleep is coming. I am getting sleepy. I am about to sleep."

Edith B. Lowry, M.D., *Your Baby*, 1915

then your legs, then your torso, arms, neck, and head.

Get out of bed, put on your robe, and sit in an easy chair in a moderate light. Read, knit, crochet, do needlepoint, work on a puzzle, until you feel sleepy. Then go back to bed.

Listen to soft music or watch TV.

Make love—the most tension-reducing, relaxing activity known to woman.

Dark splotches on your skin. Avoid the sun. Use a sun screen or sun block, especially on your face, even while walking about on a sunny day. Do not let yourself suntan or sunburn.

Wear a foundation makeup a shade or two darker than usual. Use a blusher. Choose eye makeup that is a bit brighter than usual.

The pigmented splotches will disappear after the baby is born, so camouflage as a temporary measure is the best approach. Do *not* scrub with lemon juice or bleach, or try any other home-brewed treatment that may irritate your skin. In severe cases an appointment with a dermatologist might be reassuring.

WHEN YOUR PREGNANCY REQUIRES EXTRA MEDICAL ATTENTION

Some conditions or events in a woman's life alert her doctor to the need for extra watchfulness. You are in this category if:

You are younger than 18 or older than 35 years.

You have a history of miscarriage, premature delivery, stillbirth, or toxemia during previous pregnancies.

You have a tipped uterus or other abnormality of the pelvic organs.

Your blood is Rh-negative and your husband's blood is Rh-positive.

You have an infectious disease, such as tuberculosis or venereal disease.

You or your husband have a family history of inherited diseases or genetic defects.

You have a metabolic disorder such as diabetes or hyperthyroidism, or you have a family history of these problems.

You have previously had a child with birth defects or hemorrhagic disease.

You live or work in an atmosphere containing particular chemicals or environmental pollutants (see page 191).

SOME DISCOMFORTS ARE WARNING SIGNALS

Call your doctor or nurse-midwife at once if you notice any of the following:

Swelling or puffiness of hands or face

Swelling of ankles or feet, especially early in the day, every day, or a great deal

Blurred vision, dizziness, or spots before your eyes

Breast or nipple soreness, hardness, or inflammation

A severe, perhaps sudden, headache

Pains in your stomach, back, or legs

Sudden chills or fever

Sudden weight gain

Bleeding or discharge from the vagina

Vomiting day after day

Pain or a burning sensation when urinating

Decrease in the amount of urine

A steady leak or gush of fluid from the vagina

Note that the symptoms on this list are considered significant if they occur suddenly, continually, and/or severely.

SOME DISCOMFORTS CAN BE LARGELY IGNORED

There are a number of mild discomforts associated with pregnancy. The following, unless they become severe or excessively frequent, can be ignored:

Sleeplessness *or* sleepiness

Shortness of breath, or occasional faintness

Frequent shifts of mood, as from elation to depression and back again (but do read page 280 on "How to Avoid a Postpartum Depression")

Occasional acid indigestion, constipation, or hunger

Nosebleed (if occasional)

Backache or leg cramps (but do wear a good support, and do exercise your legs)

Nausea (now and then)

Frequent urination

Slight swelling of legs and ankles, especially after work or late in the day

In fact, if you ignore such occasional symptoms, they are very likely to disappear without your realizing it.

How It Used to Be

Above all, keep all croaking companions away. You will find in every neighborhood women who delight to give in detail all the terrible cases they have ever heard or imagined, and these are the women that you should shun, and in plain words, forbid the introduction of such topics if necessary.

Mrs. Emma F. Angell Drake, M.D.,
What a Young Wife Ought to Know, 1901

EATING FOR TWO?

Taking care of your body means eating properly. If you do not provide adequate nutrition for your unborn baby, he or she will be malnourished. But so will you. You'll become more tired, less capable of going through your day's work—*and* more susceptible to disease. If you eat the wrong foods, even if you eat a lot and gain weight, you'll be malnourished. And your baby is very likely to be less than the healthy, happy infant you could have.

Malnourished babies:

Are underweight at birth.
Are more often premature.
Have fewer brain cells than
    normal babies.
Have less resistance to disease.

The evidence becomes stronger and stronger almost daily that, without good nutrition, pregnancy and childbirth are just not going to progress well, and that the baby will suffer the consequences for the rest of his or her life. It really is that important. A malnourished baby is more likely to be born prematurely, to have a low birth-weight even if born at term, and to suffer more easily from infections and illnesses. Such a baby may be mentally affected, too, since intellectual development may lag. Protein is essential to the formation of the brain cells before birth, and a "baby" seriously deprived of good nutrition in early pregnancy may have a reduced fetal brain weight. A British study found that babies whose mothers were well nourished in pregnancy and gained sufficient weight did well intellectually in later life.

The work done by a team headed by Dr. Jack Lippes with "high-risk" clinic patients at Buffalo (New York) General Hospital also bears out these findings. A group of pregnant women were selected and given special information on nutrition from doctors, nurses, and hospital dietitians. They were supplied with vitamin mineral capsules and a special nutritional supplement high in protein that added twelve hundred calories to their daily diet. This group of mothers gave birth to babies who were larger, healthier, and had greater head circumferences (meaning greater fetal brain development) than equivalent babies in the hospital.

They had a much lower rate of prematurity and easier births.

There used to be a comforting notion that the baby simply took what it wanted from the mother regardless of what she herself ate. This really isn't true. That old saying "eating for two" really *is* a much better guide to pregnancy. When you are pregnant, you need to take in enough good food to feed yourself and the growing baby. By and large, the baby relies on what you eat, and so do you.

You want to remain active and healthy and feel as good as you possibly can up to and through delivery. If you don't eat properly, you are likely to be tired, possibly depressed, more susceptible to infections and ailments, and more likely to become seriously ill during pregnancy. Your body is, after all, working very hard at this time, even if you seem to be slowing down. Your blood flow is increased tremendously; your heart is pumping harder; your respiration is deeper.

Your body is well aware of the tremendous need of your baby for energy and nourishment, and plenty of good food is essential to keep this amazing system going. If you are in good physical shape when you become pregnant, you are likely to have an easier time throughout. And this involves your lifelong eating habits. But whatever your condition when pregnancy begins, you can make sure that, during pregnancy, you both eat as well as you possibly can.

WHAT SHOULD I EAT?

The normal levels of protein, minerals, and other nutritive substances have to be considerably increased during pregnancy. You need about three hundred extra calories a day just to keep going at your normal activity level. You need around forty-five percent more protein and twice as much calcium and ascorbic acid as usual. Certain B vitamins, folic acid and B_6 particularly, are very much more important during pregnancy than they were previously. Your iron intake is vital. So you need extra calories, and they must be chosen carefully. You should have a wide variety of foods rich in protein, minerals, and vitamins, and possibly some supplements as well.

Basically, what you eat during pregnancy should come from the following major groups:

Milk and milk products
Meat, fish, eggs
Cereals, dried beans, and peas
Fruits and vegetables

Milk and milk products are the very best source of calcium, which is vital to the good development of the "baby's" bones and teeth. The baby's milk teeth form well before birth in his or her gums; in the fourth month after conception calcium begins to be laid down in the tooth buds to form tooth enamel. If you cannot digest milk properly as a result of lactose intolerance, you can still get enough calcium through eating hard cheeses, and those of us who do not like milk usually do not mind yogurt or soft or hard cheese. Four cups of milk or yogurt daily are enough to supply the right amount of calcium.

Milk, of course, supplies some of the protein you need throughout the pregnancy. Protein intake is one of the most important factors in a good pregnancy. In fact, a low-protein diet has been linked to such serious health problems for the mother as toxemia and convulsions. Also, good development for the baby is directly related to how much protein a mother has in her diet.

Since good-quality protein is so important, you will need at least three servings of high-protein foods such as meat, fish, or eggs daily. These foods also supply important vitamins. Cereals and legumes (dried peas and beans) also supply protein, though not in such high quality, and are important to a well-balanced diet, especially since your energy requirements are so great during pregnancy. Some of the extra B vitamins you need are to be found in whole wheat breads, wheat germ, whole wheat cereals, nuts, and organ meats.

If you increase your meat intake, be careful about eating too many processed meats. The nitrites in bacon, salami, and lunch meats may be a serious health hazard at any time, and there are now clues that they may cause serious birth defects. In general, it is wise to keep away from food additives if you possibly can. Now is really a vital time to check the labeling of canned and packaged foods.

Fruits and vegetables are important for vitamins and minerals. You need plenty of vitamin C, although excessive use of vitamin C capsules is not wise.

Citrus fruits and dark yellow vegetables also supply the important vitamin A. Leafy green vegetables are a vital part of your diet. That traditional childhood enemy, spinach, is a great ally in pregnancy, since it is an excellent source of folic acid and vitamin B_6. Broccoli, too, is rich in these vitamins. Since cooking decreases the vitamin content in fruits and vegetables, portions of fresh fruit and salads are preferable.

You will need plenty of liquids since your body is taking on extra fluid at this time. As I have previously mentioned, excessive caffeine is now suspected of causing birth defects, so you should try to cut down on cola drinks and coffee. Water or unsweetened fruit or vegetable juices are the best way to take in the necessary liquids. Pregnancy is a very good time to buy a juicer!

Whether or not to use salt has been the source of so much controversy that I have included special material on salt at the end of this section.

DO I NEED SUPPLEMENTS?

Many doctors do recommend iron supplements during pregnancy since it is difficult, even if you eat such iron-rich foods as liver or dried fruits regularly, to maintain a satisfactory level. You can discuss this with your doctor. If you do not think you are getting enough folic acid, which is essential in keeping your uterus in the very best condition, you might want to take a supplement for this, too. On the whole, vitamin pills are not a substitute for a good diet with plenty of variety. After all, you need calories, which you can only get from food, as well as minerals and vitamins. However, I do believe that vitamins are a necessary addition to food—because the quality of food, or even your ability to absorb its nutrients, may be quite uneven.

WHEN AND HOW MUCH SHOULD I EAT?

Since so many of us have always been so careful about *overeating*, "eating for two," which means eating three full meals a day, may seem almost illegal! But you do need to eat regularly. Much of the time nausea during pregnancy is the result of your blood sugar dropping below a reasonable level because you are hungry. This is why the early morning is classically *the* time for nausea—after the long fast of the night. So you need breakfast—especially—and lunch and dinner. Possibly you might want to take five or six small meals at regular intervals instead of three large ones. You can try this out for yourself and see if it helps you feel more energetic and less nauseated.

At any time during pregnancy, it is not good policy to allow yourself to become starving hungry. A piece of fresh fruit in the morning (bananas are wonderful for this) or some cheese in the afternoon will help keep your energy level up between meals. This is not indulging yourself—you really need the calories. Of course, if you eat cake or cookies or ice cream sodas, you are only going to take in empty calories that won't help you or the baby, and will only put on some extra pounds. How much you eat and what you eat are both very important. It is as dangerous to become overweight as it is to be underweight during pregnancy, since overweight mothers may have serious conditions such as hypertension and may have difficult deliveries. Pregnancy doesn't give you a license to buy up all the dessert topping in the supermarket.

A NOTE ABOUT BANANAS

Bananas are rich in potassium and they are a high-energy food. If your stomach is upset, if you are nauseous, and particularly if you have vomited, bananas will help. They also have other nutrients in abundance: vitamin A, thiamine, riboflavin, niacin, vitamin C, vitamin B_6, calcium and phosphorus, and iron. They have *no* cholesterol! Don't worry about their being fattening. A banana is only 100 calories.

THE NECESSITY OF VITAMIN A, VITAMIN C, AND FOLIC ACID

Dr. Tom Brewer and his wife, Gail Sforza Brewer, Ph.D., have been pioneers in the new perspective toward nutrition in pregnancy. Their influential book, *What Every Pregnant Woman Should Know: The Truth About Diets and Drugs in Pregnancy* (1977), attacks low-sodium diets and the use of diuretics and stresses the incredible importance of prenatal nutrition. Dr. Brewer has for some years traveled all over the United States on speaking engagements with his "brown bag" of nutritious foods. He has bitterly attacked the American diet of junk foods as dangerous for pregnant women and unborn children. The Brewers believe that most "problem" pregnancies would be eradicated if American women had good nutrition as children, ate well during pregnancy, used salt, and refused to follow some obstetricians' rules on dieting. Some of their advice on vitamins in pregnancy, published in their book, follows.

Three of the most important vitamins for a pregnant woman are A, C and folic acid (part of the B complex). Vitamin A has been called the "anti-infection" vitamin since the 1930's. Mothers who have a balanced diet with adequate vitamin A seldom develop serious infections of the kidneys, bladder, uterus, lungs, liver or breast during pregnancy or after delivery. . . . Vitamin A keeps skin healthy and helps the lining of the female tract, bladder, kidneys, stomach, intestines and bronchial tree resist infection by bacteria. Foods containing vitamin A, in addition to whole milk and eggs, are the yellow and orange fruits and vegetables and the dark, green leafy vegetables. There is vitamin A in butter and margarine. . . .

Vitamin C is exceptionally important. It helps the uterus grow strong, and so makes for an easier labor and birth. Poorly nourished women have thin, flabby wombs which function poorly and result in longer labor . . . In addition to the citrus fruits, vitamin C is found in many other foods. Strawberries, cantaloupes, tomatoes, broccoli, cabbage, green peppers and potatoes also supply considerable amounts.

Folic acid is part of the complex of nutrients needed to build red blood cells. Iron, protein and vitamin B_{12} are also part of this complex. The best sources of these nutrients are liver and kidney, eggs, and dark, green leafy vegetables. . . . Since folic acid is water soluble, cooking greens and throwing away the water, as most people do, results in loss of this vitamin.

Using these vegetables in salads is far better.

WATCHING YOUR WEIGHT?

If you are hungry between meals, snack on one half to a whole serving of any fruit or vegetable.

Do not fill up on pie, cake, soda, candy. Eat as little sugar or honey as possible. Even if you tend to be slim and do not have a weight-gain problem, avoid these foods, since they will dull your appetite for food with nutritional value.

If you are gaining weight too rapidly, try cutting back on the bread-cereal group and omitting dried beans and peas, dried fruits, and nuts. Eat an extra serving of yellow or green leafy vegetables instead.

If you *really* have to watch your weight, follow these suggestions for an average day's meals:

Breakfast. One orange or fruit juice; ½ cup cereal with skim milk and just a touch of sugar; 1 slice whole wheat toast (no butter); glass of skim milk; coffee or tea with milk.

Lunch. Salad of lettuce, tomato, cottage cheese, carrot and celery sticks; *or* 2 soft-cooked eggs with whole wheat toast; glass of skim milk; fruit.

Dinner. Slice of melon; average portion of broiled or roasted meat, fish, or poultry; one green or yellow vegetable; green salad dressed with lemon juice; glass of skim milk *or* tea with milk; Jell-O *or* fruit.

Snack(s). (No more than two a day.) 1 ounce hard or semisoft cheese; 2 slices Melba toast; 1 cup bouillon; 1 slice lean chicken; 1 stalk celery; cucumber sticks; a handful of raw asparagus, zucchini, string beans, or mushrooms; ½ cup cottage cheese; 1 bread stick; 4 carrot sticks; ½ tomato; 1 tangerine; fresh pineapple slice; a dish of blueberries.

From My Favorite Dessert Book
For a Sweet Tooth

Berry Ice (Nero's Pleasure)

1 pt. fresh berries	¼ c. orange or
¾ c. honey	lemon juice
¾ c. water	

1. Wash and puree berries in a food mill or blender. Strain through a fine sieve or strainer to remove seeds.

2. Combine honey and water into a syrup and boil over a low heat until thoroughly mixed. Cool.

3. Blend pureed berries, honey syrup, and juice.

4. Churn-freeze.

Nectarine Sherbet

6 fresh ripe nectarines	1¾ c. water
¼ c. orange juice	1 T. grated orange rind
½ c. honey	1 egg white
1 T. lemon juice	1 c. milk

1. Peel and pit nectarines. Puree in a food mill or blender with the ¼ cup of orange juice. Set aside.

2. Combine honey, lemon juice, and water in a small saucepan and heat for 10 minutes. Add the nectarine puree and grated orange rind to the honey mixture and continue cooking, stirring occasionally, for 15 minutes. Cool.

3. Beat egg white lightly and fold into nectarine mixture. Add milk.

4. Churn-freeze.

Robert O. Soman, *The Natural Foods Ice Cream Book,* 1975

For Health's Sake, Generally *Avoid:*

Sugar
Chocolate
Candies
Cookies
Noodles and pasta
Hot dogs
Processed meats
Ice cream and other heavy-calorie items
Liquor
Coffee and cola (much)

FOOD DOS AND DON'TS

Do keep track of what you eat every day. If you are short a serving of a major food category every now and then, don't worry. But if you are consistently avoiding fruits or any form of cereal, try to change your eating patterns and discuss this with your doctor.

Don't overeat. Don't eat candies and cakes or drink soda to excess.

Do tell your doctor if milk disagrees with you or if you have trouble getting your daily three to four cups down. You may need a milk substitute. There are several possibilities, from calcium tablets to Soyalac.

Do cut coffee or tea or cola drinking down—and preferably out. Substitute milk or fruit juice for at least one cup of coffee per day.

Don't gulp food; savor it.

Don't try to save money or time now by eating convenience or nonnutritious items.

Protein Preeminent

Protein is crucial to the development of your baby-to-be. Body *and* brain of the fetus are produced largely from the proteins that go into *your* body. The protein you eat also keeps your own body and its organs in working order and supplies the building materials you need for your own blood cells, antibodies, and new tissue for your growing breasts and uterus.

As nutritionist Adelle Davis pointed out in her 1975 book, *Let's Have Healthy Babies,* the proteins containing the largest amounts of all the vital amino acids (which are the basic elements derived from proteins, which build body structures) are called complete. And incomplete proteins need to be combined in complementary ways to be at all useful in building tissues.

According to Ms. Davis and many other nutritional authorities, animal protein, which is more complete than vegetable protein, is to be preferred. Most vegetables do not contain enough essential amino acids. (Wheat germ, soybean, some nuts, and yeast are exceptions.)

Vegetarian pregnant women should be exceptionally careful about their diets. Many are not getting enough B_{12} and iron. As a result, babies develop deficiency diseases. It's very important either to change your diet during pregnancy or to take some supplements—cautiously cautiously. If you are and remain vegetarian during pregnancy, your nutrition research should be even more extensive and thorough, however.

WHAT ABOUT SALT?

In the 1950s and 1960s when women were encouraged to keep their weight in pregnancy as low as possible, obstetricians regularly advised patients with normal pregnancies to restrict salt intake. At the first sign of edema (swelling of the ankles and hands) women were put on totally salt-free diets and often given diuretics (pills which reduce water retention). Both practices have been discredited in recent years, in part through the fierce attacks of an organization called SPUN—the Society for the Protection of the Unborn Through Nutrition, of which the Brewers were founder members.

SPUN and other nutritionists claimed that salt-free diets were doing far more damage than good, and were only causing the very conditions they were supposed to alleviate. Toxemia, which is a severe form of edema and can lead to convulsions, was believed by many doctors to be preventable when women with mild edema used a salt-free diet and diuretics. SPUN claimed that the situation was quite the opposite—that this kind of treatment led to women developing toxemia and on some occasions resulted in patients dying of the disease. They felt that studies bore out their belief that salt is necessary in pregnancy, that diuretics are dangerous, and that a woman on a salt-restricted or salt-free diet is putting herself at unnecessary risk. (They continue to feel the same way today.)

As a result of all this controversy the American College of Obstetricians and Gynecologists (ACOG) is now recommending that women use a moderate amount of salt in pregnancy. The March of Dimes Birth Defects Foundation states in a recent publication, "Salt is a necessary part of your diet if your general health is good and your pregnancy progresses as it should."

HOW THE WEIGHT BREAKS DOWN

Over one third is the baby, the placenta, and the amniotic fluid.

Your uterus, extra breast-weight, and blood and tissue fluid account for slightly less than one third.

The maternal fat stores amount to almost another one third. At the beginning the uterus and breasts will weigh proportionately more.

HOW MUCH SHOULD I WEIGH?

Ten years ago the weekly visit to the obstetrician was often a battleground over pounds and ounces. Attitudes toward weight have really changed since then. Eighteen pounds was once regarded as the *absolute maximum* amount a woman should put on during pregnancy, and some doctors encouraged women to gain considerably less. Babies with birth weights in the six-pound range were considered to be perfect babies.

During the last few years, however, nutritionists and lay and professional people interested in birth practices have been looking at childbirth in countries like Denmark and Sweden where baby birth weights are regularly around eight pounds. These informed people have been concluding that American babies would benefit considerably from being bigger. So, if your baby is born at 7½ pounds, that's no longer a "large" baby. Doctors believe that a good weight gain during pregnancy is directly linked with your baby's physical and intellectual development after birth, and considerably cuts down the risk of prematurity. A more mature baby is usually healthier and the fetal brain more developed. The medical profession also has begun to feel that women with low weight gains are robbing themselves of much-needed energy when the body is going through a time of incredible change. Since the pregnant woman needs calories, she must necessarily put on weight.

The American College of Obstetricians and Gynecologists recently revised its recommendations on weight gains during pregnancy, and now encourages women to gain twenty-two to twenty-six pounds above their normal weight. Some American doctors, such as Dr. Myron Winick of the Institute of Human Nutrition at Columbia University, feel that larger gains, twenty-five to thirty pounds, are ideal. These recommendations are for women who are at an "ideal" weight for their height and age before becoming pregnant. Seriously underweight women should try to gain around thirty pounds, since the baby is starting off at something of a disadvantage. Obese women, who used to be encouraged to diet during pregnancy, are now told to wait until after the baby is born. Undernourished obese mothers are very likely to give birth to a stillborn baby or one who dies soon after birth. Today women who are overweight when pregnancy begins are being encouraged to eat nutritiously and put on a moderate amount of weight.

Ideally, you should put on your twenty-five or so pounds steadily throughout your pregnancy. In the first three months you should gain about 1½ to 3 pounds and continue to put on 1 pound every 9 days after that. Again, it is important not to exceed a reasonable amount of weight. You won't be comfortable, and, in cases of really excessive weight gains, you are endangering yourself and the baby. The birth will probably be more difficult and the baby more likely to be distressed.

One Perspective on Calories Needed

A moderately active woman needs approximately 2,600 calories every day to meet her normal energy requirements in the last three months of pregnancy. If she is carrying twins, the figure is closer to 3,100 calories. On the kind of diet recommended for weight control by most obstetricians, she is only going to get 1,700 calories—a deficit of at least 900. (Gail Sforza Brewer with Tom Brewer, M.D. *What Every Pregnant Woman Should Know*, 1977)

The Common Problem of Obesity

An inadequate weight gain during pregnancy is almost always due to inadequate dietary intake and usually has little to do with work activity. Currently, it is recommended that a woman gain 10–12 kilograms during pregnancy. A well-balanced diet, including at least 75 grams of protein per day, should be maintained. A more common problem is obesity, defined as more than 20% above standard weight for height. Obesity and excessive weight gain during pregnancy may interfere with activity and are associated with increased likelihood of dystocia, fetal distress, birth trauma, and large birth weight. Finally, anemias and

other nutritional deficiencies may diminish the patient's resistance to infection and toxins and impair her ability to perform physical tasks. (American College of Obstetricians and Gynecologists, *Guidelines on Pregnancy and Work*, 1977)

Malnutrition of the Pregnant: Why Not Solve It?

We are prepared, and we are a rich enough country, to afford $500 million to $2 billion to prolong life for a few years in those with irreversibly damaged hearts and kidneys.

Why, then, the incredible neglect annually of many thousands of pregnant women whose malnutrition causes irreversible fetal brain damage and physical anomalies in children who will for a lifetime be a burden to themselves, to their families, and to society? These are preventable conditions due to ignorance and/or lack of the most simple nutritional essentials.

From strictly an economic standpoint, preventive obstetrical care is one of our nation's soundest investments. For each case of severe mental retardation, which frequently results from inadequate maternal nutrition, that is prevented, the economic gain to society is more than $900,000. If we are to avoid such retardation, we must insure that no mother, either through poverty or ignorance, malnourishes her children in utero.

The highest priority in American education today should be the establishment of a national program of nutrition and early childhood education. . . . It is the obligation of educators at all levels—in schools, colleges, institutions, social agencies, and medical institutions—to provide this education. It is the obligation of society to see that no carrying mother or young child is undernourished because of financial need. (Tom Brewer, M.D., and Jay Hodin, "Why Women Must Meet the Nutritional Stress of Pregnancy," *21st Century Obstetrics, Now!*, 1977)

YOUR SKIN IS MORE THAN SKIN

During pregnancy your skin is more active than usual in helping your other organs eliminate impurities. Therefore, daily baths or showers are particularly important; cleanliness will encourage the proper function of skin glands. Use a pure mild soap. Never use bubble bath or bath oil. Any skin lotion you like should be rubbed or smoothed on after bathing. In the later months, be especially careful getting into and out of the shower or tub. Try to bathe only when your husband or someone else is in the house to help out if you need a hand. Be sure there is a skidproof mat in the tub and in the shower. (During the last two months showers are preferable to tub baths because they are easier to get into and out of when your weight is tipping you forward.)

Good prenatal hygiene includes cleanliness of the scalp and hair. Daily brushing and weekly (at least) shampooing are basic—more frequent if your hair tends to be oily, or if you wear it long and loose.

STRETCH MARKS

The tendency of women to develop these varies with skin tone, complexion, weight, and each pregnancy—and probably other factors as well. Some people think creams and lotions and gentle massage work. Some people don't. There is no harm in trying. Cocoa butter has been preferred by generations of women for this purpose; massage it gently into the skin at the hips and over the abdomen as desired. Sometimes stretch marks appear on the breasts and thighs as well.

BREAST CARE

About the fourth month a colorless fluid called colostrum begins to ooze from the nipples. This means that your breasts are preparing to produce milk. If this secretion forms a crust, use a little cold cream, lanolin, or cocoa butter to soften it. Small squares of gauze worn over your nipples will keep the colostrum from wetting your clothing.

WHAT ABOUT DRUGS, DRINKS, WEEDS?

Alcoholic beverages. Your unborn "baby" will absorb the effects of your martini almost as soon as you will. While an occasional drink is believed to have no serious consequences, heavy drinking will. Alcoholism can interfere with maternal health and nutrition, thus giving the growing fetus a weak start. Children born to alcoholic mothers may have low birth weight, and may even become addicted to alcohol themselves while still in the uterus.

Antibiotics. Take only on recommendation of a doctor you trust who knows you are pregnant; do *not* automatically reach for the medication you usually take if you have a cold or other minor infection. See a doctor for severe infections.

Aspirin. Very occasional use, with a drink of water, is considered okay; heavy use is to be

---

How It Used to Be

Those who have not been accustomed to bathing should not begin the practice during pregnancy, and in any case great care should be exercised during the latter months. It is better to preserve cleanliness by sponging with tepid water than by entire baths. Foot-baths are always dangerous. Sea-bathing sometimes causes miscarriage, but sea air and the sponging of the body with salt water are beneficial. The shower-bath is of course too great a shock to the system, and a very warm bath is too relaxing.

George H. Napheys, M.D., *The Physical Life of Women: Advice to the Maiden, Wife and Mother*, 1889

avoided at all times, and particularly in the last few weeks.

Cigarettes. Stop smoking altogether. Women who are heavy smokers give birth to a disproportionate number of underweight babies. Plus, continual dosing with nicotine interferes with fetal nourishment and development.

Coffee, tea, cola drinks. Avoid as much as possible. The latest evidence is that caffeine taken by the mother-to-be can have adverse effects on the fetus. Colas and tea contain caffeine.

Hallucinogens, amphetamines, narcotics, diet pills. Don't take them under absolutely any circumstances! They weaken your system, and can cause addiction in the unborn "baby." Avoid anyone who offers them.

Household products. Be careful of some familiar household products at this time. Aerosol sprays should be avoided and anything such as spot cleaning fluid or paint thinner that carries a warning label should be handled with extreme care to avoid inhaling the fumes. This is something to remember particularly when you are getting a room ready for the baby. Look for cautions on paints or other decorating products before buying them.

Laxatives; digestive medicines, including sodium bicarbonate, antacids. Occasional single dose is considered okay, but frequent and/or heavy use is not. For chronic indigestion or constipation, see a doctor or your nurse-midwife.

Marijuana. At this point we don't know, scientifically, what the effects of marijuana on an unborn "baby" might be. Don't take the risk. Let pregnancy be your high!

Megavitamins. Eat a balanced diet and you and your "baby" are likely to get adequate natural nutrition. Take supplementary vitamins only on recommendation of a doctor who knows you are pregnant; an excessive amount of some vitamins can be harmful to your child-to-be. Do a careful check.

Tranquilizers, sleeping pills. Avoid these; put up with sleeplessness if necessary. Some tranquilizers cause birth defects. If you have a sleep problem, consult a doctor or your nurse-midwife.

WHAT ABOUT ILLNESSES?

Contagious diseases. German measles in the mother-to-be, which I deal with later in this section, is notorious for its crippling effect on the developing fetus. Other common infections such as the flu or the chicken pox or mumps may be harmful at certain points of the pregnancy. It is difficult to avoid people and places that may be infectious, but try as much as you can and talk to your doctor if you do fall ill. Many common ailments of the past *are* past, but not completely.

Toxoplasmosis. Exposure to the disease of toxoplasmosis through the mother-to-be can have extremely serious consequences for an unborn "child," including blindness, brain damage, and possibly death. The virus that causes toxoplasmosis is found in raw meat and in the feces of cats, whose diet includes raw meat (as do the diets of birds and rodents). This means that while you may have enjoyed rare steak in the past, make sure now that you eat beef or other meat heated to at least 140 degrees Fahrenheit. Do *not* clean the cat box yourself, and avoid contact with cats that live outdoors. Since many adults have had toxoplasmosis (and are therefore immune) without realizing it, you might want to reassure yourself and have a blood test taken.

Evidence Against Aspirin

Anemia developed twice as frequently among (regular) aspirin users as among non-users.

The incidence of late delivery was four times higher among regular aspirin users than among non-users.

Severe hemorrhages during delivery occurred twice as often among regular users as among non-users.

The incidence of miscarriages and still-born children was significantly greater among "aspirin addicts" than among non-users. Regular users also tended to have smaller babies, and about half the infants born to aspirin-takers showed traces of aspirin in their blood (at birth). ("Expectant Moms Hurt By Aspirin," *Moneysworth*, February 16, 1976)

◇ ◇ ◇

SMOKING AND BABIES: A DREADFUL MIX

In 1979 the U. S. government released a major report on the effects of smoking on women and unborn children. The U. S. Collaborative Perinatal Project, undertaken in 12 major hospitals, examined 50,000 pregnancies.

Pregnant women, the study found, are significantly endangering their children. Mothers who smoke are more likely to suffer spontaneous abortion, to give birth prematurely, or to have babies who die at birth. Even babies whose mothers deliver normally are likely to be smaller at birth—and remain smaller in childhood. Such babies are more likely to suffer Rh disease, or serious damage to vital organs such as the heart. And the possibility of infant crib death is increased by 52 percent by women who smoke during pregnancy.

The report advises women even contemplating pregnancy to give up smoking as early as possible. A past history of smoking can create problems during pregnancy and delivery, too. For instance, the incidence of placenta praevia, a serious birth complication caused by the placenta being attached abnormally low in the womb, is found by the researchers to be higher among women who have smoked in the past. Placenta tissue may also be adversely affected by previous smoking.

The study found a relationship between the amount smoked and the degree of risk. There was a 35 percent increase in the risk of perinatal death among babies born of pregnant women who smoked more than a pack a day, while those smoking less than a pack faced a 20 percent increase concerning this potential disaster.

Give it up. Give it up.

A WARNING

Recently my mail contained a fifty-four-page document (with over nine pages of bibliography) attempting to prove that cigarette smoking is *not* harmful to women and babies. The first pages of this apologia, *Fact or Fancy*, are devoted to pregnant women and new mothers and their babies.

Since *Fact or Fancy* has been put out by the Tobacco Institute, you should be warned that the possibility of objective reporting is slim. You also should be warned that, despite the source, there will be continuing reports in the press questioning the harmfulness of smoking, stemming from this and other efforts of the institute.

And you should *not* be fooled. At the very least, cigarette smoke cannot be proven good for babies. So why add any questionable substance other than pure food, water, and air to your baby's bloodstream? Why blow smoke into a baby's lungs when you don't have to? Regardless of all other factors, smoking diminishes the oxygen in the blood and constricts blood vessels. Both of these, it is logical to assume, restrict the growing fetus's source of food supply and of oxygen. This alone is reason enough to stop.

I think the Tobacco Institute should let mothers and babies alone.

◇ ◇ ◇

How Alcohol Affects Babies

One of the most common causes of fetal damage is alcohol, which drinkers rarely recognize for what it is—a powerful drug. The more a pregnant woman drinks, the greater her risk of giving birth to an abnormal baby. Studies show an increased frequency of stillbirths, premature babies, mental retardation, physical deformity, and behavioral problems among children born to alcoholics. The National Institute of Alcohol Abuse and Alcoholism says *there is a definite risk of birth defects when a pregnant woman drinks 3 ounces or more of alcohol a day. Drinking 1 to 3 ounces of alcohol a day may be risky* and caution is advised. Birth defects resulting from drinking during pregnancy are known as fetal alcohol syndrome. (Pauline Postotnik, "Drugs and Pregnancy," *FDA Consumer*, October 1978)

◇ ◇ ◇

Another Warning: X Rays and Pregnancy

In the May 1977 issue of the *FDA Consumer*, James L. Morrison and Mark Barnett explained why X rays are risky during pregnancy. They wrote:

Tests with animals have shown that when high doses of radiation are administered during pregnancy the risk of major malformations in the offspring is increased. This risk is greatest during the stage of pregnancy when the various body organs are being formed which, in humans, is the second through the seventh week of pregnancy. During this period the developing embryo also is most sensitive to other agents that can cause malformations, such as drugs and viruses. It is generally agreed, however, that malformations are very unlikely to occur in unborn children as a result of exposure to ordinary diagnostic x rays.

Evidence from studies of atomic bombing survivors and other groups suggests that large doses of radiation received during the later stages of pregnancy can produce severe effects on the behavior and intelligence of the child through damage to the central nervous system. The children of Japanese women who were exposed to atomic radiation during pregnancy showed more of a tendency to suffer severe mental retardation than the children of mothers who had not been exposed.

Information from animal studies suggests that smaller doses of radiation than those received by the Japanese survivors could produce slight effects on intelligence or behavior which would be very difficult to measure. It is not known whether these kinds of subtle effects might occur as a result of diagnostic x-ray exposures.

Several studies indicate there is an increased risk of leukemia and other cancer among children exposed to radiation as a result of abdominal x-ray examinations of their mothers during pregnancy. Although precise estimates of risk are not possible, the results of several studies indicate that the possibility of a child developing cancer before 15 years of age as a result of the radiation would be around one in a thousand, assuming a typical two- or three-film x-ray examination was made of the mother's abdomen. The likelihood would obviously increase somewhat if the examination involved more radiation, as with the use of the fluoroscope.

. . . any unnecessary abdominal x-ray exposure of a pregnant woman should be avoided. The physician should be able to explain the reasons for an x-ray examination and why it cannot be postponed until after the baby is born.

Should Your Baby-to-Be Be X-rayed?

The atomic scientists themselves have become very concerned about radiation. In the September 1978 edition of the *Bulletin of the Atomic Scientist*, Karl Z. Morgan writes:

> Reports of a significant increase in the risk of cancer from exposure to low levels of ionizing radiation [therapeutic radiation which is capable of altering cells] and evidence suggesting that federal agencies had attempted to squelch these reports resulted in the congressional hearings held last winter on this subject being conducted at a rather hot pace. . . .

> The Bross Study has shown a 5,000 per cent increased risk of cancer among the children who had been exposed to diagnostic X-ray in utero, and who later developed certain respiratory diseases. . . .

> Children who received in-utero diagnostic X-ray exposure have a 40 to 50 per cent increase in risk of dying of leukemia. . . .

> . . . children have a higher risk of dying of radiation-induced leukemia than do middle-aged persons. . . . The cancer risk from exposure to ionizing radiation is much greater than was thought to be the case some years ago. . . .

> *The emphasis of this article* on cancer risk is not to depreciate the seriousness of genetic risks from exposure to ionizing radiation but rather to point out that the scientific community was rather smug 15 years ago (as some scientists are still today) in the belief that somatic [bodily] risk is far less than genetic risk and that somatic risk is almost negligible at low doses. Now most of us recognize that the risk of inducing cancer at low doses of radiation is far greater than we once thought it to be and it may be as great or greater for the human race than genetic risk.

Drugs and Defects

When you take any medicine, you are dosing your unborn baby (fetus) as well as yourself. But its tiny immature body may not react to the chemical as you do. Drugs that comfort you may interrupt your unborn baby's growth or development. . . .

Most birth defects are caused during the first twelve weeks of pregnancy, when a baby's body, arms, legs, and internal organs are being formed. The wrong drug taken at this time could interrupt, or drastically change, part of the baby's development. That same drug taken at some other time in pregnancy might not affect the fetus at all. (March of Dimes pamphlet, *DATA*)

Drugs and Pregnancy: Problems from Pills

Many women have a healthy skepticism about taking drugs when they are pregnant. Unfortunately, however, we have become a nation of "pill poppers," taking medicines for minor aches and pains without really thinking about them. Thus some pregnant women take drugs, both prescription and over-the-counter preparations, for minor conditions such as colds, coughs, or nervousness when use of such drugs may not be necessary.

Some drugs can be beneficial to mother and child. Indeed, many infants owe their survival to drugs given to the mother during pregnancy. It is important to understand, however, that there are risks as well as benefits with any drug a person takes.

. . . Whether the fetus will be harmed depends on the nature of the drug itself, the time during pregnancy the mother takes it, and the amount of drug to which the fetus is exposed.

Physical defects can be caused in an unborn child by drugs taken by the mother during the early stages of pregnancy when the cells of the fetus are rapidly growing and organ systems are developing. The most publicized example of this danger occurred during the late 1950's and early 1960's with the drug thalidomide, a supposedly safe sedative that was sold without prescription in Germany and England.

. . . The use of the hormones estrogen and progestin during the first 3 or 4 months of pregnancy can increase the risk of birth defects, including limb and heart defects.

. . . Other drugs are suspected of causing some serious adverse effects on the fetus.

. . . Minor tranquilizers, such as Valium, Librium, Miltown, and others containing meprobamate or benzodiazepine derivatives, when taken by a mother during early pregnancy, may increase the risk that her baby will be born with a cleft lip or palate.

. . . Aspirin and other drugs containing salicylate should not be taken during the last 3 months of pregnancy except under a doctor's supervision. Salicylate, a common ingredient in many over-the-counter painkillers, may prolong pregnancy and labor and may cause excessive bleeding before and after delivery. (Pauline Postotnik, "Drugs and Pregnancy," *FDA Consumer*, October 1978)

An Anthropologist's View of Drugs

Virtually all drugs, no matter when or by whatever route administered, are known to have a detrimental effect upon the fetus, not to mention their frequent ill-effects upon the mother. It took the thalidomide tragedy to bring the danger of administering such drugs to the pregnant woman to the attention of the public. Nevertheless, to this day many anesthetists and obstetricians blithely continue on their unrestrained way, assaulting the fetus and mother with drugs, ignoring the literally hundreds of researches which prove beyond any question that such drugs are damaging. The consequences to the individual, to the family, and to the society resulting from such professional irresponsibility are so serious that the time is now long overdue for government intervention.

Dr. [Frances O.] Kelsey [who discovered the dangers of thalidomide] . . . attributes some 80 percent of congenital abnormalities of unknown causation to the uncontrolled administration of drugs. Everything from cleft-palate and harelip to various degrees of mental retardation has been traced to the administration of drugs to the pregnant mother. The facts are now fully documented, and it is therefore quite inexcusable for anyone, let alone alleged specialists, to go on disregarding them. (Ashley Montagu, "Social Impacts of Unnecessary Intervention and Unnatural Surroundings in Childbirth," *21st Century Obstetrics, Now!*, 1977)

ARE THERE ANY HARMLESS MEDICATIONS?

"The fact is that only medicines which are necessary to treat a specific, serious ailment should be administered, in my judgment."

So says J. Robert Willson, M.D., professor and chairman of the Department of Obstetrics and Gynecology at the University of Michigan Medical School.

"Even drugs which have been reasonably well studied and are considered to be safe during pregnancy may have an adverse effect under certain circumstances," he continues.

The University of Michigan specialist says that a totally nonmedicated pregnancy was obviously impossible with certain patients, because some require insulin, antibiotics, hormones, and other preparations.

However, physicians need to know that fetal and perinatal research has revealed a catalog of medications thought to be harmless that are being routinely and excessively prescribed, resulting often in congenital defects in the infant. Tranquilizers and sedatives, so frequently prescribed today, have been found to produce mental retardation and vitamin K deficiency in infants.

"Medicines should not be prescribed for the relief of minor symptoms, and pregnant women should be warned against the dangers of self-medication," Dr. Willson says.

Drug Effects Years Later

Last year [1977], the University of Chicago was slapped with a $77 million class-action lawsuit filed on behalf of more than 1,000 women who unknowingly took part in a University experiment some 35 years ago with the synthetic hormone DES.

. . . DES had effects, 15 to 20 years later, on the male offspring of mothers who had been given the treatment, as cases of defects in genitalia and alterations in Vitamin E levels among these young men began to surface in the '70's.

. . . DES is still being given—as the "morning after" pill or to dry up breast milk. (Dr. Robert Mendelsohn, "The People's Doctor," syndicated column, February 1978)

WHAT YOU SHOULD KNOW ABOUT GERMAN MEASLES (RUBELLA)

German measles is not the same as "ordinary" measles, which lasts longer and is caused by a different virus. German measles, also known as rubella, usually occurs in young children, and lasts only a few days. It is such a mild ailment that it is possible for someone to have it and not know it. There may be low fever and a pale pink rash that is more spread out than spotty. A more noticeable symptom is swelling of the glands behind the ears and at the back of the neck. (However, swollen glands may indicate other illnesses as well.)

A child with German measles should be kept in bed for a couple of days, or as long as symptoms are noticeable. There are no serious aftereffects.

But if a woman is exposed to rubella during the first three months of pregnancy, the normal development of the fetus may be interrupted, and the baby might be born with severe birth defects.

Fortunately, there is a reliable vaccine. *But women who are or may be pregnant should never be given rubella vaccine*, because it may act just as the disease itself and cause defective development of the fetus. All children from one year on should be vaccinated, because they are most likely to get rubella and transmit it to others. Usually pediatricians vaccinate most young children against German measles. In some communities the school system provides vaccination.

If you have not been vaccinated and are now pregnant, try not to be around children who have not been vaccinated. Do not babysit, or even teach school, or give music lessons—*unless* you have checked and made sure that the children you are with have been protected.

For information about rubella vaccination programs in your community, consult your local health department.

It may not be of help to you for your current pregnancy, but measles will soon be a disease of the past—and rubella is on the run, too.

Group W's medical correspondent William Hines reports that the date of October 1982 has been set for the final disappearance of red measles. At the same time a new rubella vaccine has been approved by the Food and Drug Administration. The new vaccine, which became available in 1979, works much better than the old one.

WHAT YOU SHOULD KNOW ABOUT THE Rh FACTOR

The Rh factor (named after the rhesus monkey upon which it was tested) is a sensitive factor in our red blood cells. It is not a defect; rather it is the interaction of two normal but incompatible blood types. Most of us are Rh-positive—which means that this factor is present in our blood system. The rest are Rh-negative. The difference between Rh-positive and -negative becomes important when an Rh-negative woman is carrying an Rh-positive child. (Her mate's blood factor determines this.) This situation very rarely causes problems in first pregnancies, but can have fatal consequences (miscarriages and stillbirths) in subsequent conceptions. (An aborted first pregnancy counts as a full pregnancy in this respect.)

In 1969 a new desensitizing vaccine began to be widely used. It replaced total blood transfusion. Scientists believe that the Rh factor will disappear in America within the next ten to fifteen years; almost 100 percent use of the desensitizing vaccine in hospitals and abortion clinics is expected. Thereafter, succeeding generations may never know this condition.

In France the Rh antigen is being given orally during pregnancy. If this method is effective, the procedure will be infinitely simplified.

The March of Dimes pamphlet *Mission Possible: A Happy Baby Summer* explains the Rh factor and what steps can be taken to avoid serious problems. Check with your library for this and other publications on the Rh factor.

EXERCISE? WHY?

For several hundred years pregnant women have been coddled, told to rest—indeed even forced to rest—and prevented from doing any real work or taking any exercise more strenuous than a short stroll. But today exercises are prescribed for pregnancy, for the labor period, and for the time after the baby comes. And it's been a very significant development—easing the whole process of having a baby, and improving appearance, too. Many a woman, contemplating a stomach gone to flab, has regretted listening to a

doctor who advised her to "wear a girdle and forget it."

Some exercises are designed to help maintain your body tone. Some will strengthen and help you control the muscles involved in labor and delivery. Special breathing exercises will also strengthen you and give you conscious control over your contractions during labor.

Any kind of aerobic exercise you do during pregnancy helps your body prepare for delivery. Carol Stahmann Dilfer, author of *Your Baby, Your Body*, explains what such exercises are and why they are important:

> Any exercise that (a) makes your heart work harder than normal for a longish period of time, while (b) causing your body to demand more oxygen, and (c) making you breathe more deeply and rapidly and use all your lung space—way down to the bottom of your lungs—in the process can be considered an aerobic exercise.
>
> Aerobic exercise improves the tone of the blood vessels, and makes them more pliable, so that they can perform their function more efficiently. And it does something even more astonishing. It can actually cause your body to open latent blood vessels and to create new ones. . . .
>
> . . . When your heart, lungs, and circulatory systems are working well, your body does not have to use so much energy for those basic functions. And so, there is more energy left for the other things you want to do. But, what is perhaps more important is what aerobics will do for you during labor and delivery. When your cardiovascular system is healthy, when your oxygen delivery system is good, and your lungs strong, your body is much more capable of working hard without tiring. And labor, of course, is hard work. Aerobically fit women labor more efficiently and feel better after delivery than do unconditioned women. It's as simple as that.

If you attend a childbirth preparation class (and I urge you to do so) you will undoubtedly be shown a number of different exercises. Be sure to find a doctor or nurse-midwife who understands the basic value of exercise. You may also be able to find a class devoted specifically to exercises for pregnancy, such as the ones Elisabeth Bing holds in New York City.

PELVIC ROCKING

This exercise may be done in any comfortable position: standing, sitting, lying down, or on all fours. It should be performed daily, and helps relieve abdominal pressure during pregnancy and lower backache during pregnancy and early labor. It can also be resumed following birth of the baby to firm abdominal muscles.

1. Tighten your abdominal wall, pulling in and up, and tuck in your buttocks. This will rock your pelvis upward, flattening your lower back as you straighten the hollow there.

2. Slowly relax your abdomen and buttocks, allowing the hollow of your back to return. Take care, however, not to accentuate the curvature of your back.

3. Repeat the exercise five or six times, maintaining a slow, rhythmic motion.

RIB CAGE LIFTING

This comfort measure may help relieve pressure under the ribs and make it easier for you to breathe. It may be done sitting or standing, but sitting tailor-fashion at the same time will also help limber joints and strengthen thigh muscles.

1. Curve your arm over your head on affected side. An alternate method is to lift first one shoulder and then the other, as high as possible.

2. Perform whenever necessary.

LEG ELEVATING

This promotes good circulation in the legs and reduces discomfort from varicose veins, leg cramps, and leg fatigue. It should be done before going to sleep at night and, if discomfort persists, at intervals throughout the day. Some suggestions for leg elevating:

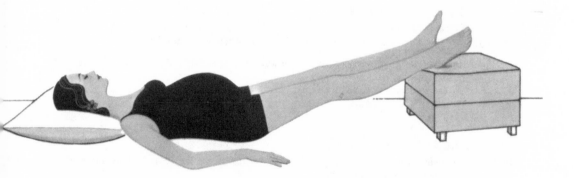

1. Lie on the floor or bed. Prop your heels on a chair or headboard so that your legs are at about a 45° angle to your body. Remain this way for a few minutes or as long as you feel comfortable.

2. When you sit, keep your legs elevated and supported so there is no feeling of pressure or strain. Do *not* sit with your knees crossed.

3. Sleep with the foot of your bed elevated or with your feet resting on pillows.

MODIFIED KNEE-CHEST POSITION

This helps relieve pelvic pressure, hemorrhoids, cramps in the thighs and buttocks and, occasionally, lower back and leg pain.

1. Kneel, keeping your knees apart.

2. Tighten your abdominal muscles slightly in order to relieve the pressure of the baby on your abdominal wall.

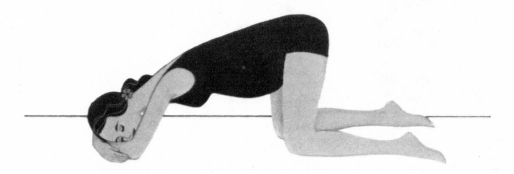

3. Place your arms and head on the floor. Your pelvis will then be higher than the rest of your body.

4. Keep your back straight. Maintain this position for no more than a minute or two.

5. Straighten up and relax. Pause before rising to regain your balance.

6. Repeat at intervals throughout the day as needed.

HEAD AND SHOULDER LIFTING

This exercise should be performed while lying on your back with your arms at your sides. The exercise helps strengthen your abdominal muscles.

1. Tighten abdominal muscles, raise your head and shoulders, and hold for a count of six. Do not hold your breath.

2. Lie back and relax.   3. Repeat five to ten times.

LEG LIFTING

1. Lift one leg slowly and without bending your knee. Bring the leg up as high as you can comfortably and let it down slowly.

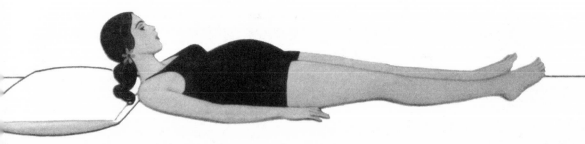

2. Repeat with the other leg.

3. Now lift both legs, but let knees bend.

4. Then try lifting your legs without letting your knees bend.

5. Repeat each exercise five to ten times.

From Preparation for Childbearing, Maternity Center Association, N.Y.

The Advantages

The woman will feel better, and her abdominal muscles and her back will become stronger, if she takes part in gymnastic exercises during pregnancy. A further advantage of a prenatal exercise program can be an easier delivery.

No one should expect that the gymnastics and relaxation exercises will automatically ensure a painless delivery. But they are one of the things a woman can do to help her take a more active part in delivery. Moreover, she will feel much better during her pregnancy. The advantages to the newborn baby of less or no anesthesia have also been emphasized by recent research.

The discomfort and back strain caused by the ever-increasing dimensions of the abdomen can be avoided with the proper exercises. The muscles of the back are exposed to greater strain because of the increasing weight in the front. This strain may cause unnecessary tension, which can be counteracted by some basic back-strengthening exercises. These should, of course, be followed at home as well as in the classes. Women with a previous history of backache or spinal disorder should consult their doctor or an orthopedist before engaging in these exercises. (Mirjam Furuhjelm, Axel Ingelman-Sundberg, and Claes Wirsen, *A Child Is Born*, 1977)

Household Design and Exercise

I think most table tops, sinks, stoves, and ironing boards are badly designed for the average woman, especially when she is pregnant. She has to bend too far down, which is difficult, or the surfaces are too high, or too wide. Whichever, it's often backbreaking to work in the kitchen. And on top of that, when one has a big abdomen, it's difficult to reach across things, and one tends to overcompensate with a hollow back. . . . Straighten the back and tuck your tail in. This will allow you to get closer to the sink, it will not overstrain the back or neglect the abdominal muscles. (Elisabeth Bing, *Moving Through Pregnancy*, 1975)

One Couple's Experience

NEIL: My wife was super healthy—riding a bicycle daily 15 to 20 miles until her stomach got too big and her knees kept bumping it; then jogging a mile and a half nightly up to the night before labor started. She had a super diet: considerably over the recommended protein intake for pregnant ladies, and she's small. Besides we knew she had a body that could birth a child. We already had one. And she had an obstetrician whose competence was cross-referenced from several other health professionals who, themselves, had reputations for excellence.

HART: Meanwhile, we had been preparing ourselves for the homebirth. We understood that something like 95% of the risks could be prevented by excellent prenatal care, so I had tried to eat 100 grams of complete protein per day and also maintained an aerobics program of bicycling and jogging. From the 4th month on, we had attended childbirth preparation classes geared particularly for homebirth parents and we read our way through a library of childbirth books. (Hart Collins and Neil Collins, "Birth in a Grocery Store," *Safe Alternatives in Childbirth*, 1976)

Reaching Up

Reaching up does not hurt a pregnant woman. There seems to be a dreadful old wives' tale that says that it hurts the baby if one lifts one's arms or reaches out. It even suggests that the baby may strangle on the cord if you stretch. So women will come up to you in the supermarkets and tell you to be careful. All this is really just superstition and nonsense. Do raise your arms. (Elisabeth Bing, *Moving Through Pregnancy*, 1975)

Sex and Pregnancy

Good Mates, Good Pregnancy

There is a strong relationship between a woman's feelings toward her mate and the course of her pregnancy.

Frances K. Grossman and her colleagues at Boston University studied 98 pregnant women in an attempt to assess the effects of their emotions. They found that women with good marital relationships were less likely to be depressed and anxious during pregnancy than women with unhappy marriages. (Niles Newton and Charlotte Modahl, "Pregnancy: The Closest Human Relationship," *Human Nature*, 1978)

THE WAYS OF SEX DURING PREGNANCY

Is sex possible—and enjoyable—throughout pregnancy? Should it be avoided at specific time periods? Must a baby coming limit your sex activity?

Today's experts believe that sex during pregnancy is possible *and* enjoyable most of the time—although there may be a few limitations, particularly if a couple has had problems in the past. But how the couple themselves feel about sex during the pregnancy period is probably the most important factor to consider.

You may well find that your sex life *is* different at this time. Obviously a woman's body goes through tremendous physical alterations during pregnancy, all of which may change her and her partner's sex life. The traditional pattern is that she will want much

less sex in the first trimester, experience greatly increased desire in the middle three months, and will find sexual interest dwindling again in the third.

There are good physical reasons for this pattern. The first three months can be a time of physical and mental upheaval which would tend to decrease your desire for sex (being nauseous, for instance, or, as one friend of mine put it, feeling generally frail). Your husband, too, may be nervous about his new role and concerned about you.

By the fourth or fifth month the enormous hormonal changes of pregnancy have made your breasts and sexual organs extremely sensitive, often pleasurably so, although some women do suffer from uncomfortably tender breasts. Many women who have never reached orgasm before do so now—and other women find they can have multiple orgasms. This may all be wonderful for your husband—or he may be somewhat overwhelmed by the physical changes you are experiencing. Many men find a woman's body extremely beautiful and desirable during pregnancy; some others find it difficult to adjust to the pregnant shape and the hormonal changes. It may take reassurance and patience for the two of you to readjust to one another.

In the third trimester both of you have to cope with the increasing clumsiness of sex. Obviously this physical difficulty is temporarily inevitable, and lovemaking positions will necessarily change to accommodate the growing "baby." The mother-to-be may also feel increasingly fatigued, perhaps anxious, and the father-to-be concerned about hurting her or the "baby." The likelihood is that you can both continue to enjoy sex until the very end of the pregnancy, but a general tapering off of sexual interest is natural, so do not be concerned about it. If this is your first pregnancy, you can look forward to the good possibility that your sex life after the baby will be even more enjoyable than it was before—thanks to permanent changes in the woman's body. The new blood vessels formed in the pelvic area with pregnancy remain and will help to increase sexual arousal.

I have described what is considered to be the traditional pattern, but of course you may find variations in your own case. In an informal survey conducted by Sam Bittman and Sue Rosenberg Zalk, authors of *Expectant Fathers,* many of the men reported that their sexual desires fluctuated considerably during pregnancy, while some felt that very little had changed from prepregnancy. Some of the expectant fathers reported increasing desire, but in general as the pregnancy advanced, sexual desire for both partners tapered off. Interestingly, the authors also found that very few of the men they interviewed actually tried extramarital sex, although many of them fantasized about it and some were urged by their friends to find a temporary girl friend. Other studies have indicated that some men do tend to look to other sexual partners at this time. You should both try to bring such fantasies out in the open if you possibly can. It is very important to talk honestly about your feelings.

In one study of pregnant women a significant group reported an intensity of orgasm at all stages of the pregnancy reflecting a sexual interest level that remained continuously high. So you may not experience fluctuations as wide as the traditional pattern indicates. And if you do find that your normal sexual activities and interest levels change during this time, this will help you find other ways to please one another.

It used to be that sex was frowned upon at various times during pregnancy as possibly harmful to the baby. Sex during both the first three months and the last three months was considered suspect. Doctors now feel that sex in the first three months generally presents no problem at all. The couples who should be careful about their sexual activities throughout pregnancy are those who have had problems in the past or who run a risk of having a premature baby. While reaching orgasm (through any means at all) will *not* initiate labor if the cervix is not ready for it, it may trigger labor for a prematurely ripened cervix. Doctors may prohibit any kind of sexual climax, including masturbation (the orgasm is particularly intense) for a woman when there is an indication of prematurity.

In addition, new findings from the Collaborative Perinatal Project (a massive and important study carried out in the 1960s which is still being analyzed) indicate that there may be a risk of infection to the amniotic fluid if couples continue having genital sex in the last trimester. The danger of a serious or even life-threatening infection to the baby is apparently much greater in cases of prematurity. After reviewing the evidence, Dr. Arthur L. Herbst of the University of Chicago recommends that couples who have had previous problems with prematurity, or in cases where the woman's cervix has prematurely ripened, should abstain from intercourse in the last three months. He does not feel that a normal couple need be too concerned.

Some final important words of caution for everyone. A man must *never* blow into the vagina during his wife's pregnancy. This may detach the placenta and cause a fatal air embolism. And don't have sex after the membranes have ruptured or if uterine bleeding is occurring.

With these few exceptions sex will *not* hurt the baby. Many men worry about this, but it is impossible for the penis to injure the child or break the "bag of waters." The most it may do is to cause some spotting or bleeding after intercourse because the cervix is more tender than usual at this time. Of course, a woman should ask her doctor about any bleeding. In the last months you should simply avoid putting any pressure directly on the abdomen. And don't worry—there's every reason to believe that the pleasure that conceived the "baby" will remain while the "baby" is growing.

What Do the Doctors Say About Love?

Some psychiatrists and psychologists advise women whose sexual desire is low (more likely during early and later stages of pregnancy) to stimulate it by listening to romantic music, or by reading books or going to sexy movies. It might be worth trying.

The woman who suffers from chronic fatigue during the first three months of pregnancy may find it hard to be energetic or enthusiastic about anything, including sex. If this is your problem, try taking a short nap just before or after dinner. It may put you in the mood for love later on in the evening. Another recourse worth considering is changing the time at which you and your husband make love. Instead of the end of the day when you're likely to be more exhausted than ever, how about morning, early evening, or, on weekends, in the afternoon?

If you find that either you or your husband is indifferent to sex, don't dismiss it as one more inconvenience of pregnancy. Discuss it with each other or with your doctor, and see if the situation can be remedied. (Alice Fleming, *Nine Months: An Intelligent Woman's Guide to Pregnancy*, 1972)

Sex and Pregnancy: A Summary

1. [Biologically] there are fluctuations in the woman's interest in sex and frequency of intercourse throughout pregnancy and the postpartum period.
2. In some respects pregnancy may enhance the woman's capacity to be orgasmic both during and after the experience.
3. There is no evidence that sexual intercourse must be prohibited during the latter part of a normal, uncomplicated pregnancy.
4. Changes in the woman's anatomy and physiology during pregnancy may make some aspects of intercourse uncomfortable.
5. Masturbation as well as sexual intercourse should be prohibited if there is fear that orgasm will initiate fetal or maternal damage.
6. Mild to moderate obstetric damage should not interfere with sexual function after delivery.
7. Changes in body contour may alter the woman's concept of herself as a sexual being.
8. Lactation can enhance a woman's sexuality.
9. Aspects of lactation may appear similar to sexual arousal in some women.
10. Responses to pregnancy are socially and culturally determined.
11. The marital role relationships are usually altered in some way by pregnancy. (Nancy Fugate Woods and Gretchen Kramer Dery, "Sexuality During Pregnancy and Lactation," in Nancy Fugate Woods, *Human Sexuality in Health and Illness*, 1975)

Expanding Sexual Horizons

Now is the time to expand your definition of "good" or "normal" sex. It's the time for exploring sexuality that involves more than genital intercourse and orgasm. If either of you is not interested in other forms of sexuality, there still is a wide range of sensual, intimate contact you can have with one an-

---

How It Used to Be

Preparation for Motherhood. Do Not Over-indulge in Bonbons.—Take Regular Out-door Exercise.—Use as Little Pastries and Tarts as Possible.—Do Not Over-indulge in Sweet-meats or Chilling Cold Drinks.—Do Not Yield to the Acceptance of Repeated Dishes.—Be Brave Enough to Say "No."—Keep in Physical Condition as do Athletes.—Discard Late Heavy Suppers.—Intemperance Not Confined to Over-indulgence in Stimulants but Applies as Well to Food.—Don't be a Gourmandizer.—Lobster Salads with Custards Are Very Dangerous.—Cake and Coffee at Late Hours Are Not Good and Possibly May Prove Disturbing.—Be a Self-controlled Young Woman.

Mrs. Emma F. Angell Drake, M.D., *What a Young Wife Ought to Know*, 1901

other. Try touching each other often throughout the day, bathing together, massaging each other's feet or hands or head, cuddling, or watching the other's sexual pleasure. What worked for you in the past may not work now, so let that be okay and look for other ways of giving and receiving sexual approval and satisfaction.

It's interesting that those couples who give each other permission not to want inter-course have more frequency of intercourse and greater satisfaction in their sexuality. Such permission eliminates the necessity of constructing avoidance schemes or pretending interest and satisfaction. (Lyn Delli-Quadri and Kati Breckenridge, *Mother Care*, 1978)

On the Job: Before and After

A Non-aggression Pact

After my first baby was born, I was back at work within about eight days. I nursed for about three months while working. We had a non-aggression pact. He slept during the day and ate all night. He didn't interfere with my work. (Nobel laureate physicist Dr. Rosalyn S. Yalow)

◇ ◇ ◇

THE QUESTION: SHOULD YOU KEEP YOUR JOB?

One of the most important areas to be talked about and planned in advance concerns work. The choice is completely up to you—both of you.

Will you be able to live on one salary? Will you, the mother, go back to work and you, the father, stay home with the baby? Are either or both of you, the parents-to-be, still completing your education? Are both of you in occupations where scheduling can be flexible so you can share both baby care *and* earning responsibilities? Are reliable relatives (or others) available and willing to provide substitute child care on a regular basis? Are you, the mother, planning to breast-feed? Where is your place of business located?

These are only a few of the possible questions that must be raised!

By now it should be clear that this major decision depends on your individual situation. There are many possible variables within that situation. Every case is different, because the personality, job history, earning capacity of both parents, and life goals of every couple are different.

In any case, *do not* let your decision be influenced by:

What others are doing.
What the neighbors are saying.
What your in-laws might say or think.

This is a crucial decision. It is one of the most important you will ever make, because it affects all of the members of your family, now and into the future. *Do not* make it hastily. For the sake of your marriage it cannot be a one-sided decision. Both of you must take everything into consideration:

The availability of really good baby-care alternatives is the first consideration—the most important consideration of all. Consider a relative, housekeeper, baby-sitter, day-care nursery, or whatever other alternatives you can think of.

Your need for additional income at this stage in your lives is next in importance. Also consider what the additional income will be needed for. Is it for the extras that can be postponed until the baby is less dependent upon you? Or is it for the most basic needs—food, clothing, the roof over your head? If money is a serious problem, and you have no alternative child care resource to look to, consider Aid to Families with Dependent Children (AFDC), a special category of welfare—a decent, reasonable, honorable alternative to working while your baby is very young. Everybody has the right to public assistance in a time of need. The proper care of your child is your primary concern.

Calculate the cost to you of working:
Cost of baby-care helper
Cost of lunches on the job
Cost of convenience foods
Cost of clothing for work—you'll need a greater variety of things than if you stayed at home
Cost of cleaning and laundering that wardrobe, and perhaps the baby's things as well
Cost of transportation to and from work

Figure out your net profit—that is, subtract costs from additional income, minus taxes. If money is your reason for working, is it enough after expenses to be worth it?

Consider the importance of work in your life. For many women today, psychological well-being depends either on the adult give-and-take of a job, or the feeling of independence gained from having a job. Without a job many women feel incomplete. This is especially true of women who have worked for several years before raising a family. For them family and children are not all-absorbing, and they have a real, legitimate need for non-child-centered activities in their lives.*

Think about your capacity to keep mentally alert as an at-home mother. Some women get so involved in their children that they forget to maintain an adult perspective and keep up with non-child-oriented activities as well. This can be destructive to a marriage, and it makes adjustment harder when the children reach school age.

Assess your personal stage of career development. Will dropping your career in midstream make it difficult to pick it up again at a later date? Not every occupation provides a built-in leave of absence as, for example, teaching jobs usually do. And some careers—medical research, for one—require keeping in constant touch with new developments, while others—such as advertising—involve maintaining personal contacts.

Consider the hours and location of your job. If you are going to spend an hour or more traveling each way to a job, your working day stretches from 8 hours to 10 or 11. Not only will you be proportionately more tired,

but you must depend on—and pay—others for longer hours of child care.

Decide whether you are going to breast-feed or not. If you will, it may preclude working, especially if you have a time-consuming commute to your place of work. While one replacement bottle (even of your own breast milk) a day is quite feasible, it is not a good idea to try to get away with two bottle feedings in a row, day after day. (In an emergency, of course, it may be necessary.) You might in this case have a problem maintaining an adequate milk supply; further, it is not good for the baby, and could very well erase the advantage you are trying to provide (and see page 146 for much more information on the subject of breast feeding). I once knew a young female executive who took a lunch-time cab home from her midtown Manhattan office every day to nurse her children. But most would find that economically impractical.

Does your place of employment provide child-care facilities? Some do; more will eventually, but this will not become the usual situation until far in the future, if at all. At a few enlightened places new mothers can now bring in their babies and care for them in the office. Some organizations set aside a mother's lounge where babies can be changed and nursed. Some factories and universities have fully staffed day nurseries for the children of their workers or staff members.

Consider whether your working situation provides flexible scheduling or whether you can arrange for part-time work. Close to twelve million women worked part time in 1978 (as opposed to six and a half million men), and opportunities for such work are going to increase, especially in retailing and the service industries. If you can persuade an employer to create flexible or part-time scheduling for you (and other women in the same situation), you'll be expanding opportunities for others as well as giving yourself the job continuity that can be essential to career development. Increasing numbers of men are looking for flexible working hours, too. This enables fathers to spend more time with their young children. And it makes it possible for

*But on Phil Donahue's NBC-TV Show of July 2, 1981, the reverse seemed true. The discontented full-time mothers were those young women who had had very little time on a job before early marriage and motherhood.

everyone to pursue other interests—sports, arts, courses, a special skill.

Discuss whether your husband agrees in principle, and whether he agrees deep down in his gut. While a disapproving husband may be wrong, and he may be an unrepentant male chauvinist, his feelings must be considered, since they will intimately affect your marital relationship.

And weigh all those other personal factors that only you can determine.

THE WORKING QUESTION

As you can see, this complicated question cannot be reduced to a simple yes or no—unless there is a compelling financial need to work. Then there is far less choice. You can clarify your own situation even more, however, by using the following checklist to get a better picture of your own home circumstances, your feelings, and your resources. Often there is no clear-cut yea or nay answer to whether you must or should go back to work after the baby is born. But there *are* many factors to consider. (See page 67)

One Woman on the Job to the Birth Time

"Two centimeters dilated and here I am at my desk," Pia Lindstrom (a television reporter with WNBC-TV), laughed during an interview just after a visit to her doctor's where she was told she could expect the baby "any time now."

She wasn't sent home to an easy chair and footstool, however, and more than a week later, looking just a little wan, she was still doing on-air interviews.

Pia, who was New York City's first pregnant "Anchorman" by virtue of her having anchored week-end newscasts, has been unabashedly frank about her pregnancy. One of her on-air outfits included a black knit shirt with a huge sequined arrow pointing downward and the word "baby" printed on it. (Jean Crafton, "Their Pregnancies May Be News to Their Fans," New York *Daily News,* March 13, 1975)

Part-time Work Force Increasing

There's a little factory in St. Paul that may be unique in the annals of manufacturing.

. . . A morning shift allows women to work while their children are in school, and an afternoon shift is filled by students. Such scheduling, although unusual in manufacturing, is part of a growing trend in the world of work: the employment of part-timers.

Today one American voluntarily works part time for every five and a half fulltime workers. A decade ago it was one part-timer for eight fulltimers, and 15 years ago it was one for 10. (Jerry Flint, "Growing Part-time Work Force Has Major Impact on Economy," *The New York Times,* April 12, 1977)

Part-time Work Is Better

Reports from employers who hire mothers for part-time work indicate that when women work fewer hours per day or fewer days per week, their energy, productivity, and accuracy increase. Absence from work decreases. (Dorothy Whyte Cotton, *The Case for the Working Mother,* 1965)

How the French Do It

In France working women are entitled to a sixteen-week maternity leave, which can be taken from six weeks before the birth to ten weeks after. Or this period can be modified through special arrangements made with one's employer: a woman may choose to take two weeks before birth and fourteen weeks afterward.

The important point is what happens next. After completing her maternity leave, the new mother can go back to her job. It will still be there for her. Or if she does not want to leave the baby, she can take an extended leave of up to one year. *At any time in that year, she still has the choice of going back to her job!*

A bill was passed to extend this option period to two years starting in 1978 for either parent. The two-year option had been in effect for civil service employees. When a woman civil servant who has a baby returns to her job after two years' leave, she is still eligible for all benefits *and* she is also entitled to any raises given during that time. The new law makes these provisions available to employees of private firms of over two hundred people. (Based on newspaper article, translated by French embassy)

Factors Leading You to Work Outside	Factors Leading You to Stay Home
There is no way you can manage financially without a job.	You can manage a decent style of living without your salary.
You can get part-time or flexible-hours work.	You will mind dreadfully if you are not around most of the time to care for your own baby.
Your husband, mother, or other close relative is going to care for the baby while you work. Or, you can make another satisfactory arrangement.	You would have to leave the baby in the hands of most inadequate caretakers.
You couldn't bear being at home all the time for more than a few weeks.	You would have to work excessively long hours, and come home exhausted.
You have a great maternity-leave plan and can return to work at a much later time.	Your office will not give you maternity leave.
Your husband is in favor of your working.	Your husband is not much in favor of your working now.
You can bring your baby to work with you.	You could not bring your baby to work— and you would have to work some distance away from your home.
You have a career that cannot take an interruption of any length of time.	You will be able to resume your career later, or you can keep up with it partially from home.
You can make arrangements to nurse for a while.	You intend to breast-feed for the first six months to a year—and do not want anything to interfere with this plan.
You have something of great significance to contribute to the world. (Should a Madame Curie stop working for a year or two or three?)	You have no earthshaking contributions to make to the world.
You aren't too fond of infants, and would make a much better part-time mother.	You like being home anyhow.

None of these answers is right or wrong. Even a pattern is not the only basis for a decision one way or the other—although it might help. Your decision to work or not might turn on just one factor—whether you plan to breast-feed or not. Essentially this checklist is only for the purpose of clarifying your own thinking.

Still, from the point of view of the author of this book, there is one overriding question that *must* be answered:

Will your baby be a lot better off—or a lot worse off—if you work outside, or stay at home?

Assuming you have choices, let your answer to this question tip the scales in one direction or the other.

*"Working" *should* include work *inside* the home; unfortunately, it doesn't.

How the Italians Do It

La signora is covered by special protective statutes as an employee—she is not to work at night; she cannot do heavy or dangerous work; she cannot be fired for marriage or pregnancy. If she becomes pregnant while working, she is entitled to four months' leave with pay—one month prior to birth, three months after. An additional month can be taken at half pay. If she is breast-feeding, she has an hour of paid time in the morning and an hour in the afternoon in which to feed the child. Any firm employing more than thirty-five women is required to have a free nursery on the premises for children. (Shari Steiner, *The Female Factor: A Report on Women in Western Europe*, 1977)

How the Germans Do It

State support for parents is explicit, orderly and relatively easy to obtain. The pregnancy leave (which is mandatory) is six weeks before and a minimum of eight weeks after the birth. If there are complications or multiple births, the postpregnancy leave is extended to twelve weeks. Employers must keep a woman's position open for her, but her wages are paid in full by the national health insurance plan, so that employers are not faced with financial penalties for hiring women. Shari Steiner, *The Female Factor: A Report on Women in Western Europe*, 1977)

Dr. Spock—Then

To work or not to work? Some mothers *have* to work to make a living. Usually their children turn out all right, because some reasonably good arrangement is made for their care. But others grow up neglected and maladjusted. It would save money in the end if the government paid a comfortable allowance to all mothers of young children who would otherwise be compelled to work. It doesn't make sense to let mothers go to work making dresses in a factory or tapping typewriters in an office, and have them pay other people to do a poorer job of bringing up their children.

The important thing for a mother to realize is that the younger the child the more necessary it is for him to have a steady, loving person taking care of him. In most cases, the mother is the best one to give him this feeling of "belonging," safely and surely. . . . (Dr. Benjamin Spock, *Baby and Child Care*, 1957)

Dr. Spock—Now

I hope that there will always be men and women who feel that the care of children and home is at least as important and soul satisfying as any other activity, and that neither men nor women will feel the need to apologize for deciding to make that their main career.

. . . [But] both parents have an equal right to a career if they want one, it seems to me, and an equal obligation to share in the care of their child, with or without the help of others. (If they want others to do it all, I'd advise against their having children.) (Dr. Benjamin Spock, *Baby and Child Care*, 1976)

Better Workplaces

Hopefully, the special needs that women may have when pregnant can likewise be the driving wedge for improved working conditions for all workers—including potential fathers and non-childbearing adults. (Jeanne M. Stellman, "The Hidden Health Toll, A Cost of Work to the American Woman," *Civil Rights Digest*, Fall 1977)

HIDDEN JOB HAZARDS

There is a hidden hazard to some jobs. This is the effect of environmental substances or conditions upon your unborn baby—toxic exposures. Today any workplace that uses lead, photographic chemicals, X rays, or anesthetics, and employs pregnant women runs the risk of government action. In a landmark 1979 case American Cyanamid was cited and fined by the federal Occupational Safety and Health Administration (OSHA) for a "willful violation" of government regulations designed to protect worker fertility and genetic structure. One high federal official commented that the more we learn about the effects of environmental toxic exposures, the more we suspect that many of the large numbers of stillbirths and deformed children in our country are a result. In fact, we are probably only just beginning to learn about the effects on fertility of some widely accepted substances. For instance, nitrous oxide gas, used by many dentists, is now shown to be harmful—not to the patients, but to the dentists' and dental technicians' unborn children. A Stanford University study found a high miscarriage rate among the wives of dentists and dental technicians who frequently used the gas.

Obstetricians have been more attuned to environmental hazards to mother and baby than many of the rest of us. The American College of Obstetricians and Gynecologists (ACOG) printed a most significant booklet in 1977, entitled *Guidelines on Pregnancy and Work*. You may be able to get a copy by writing to ACOG (see Resource List).

One of the recommendations of ACOG is that every obstetrician take a detailed profile of his or her patient's workplace. This would cover all possible sources of potential harm, including such ordinary items as slippery floors.

With more and more information available today about safety and preventive health care, I would advise every pregnant (or about-to-become-pregnant) woman to avoid working in *any* place where there are concentrations of lead, asbestos, benzene (used in rubber cement), or other substances in the atmosphere which are harmful; and to check far beyond your doctor. Try OSHA at 200 Constitution Avenue NW, Washington, D.C. 20037, and NIOSH (the National Institute of Occupational Safety and Health) at 5600 Fishers Lane, Rockville, Maryland 20852. If you are concerned about conditions at work, the law provides that you have the right to request OSHA to inspect your workplace and you can remain anonymous if you so wish. Legally no worker can be discriminated against for taking this action.

You should also read the literature carefully and thoroughly to see what your risks in your workplace may be. Be sure to get a copy of Jeanne Stellman's revealing and startling book, *Women's Work, Women's Health*.

Workplace Problems for Babies-to-Be

Chemicals in the workplace can affect reproduction at many levels and in both sexes. Mutagens can affect ovary and testes tissues before conception, causing chromosomal abnormalities that lead to poor fertility and early miscarriages. Carcinogens can cross the placenta, affect growing tissue of the fetus and bring about cancer in the child. Teratogens usually kill cells of the conceptus during the very early stages of development (the third to the eighth weeks), and cause either miscarriages, stillbirth defects.

An epidemiological study of more than 400 children who died of cancer before the age of five found "over-representation" by their fathers in industries involving hydrocarbon exposure.

Constant exposure to gas anesthetics in hospitals is correlated with more stillbirths, malformations and spontaneous abortions among operating room nurses and among the wives of doctors. (*Science News,* April 8, 1978)

What Has Not Been Studied

Of the more than 15,000 chemicals in industrial and home use today, only relatively few have been tested for toxic effects on growth and development. There have also been very few large-scale studies of the effects on people and their offspring of exposure to most environmental pollutants. Physical workplace hazards, such as noise, vibration, radiation, and heat stress, are similarly unstudied and poorly understood. (Jeanne Mager Stellman, *Women's Work, Women's Health,* 1977)

Men As Well As Women

The exposure of men and women to environmental hazards and drugs during the peri-conceptional period has been associated with genetic abnormalities which are generally not detectable prenatally, including spontaneous abortion, stillbirth, congenital malformation, and carcinogenesis in the child's later life. In some cases, such as exposure to lead, mercury and ionizing radiation, a relationship is relatively well established. In others, the relationship is strongly suggested by epidemiologic studies as in recent studies of women exposed to anesthetic gases in operating rooms. Data on abnormalities in the infants of male anesthesiologists suggest that this may be a problem for both sexes. Finally, many substances have been shown to produce genetic abnormalities in laboratory preparations and experimental animals, but there is no evidence that they produce similar effects in humans. (American College of Obstetricians and Gynecologists, *Guidelines on Pregnancy and Work,* 1977)

KNOW YOUR JOB RIGHTS

Early in your pregnancy discuss your intentions with your employer. Find out what your company's insurance policy provides for you. If you return to work after the birth, are the maternity benefits different from what they would be if you resigned?

On the job don't keep your condition a big secret. But don't make a "thing" of it, either. Make your announcement matter-of-factly, at an appropriate time. When you do tell the boss, try to give your plan about staying on until whatever time you and your husband have decided upon. This avoids misunderstandings, and gives you a chance to provide on-the-job training to your replacement, if necessary. If you plan to take maternity leave and then return, announce that, too. Don't anticipate problems that may not exist. You may get no hassles at all.

But—some companies have rules, written or unwritten, against employing pregnant women. The concern may be about your safety on the job, or the company's insurance liability in case of an accident. Or your employer may say something about your appearance "at this time" not being appropriate for "facing the public." This is nonsense. You should be able to work as long as you and your doctor feel comfortable about it, depending on your health, the nature of your work, and the legal liability of your employer.

In one recent instance a woman employed by the First Women's Bank of New York (of all places!) charged that she was first demoted and then dismissed after her pregnancy became known. This kind of discrimination has been widely practiced, with employers routinely dismissing pregnant women or forcing them to take unpaid time away from work. Then, when women have gone back to work, they have sometimes found themselves demoted, even after years of work for their company.

In the last few years, the courts have heard various discrimination cases on pregnancy-related issues and one Supreme Court ruling came out strongly against the payment of maternity benefits. But the situation is changing. In 1978 the federal government held a series of hearings on discrimination against pregnant workers and as a result an amendment to the Civil Rights Act of 1964 has been passed. This amendment makes it illegal for employers to discriminate against women workers on the basis of pregnancy. In other words, if your company offers paid sick leave as part of its benefits, you can claim it if you are pregnant, and your position in the company cannot be endangered.

The hearings pointed out the ludicrous situation of men being granted paid time off for minor surgery (hair transplants were even mentioned!) while women were forced to take unpaid leave for a condition as important as pregnancy. It is interesting that the hearings also recognized that many women with children are now in full-time work.

Do find out what kind of leave provisions your company has and *insist* on receiving your benefits. If you are not satisfied with the responses of the organization you work for, or if you have questions about your rights as most recently defined by the Civil Rights Act or any court rulings in your state, consult your lawyer, the local Legal Aid Society, American Civil Liberties Union, Equal Employment Opportunity Commission office, or a local women's group.

The times are changing—but still slowly. You may be able to raise issues that can be resolved in a way that will benefit other women. Fair benefits for pregnant women and working mothers help husbands and children, too—a point that has been ignored through the ages! Find out what your rights are and insist on them—or try to change them.

◇ ◇ ◇

The Big Surprise!

The unexpected desire to be with the new child, the unforeseen mutual attachment between mother and infant seem to be the overriding sentiments of women who change their minds about going back to work. (Sue Mittenthal, "After Baby, Whither the Career?" *The New York Times*, February 14, 1979)

◇ ◇ ◇

BABY NOW, WORK LATER

If you decide to stay at home with your baby, it is not the end of your working life. Women can and do return to work—when the children are in nursery school, elementary school, junior high, or later. Sometimes women return to better jobs, bringing to bear their total experience in community activities and executive-quality household management. But all too often women return to lower-level jobs—if their skills have become rusty, their contacts fallen off, or if a shift in the national or international economic situation has created fewer opportunities in their fields.

These are the realities. But—you can usually go back to work, and perhaps you can retrain for a new field. Women *can* work themselves up the corporate ladder a second time around, often in an entirely new field.

Returning to work, you'll probably have a better idea of who you are and what you really want to do with your life. You'll have more perspective than you had a few years earlier straight out of school. You'll have the advantage of added maturity. And believe it or not, you'll have more "people experience"—yes, being a full-time mother for even six years will give you *lots* of dealing with people, and not just pint-size people.

For your future work plans it's important to anticipate the occupational outlook in your field ahead of time, and make plans accordingly. (This is, of course, not always possible.) Try to get some additional training—one course at a time, perhaps—during your nonworking years to help you keep up with new developments and trends.

Another possibility: Try to get a maternity leave, and a promise of reemployment after a specified period, from your current employer. You might well be breaking new ground for other women, as well as cushioning your own career future. If you have made yourself indispensable to your employer before your baby is born, you will have a much better chance of getting concessions made in scheduling. It has been done—often, but not nearly often enough.

Further, women are not just sitting back and taking it anymore. They are going to court to demand equal rights—and maternity leave with a guarantee of employment is being viewed increasingly as a right.

Men—fathers themselves—are coming to realize that benefits for mothers are benefits for the entire family.

All of these are trends—the wave of the future. They will continue. You can hasten these trends.

Naturally, women's labor will be more valued in an expanding economy than it has been during the recession years of the 1970s—and maybe the early 1980s. When millions of men are out of work, even the most equality-minded employers are not likely to break new ground of their own accord by providing special working hours for employees who happen to be young mothers. Activism, from mothers and fathers, will continue to be necessary for the foreseeable future.

SUPPORT FOR THE WORKING MOTHER

There are agencies and organizations that can help you decide on your present or future career. You might want to contact one of them for assistance and information about the situation in your region, and prepare yourself realistically by reading books and periodicals.

AGENCIES

Women's Economic Round Table
860 United Nations Plaza
New York, New York 10017
(212) 759-4360

Since economic issues are vitally important for young women to begin to understand, I am including this basic and most prestigious new organization. WERT, a national organization, holds periodic forums with national leaders on the most significant financial factors which affect everyone. You can join and learn. Transcripts of programs are available at minimum cost.

Business and Professional Women's Foundation
2012 Massachusetts Avenue NW
Washington, D.C. 20036
(202) 293-1200

With a vast nationwide membership, this organization helps both the woman in business and on the job.

National Commission on Working Women
1211 Connecticut Avenue NW Suite 310
Washington, D.C. 20036
(202) 466-6770

Eighty percent of all working women are employed in factories, restaurants, supermarkets, and in other blue- and pink-collar jobs. In 1977 the National Commission on

Working Women was founded to help this enormous and underrepresented group of women. It acts as a spur to legislation and as an information and referral center.

This list is just a small sample of the many other helpful organizations for women who are working or want to work outside their home. NOW (the National Organization For Women, 425 Thirteenth St., N.W., Washington, D.C., 20004) is one example. To find others, consult the over 500-page Civil Rights Directory 1981 (the U.S. Commission on Civil Rights published this) or the 32-page Guide to Women's Resources (put out by the White House in late 1980). If your library can't find them, bother your congressional representatives for photocopies from the Library of Congress.

NO NEED TO STAGNATE

Most women will elect to stay home with their infants and very young children. But daily, day-long child care *can* become stultifying to some. If you anticipate this reaction, you can do something about it.

Plan a regular "day off," or perhaps two half-days off. Get a relative, friend, or other caring substitute to take over while you see former colleagues or friends, go to museums, take courses.

Join or organize a women's group that meets regularly for serious discussion (which provides regular conversational meetings for women out of the job market). If baby-care substitutes are scarce or too costly, combine your own day-nursery with your discussion group and keep your eyes on the tots and tykes while you and several like-minded women discuss world events, local politics, art history, and child-care issues.

Take the baby with you as much as possible to things you want to do. The new baby-carriers and folding strollers, more acceptance of breast feeding, and the use of disposable nursing bottles and diapers, make baby more portable than ever before—and mother more mobile. Museum- and library-going, shopping, sightseeing, and visiting are all possible with baby in tow.

Set up an exchange daytime baby-sitting service with other women in your neighborhood who have young children. Two women in a New York apartment house did exactly that, giving each a free day one day a week or in case of emergency. The arrangement worked out so well that they expanded it to include their husbands and evenings, and then to provide for occasional entire weekends off.

THE AUTHOR'S OPINION

Mothers and fathers of infants, tots, and toddlers who work full time outside the home are missing some of the loveliest moments of parenthood, some of the times that make everything they have given up worthwhile. Children, too, are missing something: more rested, less frantic parents who can give more of their undivided attention to being creative parents.

And despite the prevalence of the sentiment that it's not the quantity but the quality of the time spent, it is my opinion that this view is highly oversimplified. How can there be any quality without *enough* quantity? I even subscribe somewhat to what Selma Fraiberg (author of *The Magic Years*) said, that there is no real substitute for a full-time mother in the home during the first few years of life. (My only exceptions would be the substitution of a father or a grandmother as the primary care-giver.)

Still, we have a society that does not provide a reasonable alternative for most people. There are a few experiments which seem to give some of the best of both the work and child-caring worlds. Among these are some of the communes in the United States and the kibbutzim in Israel. They provide work for men and women right where they live, easy access to parents and often grandparents.

One example is the Kibbutz Kfar Blum in northern Israel which I visited in the winter of 1975. At the time, I interviewed a number of young families and grandparents, too.

"This is a paradise, a paradise for children," a young father told me. Since he himself had been raised in the very comfortable suburb of Great Neck, New York, I was quite startled. Here, on the kibbutz to which he had immigrated, much work was in the fields and orchards; the apartments were quite small and simply furnished, and guard duty at night was essential. The lifestyle did not seem that idyllic.

"Why? Why?" he went on. "Because the

children are safe and they're free. They can run anywhere without getting hit by cars. There're always grown-ups around to see that they're all right and to help them. And they have so much time with their fathers, not only their mothers. I pick up my son from the children's house about three thirty or four and have all the time before dinner to play, and the time after as well."

The fact that there is a children's house which provides excellent daytime care (children now sleep in their parents' homes) on the grounds gives mothers the ability to work at jobs other than baby or child care.

Ideally, our society should pay a mother (or father) to stay home after the birth of a baby for two to three years—without jeopardizing her or his return to work, or career potential. Or it should provide part-time work and flexible hours for both parents.

Even more ideally, only those mothers should be employed outside the home in the first year or two who do not want to breast-feed and really cannot bear taking care of an infant.

But why can't we aim for a kibbutz kind of solution? We could have an urban U.S.-style kibbutz, where caring for an infant, baby, and child is the most important kind of work anyone can ever find—but where there's sharing and cooperation among all adults, and, above all, the active presence of all age groups. For those realists among us who look at the practicalities involved, the best hope for change today is through employers. Employers could provide ways for mothers or fathers to bring a child to the job, and they could also arrange much better maternity benefits and part-time work schedules.

Travel During Pregnancy

VACATION
WHILE YOU WAIT?

Although you're working, watching what you eat, and keeping a careful check on yourself, you should seriously consider taking time away now—during pregnancy. Of course, you may think that a vacation—long or short—is an impossibility. You are, indeed, (1) far too busy, (2) saving every penny, (3) very involved in baby preparations, (4) afraid to leave your doctor, (5) not yet due for vacation time, (6) too uncomfortable. Ah, but these are among the excellent reasons why you and your partner should have a happy, carefree, even luxurious time-out from the baby-making process. Such time, if it is financially feasible, is among the prescriptions for better marriages. In fact, time together, time alone, time when you both feel easy and at ease and pampered is a must before and after the baby's birth. But after the baby arrives, time away and alone is, for a long time, usually limited to an hour, an evening, or an occasional day. Leaving an infant or tot behind for long vacation periods is definitely not desirable. Carrying along an in-utero not-yet baby is very desirable, a relief from impending responsibility, an opportunity for heightened romance.

Where to go? When to go? How often? These questions all depend on your jobs, budget, distance travel capabilities. One of my own happiest recollections is a very big-belly two-week summer vacation with friends far from home in the Cape Cod sun. Others may prefer resorts or nonbeach areas, shorter periods of time, and closer-to-home places.

One lovely solution to mounting pressures and the need for fun and peace is a weekend in a nearby luxury hotel in your own city! You may think it odd to leave the comforts of your own home to travel only a few miles for the "privilege" of spending two or three hundred dollars in a hotel. From my own experience, though, it is a marvelous relief and comfort! Home, as familiar and pleasant as it may be, brings mail, telephone, visitors—and most of all, the reminders of chores and errands and cleanups and work. A luxury hotel is away from that. It is adventure and privacy and romance and someone else's chores! It provides an island of time-out from baby-and-job-and-home preparations.

The idea of mini-vacations right where you live means choosing hotels where you are bathed in the comforts and delights of Old (or New) World elegance. Some of these hotels may have great views, great restaurants, or just great facilities (for example, the Ritz Carlton in Chicago or Boston). During the vacations get away from baby planning as much as possible. Think *you* and the *other you*.

There are many other ways to have a vacation. And unless there are medical reasons not to, you may want to venture farther afield. Wherever you go, you should take along some brief medical data, written down and available in case it is needed. The handiest method of doing so that I have seen is a pocket-size booklet called the *American Express Med Chart*. The only thing I would add, and staple to the inside front cover, is a typed note that says:

I am pregnant, and expect my baby in the month of _____. I do not want unnecessary drugs.

The chance of your having a vacation-time medical problem is minimal, however. And the chance of your having a great prebaby filled-with-fun time is very high! Just remember not to overdo, and not to try new athletic activities!

You may want to try something new, however. The Palm-Air Spa in Florida has had at least thirty (as of 1979) very pregnant women making use of part of its marvelous program of exercise, massage, whirlpools, swimming, and walking.

Wherever you go, do take pictures, pick up menus and mementoes. These are wonderful beginnings for the start of your baby book. Some years from now when she or he takes out his or her very own book, it will be so warm and lovely to see the evidence of happy prenatal times together.

TRAVEL CAUTIONS

There are only two arguments against travel during pregnancy:

First, abortion or labor can happen at any hour on any day, and it is nearly always impossible to predict the occurrence. If a pregnant woman is traveling at the time of such an emergency, or if she is living in a community other than her own, the inconvenience and fright may be strong. One way to lessen the difficulty is to take along names of medical people (obstetricians, nurse-midwives) living in the area you plan to visit. Ask your own doctor or nurse-midwife for a referral. Sometimes a nonmedical resource can be most helpful. I have found that family agencies (see "Family Service," "Family Counseling," or "Child and Family Service" in the Yellow Pages) often know appropriate doctors. If you're traveling abroad, there are two organizations that supply names of English-speaking doctors. You probably won't need the names—but why not have the resources in case. (See Resource List.)

Second, traveling can be fatiguing and uncomfortable, especially in late pregnancy.

This is particularly true of automobile travel. The only antidote for this is to break up the trip every fifty miles. Get out of the car, walk about for a few minutes, go to a rest room. Pregnant women should not travel more than three hundred miles a day in a car.

Decisions about travel during pregnancy should be governed mainly by common sense. For example, if the woman is prone to motion sickness, a train is probably best. Long distances are usually accomplished with the least fatigue and discomfort by air. Avoid planes with nonpressurized cabins.

TRAVEL TIPS
FOR PREGNANCY

Stay close to home during the last three months.

Move around a lot—even while you're sitting down. Wiggle your toes, move your arms, turn your head.

Stick to bottled water or hot tea or club soda in places where you're not sure about the water supply.

If you're in a car, be sure to stop at least every hour (and preferably at shorter intervals) so that you can get out and stretch.

In plane, train, or boat, walk up and down aisles or corridors frequently.

If yours is a long trip, bring along extra shoes to change into—or even a pair of slippers to wear en route.

For cool weather travel, bring warm socks, sweaters, and gloves. Keeping wrists, ankles, and neck warm can help a lot.

Keep to light *and* cooked foods while traveling: omelets and chicken, steamed vegetables, and fruits. If you eat fresh fruits, peel the skins.

Travel light. Luggage can be a huge burden. Try to limit yourself to essentials.

Seat belts are a problem. Some people don't believe in their use for pregnant women. Others recommend either wearing the belt low across your pelvis, or using a shoulder belt. (Don't put a seat belt across your middle, where the baby is.) In a plane, you don't have any choice at all. You must wear the belt.

Alert the airline or the railroad to your condition ahead of time. You may not need to stand in line for tickets, space, or whatever. You'll also find out if your airline has some peculiar rule regarding pregnant travelers. Some have in the past.

Avoid any medications, even if you get sea-, air-, or car-sick.

Let your doctor (or midwife) know about your trip in advance. Either may have some important advice for you.

Also, be sure to ask for a reliable medical source along the way and at your destination.

Clothes for Waiting and Growing

MATERNITY CLOTHES

Maternity clothes—does the term sound mature, unstylish, even dowdy? Then you're in for a surprise, a big one. Maternity clothes are high fashion today. Their object, as it used to be even as late as the 1950s, is no longer to hide your body's burgeoning contours. Their purpose is to provide you with a convenient but stylish, healthful but active, wardrobe for a today life-style. It *is* more convenient to wear clothes that leave adequate room for a new "baby" belly, but these clothes are right up there with the latest styles and trends. (Read on for examples.) It *is* much healthier for you, and safer for your unborn darling, to wear special clothes with a purpose—bras and support hose and low-heeled shoes. But these and other items will give you the best ability to stay active, to stay involved with your life's activities.

So give maternity clothes a new name, if you like—Clothes-For-Growing, for instance. Or give the old term a new attitude, a new polish. And either way, you'll relish planning and shopping and borrowing for new clothing for you-with-child!

WHEN TO BUY

As soon as you know you're pregnant, start looking at maternity clothes. An exploratory trip to the nearest maternity boutique or department will give you an early chance to scout the styles. Then you can plan your wardrobe more systematically.

Scout the mark-down racks, too. You'll find leftovers from last season—which, incidentally, had the same weather as the season of your last few pregnancy months. If you see anything on sale that appeals to you, scoop it up. You may save a lot! You may even find such basics as tops, bras, and support hose marked down as irregulars.

Next, try borrowing from friends and relatives. No one ever wants to wear maternity clothes after the baby comes, and your friends may be delighted to share their wardrobes with you. (The new high-style clothes may be changing attitudes.)

For real penny-pinching in maternity clothes, some women's organizations or nursery school parent groups run maternity exchanges. There are thrift shops, too.

But don't try to be too thrifty: buy at least two new and charming outfits, just for pleasure. The big-belly months seem long at times and there will be occasions when you'll want to feel your most attractive.

Regular clothing departments, a good source, will have capes, caftans, peasant-style tunics and overblouses, A-line or tent dresses, and jumpers—any of which might be ideal for maternity wear, too. Every month or so look in a maternity boutique for bargains or for fill-in needs.

By the fourth or fifth month, you'll probably need to put away your usual clothes and use your maternity outfits. By the way, if you're thin, you're likely to need your waiting-for-baby clothes sooner. On slim women, practically every additional ounce shows! Women of heavier build may have a few more weeks of clothing-as-usual.

WHAT TO BUY, WHERE TO BUY IT

Everything you have has a maternity version—jeans, body suits, tennis dresses, and bikinis! The big news in maternity fashion is the same boutique look you have been wearing right along. In shopping centers across the country, maternity chains are selling contemporary styling in waiting-for-baby wardrobes. You'll find denim and corduroy, oriental and peasant styles, and now an active sports collection, particularly jogging clothes.

There are a number of chains. The Motherhood Maternity Shops of Santa Monica, California, have 232 branches in 40 states, and Sears, Roebuck's and Montgomery Ward's catalogs have special sections for maternity clothes. The Lady Madonna has more than 100 branches in the United States, Canada, England, Puerto Rico, and Japan. Their specialty is interpreting current fashion trends in a way that accommodates the pregnant silhouette. One variation is an extensive wardrobe for exercise, as well as uniquely glamorous evening fashions.

One of the most fascinating signs of change in social mores is the Lady Madonna pregnancy bridal gown! It was shown as a gag a few years ago. But the maternity wedding dress brought a surprisingly large number of inquiries. In some of the company's past semiannual fashion shows, the presentations ended with a pregnant bride, just as the Parisian couture shows traditionally end with a bride. One show-stopper was in a tropical mood. The full, tenty off-shoulder dress, lavishly ruffled on top and bottom, was an exquisite confection of white-on-white embossed georgette. Everything is up front.

Mothercare, Ltd., is a British maternity wear and baby goods chain with 161 shops in the United Kingdom and a dozen more throughout Western Europe. Mothercare has a cost-conscious perspective. The chain tries to make childbirth and parenthood more affordable and more manageable for today's young families. It was actually founded by a father astounded at the high cost of parenthood. Now Mothercare has come to the United States. The American stores, located in shopping centers across the country, operate under the names of Mother To Be and Maternity Modes, as well as Mothercare.

Mothercare products range from A to Z— with everything for the expectant mother and young children (except baby food) that could possibly be required under one roof. For the mother-to-be, it features a complete line of moderate- to higher-priced maternity clothes and accessories. Catalogs of all merchandise available, patterned after the British Mothercare catalog, which serves as an aid to purchasing in the stores as well as by mail, have been published here. Write: Mothercare-by-Mail, P.O. Box 228, Parsippany, New Jersey 07054 (201-366-1199).

WHAT WILL YOU NEED?

This is a very full suggested list. Some items are really vital for your future health and well-being. These are starred.

UNDERWEAR

Support hose *or* pantyhose. Three or more pairs.

Special maternity support pantyhose will help avoid varicose veins and tired legs. They're available in regular standard sizes; usually made of semisheer nylon and spandex elastic, with a stretch lace panel covering the panty part for comfortable expansion. Order by regular size.

Panties, expansion-style. Three pairs.

Girdles or panty girdles. Two to three.

Even if you never wear a girdle, you may be more comfortable with some extra support when you get to the larger-size months. Girdles give lightweight gentle support or firm back support. Back-support models have extra fabric panels crisscrossing the back, and are a particular comfort if you have backaches. Or they can prevent backaches later on. Do not buy *any* that are tight on your legs or thighs; this type can lead to varicose veins. Order girdles by prepregnancy waist size.

Maternity bras and/*or* nursing bras. Three or more.

Maternity bras are made with stretch elastic inserts to grow as your breasts do; they should also have four hook adjustments in back, and be a little longer underneath the cup than your usual bra may be. Maternity bras can be nursing bras as well. They have a special hook mechanism over each cup so you can open them for convenient nursing later on.

Disposable gauze pads (nursing pads).

When you're pregnant, there is likely to be some leakage of colostrum from your breasts; when you are nursing, there is likely to be some leakage of milk from your breasts. Inserting a gauze pad in each bra cup once or twice a day will keep you dry and fresh.

Slips (noncling fabric).

Even if you don't usually wear a slip, you may want one now. Many maternity skirts are unlined and a slip will help them drape better. If you perspire a lot during pregnancy, you'll be more comfortable with a slip on.

At-home gowns, negligees, nightgowns, robes.

You may well have enough loose items here to carry you through.

OUTERWEAR

Shoes, *sensible*

Low or medium heels are essential. You'll teeter too much on high heels. Avoid platform shoes; they'll affect your balance badly. If your feet and/or ankles have swollen, get a larger size than usual. Be sure to get arch supports inserted, if you need them. Fit and comfort are most important. What good are shoes if you can't walk around in them?

Pants for every day, including jeans; or pantsuits

Evening skirt and tops

Dresses, either one-piece or a coordinated tunic-and-skirt style

Skirts or jumpers or shorts

Bathing suits

Sport tops or T-shirts (summer)

Pullovers or blouses (winter)

Coat, loose fitting. Preferably with raglan sleeves—warm, winter-weight; light, all-weather

Avoid a coat with a waist, or a single-breasted fitted coat which can't be buttoned over your growing middle.

HOW MUCH TO BUY

Before you buy, here are some pointers to help.

Don't overbuy. Buy less rather than more. You can fill in as needed. And for the second time around, you'll want to get some new things anyway.

On the other hand, *buy enough.* Naturally, you don't want to wear the same thing every single day—or even every other day. Twice a week is probably enough. Don't bore yourself with the same old clothes, or the same new ones. If you look well, you're more likely to feel good.

Consider the season. Let's say it's summer and you live at the swim club or beach. Then you'll need at least two bathing suits and several sunsuits and sets of shorts. But if you can only get to the beach for an occasional day outing, one bathing suit and a cotton skirt or jeans will do. In winter you'll need at least one warm sweater and a warm coat. (And don't forget boots. If your shoe size has changed, you may need new boots, too.)

TIPS AND HINTS ON COMFORT AND COLOR

To look and feel trim, choose jackets and tops that are wrist-length or longer. Avoid short maternity blouses or tops that end at the widest part of your stomach, giving you a profile like an abrupt cliff.

One-piece dresses or tunic-skirt outfits should not be shorter than mid-knee. Generally, maternity skirts are cut a little longer in front than in back so they won't hitch up as your abdomen grows.

Whatever you do, don't make the mistake of buying anything a size too large. Look for perfect fit in the shoulders and across the top of the bust. This part of you will not change. A too-large item will droop over your shoulders and make you feel droopy all over. The right size will look trim, too, even when you're the largest you'll be.

Color is the key to economy and style. In a color-coordinated wardrobe many parts are interchangeable, giving you more outfits

Not An
Extra Expense!

Lane Bryant
Maternity Dresses
Will Do Just as
Well When Your
Figure Returns
to Normal

5 C 104
98¢

5 C 105
$2.49

CHAMBRAY

LINENE

5 C 104—This is *not* a regular house dress. It is a Lane Bryant Maternity House Dress, which means it is cut extra-full over bust and through the hips and abdomen, to allow room for necessary expansion.

One-piece style; of solid color Chambray, trimmed with checked gingham in matching color. Kimono sleeves. Adjustable sash.

Blue, rose, tan or green. SIZES: 34 to 46 bust. Entire length about 52 inches. Price.... **98¢**
Post. 5¢ extra.

5 C 105—At all times during the maternity period you will feel comfortable and look well in this straight, one-piece Dress of fine quality Linene

Bands of contrasting color self material trim the collar, front opening, cuffs and the pockets. Novelty buttons. Adjustable self-material sash.

Brown with tan, green with white, or blue with white. SIZES: 34 to 46 bust. Entire length about 52 inches....
Post. 5¢ ex. **$2.49**

Open-Front Model for Nursing Mothers

5 C 103—Maternity House Dress of serviceable quality Checked Gingham. Simple to adjust, and most effective in concealing the condition of your figure.

A one-piece model with kimono sleeves and a detachable surplice front. Surplice allows extra room for adjustment during maternity period, and makes it convenient for nursing later. White rick-rack braid trims it.

COLORS: Blue-and-white, black-and-white or lavender-and-white check. SIZES: 34 to 46 bust. Entire length about 52 inches. Our price....
Postage 5¢ extra. **$1.49**

Maternity clothes—then and now
a)   1925
b)   1980

from the same number of parts. Since many designers now think in terms of mix 'n' match, a little advance planning will help you buy wisely. Look for one great outfit and then let it set the color key for most of your other purchases.

Shoes can't be emphasized enough. Even if you're used to stilt-high heels, you won't like them when your abdomen expands and your balance shifts. Your center of gravity moves forward and down. If you must wait to see, then as soon as you feel yourself the least bit tottery, buy something you can *walk* in. Flat sandals, if they have straps so they don't slip off your feet, are a good warm-weather solution.

In any case, buy the smartest styles that are comfortable; buy two or three pairs so you have a change. Changing shoes from day to day is good for your feet, as well as fashionable. Color-key your shoes to the basic colors of your wardrobe—black and camel, or brown and navy, or whatever your color scheme is.

Money, Family Budgeting, and Insurance

THE MONEY SITUATION

Money is a key factor in having and raising a child.

Of course you're absorbed with the love and wonder and beauty of producing and nurturing a new life. But sound planning and knowledge about money can only add to the experience. Conversely, appreciation of a baby can be diminished by debts and money worries. For your baby's sake—and for your own sake—both of you have a vital obligation to learn and understand money management. In economic terms, your family is very like a business. There is gross income and net income. There is purchasing "raw" supplies and services. There are sometimes cost overruns. There are, hopefully, profits and dividends. There is bookkeeping and a balance sheet—even if it is invisible. There is a product—not for sale, but definitely of value.

The economic side of child care and family life should not dominate anyone's feelings or relationships. But if money management is a smooth, understood, non-emotional process in your family, there is more likelihood that the other delights in living together *will* prevail.

To too many of us money represents more than it really is. For some it's a weapon, for others a way of control, for still others a symbol of love. All of these attitudes can lead to trouble. For you and yours, try to place money—and learning about it—in a helpful perspective.

Money for you should be another important tool for an easier daily life with your new baby and child—and for a pleasant, developing future. To know where you stand financially can only help you in that goal.

For specific information:

- Read some money management books— Jane Bryant Quinn's *Everyone's Money Book* or Sylvia Porter's *The New Money Book for the 80's* are two of the best.
- Check the magazines for helpful information.
- Take an adult education course in money management and/or bookkeeping to give you a firmer grasp.
- Consult family financial specialists or credit management experts.
- Listen to experts on the radio; I like John Scheuer on New York's WMCA.
- Talk to friends, neighbors, and relatives about working out budgets, what to buy and what not to buy, and how to save on costs.

Also, do realize that things do *not* stay the same. Inflation gallops or deflation hits. Babies grow into children. Needs expand. For this reason, *any* money planning you do needs to be reevaluated *at least* once a year— and better yet, every six months.

YOUR NEW FAMILY BUDGET

You will soon have:

An extra mouth to feed

Extra doctor bills

Extra clothing expenses

Extra laundry costs (including diaper service or disposables, plus the laundry you will do yourself)

Extra entertainment costs (because you may need to hire a baby-sitter every time you go out)

And just plain extras

Let's face it, having a baby will increase your costs on a day-to-day and a week-to-week basis. At least after the beginning, the rest happens gradually. It doesn't come upon you all at once, as baby-connected expenses do.

How It Used to Be

Here is a typical young couple's post-World War II monthly budget (1947) just before the baby came:

$60—rent (including gas, light, and electric)
$25—savings
$65—food
$10—smoking
$10—laundry and household supplies
$ 5—cleaning and clothing repairs
$10—newspapers, carfare
$ 5—personal incidentals
$ 5—insurance
$10—entertainment, movies, books, magazines
$ 5—packages to Europe
$ 5—clothes, travel money
$ 5—phone
$220

Truly another world.

THE COST OF HAVING A BABY

The cost of raising a child begins even before the baby arrives, as you have undoubtedly found out by now. Just note these categories in which you will be spending money, now and only until the baby is one year old.

Maternity wardrobe for mother-to-be

Lost income of mother-to-be who leaves outside employment before the baby is born (3 to 6 weeks)*

Obstetrical care (minus whatever you are reimbursed by your medical insurance plan)

Medication, if any, including laboratory tests and vitamin supplements

Hospitalization (minus, of course, whatever you are reimbursed by your medical plan)

- Room cost per day multiplied by 3.3 (average stay)
- Labor room
- Delivery room (some hospitals charge for this)
- Laboratory tests (and drugs)

*In New York State, disability is provided for some weeks by employers.

- Anesthetist (always billed separately; even if you have a prepared delivery, an anesthetist is on hand in case of emergency in most hospitals)

In-hospital pediatric examination

Circumcision or other special procedures

Baby's layette

Furnishings for baby's room, including crib and carriage

Nursery supplies (includes everything from sterilizer and bottles to diaper rash ointment and cotton balls)

Announcement cards and postage

Pediatric fees

Annual fee or retainer, or per-visit charge

Extra charges, for house calls, inoculations

On a special WCBS-TV news report in July 1980, entitled "Baby's Bottom Line," it was estimated that the cost of a baby the first year—to birth and feed and dress him/her—could run as high as $7,000. (Obviously, this figure is considerably higher today because of inflation.) This included approximately $950 for furnishings, $600 for clothes, $500 for clothes for the mother, $1,300 for diapers, baby formula, and food (depending on whether the mother breast-feeds or not and what kind of diapers are used), $2,000 hospital charges (at a major New York hospital where a semiprivate room averaged $225 a day and a private room $310), plus the private doctor's fee, the first-year pediatrician fees and the cost of a baby nurse.

This is a staggering figure, but happily, there are some ways to cut costs.

HOW TO HAVE A DOLLAR-WISE PREGNANCY

SCHEDULE THE OUTGO TO KEEP UP WITH THE INCOME

When you find out what your hospital, obstetrician and pediatrician—or your home, nurse-midwife, doctor—charges are going to be, find out also the schedule of payments you are expected to meet. Then draw up a timetable for yourself, so that you can distribute these costs over a period of time according to your income. Plan your other major expenses, such as furniture purchases, so that they too may be distributed.

LOOKING FOR MEDICAL-CARE SAVINGS

Investigate clinics for prenatal and pediatric care. Seek out a birthing facility (see page 114) instead of a hospital for delivery. Or think about home delivery. But plan very carefully. Always compare quality of the lower-cost medical service to be sure there is a real savings. If, for example, you have to take a day off from work every time you have a clinic appointment, and your employer does not pay for medical time off, you might not be saving very much over the cost of a private or group-practice obstetrician. Or if you are uneasy about delivery at home, you might decide the cost of a hospital will buy you peace of mind *and* possible emergency protection.

HOSPITAL CHARGE POLICIES

Establish your credit at the hospital with your down payment. Find out if personal checks, credit cards, or only certified checks are accepted.

MEDICAL PLAN REIMBURSEMENT PROCEDURES

Find out what the reimbursement procedures of your medical plan(s) are—whether the hospital receives payment directly from your insurer or whether you must lay out all monies first, to be reimbursed later.

HOSPITAL ROOM SAVINGS

Save by reserving a semiprivate room; it's a lot more fun, anyway! Unless you are an extremely reserved person, you'll get lonely in a private room. Two to four beds to a room is usually comfortable—and these days you may well find only two women in a four-bed room and the nursery filled to only about half of its capacity.

ESTIMATE AND SAVE ON DIAPER COSTS

Compute and compare the probable costs of diaper service versus disposables. A baby needs approximately 4,000 diaper changes during the first year of life! Look at packages of disposable diapers and compare costs of regular and large economy sizes. Divide each cost per package by the number of diapers per package to get the per-diaper cost. Then multiply by 4,000 to get the annual cost. Call your local diaper service(s) to find out their cost per year. This is usually figured on a monthly basis according to the number of diapers used per week. So ask for a cost estimate based on an average of 80 diapers per week. Then compare. Even if you decide on a diaper service, you'll probably also use disposables for trips away from home and as an emergency supply. If the diaper service comes out ahead—that is, less costly—you'll have to judge by your life-style and convenience factors which to use on a regular basis.

BUDGET FOR BABY EQUIPMENT

Look at our lists of layette items (on page 171), equipment, and furnishings. Decide which are essential to have now, which can be bought anytime before the baby comes, which can be bought after the baby is born, and which would be nice to have but are not necessary. Before you buy, comparison-shop to determine the price range in your community of each item on the list. Then plan your own schedule of purchases and payments. Shop for essentials from the fifth month on, pick up the "anytime-before items" if you can get them at good prices at the same time, but fill in later on.

SAVE ON BABY EQUIPMENT

Department stores usually hold baby-supply sales sometime during the year. Watch for special purchases and markdowns of essential and before-the-baby items. Look for these, too, in thrift shops and at school or church bazaars.

TAX SAVINGS

It may be small compensation for the large outgo, but you do save on taxes in two ways. First, a new family member, even a tiny one, entitles you to an exemption of $1,000 on your income tax return. If you are in the 15 percent bracket, you'll have a saving of about $150; more if your taxable income is higher.* And if your taxes have been withheld, you'll probably see this saving in the form of a re-

fund check that arrives in May or June of the year after the baby's birth. Second, if you itemize deductions, your considerable medical expenses for mother and baby both, including hospital, doctors, medications, travel expenses connected with medical care, and even vitamins, when prescribed, are deductible.

Costs of Being a Parent

In 1977, Thomas J. Espenshade, a senior research associate at the Urban Institute in Washington, created a stir when he reported that it cost $64,215 to raise a child to age 18 and send him or her to a public college. In October, 1980, he redid his calculations for the Population Reference Bureau, Inc., a Washington educational concern, and found the costs of raising a child have risen about 33% since his earlier study. "Seeing a child through birth, 18 years under the parental roof, and four years at a public university now costs the average middle-income U.S. family about $85,000 in 1980 dollars in direct, out-of-pocket expenditures," Mr. Espenshade reports. But there is a second kind of childbearing cost to be considered—the "lost" earnings of the mother who chooses to stay home with her children. Adding the two costs—direct and opportunities lost (what economists call the money a woman might have earned if she had worked instead of staying home), the total cost per child in 1980 for middle-income families was approximately $140,000. (James C. Hyatt, "Costs of Being a Parent Keep Going Higher," *The Wall Street Journal,* October 2, 1980)

Author's Note: I include this information not to frighten you, but rather to help you prepare realistically as much as possible.

WHAT PARENTS-TO-BE SHOULD KNOW ABOUT INSURANCE

With a baby on the way, you're likely to think differently about insurance from the way you have in the past. Somehow a baby

*1982 figures.

begins to make us think of providing for our very own child's future just in case. . . . We also tend to think about money much more.

Insurance is one way of trying to protect your family against unexpected events that might require substantial sudden expenditures which could interfere with your continued earning ability. It can be a financial lifesaver. But it can be costly right now.

What should you do?

First, you have to decide whether you can afford to have—or *not* to have—insurance. Second, you can seek out various sources of information. Third, if you are going the insurance protection route, you can investigate the various possibilities of particular kinds of insurance.

The four primary types of insurance which every family must consider are: health care, homeowner's protection, automobile insurance, and life insurance. If you own a home or automobile, you will probably already have the appropriate insurance. But you should check your homeowner's policy to see if you're covered for a baby-sitter's liability—or get a VIP special policy attachment. If you live in an apartment, you should also be sure that you're covered for liability.

When a baby is on the way, every family thinks about health and life insurance. This is only natural, since both are important to the security and well-being of a growing family.

If you do not have life insurance, you should investigate the various types of policies available. The basic, least costly policy is savings bank life insurance—also known as SBLI—sold at banks in some states. SBLI premiums are often lower than commercial insurance company premiums. You should inquire at your bank for the details applicable to your needs. Other life insurance policies can be bought, of course, through licensed insurance agents.

Whatever policies you buy, be sure to examine them closely. Read the fine print, and ask questions about anything you don't understand. Research your options by consulting reliable money management books, and ask advice of friends or relatives.

Whatever you do, don't forget that women should have life insurance policies as well as men—whether or not they work outside the home. Replacing a mother's services can be very costly.

After you make your decisions, review all your insurance policies regularly to determine if circumstances indicate that changes should be made in your coverage.

Insurance Coverage for Infants

The last thing that parents want to think about before the arrival of a baby is possible medical complications following the baby's birth.

Most parents push such fears out of their minds, and few consider the possibly disastrous economic consequences of congenital defects in their baby, or serious illness.

Sophisticated medical technology makes it possible today to sustain the lives of thousands of newborns who would have died in the past. But the medical bills can be crushing, if parents do not have health insurance covering the newborn period.

Laws requiring that insurance companies provide coverage for infants from the moment of birth have been passed in all states except North Dakota, Rhode Island and the District of Columbia.

Many of the laws are based on a model law on newborn health coverage developed in 1973 by the American Academy of Pediatrics (AAP) and the Health Insurance Association of America. An AAP study found that the State laws are generally satisfactory, and that major insurance companies are moving quickly to provide the required coverage.

But parents must make sure that they are covered. According to an article in the AAP's *News and Comment*, people with policies issued before the State laws took effect may continue to be without coverage for newborns.

Review your policy carefully and discuss any inadequacies with your agent or with the person in your company or union responsible for insurance.

If you're not covered for all dependents, purchase the needed health insurance immediately.

If you expect a baby and your policy has an exclusionary provision, take out additional insurance for the uncovered period of time.

Sidney Rosendorf, ed., Children's Bureau, Department of Health, Education and Welfare, 1978

LIFE INSURANCE FOR CHILDREN

The purpose of life insurance is to provide money for the survivors should the primary working member(s) of a family die. Since children are seldom earners, the other family members hardly need to be protected against the loss of their income, and life insurance for them is usually a waste of money.

There are, however, many who advise it. They usually argue that the premiums are lower because you start at such a young age. But this is not really so. Because you will be paying them over a longer period of time, it will actually prove *more* expensive in the long run.

It is also argued that a life insurance policy would provide money to pay funeral and related costs in the event of death, and that the money could otherwise be used for college. But the chances of a child dying are statistically very small. And you would actually accumulate more money by investing the amount of the premium regularly in a savings account, especially in a term account paying a high rate of interest.

Still, there is one important purpose in buying life insurance for a child. For a small additional premium you can provide in advance for your child's right to buy additional insurance later in life. If there is a family history of severe illness or genetic ailments, such a policy could provide insurance for a child who, as a young adult, might otherwise not be able to buy any. Only about 3 percent of those who seek insurance cannot get it for medical or other reasons. But while there is little chance of a child becoming an uninsurable adult, it can be quite upsetting when it *does* happen.

In general, however, it would be better to invest the same amount in savings, or add it to the premiums to purchase additional insurance for the parents.

Part Three

THE CHOICES IN CHILDBEARING

Having my first baby was the beginning of my ego. It was as if I'd given birth to the sun.

DORIS HAIRE

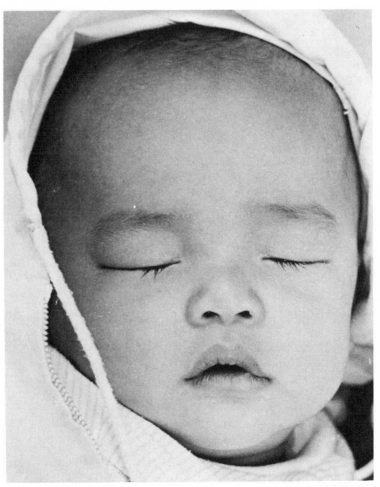

Daniel Kaufman

Who Will Deliver the Baby?

DOCTORS AND OTHER BIRTH ATTENDANTS

Obstetricians (OBs) care for women during pregnancy, at delivery, and immediately following the birth of the baby.

Gynecologists care for women throughout their lives, in relation to the health and functioning of their reproductive systems. Most OBs are also GYNs. Thus, you may go to an OB-GYN, as they are called in common parlance. Many of these specialists are *board certified;* that is, they are accredited by the American Board of Obstetrics and Gynecology.

Others are *fellows* of the American College of Obstetricians and Gynecologists (ACOG). Being a fellow means that they have:

- Demonstrated high ethical and professional standards.
- Graduated from an approved medical school and completed postgraduate training in the specialty.
- Practiced obstetrics and/or gynecology exclusively for at least five years.
- Successfully completed an examination in the specialty.

Many specialists are both board certified and fellows of the American College of Obstetricians and Gynecologists. Usually there will be certificates testifying to their credentials in their offices.

However, for one reason or another, many equally skilled physicians are neither board certified nor fellows of the American College of Obstetricians and Gynecologists.

General practitioners, or family practice doctors, may also care for women during pregnancy and deliver babies. They are not specialists. If yours is a general-practice doctor, you should ask him or her if s/he will call upon a specialist at the time of birth in the event of complications. Also ask if your doctor is a member of the American Academy of Family Physicians.

Nurse-midwives are well qualified to deliver babies and, unlike many obstetricians, will remain with the mother throughout labor, and provide psychological as well as medical support. They must be graduate registered nurses with one year's experience in obstetric nursing. They must complete a course (one to two years) in nurse-midwifery (mid-WHIFF-ur-ee) recognized by the American College of Nurse-Midwives. They must also pass the national certification examination given by the American College of Nurse-Midwives. This entitles them to use the initials C.N.M., Certified Nurse-Midwife, after their names.

In the course of their training, nurse-midwives assist in at least 40 births and handle at least 20 alone under an obstetrician's supervision. They specialize in normal deliveries; there is usually an obstetrician on call in case of complications.

Lay midwives do not have a nurse's training. But many are highly experienced, very ethical, and work out of a center or in conjunction with a nurse-midwife. Some are practicing illegally—although recognized by their communities as valid birth attendants—because state law does not certify them.

GROUPS AND TEAMS

One solution to the problem of the busy specialist is the obstetric-gynecological group, which includes two or more specialists, each of whom you will get to know during your pregnancy. Such groups also include obstetrical assistants and nurses, all of whom share the responsibility for the care of every patient. Thus, you as the patient can be reasonably assured that there is always someone on call who knows your case.

There are several variations on the group or team theme. A clinic is, by definition, a group. But some private practitioners work in groups, too. A hospital will be able to tell you about its clinics, and give you the names of the physicians affiliated with it who practice in a group.

Since the American College of Obstetricians and Gynecologists now formally acknowledges the value of nurse-midwives as members of obstetrical teams, physician groups have expanded to include them as well as obstetrical nurses. And groups of nurse-midwives have become affiliated with hospitals which provide obstetricians on call constantly.

Some group variations include:

A group of nine nurse-midwives backed up by six obstetricians able to manage as many as sixty deliveries a month

Two obstetricians and two nurse-midwives in private practice

Four nurse-midwives operating a hospital clinic

Five nurse-midwives operating a private service but working through a hospital which provides office and examination facilities able to handle up to 200 deliveries a year

LOCATING A DOCTOR

Common wisdom and the medical profession both advise that the best recommendation for a doctor is word of mouth, preferably from a satisfied patient. The author of this volume has other ideas. You can't possibly cover any doctor's clientele thoroughly enough to know how good (or bad) your doctor may be. Yet, it is very important that you do know in advance. Therefore,

here are a few ways you can play Ralph Nader ahead of time:

Do ask other women about their doctors and their experiences with them. Get details. Ask both women who have had babies recently and older women who visit gynecologists.

Ask your family physician or general practitioner to recommend a colleague. This is the second most frequent source of referrals. Try to find out who *other doctors* use for their own childbirth experiences.

Call your county medical society, which will make several recommendations. Then check the credentials of each name on the list, and check also with the hospital with which each doctor is affiliated. Try to get the names of previous patients.

Check your local Lamaze or other natural childbirth class teachers.

Write to the International Childbirth Education Association (see Resource List on page 320).

From a local hospital with a maternity department get names of specialists on its staff and/or information about its clinical services. Find out exactly what facilities your hospital offers and the practices it prefers or discourages.

From your local public health department get information about hours and locations of any prenatal-care clinic in your community.

Find out if there is a women's health center or women's service in your community and if they run a prenatal-care clinic, and/or get their recommendations of obstetricians, midwives, and clinics.

Write to: The American College of Obstetricians and Gynecologists (ACOG), 1 East Wacker Drive, Chicago, Illinois 60601, for the names of specialists in your community. Also: write to the National Association of Parents for Safe Alternatives in Childbirth (NAPSAC), P.O. Box 267, Marble Hill, Missouri 63764, for their directory of alternative birth services; to the American College of Home Obstetrics (ACHO), 347 West Harrison Street, Oak Park, Illinois 60607; to the American College of Nurse-Midwives, 1522 K Street NW, Washington, D.C. 20005; to the American Academy of Family Physicians, 1740 West Ninety-second Street, Kansas City, Missouri 64114.

Look in the *Directory of Physicians and Surgeons*, published by the American Medical Association, which you can probably find on the reference shelf at your local library. Hospitals are likely to have a copy, too.

If you decide to use an obstetrician, you should telephone several and make appointments to meet with them. Actually, *before* you decide on the person *or* the place, you should check out three or four possibilities. And if you are new to the community and have few clues to go on, you'll need to put in more time and money on research. It may be a vital investment in your baby's future.

TIPS TO HELP YOU
MAKE A SELECTION

On the following pages several kinds of doctors and other birth attendants are described along with various types of childbirth experiences. This will give you some idea of the childbirth options. Here are some tips, hints, and just plain old-fashioned advice.

First and most important, keep a special notebook with you all the time. Jot down all the questions that you would like to ask a doctor or other specialist in childbirth. Leave several pages blank so you can add additional questions as you think of them.

On another page make your own checklist of what you expect from your doctor, qualities you might look for in any skilled person with whom you expect to share this important part of your life. (See the lists of doctor qualifications later in this chapter for some ideas to get you started.)

As you get the names and phone numbers of doctors or hospitals, write each at the top of a separate page. Immediately after you phone or visit, note down your impressions and the answers given to your questions. After you have spoken to three or four people, your reactions are likely to blur. This record will be a handy jog for your memory and will help you recall things you might otherwise forget.

When asking for recommendations or when visiting doctors, always ask *specific*

questions. (Carry your notebook of questions with you.) If you want a natural childbirth (see page 99), ask about doctors who are committed to this approach. If you want your husband present (or even helping to deliver the baby), ask for a doctor and hospital that agree. Today, most doctors prefer a moderate approach to labor and birth, using the minimum anesthetic believed necessary in each individual situation. But there are doctors who encourage a completely natural labor and birth, and who follow Leboyer birth practices.

If you feel strongly about a particular approach or method, be prepared for some extra searching before you find a compatible obstetrician. Don't be discouraged— by all means, look around for a physician who shares your views. It's much better to take the time early on and not have any regrets later. *Start the search as early as possible in your pregnancy. Don't* wait until the last minute—or the sixth month—to decide who will help you have your baby.

DOCTOR'S
PERSONALITY CHECKLIST

No, it's not a popularity contest. But your doctor *is* someone with whom you will have an intimate relationship for a long period of time. Naturally, you want him or her to be the kind of person who is sensitive, and who respects your rights as an individual.

Here are some ways to judge whether your medical expert is simpatico:

• Does your doctor answer even your first questions fully? Or are his or her answers "clipped," too abrupt?
• Does your doctor ask you about your family situation, about your personal preferences?
• Does your doctor take your knowledge and background into consideration, or does he or she *either* talk down to you so you feel like a child, *or* over your head so you come away befuddled?
• Does your doctor refer you to appropriate courses, written material (books, pamphlets), and other sources of additional information?
• Does your doctor explain costs in detail,

and perhaps even make suggestions about keeping costs down?

• Does your doctor show respect for your rights by promising certain basic considerations that may be important to you, for example, not to use an anesthetic unless it is absolutely necessary? *Or,* are your encounters with your doctor impersonal, his or her responses routine?

• Do you *like* the man or woman? Is he or she humane and kind?

• Is your doctor too busy? If your doctor delivers 500 or more babies a year, he or she may be too busy to give you and your baby adequate care. Another patient may go into labor just when you have an appointment, or, worse, just at about the same time *you* go into labor. The office may be quite crowded whenever you arrive, and you may have to wait an hour or more each time. Or, you may continually have trouble reaching your doctor by phone.

Obviously, all of these things may happen occasionally, unavoidably, even to a doctor whose practice is of moderate size. But when they occur regularly—when you always have trouble getting through—you should be concerned and start to think about changing to a less busy physician.

COSTS

Costs are important. *Always* ask what they will be. Costs vary and change from one part of the country to another, from one hospital to the next, and from one doctor to another. The solution is—comparison shopping! Some shopping pointers:

Private-care costs are highest. Group or team private practice may lower the cost somewhat.

In general, clinic costs are lower. But there may still be considerable variability, from moderate or pay-what-you-can-afford to low or no-cost-at-all for families with minimal incomes. Ask questions; state your circumstances.

Some medical insurance plans cover physician services. Always check to see what coverage your policy provides *before*

investigating doctors and alternative services. You may be surprised to find you are better off financially with more expensive private care if it is covered by your group insurance policy than with moderately priced clinic services which may not be covered.

IMPORTANT QUESTIONS TO ASK A DOCTOR

• How much weight should I gain?
• Do I have to restrict my diet? If so, how?
• Should I nurse?
• What can I do about breast care beforehand?
• How important is exercise?
• What kind do you recommend?
• What if there are problems? What kind of services can I count on, at what times of day or night?
• How do you feel about prepared childbirth?
• What types of analgesia/anesthesia do you use?
• Do you advise my seeing a pediatrician beforehand?
• If you're not available when my baby is ready to come, who will take care of me? Can I meet him/her beforehand? How often?
• Does your hospital allow husbands in the labor room? Delivery room? Do you?
• Must I be prepped? Have an enema? An IV? An episiotomy?
• Can I be propped up in a semisitting position during delivery?
• Do you routinely use electronic fetal monitoring?
• Will I be able to walk around during labor?
• Will I be able to hold my baby right away, and for how long?
• Under what conditions would you perform a cesarean?
• If there are no problems, how soon after the baby is born will I be able to leave the hospital?
• If there are problems, will I still be able to care for and nurse my baby?
• How often are there problems in your experience?
• How many cesareans do you perform in a year?

DON'T LET
YOUR DOCTOR TREAT
YOU AS AN OBJECT

There is no reason for any woman to accept patronizing or impersonal medical care. If at any time during your pregnancy you become uncomfortable with your doctor and the quality of care you are receiving, stop! Think *hard*! Many women have later regretted not leaving an obstetrician whom they came to dislike, or whose attitude somehow rubbed them the wrong way.

A woman doctor is not necessarily a guarantee of compatible, empathetic care any more than a male doctor is necessarily a male chauvinist. Treat each doctor as an individual, as you wish to be treated. But don't put up with what you shouldn't, either. During the early months of pregnancy you will be able to judge your doctor's attitude toward you as a person. If you are dissatisfied, you will have plenty of time to investigate other doctors and make a better selection.

Ask yourself:

• Is your doctor understanding? Are you treated as an individual—and not just another pregnancy?
• Are you addressed as "Mrs." or "Ms." according to your preference, and not by your first name—unless, of course, you are on a mutual first-name basis with your doctor or prefer to be called by your first name.
• Does the doctor keep appointments promptly—except, of course, if someone else's baby arrives? Or must you spend half a day in the waiting room?
• Are all your questions answered patiently and clearly, even when you ask them a second time?
• Are the next stages of your pregnancy explained to you in advance, even if you don't ask?
• Are you examined with consideration? Some minor discomfort is to be expected during an internal examination, but there is no need to be poked or prodded, inside or out, or to have an ice-cold speculum used.

I am not encouraging you to spend nine months doctor-shopping. Rather, I hope to show you what to expect from a caring doctor, so you can judge early on whether you are receiving the quality of care you want.

HOW TO TREAT
YOUR DOCTOR

Patients have been known to be inconsiderate themselves! You're probably not the sort who needs this kind of advice—but just for the record, here are a few reminders:

• Keep appointments promptly; if you must change your schedule, call as far in advance as possible.
• Be understanding when the doctor is rushed or must change your appointments (as long as it doesn't happen every time). His/her other patients may have emergency needs, and you would want yourself attended to promptly in such circumstances.
• Be sure to write down questions in advance.
• Follow instructions carefully. This will save time and money.
• Answer the doctor's questions clearly and fully.
• Tell your doctor frankly what's on your mind; don't keep questions or opinions bottled up till the seventh month.
• Pay your bills as promptly as possible. If there are financial problems, discuss them openly at the first opportunity.

Not So Old-time Doctor's Orders

Doctor's orders are supreme. In *Vienna ten years ago,* I was the only woman in the maternity ward not bound into a corset and kept in bed for two days after the delivery. The nurses were astonished and disapproving at my relative liberty, but *Herr Doktor* had left instructions, and they dared not disobey. Nor did they investigate his reason for the order, which was that I had not gained *the fifty pounds then popular in Vienna* and consequently didn't need so much "shoring up." The practices of corseting and lying-in have now largely disappeared in the Germanic countries, but the initiative for the innovation came strictly from the doctors. Nurses and mothers are not supposed to have opinions, much less to seek an analysis, of the situation. (Shari Steiner, *The Female Factor: A Report on Women in Western Europe,* 1977)

◇   ◇   ◇

WHAT IS NURSE-MIDWIFERY?

The first midwife in North America arrived on the *Mayflower,* and for hundreds of years most births were assisted only by such practiced, but not formally trained, women. In essence, these were lay midwives. Only centuries later, in 1931, the Maternity Center Association started a school for nurse-midwives for the rural communities of eastern Kentucky, which were then almost without medical care.

Today nurse-midwifery is a skilled profession, with 2,000 midwives certified by the American College of Nurse-Midwives, although the college does not know how many of them practice regularly. Interestingly, 12 or 13 of these are men. A prospective nurse-midwife must be a registered nurse with at least one year's prior obstetrical experience. Further, a course of study must be completed at one of the sixteen schools accredited by the American College of Nurse-Midwives.

Elsewhere in the world, where *80 percent of all babies are delivered by nonphysicians,* the midwife—not necessarily a nurse, too—is a well-known figure in most communities. In the United States the nurse-midwife is rapidly becoming recognized as a key member of the modern obstetrical team. She functions in the hospital—and in the community—offering personalized health care for *healthy* women in all phases of childbirth, baby care, parenting, and family planning. She may be the first to diagnose pregnancies with a risk, and she will then refer such women to obstetricians.

According to Dorothea M. Lang, C.N.M. and president of the American College of Nurse-Midwives:

"The uniqueness of the midwife program is that the midwife provides each woman with preventive and personalized health care, which includes direct supervision during pregnancy, labor, and the postpartum period. She cares for the newborn and provides guidance on family planning, as well as teaching classes to prepare parents for childbirth and parenting. In the United States the nurse-midwife always functions within the framework of a medically directed health service, and handles only normal deliveries."

For information about courses in nurse-midwifery or for referral to a childbirth-preparation center staffed by nurse-midwives in your community, write to American College of Nurse-Midwives, 1522 K Street NW, Washington, D.C. 20005.

WHY GO TO A NURSE–MIDWIFE RATHER THAN TO A DOCTOR?

At a recent nurse-midwifery conference in New York City, I asked Adele Treible, C.N.M., why a woman should choose her services rather than those of an obstetrician. Her answer:

"If I had the choice I would rather go to a nurse-midwife because I feel that the regular obstetrician treats you like you're in and out, like another number—there is no personal care. The nurse-midwife cares—she is with you, she listens—she answers your questions. You do not get that feeling from an obstetrician."

"But," I suggested, "suppose there is a complication or some kind of problem?"

"Then I would advise going to see a regular obstetrician."

"How can you tell? At the last minute a problem may develop. . . ."

"Doctors are available at delivery. Either they're on call or they're right there. If a woman has had two miscarriages, then I recommend that she go to an obstetrician. But if she had two healthy childbirths, or no history of any problems, there is no reason why she shouldn't go to a nurse-midwife."

Then I spoke with Dr. Morton Shiffer, an obstetrician-gynecologist with the Jewish Hospital of Brooklyn, New York. I asked, "Why would anyone go to a nurse-midwife instead of a doctor?"

He replied, "Well, I think a nurse-midwife is more sympathetic, has more empathy, is more dedicated, gives the patient greater security."

"But," I persisted, "I would be nervous because of the question of expertise. . . . If anything went wrong . . ."

"They know exactly how far to go and they know when to call the doctor," Dr. Shiffer responded. "I don't know all of them but the ones I know are very, very careful about what they can do."

See page 118 on home births for more information on midwifery.

THE LAY MIDWIFE

You may choose a home birth and a lay midwife. Some certified nurse-midwives attend home births with a lay midwife as an assistant. And there are some doctors who will attend a home birth. However, the majority of home births seem to be attended by lay midwives. These women have had on-the-job training, and sometimes Red Cross training in resuscitation techniques. Some may have had nurse's training without a midwifery background. At present there seems to be no organized training group or school for the lay midwife.

There are some specific advantages to the use of such a person if you decide on a home birth. The first is ready availability. The second is identification with the mother-to-be, and a resulting warmth. The third is that she will have seen a number of births—unlike you and your husband.

Here are some guidelines for choosing a lay midwife:

IMPORTANT QUESTIONS
FOR THE LAY MIDWIFE

- How much experience has she had? How many babies has she brought into the world?

- What has been her training? Any medical background?
- If there is an emergency, who and what would she call on? Is she able to get you to a hospital? How?
- Does she prepare you for possible complications for you or the baby?
- Is she prepared to help you in prenatal care, or to refer you to other sources of help?
- Can she screen you in advance for possible complications? Under what conditions would she forgo you as her patient?
- What equipment does she carry to the birth?
- What arrangements does she make to check the baby?
- Is she listed in the NAPSAC (National Association of Parents and Professionals for Safe Alternatives in Childbirth), or other directory? Is she part of any home birth organization?
- How much does she charge?

Some states do not legally allow lay midwives to practice. According to Tracy Hotchner in *Pregnancy and Childbirth* (1979), some nineteen states do allow lay midwives to practice. These are: Alabama, Alaska, Arizona, Arkansas, Delaware, Florida, Hawaii, Louisiana, Maryland, Minnesota, Mississippi, New Mexico, North Carolina, Oklahoma, Rhode Island, Tennessee, Texas, Washington, Wyoming. To be sure, you should check with your local or state health department.

Different Ways to Have a Baby

*Laughter is the one great distinguishing
characteristic in natural-birth rooms.*

    ROBERT A. BRADLEY, M.D., *Husband-Coached Childbirth,* 1974

A New World

I am very conscious of the small fraction of
total knowledge that is within the compre-
hension of man. To me, childbirth is a sa-
cred event and brings humanity nearest to
the spiritual and metaphysical world around
it. It is a moment of emergence of new life
with unknown potentialities.

    When I see a baby born to a happy,
healthy mother and witness the superhuman radiance that carries her to a new world
of mystery and possession, I say to myself,
"What sort of an idiot thinks he can make
anything of this life without the hand of God
to guide him?" (Grantly Dick-Read, M.D.,
Childbirth Without Fear, 1944)

Awake! Awake!

    Childbirth is one of the enormous events
in a human being's life. For a mother to sleep
through it, for a father to be excluded, is a
real tragedy. (Elisabeth Bing, New York
Daily News, November 22, 1976)

PREPARED CHILDBIRTH:
A LITTLE HISTORY

Childbirth has had an odd history for several reasons. Traditionally, it has been regarded with great fear in Western societies.
In addition, until very recently, the procedures of childbirth were designed to suit the
convenience of the attending physician. The
position of the mother, the place of birth,

who was present, and, in fact, all the important factors were decided by the doctor. An
anesthetic was used for the first time in 1847.
With the introduction of anesthetics and
their later widespread use after the turn of
the century, some of the fear diminished. But
this led doctors to claim childbirth as their
own province. Each time a new element of
technology (from forceps to fetal monitoring) has been introduced, the male medical
profession has tended to replace the female
midwifery profession in the baby field.

    Once painkillers came into general use, the
medical profession used them excessively.
Doctors began medicating everyone for
quick, quiet deliveries, not realizing until
many generations later that the drugs given
to the mother crossed the placenta into the
fetal bloodstream and could, and often did,
depress the baby's breathing. The use of anesthetics as well as other technological "advances" in delivery reduced the woman in
childbirth to a passive recipient of medical
intervention, rather than the active producer of the baby.

    It took nearly a century for the male-dom-
inated medical profession to recognize that
a mother's emotional condition and her active cooperation played an important role in
childbirth; and that moral support, comfort,
loving care, and knowledge might be as
helpful in delivery as analgesics and anesthetics. And infinitely better for the baby.

    Even today, unfortunately, many doctors
do not subscribe to these principles. Some,
in fact, still call a mother in labor names, or
cast aspersions upon her abilities. "Your
baby is as stubborn as you are," one noted
obstetrician recently told a young woman

whose labor was prolonged. Under other circumstances if someone offended you, you could get up and walk away! As it is, you must put up with the peccadilloes of your doctor—unless your husband is present and ready to speak up in your behalf.

HOW "NATURAL CHILDBIRTH" BEGAN

The major changes in childbirth began earlier in this century, but did not involve many women until mid-century. And it's only during the last decade that the popularity of new childbirth principles has become widespread. It all began with an English physician, Dr. Grantly Dick-Read, who has come to be known as the father of natural childbirth.

In 1919 Dr. Dick-Read, a senior resident in obstetrics at London Hospital, wrote a brochure on natural—not, he emphasized, pain-free—birth. This paper grew out of an experience he had had before the First World War. A woman he attended at a home birth in a London slum refused the chloroform he had brought with him—the first time this had ever happened in his medical practice. The woman seemed absolutely in control of herself and the birth was free of the usual confusion and unbearable pain. After the delivery she said: "It didn't hurt. It wasn't meant to, was it, Doctor?" This so shook Dick-Read's conservative medical thinking about childbirth that, over a period of years, he began to reexamine the whole nature of pain. But not until 1933 was anyone willing to publish his theories.

Dr. Dick-Read started by insisting that the phrase "labor pain" be expunged from hospital vocabulary and replaced with "contraction." He divided labor experiences into three categories: (1) normal or natural, (2) average or cultural, and (3) abnormal or surgical.

To Dick-Read the category of "normal or natural" refers to a labor in which no physical, chemical, or physiological condition is likely to disturb the normal sequence of events. An important adjunct to this condition is the education of the mother. She must know what the sequence of events will be, and how she can help herself during the various phases. That is why this type of birth is often referred to as a *Prepared Birth*.

The mother-to-be, according to this pioneer of childbirth, should also be surrounded by people—including the father-to-be—who understand labor and how it progresses, those who can give her the emotional support she needs to overcome any fears she may have. Dick-Read believed something we all know today: Fear causes tension; tension affects muscles and nerves, thereby resulting in more than normal, tolerable pain. Dick-Read also believed that preparation through physical exercises, breathing exercises, knowledge, and emotional calmness would lead to a Prepared Birth without the need for medication during labor.

The second category of experience, cultural labor, refers to women who are physiologically and mechanically well-equipped to bear children but emotionally and intellectually unprepared. They have doubts and fears and understand little of what is going on. Put simply, they are scared.

Fear, says Dick-Read, inhibits the normal sequence of events during labor. The Fear-Tension-Pain syndrome is present and produces *real* pain. In addition to a woman's fear of pain, hospital practices can increase such fear. Many medical staffs leave the laboring woman alone during the first stage. Solitude can be very frightening, and this only increases the pain. Such a woman, says Dick-Read, should certainly have analgesic or anesthetic relief. Whether the pain was necessary or not, she has it and it should be eased if she so desires, even though in ninety-five percent of the cases, had she been properly prepared, she would neither need nor want anesthetics.

And finally there is the minority of women who make up the third category, those with physiological problems—a disproportion or malpresentation—which require instruments or surgical deliveries.

Dick-Read believed in some important keys to laboring with minimal discomfort: good health, good muscle tone, relaxation, and proper breathing. He advocated that women reduce the tension of their contractions by using deep abdominal breathing patterns. In addition, fairly strenuous special exercises were practiced to strengthen the body. More and more Englishwomen were attracted by Dick-Read's humane approach to childbirth, and in the 1940s the Maternity Center Association sponsored several lecture tours for him in the United States. Educated women began to go to classes teaching Dick-Read's methods in the 1940s and 1950s, but the movement which really gained widespread adherence in the United States was the Lamaze, or Psychoprophylactic Method.

Dr. Fernand Lamaze was a French physician who derived his theories from practices he saw on a visit to the Soviet Union in 1951. According to Dick-Read, Russian doctors learned of his ideas long before they were adopted in England or the United States, used them enthusiastically, but claimed them as their own "Pavlovian" methods. Dr. Lamaze learned his prepared childbirth from the Russians and credited them with the innovation. There was immediate interest in his teaching throughout France and Europe, and his methods were formally sanctioned by the Catholic Church in 1956. Three years later, after an American woman, Marjorie Karmel, published her experiences of having a baby in France by the Lamaze Method, Lamaze classes began to spring up alongside the Dick-Read classes in the United States. The interest was immediate and tremendous and the American Psychoprophylactic movement was born.

This Lamaze Method was said to be inspired by the Pavlovian concept of conditioned response; that is, it is possible to be conditioned away from pain. When pain is perceived, there are other simultaneous sensations—visual, auditory, or tactile. By concentrating strongly on one or more of the latter (such as beating out the rhythm of a song on your thigh) pain becomes less overwhelming. The theory is that the brain blocks out the pain signals. This is similar to the rationale behind the Chinese use of acupuncture as an anesthetic. Its theory is that the rotating acupuncture needles fill the pain centers with a tolerable pain so there is no room for the intolerable pain of the surgery. (But some people feel no pain at all from acupuncture needles.)

The untrained response to a uterine contraction is an instinctive tensing, first of the surrounding muscles, and ultimately of the whole body. This overall tensing creates a greater force against which the uterus must push to do its work, and, as a result, a stronger uterine contraction and increased "pain." By training and practice a woman can learn to relax the rest of her body with each contraction. This deliberate relaxing minimizes the tension of the contraction.

Lamaze recommends as distractions (1) breathing patterns (some of which are difficult), requiring extreme concentration, (2)

use of a focal point during contractions, and (3) *effleurage,* or a light massage on the abdomen which is soothing and comforting as well as distracting.

The Lamaze Method relies heavily on a trained labor coach with whom the mother-to-be has already established a close relationship, and during pregnancy has devised a workable system of stimuli and responses for use during the different phases of labor. In America the father-to-be usually acts as coach. This not only benefits the mother but creates a closeness and a shared birth experience which often results in a binding force in their future family life. If the father is not going to be the labor coach, then the mother can choose another kindred spirit such as her mother or a close friend who has had a baby.

The distinctions between the Dick-Read and Lamaze methods were not that significant. The role of a labor coach was one basic difference. Another was the attention Dick-Read gave to cultural factors, as opposed to Lamaze's more physiological perspective. Dick-Read believed that education about having a baby combined with conscious relaxation would dispel the mystique and fear of childbirth. Lamaze used a more programmed approach to keeping the mind occupied during labor. They both used breathing techniques, but Lamaze's methods were more aggressive and did, at first, sometimes cause hyperventilation. Dick-Read's patients were more tranquil, Lamaze's more active.

Today the distinction is remote. In essence, the popularization of the Lamaze rather than the Dick-Read theory of Prepared Birth seems to be a historical accident. Nonetheless, in the United States the Lamaze Method is extremely popular and is the basis for most natural childbirth classes.

Gaining in popularity is another offshoot of Prepared Birth: Husband-Coached Childbirth, developed by Dr. Robert Bradley of Denver, Colorado, who in over thirty years has delivered more than 13,000 babies, administering pain-relieving drugs in less than 5 percent of the births.

Bradley, like Dick-Read, believes in the positive power of serenity, but he doesn't find serenity and excitement mutually exclusive. Giving birth *is* exciting but one can approach it serenely. Bradley's method is based on imitating the behavior of mammals in labor.

Mammals instinctively relax during labor

and appear to experience no pain. Bradley disagrees with Dick-Read's contention that the instinctive reaction to a contraction is to tense up. He has developed his own childbirth-preparation course, which emphasizes the intimate participation of the husband in all phases of the pregnancy and birth. During the course (which lasts for six months instead of the three for Lamaze preparation, and the six to eight weeks common elsewhere), husband and wife are both taught to recognize indications of tension in the mother and to eliminate the tension. This is done by a simple touch or caress, by massage, by willpower, and other techniques.

Bradley believes that controlled breathing should follow animal labor behavior patterns. Like many other experts he believes that the natural contractions of the uterus, the strongest muscle in the body, function best with athletic, deep chest breathing in the second stage of labor.

Bradley holds regional training seminars and classes all over the country.

WHEN YOU TAKE A CLASS

If you choose prepared childbirth, you will probably start your classes around the seventh month. (If you possibly can, start much, much earlier.) Six to eight weeks of practice is required before you can use the techniques successfully during labor. Generally, classes are limited to six or seven couples and meet for two-hour sessions once a week for six weeks. Your husband, or whomever you choose as labor coach, attends with you.

The three stages of labor (see page 222) will be discussed in the first class session, with visual aids, so that you will be able to recognize the characteristics of labor at any given point and will know what to expect when. The second session concentrates on muscle-relaxing techniques. In sessions 3 and 4 the three phases of contractions are discussed along with the tempo and depth of breathing to be used for each. (The rate of breathing is timed to the contraction.) The couples are then taught how to massage the abdomen and back during strong contractions.

The fifth session concentrates on the birth itself, the second stage of labor, how *not* to push (until the cervix is fully dilated), the actual delivery, and the husband's or labor coach's role. And in the final session you learn how to recognize real labor, what to bring to the hospital, and the hospital routine and procedures. Breathing patterns are reviewed and the use of medication discussed and you are prepared for the great moment.

In order for psychoprophylaxis to work well, the hospital team must cooperate. Your husband or coach must be allowed in the labor *and* delivery rooms. The hospital staff must agree to your wish to avoid anesthetics, unless there is a compelling medical reason to use them. To prepare for this eventuality, an anesthetist is always present.

Among all the newer birth methods there are some common denominators. They all stress body building and physical fitness, muscle relaxation, and specialized breathing for the different phases of labor. But the sine qua non for all is knowledge, awareness, recognition of what is happening and elimination of the fear of the unknown. If fear can bring pain, the absence of fear goes a long way toward minimizing it.

If, however, during the course of your labor you decide that the pain is more than you can tolerate, don't feel ashamed or a failure. Different people have different tolerances, and the time and intensity of labor varies. Besides, you may have been unrealistically ambitious. If you or your doctor feel you should have some medication, chances are—because of your preparation, knowledge, and lack of fear—you will need half the amount of painkiller you might have needed otherwise. On the other hand, you should also know that you may change your mind about an anesthetic in mid-delivery, and find that your doctor is unwilling to give you medication, for the sake of the baby's welfare. If this happens, you will simply have to accept the doctor's judgment at that crucial time.

Prepared Childbirth is becoming more available, especially in big cities. And increasingly, parents-to-be are becoming interested in Prepared Births as they become aware of how joyful it can be to see their own babies emerge into the world. Prepared Births also seem more desirable as we all become educated to the dangers of childbirth drugs to the babies.

For more about the Lamaze method, read *Painless Childbirth* by Dr. Fernand Lamaze (Pocket Books, 1977). Write to Childbirth Without Pain Education Association, 20134 Snowden, Detroit, Michigan 48235.

For more about the Bradley method, read *Husband-Coached Childbirth* by Dr. Robert Bradley (Harper & Row, 1974). Write to American Academy of Husband-Coached Childbirth, P.O. Box 5224, Sherman Oaks, California 91413.

HOW TO CHOOSE A CHILDBIRTH CLASS

The best checklist I've seen for choosing a childbirth preparation class is excerpted below from *Our Bodies, Ourselves: A Book By and For Women* by the Boston Women's Health Book Collective.

1. Make sure the class is small—although it's hard to find a class with fewer than ten couples.
2. Compare the prices of the classes with the quality of teaching and attention to your needs as an individual.
3. Make sure the class will include adequate discussion, detailed information, plenty of rehearsal to learn physical techniques. Six weeks is minimal; eight to ten weeks better. . . .
4. Be sure the class encourages fathers and/or friends to participate. The class should be built around the expectation that someone who is as trained as you will always be with you throughout labor and delivery.
5. The class should discuss feelings and attitudes as well as techniques. . . .
6. Find out as much as you can about the organization that sponsors the classes. . . .
7. If your class is to be part of any research study, find out as much as you can about it. Don't consent to anything you don't feel comfortable with.
8. Look at the qualifications of the instructor. A reputable teacher needn't be an R.N. (registered nurse), but she should have a detailed sheet of her qualifications and experience ready to give you. . . .
9. Find out whether any professional board is affiliated with the class program and who is on it. . . .

◇　◇　◇

Childbirth and Energy

Childbirth without pain does not mean childbirth without effort. Childbirth de-

mands of a woman a great expenditure of energy. You will be asked to put forth great efforts, and you will succeed—provided you have prepared for it. . . .

To all of you joining in the preparation delivery will be an *active event*. When you are admitted to our labour ward, you will come in to complete an action. After you have taken full cognizance of your maturity, you will have a chance of *analysing* it, of *controlling* its progress and of *checking up* at each stage the benefit arising from what you have been taught. You will give *impetus* to your delivery by remaining its *driving force*. . . .

. . . In the days to come we shall talk to you about the position of your genital organs, as well as the work of those specially involved in delivery. We shall study their relationships and we shall tell you how they function.

You will realise that:

1. These organs are made to hold and shelter the child.
2. After holding and sheltering it, they can expel it.
3. Your pregnancy and delivery are part of your life, being two natural and physiological phenomena.
4. Pain is no more essential to labour than it is to pregnancy, and that it is harmful to delivery as it would be to pregnancy. . . .

. . . You will have been handed a stock of information, amply sufficient to allow you to give birth, with *full knowledge* and with joy. (Dr. Fernand Lamaze, *Painless Childbirth*, 1977)

◇　◇　◇

THE BACHELOR WHO CHANGED CHILDBIRTH

Dr. Frederick Leboyer is a very successful (currently nonpracticing) middle-aged French obstetrician who has helped to revolutionize childbirth. After a long and very painful psychoanalysis, Dr. Leboyer's thinking-feeling about baby birth changed dramatically. In the late 1960s he set out to find better ways for babies to be introduced into the world.

His study led him to advocate dim lighting and quiet in the birth room; the mother moving around freely; talking to the new-born infant and explaining every procedure; massaging the infant; letting the cord pulsate for four or five minutes; immersing the infant in a small bath of warm water a little after birth; keeping infant and mother close together; not laying the baby flat on the back.

Dr. Leboyer let the world know his perceptions of the way a baby should be born in an extraordinary volume published in 1975, *Birth Without Violence*. Since then he has published two other books: *Inner Beauty, Inner Light: Yoga for Pregnant Women* and *Loving Hands*, the latter about baby massage.

A four-hour film-and-conversation session with Dr. Leboyer was sponsored on November 5, 1978, by the East–West Center for Holistic Health at New York University. The audience consisted of health students and professionals (nurses, midwives, even obstetricians), teachers, many parents, grandparents—and children and babies.

Dr. Leboyer does not lecture. He engages in conversations—then a dialogue ensues. At first he appears to be *l'enfant terrible*—because he answers no questions of the mind, or even of fact.

Although he might deny it, Dr. Leboyer's perspective seems basically emotional. His belief is that feelings and the body are all that matter in childbirth. Knowledge and its acquisition is anathema. He pooh-poohs such standards as preparation-for-childbirth classes or the significance of studies and statistics. Those of us who have come to our opinions and biases from what we regard as the infallible evidence of science, and the incontrovertibility of proof, might be shocked by his seemingly antiintellectual, antithinking stance on having a baby.

Observing him before an audience, one realizes that Dr. Leboyer is trying to provoke us into a state we all too often forget: feeling. The naturalness of feeling, doing things largely the way that nature provides are high values in his lexicon. And his thesis seems to be that modern science and technology have developed a screen and large barriers against doing what comes naturally. We now have "techniques"—and the revolutionary doctor is opposed to "techniques" in childbirth. He believes in freedom of choice by mother (and father), the personhood of the baby, and following natural paths. Animals lick their babies, we

should rub and stroke and bathe ours. Mothers need to concentrate on birthing, babies need to hear pleasant sounds; the birth room should be silent except for breathing sounds.

Dr. Leboyer is opposed to many of the so-called standards of modern medicine: fetal monitoring, episiotomies, anesthetics, forceps (unless essential), cesareans (again, except when essential), clearing out the air passage of the newborn, putting silver nitrate into the eyes. Circumcision appalls him, except when it is performed for religious reasons.

Dr. Leboyer: "l'enfant terrible"? Hardly. Somewhat controversial, though. There are a fair number of women who criticize him for being too authoritarian and not giving mothers a sufficient role. But my own impression is that this criticism is largely irrelevant. He has given all babies the opportunity to be treated as sensitive human beings during and just after birth, and thereby has helped to minimize the physical and emotional traumas of childbirth. Birth will always be a dramatic change, a crisis; but Dr. Leboyer has shown us that birth can be beautiful for the baby, too.

After hearing Leboyer speak, when you see the huge circle of women who gather around him and watch the young mothers with their babies and the young pregnant women embrace him with great emotion, you realize that this guru of childbirth has brought something unique into their lives. Something irreplaceable: the feeling that having a baby is too precious an experience to squander on the mechanics of the technicians of birth.

LEBOYER BABIES LATER ON

French psychologist Danielle Rapaport studied 120 young children who had been Leboyer babies. She found that the children were unusually well advanced for their age, walked earlier, had no problems with toilet training, and, most surprisingly, were more or less ambidextrous.

Dr. Leboyer himself has linked ambidexterity in babies with an unusual amount of curiosity and lack of fear, qualities which the Rapaport babies also exhibited to a pronounced degree.

Are these findings the result of a Leboyer birth? Or are they the result of child rearing by the specially aware group of parents, exceptionally motivated to provide an ideal climate for their children from the moment of birth onward?

It's too soon to tell. This is a preliminary finding only. If Leboyer's method appeals to you, and if you can locate a birthing facility that will provide it, then by all means try it. But don't feel bad if you can't. Although it is the belief of this author that the type of birth *and* the atmosphere in the delivery room can make an essential difference in a baby's life, still a stimulating yet gentle and loving, encouraging climate during infancy and childhood is also a crucial key to physical and psychological well-being. In other words, what happens *after* the baby's first hours of life is something you *can* influence—even if you cannot affect the birth experience.

HOW TO FIND A LEBOYER DOCTOR

Doctors who practice Leboyer's way are multiplying. To find one, you need to check in your local community. You might find out if any of the doctors who practice alternative birth methods (see Resources List) know a Leboyer obstetrician. In addition, write to the National Association for the Advancement of Leboyer's Birth Without Violence, Inc., at NAALBWV National Headquarters, P.O. Box 248455, University of Miami Branch, Coral Gables, Florida 33124.

A SWIMMING CHILDBIRTH

The latest word on painless childbirth comes from Russia. In 1979 they delivered babies—hold your breath—*underwater!* Only their expert women swimmers were involved. A woman in labor entered a tank of warm water along with a midwife, both naked. The baby was born under the water and floated in the water before being brought up for air. This type of delivery has been practiced in the United States since 1980 by people devoted to conscious birth. An NBC Phil Donahue Show on January 19, 1982 described and demonstrated the process.

How the Swedes Do It

Although childbirth education is still considered somewhat of an innovation in the United States, it has long been an integral part of maternity care in Sweden, a country frequently commended for its low infant mortality rate. In no state does the death rate approach Sweden's low rate, including Utah, the state with the lowest infant death rate. One of the most noticeable differences centers around Sweden's approach to childbirth. In Sweden every expectant mother who wishes, is educated and trained for childbirth. The average Swedish mother is

---

How It Used to Be

Time was when the little one and its comfort was not so thought of as it is today. It was not considered that the little one in its tedious birth journey had become tired and needed rest; or that its change of abodes and climates is so marked that the transition is not an easy one. It was plunged into a full bath, or exposed to the air, was sponged over, often with soap that was not too pure, and the only resulting virtue was the full expansion of lungs, because of the lusty crying from such rough handling.

To-day many physicians advocate wrapping the new baby in cotton batting, covering it quite closely, and laying it away in a warm corner for several hours, until it becomes in a measure adjusted to the change of residence. Then, instead of a thorough washing, it is treated to an oil bath before a warm fire, with only a small part of its body exposed at one time.

Mrs. Emma F. Angell Drake, M.D., *What a Young Wife Ought to Know*, 1901

---

prepared for conscious childbirth, and labors spontaneously with little or no medication. (American Hospital Association, *Family Centered Maternity Care: An Alternative Obstetrical Approach*, February 1978)

Relax and Breathe

Birth is or can be a tough, demanding (even athletic) process; so there is strong emphasis on physical training, relaxation, and learning the breathing techniques so well that they are automatic when in labor. A class goal is to achieve a conditioned response to uterine contractions of RELAX and BREATHE rather than a response of tension and pain. These responses, because of their complexity, require a concentration that shuts out much of the discomfort.

The method is not typically "natural" or "painless" childbirth. And, contrary to one widely held bit of misinformation, it *is not* necessarily childbirth without medication. In the course of the classes, the subject of medication is covered. Various types are explained, regarded as tools to aid labor,

available when needed by the patient or deemed necessary by the physician. The patient is not made to feel that she has "failed" should she or her physician feel an anesthetic is required. There is, however, emphasis on being awake and aware during this very significant life experience. (American Society for Psychoprophylaxis in Obstetrics, *The Psychoprophylactic Method of Childbirth: An Introduction*, 1977)

Movements that Helped

Here is one of Grantly Dick-Read's first pregnancy and breathing exercises:

> Stand with the feet comfortably apart, the hands at the sides, palms to the front. Raise the hands in front of the body to shoulder level at the same time rising on the toes. Swing the arms outward, throwing the head slightly backward. Complete this movement during deep inspiration, slowly resuming starting position with expiration. Repeat six times.

Different Places to Have a Baby

Most people in the field of childbirth recognize that there has been a recent movement away from hospitals on the part of parents-to-be. This, together with the large drop in the birthrate, has resulted in many empty obstetric beds in some hospitals, and has caused much worry on the part of hospital administrators. An effort to make the hospital more attractive has coincided with the spread of more knowledge about the best way to have a baby for mothers, fathers, *and* infants. The result? A lot more interest in *family-centered care in the hospitals themselves*, and many hospitals changing their practices. For example, San Francisco General Hospital has reported an increase in births from 30 a month to 132 since the Alternative Birth Center within the hospital was opened. Many of the patients do not meet the criteria for the birth center, but are given family-centered care in the once-conservative delivery room.

Alternative birth centers are also a fairly new development which bring to parents much more of the benefits of homelike care outside the home. No one knows how many centers there are throughout the country. And their practices vary somewhat. But there should be enough of them around the country to start their own association—something that hasn't happened yet.

Finally, there is the real thing—instead of an approximation. This is the *home birth*. There is a growing and vocal minority in favor of home births—including many of those who have either had a baby this way or have been present during such a birth. In fact there are organizations supporting the home birth movement. One of these is Home Ori-ented Maternity Experience (HOME) in Washington, D.C. Another is the National Association of Parents and Professionals for Safe Alternatives in Childbirth (NAPSAC) in Marble Hill, Missouri.

You may opt for one place of birth and not be at all interested in other possibilities. On the other hand, you may decide to look into the alternatives. I hope the material in this section will help you decide.

CHANGE YOUR WORLD

Some books should change the world. Some do, of course. But others, which are equally significant, remain in the backwaters of our lives. Oh, of course, these "unnoticed" volumes do influence and affect some people—usually a small number of an avant-garde of any field. And that small number, through the years, can grow. But basically, many significant books remain for too long without enough attention, without that pointed influence—the ability to effect considerable change.

Such a volume is Suzanne Arms's *Immaculate Deception*. After reading this volume, my reaction is: "Why do we have so many hospital births—still? Why are male doctors, instead of female midwives, so prevalent during birth? Why don't women control their own bodies during birth?"

This book is a revelation and revolutionary—and should be in the vanguard of a movement to change the present American experience of birth.

Other landmark books which are part of this movement are:

Doris Haire, *The Cultural Warping of Childbirth* (booklet)
Sheila Kitzinger, *The Experience of Childbirth*
Robert A. Bradley, *Husband-Coached Childbirth*
Gail Sforza Brewer, *What Every Pregnant Woman Should Know*
Grantly Dick-Read, *Childbirth Without Fear*
Fernand Lamaze, *Painless Childbirth*
Frederick Leboyer, *Childbirth Without Violence*
Ashley Montagu, *Touching*
NAPSAC's two volumes of *21st Century Obstetrics, Now!*
Lyn DelliQuadri and Kati Breckenridge, *Mother Care*

This body of books should be read by everyone. Even those of us long past the direct experience of having babies would benefit enormously from a different perspective on that most vital aspect of human life, giving birth. A different perspective on childbirth could help to change our culture, not only for those about to have babies—but for all of us involved at any time of our lives with a medical establishment devoted to money and techniques, and not enough to people.

For young parents-to-be and for grandparents-to-be, the books I've listed are vital for the best kinds of birth experience. Not everyone needs to have a baby at home to have this experience. Not everyone needs to have babies in the same way, same place, same positions. But everyone has the right to know what they are choosing, and why.

And everyone also has *the right* and *the need* to have their birth treated with the greatest respect. Every *birth-giver* has *the right* to be surrounded by the best physical and emotional ambience. Everyone giving birth should have the right to choose the circumstances that provide this condition.

So if we continue the hospital way of birth—for whatever economic, medical, or personal reasons—then hospitals and their staffs should change radically. A little change is not enough. A lot of change is essential.

◇ ◇ ◇

A New Approach

Choices for Parents:
A Different Way of Giving Birth

The organization NAPSAC has sponsored several national conferences on childbirth practices. At the second such conference, held in Chicago in 1977, Ruth T. Wilf, a nurse-midwife at Philadelphia's Booth Maternity Center, was a speaker. Her remarks were printed in the proceedings of the conference, titled *21st Century Obstetrics, Now!* In her discussion of the work of the Booth Maternity Center, Ruth Wilf also defined those groups of women for whom a traditional hospital birth was most advisable. Her remarks are as follows:

I believe that there should be a full range of options available to *all* parents in *every* community, including a high-risk center, a low-risk community hospital, an out-of-hospital birthing center, and responsibly organized home birth. Of course, all of these would offer a family-centered, parent-oriented approach. Then the optimal place for each family to give birth could be chosen flexibly according to individual wishes and medical needs.

As I see it, there are four groups who need to utilize hospitals for births:

Number one, women who have a medical problem. In the cases of these women and their families, family-centered maternity care is essential. The higher the risk, the more these parents need to become intelligent participants with their health care providers in understanding their problem, in planning jointly how to deal with it, and in becoming responsible for their own health care needs.

The second group are those who have a normal pregnancy, have planned responsibly, and plan to give birth in an out-of-hospital setting, but have some difficulty in labor which brings them to the hospital.

The third group are those who, because of cultural values, assume that of course you go to the hospital to have your baby. This group may or may not be attuned to the values of family-centered maternity care.

The fourth group who need the hospital are those who have not been ready, willing or able to take responsibility for their own care. They need to be helped toward doing so through the style of family-centered maternity care.

The sense of achievement from a good birth experience is the strongest stimulus I know to greater self-esteem and effective functioning. It is vital for us all, and super-vital, especially for those who have not had much opportunity to achieve in their lives. What a fabulous surprise and source of pride! Of course, there is also an authoritarian style of care that is threatened by parent participation, and attempts are made to intimidate parents. These establishments should be labeled, "Dangerous to your health!"

The health care team must include parents as equal participants as well as professionals. It is *our* bodies, and they are *our* babies.

THE HOSPITAL OPTION

How It Used to Be

A Few Hospital Rules in Early America

No dirt, rags, or bones shall be thrown from the windows.
Sheets are to be changed once in two weeks, and night shirts once every four days.
All nurses who get drunk, neglect their patients, quarrel or fight with other nurses, or quarrel with men shall be immediately discharged.

Dr. Palmer Findley, *The Story of Childbirth*, 1933

The New Family Way to Have a Baby in a Hospital*

The material that follows is being reprinted with permission, from an unpublished paper ("Family Centered Maternity Care: An Alternative Obstetrical Approach") prepared by the the American Hospital Association in February 1978. In addition to a mailing, twenty-five hospitals (including two alternative birth centers) in urban areas of seven northern states were visited by a representative of the AHA in preparation for this report. The headlines are largely mine.

Throughout the country, the traditional concept of maternity care practiced by most hospitals is undergoing a significant change towards Family-Centered Maternity Care. In recent years, health care professionals have become increasingly aware that dissatisfaction with the present system of maternal health care delivery exists on many social levels.

Although many physicians, administrators and nurses have recognized the need to modify the present system of maternal health care and have been responsible for initiating and implementing many new ideas, the main impetus for change has come from the consumer. "Expectant couples are requesting, in increasing numbers, more personalized, family-centered care," explains Katherine Brown, R.N., maternal and child health coordinator at Evanston Hospital in Evanston, Illinois. "Our family-centered maternity care program, established in the late 1950's attempts to respond to the ob-

---

*What follows presents hospital practices in a very favorable light. However, many, many hospitals, unfortunately, are still following outmoded and very harmful procedures.

stetrical needs of the complete family unit in a safe, home-like atmosphere."

The concept of family-centered maternity care includes such procedures as natural childbirth, fathers present during labor and delivery, childbirth education classes, childbirth preparation techniques—Leboyer, the Lamaze Monitrice System, Rooming-in, sibling visitation of mother and baby, birthing rooms and alternative birth centers, and early discharge of mother.

WHAT IS FAMILY–
CENTERED MATERNITY CARE?

Family health care is the term usually applied to services in some respects, which are available to more than one, or to all members of a family. The term evolved from the concept of the family as a "unit," whose members interact in such a way as to affect each other's health to their advantage or detriment.

Family-centered maternity care is a flexible concept of quality: individualized health care that recognizes, focuses on, and adapts to the physical and psycho-social needs of the mother, her family, and newborn. The emphasis is on the provision of alternative maternity care which maintains physical safety as well as family unity. The important teamwork effort involves the woman and her family, obstetricians, family physicians, certified nurse-midwives, pediatricians, nurses, nurse practitioners, and requires cooperation and understanding to be effective. . . .

The father is not treated as a visitor but is considered an integral part of the family unit and is permitted to provide his wife with the emotional support the couple feel she needs in the days surrounding birth. The husband's participation also aids in the re-establishment of the family relationship on a cooperative basis. Modified rooming-in, an important part of family-centered care, allows both parents to acquaint themselves with their baby during the postpartum period, under the guidance of trained, sympathetic personnel.

Some programs [surveyed] included pre-delivery classes for parents; some have private nurseries next to the mother's room with a connecting window as opposed to a general ward nursery for use when the mother chooses to rest. Some consist of private and semiprivate rooms. Some have semiward arrangements and some hospitals allowed other family members (grandparents, older siblings) relatively unrestricted visitor privileges to non-high-risk mothers. Early labor lounges, and alternative birth centers, free-standing care facilities offering comforts of home with advantages of operating and emergency facilities nearby, are available in some settings.

Many hospitals have decorated postpartum units to resemble an average home. One hospital placed a rocking chair in each room, as the universal symbol of family-centered care. Other hospitals provide cheerfully decorated family waiting rooms, early labor lounges, and recreation areas. They usually contain small libraries, television sets, and quiet corners for conversation. Snacks, juices, cold beverages, and coffee are provided for parents and children on a self-service basis to encourage interchange with each other and other families. These arrangements have been found conducive to providing learning and support between groups of parents as they form friendships, exchange child-care hints, and relax. Again, procedures in hospitals vary.

Usually, the prepared couple is then free to share the birth experience, as long as they comply with requirements determined by the medical and nursing staffs. . . .

These requirements usually follow a similar pattern:

—the couple wishing to be together must have the permission of their attending physician;

—the husband and wife must have attended childbirth education classes or received some advance preparation;

—the husband must agree to leave the labor/delivery area if the delivery will require a complicated operative procedure other than an episiotomy;

—the husband must be aware of the importance of maintaining privacy of other patients in the labor/delivery area and agree to stay in his wife's room or in a designated area while his wife is being examined.

Family-centered maternity care programs are generally for low-risk, normal healthy mothers and newborns. Parents are informed that adequate prenatal care and participation in childbirth education classes are prerequisites.

WHAT SHOULD BE ACCOMPLISHED?

The goals of a family-centered maternity care program are:

—To ensure that the mother has a good experience during labor, birth and her postpartum stay.

—To enable the husband to share in this experience to whatever extent that he and his wife desire, if there are no contraindications.

—To ensure that every mother leaves the hospital confident in her ability to care for her baby.

—To accomplish these objectives without jeopardizing the health and well being of mother and child.

FATHERS IN THE DELIVERY ROOM, EVEN FOR CESAREANS

One of the most controversial aspects of family-centered maternity care, fathers in the delivery room, has gained in demand and acceptance as more hospitals accept trained couples. Criticisms and argument against the practice stem from the belief that fathers present a considerable infection hazard to the mother and newborn; another source of concern is that the number of malpractice suits against physicians will increase. Most hospitals have successfully contradicted these beliefs through evidence offered by physicians thoroughly experienced in this practice.

Recent well-controlled research shows that not one advance in family-centered obstetrics has sacrificed the gains of modern obstetrics or methods of preventing infection. Dr. Robert Bradley, author of the book *Husband-Coached Childbirth* (1974), has had over 7,000 fathers in the delivery room with no increased evidence of infection. This is well documented in the literature. A study conducted by the California Department of Health (1974) found that, in 45,000 cases collected in surveys, there was not one infection traceable to this practice and not one malpractice suit.

ROOMING–IN

Rooming-in is a hospital arrangement whereby a mother and her newborn are cared for in the same unit. Almost any adequately arranged physical facilities for maternity care can be adapted to rooming-in care. However, it reaches far beyond physical facilities and signifies an attitude in maternal and infant care and a general plan of supportive parent education which are based on the recognition and understanding of the needs of each mother, infant, and family. It is a plan to maintain natural mother-infant relationships, to reinforce the potentialities of each mother and infant, and to encourage the family unit. The specific overall objective is to foster a natural, healthy start of family life.

Special features of rooming-in are that it (1) provides for the mother and infant relationship beginning immediately after delivery when the mother is capable of assuming the care of her infant, (2) fosters feeding on the permissive plan,* (3) facilitates instruction of mothers and fathers in infant care, and (4) reduces the incidence of cross-infections among infants.

The American College of Obstetricians and Gynecologists' *Manual of Standards* (1965) states:

Facilities for rooming-in should be provided for those patients who want it . . . modified rooming-in has much to commend it and usually requires no specially constructed facilities. . . . Lower infection rates in rooming-in arrangements than those in conventional nurseries is in no small measure attributable to the rooming-in nurse.

THE BIRTHING ROOM

Some few hospitals are making an attempt to get away from the usual "hospital image" by establishing birthing rooms, in which delivery as well as labor can take place. The birthing room is intimate in size, designed to have a homelike atmosphere. It is furnished with curtains and perhaps wallpaper, and an easy chair for the husband, who is expected to remain. The mother rests in a bed with a back support, and stays in it to give birth. Equipment is kept handy in a cupboard or on a wheeled cart, to be

*Mothers feed their infants as the baby seems hungry.

used as needed. In case complications arise, the mother can quickly be wheeled to the nearby delivery room and the infant removed to the appropriate department for specialized care.

WHY SHOULD A DOCTOR OR NURSE CHANGE?

The major advantage of family-centered care for physicians is the marked reduction in telephone calls from anxious parents after they return home. One study . . . showed this system reduced the number of telephone calls by 90 percent. . . . The training received by parents under the guidance of hospital personnel significantly increases their confidence in caring for their newborn, according to another study. . . .

It must be emphasized that many hospitals reported that turnover in personnel was significantly lower after the implementation of family-centered care. Attributed to this fact was the deepened sense of caring and satisfaction gained by personnel. "Sometimes family-centered care is theoretically accepted by nurses, but not emotionally, where it's most important," added one nurse.

Many hospitals now have classroom demonstrations and discussions given by their obstetric nurses, attending staff members and International Childbirth Education Association instructors from other agencies with qualified educational programs other than the hospital. Classes cover a full range of topics, depending on the personnel and facilities available within a given community.

Certified nurse-midwives function in some hospitals, while others do not actively utilize their services. Legislation varies from state to state, and controversy regarding lay midwives and certified nurse-midwives remains an important issue, as does reimbursement procedures. The monitrice, an obstetrical nurse specifically trained in the Lamaze method, has been used. She may also be an ASPO (American Society for Psychoprophylaxis in Obstetrics) certified childbirth educator. Her capacity is similar to that of a private duty nurse.

Some certified nurse-midwives are practicing in the hospitals surveyed. Boston hospitals, such as Beth Israel and Boston Hospital for women (Lying-In Division) deliver over 3,000 babies annually and use certified nurse-midwives. Family Hospital in Milwaukee, Wisconsin, and Northwestern Prentice Women's Hospital also use certified nurse-midwives.

PREGNANT FEMINISM

There are few lengths to which some people will not go to make sure that there is equality between the sexes. Consider this sign on a hospital room door:

This Room Is Reserved Exclusively for Pregnant Persons!

Jumping into Bed

"We have a twenty-four-hour visiting room for father and baby—whether he's married or not doesn't mean anything—and that's created a problem because we have some fathers who won't go home for one hour out of the twenty-four! They get to be a first-class pain in the neck. They'll take showers in the patient's room, and if it's a two-bed room, the patient in the other bed gets very spooked about this guy being there all the time. She's afraid to go to the john because she's afraid he's listening to her pass gas or something. They complain about that. We had one husband who took advantage of the twenty-four-hour rule and slept in the bed with his wife, and that had our nurses spooked, the patient in the other bed spooked, and [the wife] claimed she just couldn't sleep unless her husband slept in the same bed with her. Well, these are some of our problems." (Saul Lerner, M.D., Press Conference, American College of Obstetrics and Gynecology Convention, 1979)

ONE FAMILY–CENTERED HOSPITAL

At Roosevelt Hospital in New York City there is both a midwife program and a birthing room. The birthing room is the newest development. It is a small private comfortable room in which the mother can have her baby, attended by a nurse-midwife and with her husband present.

The midwife program itself has been

available at Roosevelt for around ten years. This private midwife service can be requested by anyone, no matter how poor or how rich. The nurse-midwife takes full charge of births and no doctor is present. Of course, she is always in consultation with the hospital doctors and there is a backup medical team immediately available in case of need.

Using a nurse-midwife for childbirth is much cheaper than delivering with a doctor since doctors at Roosevelt charge about $750 and the nurse-midwife program costs approximately $500. But the patients seem to prefer to use the nurse-midwife for other than financial reasons. Often women feel much more confident with the midwife's attitude toward delivery. The nurse-midwife appears to have more time for her patients.

She will sit and talk with them, is willing to discuss breast feeding and other matters, and in general, seems to take a much more relaxed and personal interest.

A sign of the success of the midwife program, as well as the birthing room, is that it is popular even among the Roosevelt staff who make use of it for their own families. That doctors' wives like the midwife service bears out the findings of a 1977 study, which indicated that women who make use of nurse-midwives are more educated than those who request ordinary deliveries.

Not all the patients at Roosevelt Hospital take advantage of the nurse-midwife program or the birthing room. Some prefer more traditional practices and some cannot use the service, since nurse-midwives do not deal with high-risk patients. The hospital has a

And in That Enlightened City

HOSPITAL SURVEY,* ACOG, DISTRICT II (NEW YORK), 1977

Total Hospitals Surveyed: 225	Total Responding 129
Questions	*Results*
Does your hospital provide an option for family-centered care?	YES—77%
Do you allow fathers in the labor rooms?	YES—99%
Do you allow fathers in the delivery rooms?	YES—96%
Do you allow mothers to be with their baby and the father in the recovery area after birth?	YES—80%
Do you have rooming-in?	YES—59%

Does your staff generally encourage:
    Expectant parents' classes?
    Prepared childbirth?
    Breast feeding?
	YES—98%
	YES—97%
	YES—97%

Does your maternity facility have a "birthing room" as an option for labor, delivery, and recovery in the same room?	YES—14%
Are you considering such a facility?	YES—24%
Are certified nurse-midwives working on your maternity service?	YES—17%
Do you find it possible to allow for early discharge after delivery?	YES—51%

If so, the discharge is usually:
    Within 12 hours?
    12–24 hours?
    24–48 hours?
	YES— 1%
	YES— 4%
	YES—95%

*This survey was conducted by Richard H. Aubry, M.D., in 1977. Some hospitals had not yet responded. It was reported in *21st Century Obstetrics, Now!*, 1977.

large OB-GYN staff with 35 physicians and 12 residents. But the six midwives who run the nurse-midwife program see about a thousand patients a year out of an average of 2,200 births a year in the hospital. Since the nurse-midwives deliver almost half of the babies, this is a sign of the considerable success of this service.

The staff is highly trained. Prospective midwives must have their R.N. and, in most cases, a bachelor's degree, before applying to train in the nurse-midwife program. The nurses then spend one to two years in obstetrics and eighteen months to two years in a midwife program before becoming fully qualified nurse-midwives. In the hospital they are available on call at all times, although the ordinary work day is 8 to 4, with one nurse working the midnight-to-eight shift.

Besides the midwife program, Roosevelt Hospital has tried to encourage some other important aspects of family-centered care. The hospital teaches the Lamaze method to prospective parents to help prepare them for the birth. Husbands are encouraged to come into the birthing room and the ordinary delivery room even if the baby is to be born by cesarean section, and small children are able to visit after the birth to see their mother and new sister or brother. Fathers are very involved at Roosevelt: 100 percent of the husbands are present in the birthing room and ninety percent in the ordinary delivery room!

THE HOSPITAL AND NURSING

You may find that practices in your hospital make it more difficult to start off nursing your baby successfully. The best way to initiate nursing is to begin immediately after birth, on the delivery table, if possible. If the baby is routinely taken away to a central nursery and not brought back to you for 12 hours, you lose the first natural period of contact. The initial feeding of the baby is then, not your colostrum, but the bottle of glucose and water given in the nursery to judge the baby's sucking capacity.

Without rooming-in, it may become difficult for you both to enjoy successful nursing. The best way to feed a baby is "on demand" and this is obviously impossible if the baby is simply brought in from a central nursery every 4 hours. By the time the baby gets to you, he or she may have already gone through a pattern of waking up, crying, and going back to sleep again and be really too tired to nurse successfully.

Where hospitals have encouraged staff to help women breast-feed (rather than simply present them with their babies and leave them to it), nursing mothers have done extremely well. The American Academy of Pediatrics, which has come out strongly in favor of nursing, believes that hospitals should change their practices to support the nursing mother.

In making your own plans, try to find a hospital where mothers breast-feed regularly, with rooming-in if possible, or at least one that might allow you to feed your baby on a 3- rather than 4-hour schedule. Emphasize in making arrangements with your doctor that you consider physical closeness with your baby in the first hours to be very important to you both. (These are all areas in which American Academy of Pediatrics policy would support you.) If you are having problems, the La Leche League in your area may be able to help you. Look up their number in the phone book.

The Prohospital View

A delivery can only be called absolutely perfectly normal *after it's all over* and the baby is out, crying and healthy. Until that point, there's no way of being certain that everything is going to be completely smooth 100 percent of the time. There is *no way* to guarantee it to anyone.

Though the vast majority of births are normal and simple, there is always a small risk that the particular birth in question won't be; for that reason, only a few nurse-midwives will deliver babies at home. We want to know, and you should, too, that there's a doctor available, a blood bank downstairs, anesthesia at the head of the table, an operating room, and an intensive-care nursery down the hall, though we rarely need to resort to them. If a patient doesn't need any of these things, I'll barricade the doors and fend them off with my life, but it's important to know they're out there just in case. When something goes wrong in childbirth, it can happen very fast. . . .

Home delivery can be a very risky business. In most Western European nations, the majority of normal deliveries are managed at home, but there are extensive systems of trained midwives and traveling obstetric flying squads, mobile units that can be summoned immediately to provide blood or perform surgery in an emergency. In this country, a woman whose birth suddenly becomes complicated must be taken to a hospital, often too many traffic jams or miles away for comfort. . . .

Just as an example, a baby with respiratory distress syndrome would need the facilities of hospital equipment for resuscitation, as well as the quick attention of a neonatologist. Or the mother may need special care if, for instance, she has severe postpartum hemorrhaging because the uterus does not contract immediately after delivery. Oxytocins, which help the uterus to contract, or perhaps even blood transfusions might be needed. (Barbara Brennan, C.N.M., and Joan Rattner Heilman, *The Complete Book of Midwifery*, 1977)

HARD QUESTIONS FOR THE HOSPITAL

- May I/we see a room in the maternity department?
- May I/we see the nursery?
- Do you have a birthing room, or are there separate rooms for labor and delivery?
- Can my husband/partner stay with me during labor? In the delivery room? (Can I stay with my wife?)
- Will I/we be able to see my baby right away whenever I/we want to?
- Is there a rooming-in plan?
- Will you help me breast-feed? How?
- Do you offer courses for prepared childbirth?
- Do you permit a Leboyer birth?
- Do you have nurse-midwives on staff?
- Are you approved by the Joint Commission of Accreditation of Hospitals?
- How many beds are there altogether in the maternity department?
- How many deliveries do you handle per year?
- Do you have a premature nursery?
- How many beds are there in the room I have chosen?
- What are visiting hours? What limitations are there on visitors, if any?
- What restrictions are there on the hours when telephone calls may be received?
- How much will it cost?
- If there are no problems, how soon after

the baby is born will I be able to go home? (Some hospitals require a minimum stay, and even charge for it if you insist on leaving earlier!)

ALTERNATIVE BIRTH CENTERS— SOME DEFINITIONS

Alternative birth centers are proliferating around the country. No one knows exactly how many there are, but, as of 1981, there were 100 to 150 such centers in 27 states. They are clearly growing fast, since the first of the centers did not open until 1975. At present the definitions of what a birth center is vary considerably.

There is a doctor in Connecticut who calls his facility a "birth center" but forceps are routinely used, and episiotomies are performed. The pretty wallpaper does not, in the opinion of many professionals, make an alternative birth center.

The criteria which seem absolutely minimal for such a center are the presence of one-to-one care and very, very little medical intervention.

Eunice K. ("Kitty") Ernst, a certified nurse-midwife, is a consultant to birth centers and has helped found several. She defines an alternative birth center as an out-of-hospital unit.

"To me there are no birth *centers* in hospitals. There are birth *rooms* in hospitals. And they are an adaptation of the hospital to a homelike setting—to make a hospital room look like a bedroom. A birth center, to me, is out-of-hospital and it is an adaptation of the home in that it has some of the accouterments of the hospital, some of the emergency supplies—IV fluids and oxygen resuscitation equipment. The program is set up rather tightly with good consultation and backup."

You can have different standards for home births, too. "For example, when the nurse-midwives of Reading, Pennsylvania, go to a home, they take emergency equipment with them. But other nurse-midwives and lay midwives do not."

Other professionals, of course, might consider hospital settings as alternative birth centers. Booth Memorial Hospital, for example, is a "free-standing" maternity hospital—unassociated with any other institution. However, babies are delivered by nurse-midwives and the physical setting is different from the usual hospital. Booth is capable of doing cesareans while out-of-hospital birth centers usually are not.

Practically all alternative birth centers use nurse-midwives during childbirth. The out-of-hospital centers generally follow the criteria of New York's Maternity Center Association. Only low-risk mothers are accepted. Usually parents must enroll with the center early in the pregnancy. They must meet other criteria for admission. These include: attendance at prepared-childbirth classes (or in-depth private instruction), definite plans for a support person who can function as coach to be available throughout the delivery, an agreement to go to the hospital if the attending physician or the nurse so advises, locating a pediatrician well in advance of delivery who will agree to see the infant within twenty-four hours.

They will not admit: women over 40 years of age for a first baby, forty-five for a second; anyone with a preexisting medical disease such as hypertension or severe obesity; women with other out-of-the-ordinary conditions, such as multiple births, prematurity, or pelvic measurements that are inadequate. Some women are transferred to the hospital during labor if certain problem symptoms occur.

The movement of alternative birth centers started in the early 1970s as a result of growing dissatisfaction with hospitals and a large trend toward home birth. The centers began because the nurse-midwives and some doctors felt that a centralized service was easier, safer, and very satisfying for childbearing couples. In big cities safety of midwives in traveling to homes at any hour was a prime factor leading to the establishment of centers. In addition, many couples felt (and feel) safer in a center with backup medical and hospital services quickly available and organized for them. Most urban centers are close to a hospital and have an arrangement with them, as well as with one or more M.D.'s.

Most out-of-hospital centers are located in big old houses—a fact which lends the feeling of home even more.

WHO SELECTS OUT-OF-HOSPITAL BIRTHS?

In an address presented at the Twenty-Fifth Annual National Health Forum in March 1977, Ruth Watson Lubic, General Director of the Maternity Center Association, gave a rundown on what type of family chose out-of-hospital births:

Who are the families selecting our out-of-hospital births? Do they represent some "lunatic fringe"? Preliminary data from a sample of our population revealed the following:

The families spanned nearly all ethnic groups and religious affiliations.

Most of the women coming to us—nearly 90 percent—were married.

For about one-third—35%—it was their first pregnancy.

Age range was from 16 to 37, with a mean of 28 years.

Education ranged from 8 to 22 years completed, with a mean of 15 years (3rd year of college).

In terms of family income, about 55 percent averaged $15,000 annually or less, and about 45 percent were above that figure.

Only about 20 percent had no form of health insurance.

By place of birth, about 20 percent were born outside the United States (Western Europe and Asia).

The majority of women—76 percent—were non-smokers.

The expectant mothers and fathers showed a wide range of occupational backgrounds, with most in the professional or clerical groups.

PHILOSOPHY OF CARE

The philosophy of the Nurse-Midwifery Division of McTammany Associates (Reading, Pennsylvania) an alternative birth center, embodies the following benefits:

• That childbearing families have a right to comprehensive maternity care.
• That women have a right to seek care that not only is medically safe for themselves and their baby, but that fits their life-style and recognizes and respects their individual, social, spiritual, and economic needs.
• That because the family is the cornerstone of our social structure, maternity care

must support and promote unity within the family.

• That childbirth is a peak life experience. It is viewed as a healthy process. Confidence in the physiological function of the body to cope with childbirth is promoted in all aspects of care.

• That childbirth is a critical period in the initiation of positive family-child relationship. Separation of family members, therefore, is to be avoided unless medical intervention is indicated.

• That nurse-midwives have a responsibility to inform women and childbearing families of their options in the form of care plans, all procedures, and treatments. The family has the responsibility to make informed decisions about their care.

• That education is an essential, integral part of midwifery care and that childbearing families are able to assume responsibility for health maintenance and effective utilization of medical care.

• And that maternity care should be provided at cost.

The Oklahoma City Birth Center

What is the "Birth Center"? The Birth Center is a birth option available to parents receiving prenatal care at this office. We do not advertise the Birth Center. The Birth Center idea was conceived out of a demand by consumers for an alternate to hospital birth. A great number of parents were wanting home birth. We felt that the Birth Center was a reasonable compromise for home birth. The Birth Center combines aspects of both hospital and home birth.

The Birth Center is not a hospital, and is not intended to provide full hospital services. The Birth Center is for normal birth without complications. If any complication of pregnancy, labor, or delivery should arise it would necessitate going to the hospital, or transfer to the hospital.

. . . Only normally progressing mothers (are allowed) to continue to labor at the Birth Center.

The Center consists of a large family living room, a kitchen and dining area and two homelike labor/delivery rooms. Parents are encouraged to bring along food to prepare either during labor or after delivery.

At all times during your stay at the Birth Center you will be watched closely by a nurse skilled in obstetrical nursing and labor-coaching. Your progress will be reported to me by phone. I do not routinely order perineal "preps" (shaving the pubic area), enemas, or I.V. fluids. During your labor you will be free to walk about the Birth Center, in fact, an upright position is encouraged as it aids the descent of the baby's head. During the second stage of labor (pushing) you can assume any position comfortable to you. Many mothers seem to enjoy side-lying or squatting position for pushing. At this point in labor we do ask that you retire to one of the labor-delivery rooms.

Episiotomies are not routinely done and it has been my experience that a well prepared mother who is able to avoid pushing at crowning can usually deliver without an episiotomy. After birth the infant will be placed immediately on your abdomen and covered with blankets. The umbilical cord will be clamped after it has stopped pulsating and the placenta will be delivered and you will be free to get acquainted with your baby. The nurse will be watching both you and the baby closely for the first few hours. After you have had a chance to rest, bathe, eat, and drink something you will be given instructions on care of both yourself and the baby. When the nurse feels you are physically ready you will be allowed to go home for recuperation. A nurse will be available to you at all times by phone should you have any questions or concerns. (Charles D. Taylor, M.D., and the Birth Center Staff, *NAPSAC News*, Spring 1978)

THE CHILDBEARING CENTER: A NEW PROGRAM

The Maternity Center Association pioneered in establishing the first school of nurse-midwifery in the United States in 1931. The association is pioneering again more than forty years later. In the small building it occupies in New York City, a Childbearing Center was set up in 1975 to provide total care for families. Here, about three hundred couples—with grandparents and siblings if they wish come each year for the birth of their babies. The numbers are small, but the center is designed as a demonstration project for out-of-hospital birth and is visited each year by hundreds of interested professionals (nine hundred the first year alone). A team of nurse-midwives and nurse-midwife assistants, aided by an obstetrician, a pediatrician and public-health nurse, work with the parents-to-be. All the deliveries are supervised by the nurse-midwife team. Costs are moderate: the fee, which includes two post-baby visits at home, was $1,000 in 1982.

Families who want to give birth here must apply not later than the twenty-second week of pregnancy, so there will be enough time for an acceptance decision, for interviews, and a series of weekly preparation classes. Time is needed, too, for a complete medical observation of the pregnancy. (The center's obstetrician sees women on their first visit and again at thirty-six weeks—otherwise the nurse-midwives supervise examinations.) Prospective parents are screened and selected for this program only if the prospects for uneventful pregnancies and deliveries are fairly certain. The center's definition of unacceptable risk includes: a first birth for women over forty; a history of diabetes, repeated miscarriage, Rh sensitization, or a serious medical condition.

Parents-to-be are both involved constantly in all classes, and the center is now pioneering parents' active involvement in self health care during the pregnancy period. The nurses have found that informed parents are very quick to spot possible problems, sometimes before the professionals themselves do. The classes start with examination of emotions of early pregnancy and its nutritional and physical demands, and go through a full preparation for the birth and adjustment after birth.

The center is *not* a hospital and has no facilities to deal with cesarean births or other conditions that need specialized medical equipment. In fact, a couple must select a hospital in advance and be prepared to transfer to that hospital during labor if the staff considers it to be necessary.

If a couple is accepted into the program, they may be asked to transfer out for medical or other reasons—detection of multiple births, abnormal weight gain, or the staff's feeling that they are not really committed to the program. Of the final group that comes in for labor, about twelve percent (1980) have had to transfer to the backup hospital they have selected, generally because labor fails to progress rather than for life-threatening

reasons. So far the center has never had a medical emergency.

The atmosphere at the center is extremely informal. The upstairs part of the building still looks something like the grand private home it once was—except that there are toys and models and pictures of baby development in the ballroom. Births take place in the "kitchens" downstairs—or what once were the kitchens. The rooms are modest. ("Just like my home," was the comment of someone behind me when I went to visit.) There is a *real* kitchen where parents can cook and eat meals during early labor. "About the only food we discourage is lasagne," said one of the midwives. "It's a little too heavy on the stomach." The midwife herself was dressed in street clothing and changed to clean clothes but not surgical greens for births.

When families come in for labor, they move around the garden floor and the garden during the early stages and then go to one of the birthing rooms as labor progresses. The beds are ordinary hospital beds (not delivery tables or the new birthing beds) and the mother takes whatever position she feels most comfortable in for pushing. Often this seems to be a side-lying position with one leg supported.

Prepared members of the family, including children, are part of the birth, and the father usually acts as a labor coach. The staff keep a Leboyer-like atmosphere, with just a spotlight on the bed and as little noise as possible. The bath is there, although many couples do not use it—they are too reluctant to let go of the baby.

As long as the baby looks healthy, the routine examination by the pediatrician, which is done in the presence of the parents, is delayed until just before the family goes home, and the staff tries to leave the parents alone with the baby for the twelve hours after birth to give them all a quiet time together. Once the family goes home, a public-health nurse visits them and telephone calls are encouraged. Babies in doubtful condition for any number of reasons are transferred from the center to the backup hospital—less than one percent.

ONE WOMAN'S VIEW

"I see my birth experience taking place in a homey, relaxed atmosphere where, with the help of my husband, I can get loose enough and feel comfortable enough to follow my instincts and pay attention to what my body is telling me. I know this is a big baby and labor will probably take a while, and I see myself free to walk around, stay active, visit with the people I love, have my daughter, my sister-in-law, and maybe my mother there, too. I want to be able to relax in warm water, feel at home, have my husband scrub my back.

"I see the experience being directed not by hospital routine, but [by] the baby, my labor, and my husband's and my efforts. I see a midwife that's warm and supportive and has a great sense of humor standing by to help us if we need it and who lets us alone when everything is going okay, who keeps me informed and listens to our evaluations, too. I see myself being free to try different positions, get naked if I want to, having my husband crawl in bed with me and cuddling; I see myself touching and being touched.

"I would like to try doing what feels right, and have the midwife help me by telling me how I'm doing and making suggestions.

"I see a lot of pushing needed with this baby. I had to push a lot with my last but it was great. I liked doing it and I did fine. My husband will give me his strength and help me push and when the head is out I'd like him to help the body come out. I want the baby on my skin right away, as soon as it's breathing, and I want it to nurse if it wants to. I'd like my daughter to be there when the baby comes out so she can see it right away, too. I'd like us all to be together for a while, then I'd like to take a bath and rest, and then go home with my family.

"I chose the nurse-midwifery birth center for the birth of my baby because I wanted a warm homey atmosphere for the birth, but also I wanted to be close enough to the hospital to be safe. I'm in very good health and this has been a good pregnancy and I feel strong and confident. Ideally, I'd just like to have this baby at home, by ourselves, but there's that one percent chance of needing medical care, and the birth center seems like a good compromise. I feel comfortable there, I trust the midwives, and they have big double beds, so my husband can get in bed with me. I feel that giving birth is a natural process and shouldn't, unless absolutely necessary, take place in a hospital. Babies should come out surrounded by family and

other people who love them." (Kathleen Houser)

HOME BIRTH

WHAT IT MEANS TO ME

When I was a child, being born in my grandparents' house seemed to me the best of all ways to be born. I had been born in a hospital. My entry into the world was accompanied by a raging night snowstorm, a taxi slipping on the high icy hill where the hospital was, my father and the driver pushing the cab up the hill to the top, my mother inside the car with me almost ready to be born.

My older brother and sister (much older) were both born in my grandparents' friendly, comfortable, old-fashioned house—with family members eagerly awaiting the birth of the first and, a year later, of the second grandchild in the living room adjoining the large, light bedroom.

I adored my grandparents' home—and I felt very left out throughout my childhood because this lovely birth had been denied to me.

Still, I will not claim, as some will, that my birth deprived me of a much better subsequent life than that of my brother and sister. Too many other factors were of more significance and had stronger effects upon each of us.

But even today I wish that my grandparents' house, rather than the inaccessible, impersonal hospital I never saw again, had been my birthplace.

Why shouldn't children be born at home? Their parents' or grandparents' or aunt's home? A home where life seems rooted and valuable, where it's possible in later years to show one's own children "the place where I was born."

There were reasons—and there still are good reasons—why hospital births have had value. The huge effort in the latter part of the nineteenth century and the early years of the twentieth century to lower the number of deaths of women in childbirth and the number of dead babies can only be applauded—and greatly appreciated by all of us who take a safe passage to motherhood pretty much for granted. I will not deny hospitals *some* credit for this. Hospital births were a factor, it seems to me—because antiseptic conditions were eventually far more possible there, and because medical knowledge and equipment were much more available in hospitals.

The ability to provide greater safety for troublesome, difficult birth situations—and for high-risk babies—was, and is today, much more possible in hospitals.

But all the rest of it—the emotional factors of childbearing for mother, father, and baby—are on the side of home births. And this is a not inconsiderable part of the process. In fact, it may be most of childbirth. The emotional, from what we now know, has very strong effects upon physical factors.

Is it possible for the emotional condition of parents-to-be to influence the entire physiological process? Could a totally happy mother-to-be still have a severe physical problem during childbirth—severe enough to make on-the-spot hospital equipment and highly trained personnel essential for life saving? Or could it be that most of the complicated, difficult childbirth cases are more the result of emotional factors—nonacceptance of the pregnancy or ambivalence about it, unhappy feelings about approaching motherhood, resistance to proper nutrition and body care, difficult feelings about the partner who brought about this state of affairs?

As yet, these speculations lack grounding in fact. But it is this author's opinion that with home births more possible and probably occurring at a greater rate, perhaps there will actually be fewer complications of childbirth at the present time. Because, as corny as it is, home really is where the heart is.

Are they safer? Or as safe? There is a dispute between the proponents of home births and the advocates of hospital births. The home birth believers declare that home births are truly as safe as, if not safer than, hospital births for most women and babies. The hospital believers (most doctors, certainly) declare that home births are unsafe, that in the cases where complications occur (a low percentage, by the way), there's sometimes a split second to deal with a problem that could *not* be anticipated.

Distinguishing right from wrong is hard in these circumstances. The greater rate of cesarean births in hospitals makes for greater

risks, as there is a risk in all major operations (that is, more women die during cesareans than die during regular delivery). Still, one reason for cesareans is the fact that difficult births would often end in the baby's death *without* the operation. The rate of maternal mortality is up somewhat, however, in recent years—doubtless the result of the increase in cesareans.

Hospitals *are* equipped with breathing equipment for mother and baby should it become necessary. They *do* have all of the other sophisticated paraphernalia, as well as very skilled personnel, for times of trouble. This is very valuable—in fact, invaluable when it is necessary to use any of it or them.

Could homes be so equipped? So far they have not been. Yet in the Netherlands, where over half the population is born at home, trained nurse-midwives bring in such equipment. Their infant mortality figures are much lower than ours, too.

Why couldn't there be a fully equipped ambulette waiting outside the home with resuscitation equipment? In case anything is needed, or a trip to the hospital is called for, this vehicle would be prepared. And why couldn't doctors or nurse-midwives go to the home so equipped?

As described earlier, some hospitals are starting to compete with themselves and homes. They are attempting to borrow homelike characteristics—a living-room atmosphere; relatives present, even children during labor; the use of nurse-midwives—to make mothers and fathers and other family members feel at home. And of course, birthing centers have been trying to be an alternative to the depersonalized hospital atmosphere.

Anything that makes the process of giving birth pleasanter, easier, more homelike, and personal is to the good. Those hospitals which have changed their ways are to be applauded.

But why can't most babies be born at home? Safety? Maybe, but I doubt that this is the only reason. From the studies thus far, home births for the healthy woman seem to be as safe as or safer than hospital births.

Dr. Lewis Mehl and his associates at the Institute for Childbirth and Family Research, Berkeley, California, compared over 1,000 home births with the same number of equivalent hospital births—matching pair for pair, mothers of the same age, number of previous children, income, education, state of health, and medical history. The home birth group consisted of couples who had planned a home birth and had begun to labor there, even though in a few instances some had to be transferred to the hospital. In these few cases, even though the birth was completed in the hospital, the data were included with the home birth statistics. The results were astonishing: In the hospital the fetus had a 6 times greater incidence of distress in labor, babies were caught in the birth canal 8 times more frequently, and mothers were 3 times more likely to hemorrhage in the hospital than in the home. Furthermore, 4 times as many babies in the hospital needed resuscitation, infection rates were 4 times higher, and chances of permanent injury at birth were over 30 times greater in the hospital. Mortality rates were the same for both groups. Home births could be even safer if the medical establishment cooperated in providing better services. Fashion? There is something to this. Most women go where their friends go.

Basically, however, the real reason why we have so few home births is that hospital births are easier (and more lucrative) for the medical staff. They also contribute toward keeping hospitals in business. I don't minimize these factors. They are important in our society for other health reasons.

But having a baby is not an illness. It's part of living. Hospitals cannot get away from a "sickness" connotation with all the pretty homelike curtains in the world. For people about to have a baby, thinking sickness—even subconsciously—is harmful, in my opinion.

And let's forget the convenience and comforts and preferences of the adults. Let us turn to the baby. When we do, I say let's bring portable equipment and trained personnel *into the home*. Let's make the home as safe as possible. Let's *not* bring babies into a hospital world. Let's give them the best start in life in the place where everything matters the most for their future—their very own home.

This volume, and much of its advice, is geared to parents who are going to have a hospital birth. The reason for this is that most people still give birth in hospitals—and it will take far more than this book to change that reality to any large degree. The economics of the situation alone prevent it. I have had to recognize this and attempt to help the 97 percent or the 99 percent of you out there with a fact of your life. But, if there is any way that I could help everyone toward a completely safe and communal (not lonely) home birth (a condition which does *not* exist in hospitals, even subtracting cesareans), then I would do so.

Short of this, you will have to evaluate the options for yourselves. There is no doubt, whether you have a home birth or not, that prenatal care is essential, and that anyone with a physical problem is better off with the most skilled medical care available. Despite my bias in favor of home births and out-of-hospital birthing centers, I have tried in this book to present different perspectives on where to give birth.

You should have on hand material about having a baby at home in any case, particularly if you live in a more isolated area. One step-by-step account to consult on how to deliver your baby at home, either as planned or in an emergency, is Judy Wilson, M.D., "Assisting at Emergency Childbirth," *Woman's Almanac* (Philadelphia and New York: J.B. Lippincott, 1976). Reprinted from Dr. Wilson's *Mother Nature's Homestead First Aid* (Willits, Calif.: Oliver Press, 1975).

On Hospital Childbirths:
A Negative View

Hospitals are the worst place to have a baby because (a) doctors are taught in medical school that patients are sick—and that childbirth is not natural—and (b) the baby and mother are separated right away and this starts the first of the awful separations which lead to the separateness and alienation of our society. (Ashley Montagu, Speaking on NBC-TV, February 12, 1977)

FACTS TO CONSIDER

There are state laws regulating those who may attend a woman during childbirth. Everywhere it is legal to have a baby at home with no assistance—but who can help you is a legal question that changes with location. Some states do not allow anyone to assist except a doctor. Some permit lay midwives to preside at a home birth. (See page 97 for a tentative list and more information on midwifery.) Some states require midwives to work under the supervision of an obstetrician. Other people, *even including the father*, may find themselves accused of practicing medicine without a license!

In the event that either the baby or mother are injured or die during a home delivery, there would not only be severe guilt on the part of the surviving parent(s) but possibly legal culpability as well. In her informative book *Childbirth at Home*, Marion Sousa points out that "there is no apparent history of prosecution on this point, but this does not mean that those who want a home delivery should be unaware of the possibility. In the states that prohibit all forms of midwifery, anyone besides a doctor who assists at a home birth could face manslaughter charges if a death occurs."

LEGAL MUMBO–JUMBO?*

Can parents legally choose to have their babies at home? The legal situation is muddy. ACOG has embarked on a policy of calling home births "child abuse"—a patently fallacious label. George J. Annas, M.D., director of Boston's Center for Law and Health Science, said in 1978 that there is no law anywhere in the United States forbidding home birth, or specifically requiring a woman to give birth in a hospital. There is a catch: Many states consider childbirth the "practice of medicine" and therefore hold only licensed physicians competent to conduct births. In the other states, parents are freer. (Check your state health department.) It is possible, however, for parents to be prosecuted (under the child abuse laws) if the newly born infant appears to have suffered from the lack of special medical care. A key issue is now the matter of proof—proof that the home *is* as safe. This could be established—*if* a government body conducted an official, carefully researched survey.

Dr. Annas reports that he has heard from all over the United States about home birth couples being accused of "child abuse" by local medical opponents of home birth. One woman was actually forced to go to the hospital in a police car while in active labor. In

another case (in 1978) a California midwife was accused of manslaughter when a baby died in childbirth at home. The judge who threw the case out of court stated, "I really feel that we have a segment of our society that wants to choose an alternative to what the California Medical Association . . . wants to provide . . . and I think these people probably have that right under our constitution."

Perhaps *hospital* births—by pulling the family apart, by using harmful intervention techniques, can fairly be accused of "child abuse" as much or more than home birth parents. Besides safety, there is the quality of life, and family stress versus family cohesiveness, to consider. Are these so intangible when they have such concrete results? Can love and family warmth be an intangible when their presence is practically palpable?

The Personal Experience of a Home Birth Leader

David Stewart is the founder, with his wife, Lee, of NAPSAC (National Association of Parents and Professionals for Safe Alternatives in Childbirth), in Marble Hill, Missouri. He writes:

We got interested in learning about childbirth 16 years ago with our first pregnancy. We knew very little, but did know enough to know that drugs in labor affected the fetus and we wanted our child to have every brain cell to which it was genetically entitled. Lee also wanted to have no separation from the newborn; this seemed cruel and unnecessary. I also wanted to be present. I had never heard of a father being present at birth, but for some reason, I just wanted to be there. After being rudely asked to leave a doctor's office upon asking for these three requests, we began library research and found that hospitals were genuinely dangerous. I found this out most convincingly by simply reading a regular obstetrics textbook written for nurses. We had originally

---

*The latest absurd wrinkle, as of this writing, turned into a front page *New York Times* story on December 2, 1981. Establishment medicine continues to fight the rise in home births in new ways. The New York State Health Commissioner suspended the medical license (for sixty days) of Dr. George Wootan, and his hospital privileges were removed by both Kingston (N.Y.) hospitals. Why? Because Dr. Wootan has delivered a number of babies at home–thereby providing his medical expertise to help increase the safety and benefits of home births. How *Alice in Wonderland* can the world get?

planned a hospital birth, but the more we learned, the more we realized the dangers. Since Lee was perfectly healthy and had only good signs during pregnancy, after much soul searching and a futile search for a midwife or physician to attend, we elected an unattended home birth. People said we were taking a risk. We felt that the risk was greater in the hospital. We had no data then, but we do now. Since then we have had 5 children—all at home—all medically unattended. This was not our preference. We had prenatal care and a physician willing to meet us at the hospital if needed, but we never found a qualified and willing home birth attendant. For 11 years we minded our own business and rarely told anyone about our home births. What we did was right for us, but we did not feel it would be right for very many others. Even so, people found out. We began to get letters and phone calls. People would drive a hundred miles just to talk to someone who had had a home birth. We started NAPSAC (National Association of Parents and Professionals for Safe Alternatives in Childbirth) with a couple of friends, Stephen and Cedar Koons, in November of 1975. In May of 1976, we held our first major conference in Washington, D.C. 528 people came from 27 states and Canada. We were overwhelmed. The result was Safe Alternatives in Childbirth, which then won a 1976 Book of the Year Award from the *American Journal of Nursing*. In 1977 we held another conference in Chicago with about 1,100 in attendance and this May [1978] in Atlanta we held a conference with 1,300 attending from 44 states, 6 provinces of Canada, England, Mexico, and the Virgin Islands. Lee and I are not medical professionals. Lee has degrees in music and business and my degrees are in physics, mathematics and earth science.

Pediatricians Are Pro Hospital Births

The American Academy of Pediatrics (AAP)—Standards and Recommendations for Hospital Care of Newborn Infants, 1977— has a page on home births. It states: "Life-threatening problems cannot always be predicted during the perinatal period; therefore, optimum care for the mother, fetus, and newborn infant can be provided only in a hospital. . . . Although there is a current movement to encourage home deliveries

because they are less expensive and often more pleasant for the mother and family, they are inherently dangerous. . . . The committee (on Fetus and Newborn, of the AAP) recommends hospital deliveries for all pregnant women." (Reported in *NAPSAC News*, Winter 1978)

Helping Families Through Home Births

You who are starting out by having babies at home are not only helping your baby to a healthier life and decreasing his chances of minimal brain damage, learning disabilities, and everything else, but you are also helping yourself, your husband, the grandparents, the aunts, the cousins, and everybody else in the family. (Robert S. Mendelsohn, M.D., "Childbirth Alternatives and Infant Outcome: A Pediatric View," *Safe Alternatives in Childbirth*, 1976)

◇ ◇ ◇

Surrounded by Love

Home births were for me custom-made deliveries. During labor I was no longer confined to a small room but could sit or walk around inside or out of the house. There was none of that apprehension I felt in the hospital when strange people, calling me "mother," came in and poked and prodded, but never could tell me what was going on because "only the doctor could do that." I had found it frightening in the hospital to be alone and at the mercy of strangers during such a crucial time. At home we could make most of the decisions, including who would be present. My husband was with me, both for the support which I needed and to share the awe-filled event. No one could take my baby away from me at a time when we both needed each other. And while our other children were never in the room during the delivery, they usually were there minutes afterwards. . . .

I know it's not fashionable to talk about things that can't be measured scientifically, yet many of the advantages of home birth belong in that category. Unless they've experienced it you can't expect people to understand what it means to give birth to a baby in your own bed, surrounded only by people who love and care about you, and to be in a position to truly celebrate a birth rather than just bravely endure it. The effects of these unmeasurables should not be underestimated. (Marian Tompson,* "Custom-Made Delivery," *Safe Alternatives in Childbirth*, 1976)

Who Chooses Home Births?

In the South and Southwest, parents who have their children at home tend to be poor rural blacks or Latinos who are not served by hospitals. Elsewhere in the country, however, families choosing home births fit a standard, middle-class pattern. According to a 1975 ethnographic study conducted in San Francisco Bay area, not even 10 percent of families who chose home birth could be described as "hippies" or members of the "counterculture." . . . most of the 300 families studied were supported by gainfully employed fathers and lived in single-family dwellings with one or two cars in the garage. (Susan Stern, "The Fight Against Home Birth," *Inquiry Magazine*, 1978)

A Home Birth Service

We have a very active and growing home-birth service here in the Washington Metropolitan Area and it is incorporated. One of the reasons it is incorporated is that the State of Maryland specifies that nurse-midwives may not practice independently nor collect a direct fee for their services. One thing we cannot do, as yet, is to collect third party payment from Blue Cross-Blue Shield. However, some of the other agencies will pay nurse midwives—for instance . . . some of the small union insurance companies. We feel we are making some headway in terms of this sort of recognition and expect more such companies will agree to pay for our services in the future.

Our services include caring for *normal* women and their families. I want to stress the term, *normal*. . . . There are physicians and some kinds of nurses who are very concerned with unhealthy people and I think this is also very important. But I think that the healthy lady, or the healthy "anybody" for that matter, can sometimes be thrown aside and neglected.

We don't call our women "patients." We call them "clients" because they are healthy people who have just come to us for advice and assistance. If we do find a "client" who is not healthy, we refer her to an appropriate physician.

One thing we try to offer at MCA is a lot of options. In so far as the situation remains normal, our clients can do and suggest almost anything. We have had clients want to use a variety of different positions in labor, want to handle their babies in particular ways. So long as we see that things remain normal, we are very broad. We will use some of Leboyer's methods—as much or as little as the individual wants. We will turn out lights, turn on lights, bathe, not bathe. It really doesn't matter to us. We consider ourselves just as hired experts only there to help and to monitor things so that everything goes well.

We usually try to make one visit to the client's home before she goes into labor just so that we will know how to get there at 3:00 in the morning when it is snowing a blizzard outside. Also, we try to establish a very warm, friendly, close relationship so that we are always on a first name basis. We don't wear uniforms. When the woman is in labor, we have a shirt that Marion and I wear that says on it, "THE HAPPY BABY HOME DELIVERY SERVICE." We wear that shirt with blue jeans which helps to keep things casual and optimistic.

The lay midwives in our area have become a tremendous asset to us in helping us to provide care for clients who wish to deliver at home. I must admit, I have become spoiled and that I will just not go out on a home birth without one.

We are guests in the client's home. We expect that she will have a place for us to sleep and some sort of small amounts of food to eat if the labor and the delivery is long. . . .

Regarding finances, we charge our clients $450. This includes *all* prenatal care, prenatal visits to the home, labor, and delivery at home, as well as postpartum care and a postpartum visit. The postpartum care includes a 2 week check-up, a 6 week check-up, a 6 month check-up, and a one year check-up. We also have postpartum groups run by a psychiatric nurse practitioner who sees our clients for 3 group sessions. . . .

Our home birth service is extremely active—20 births per month. We are very

---

*Marian Tompson is the Founding Mother and president of La Leche League International. She also is the mother of seven children, the last four born at home.

happy with our results. Client satisfaction seems to be high. We encourage these women to review their own charts and express their needs to us. (Janet Epstein, R.N., "Brief Description of the MCA Homebirth Service,"* in "A Safe Homebirth Program That Works," *Safe Alternatives in Childbirth,* 1976)

Threatened OBs?

But in an era of smaller families and a surplus of maternity beds in hospitals, fewer and fewer obstetricians will willingly take part in home births. Instead, most obstetricians and many hospitals show signs of feeling threatened by the trend.

. . . In 1976, for example, the chief of obstetrics at Yale-New Haven Hospital notified the other obstetricians practicing there they would lose their patient-admitting privileges if they participated in home births unless it was an emergency.

. . . Nonetheless, home birth does not appear to be a passing fad. In Oregon, one of the few states that keeps reasonably good statistics, one of 300 births took place at home in 1967, and by 1977 the number had jumped to one in 23. (Judith Randal, "Childbirth at Home—It's a Serious Problem—for the Medical Profession," New York *Daily News,* January 11, 1979)

For a Home Birth

General Instructions

Check with the midwife a few weeks prior to your delivery date and she will give you instructions regarding the prenatal home visit and when she is to be notified.

It is wise to preregister and tour the hospital you would use as an alternative to homebirth. Also, pack a bag in the event that hospitalization is necessary.

Select a pediatrician who will agree to see your baby within the first 24 hours after delivery either at your home or in his office. Give the pediatrician's name and telephone number to the nurse-midwife two weeks prior to the delivery date.

Have all supplies ready three weeks before delivery date.

Take classes in Preparation for Childbirth.

Make up delivery bed in the following manner:

A. Cover for mattress, if desired
B. Clean fitted sheet
C. Plastic mattress cover or shower curtain
D. Clean fitted sheet

After delivery, the top fitted sheet and plastic mattress cover are removed and a clean fitted sheet is then readily available on the bed. (Janet L. Epstein, Marion F. McCartney, James D. Brew, and Ludovic J. DeVocht, "A Safe Homebirth Program That Works," *Safe Alternatives in Childbirth,* 1976)

Nice and Easy

The way Dr. White has always done deliveries is nice and slow, letting the baby deliver itself—just being there to gently hold the baby as it comes out—no holding back and no pulling on the head. There is no reason not to let a baby take its own time in coming out even if it just sits in the birth canal for a few minutes. The baby's head can be born for 10 or 15 minutes before the rest of the body is born without any problems. It will rotate by itself—no need to pull the baby to rotate. Just gently making sure it will gently ease out, that's usually all you need do.

We never suction babies routinely. That is something that should not be done. That's wrong. You worry about it only if the baby is not breathing. The baby that's breathing spontaneously has no business being suctioned because the mucous secretions have a very positive effect. Newborns have a tendency once in a while to stop breathing and the mucous secretions actually are a stimulant to breathe.

We always give the baby to the mother immediately after birth with the baby crying spontaneously. This is the type of scene I just love so much: Father and mother holding each other, kissing themselves seconds after the baby is born, them holding the baby. Another thing we have found valuable is to make sure that every woman gets up right after the baby is born, preferably

---

*This Maternity Center Association is headquartered in Bethesda, Md.

within the first few minutes. Lying down or sitting for a long time causes stasis of the blood while moving prevents blood clots afterwards. (Mayer Eisenstein, "Home- births and the Physician," *Safe Alternatives in Childbirth*, 1976)

Pain and Anesthetics

IS PAIN NECESSARY
TO BABY BIRTHING?

Before the middle of the last century this question could not be asked. Pain was a constant feature of childbirth. It affected some women far more than others, but if the birth was difficult, there was no known way to ease, alleviate, or dispense with the concomitant pain.

Then came anesthesias. First, chloroform. It was not used very much from 1847, the year of its discovery, up to the turn of the century, when it came into very popular usage. With chloroform the movement toward hospital births leaped ahead. Other anesthetics followed, and by the 1920s women in the United States were routinely having babies in hospitals under full anesthesia—without pain.

Isn't this the best of all possible worlds? Why not avoid pain if you can?

Unfortunately, for every benefit there always seems to be a tradeoff. As progressive and great a discovery as anesthesia *was and is*, there are potential problems in its use in childbirth. With anesthesia come greater risks, particularly for the baby. Also, full anesthesia prevents a woman from the total experience of seeing/hearing/feeling the final push to human life that her baby achieves.

By the time Dr. Grantly Dick-Read published his seminal volume—*Childbirth Without Fear*—there were several generations of mothers who had not known the "pain" of childbirth, and who had not fully known the ecstasy of giving birth. Their daughters in the 1940s and 1950s sometimes opted for the latter, now that Dick-Read's natural childbirth held the promise of full consciousness without the fear of pain, or with minimal pain. Later followers of Dr. Dick-Read and Dr. Fernand Lamaze have helped to popularize and extend the entire concept of natural, fearless childbirth.

Today a very large percentage of educated urban parents-to-be are going to Lamaze classes and having babies in the "natural" way. How many? No one really knows. But one obstetrician (Dr. Allan Charles of Michael Reese Hospital in Chicago) estimates that approximately 80 percent of his patients have had Lamaze training, which he believes makes childbirth easier.

Nowadays, too, other nonanesthetic pain-and-fear relievers are tried: acupuncture, hypnosis, self-hypnosis. The practitioners of these methods claim a fair degree of success among mothers-to-be in relieving or eliminating pain.

Further, the present science of pain relief has made some significant strides. No longer is full anesthesia necessary during birth, even in those situations where the use of an anesthetic seems essential. There are analgesics which dull feelings of pain without loss of consciousness. There are epidural injections during the birth itself which block pain in the delivery area. On the horizon of the pain field is the transcutaneous stimulator, a small electrical machine which holds promise for arthritics and others with constant debilitating pain—and which may become adapted for childbirth in the future. In fact, a recent (mid-1981) report claims totally painless childbirth in Vienna through electrical stimulation of the brain. Dr. Eduard Gitsch's study of a small group of women is very promising.

But do most women still have pain? Will you?

There are some women who find that childbirth is painful, regardless of their training, aids, frame of mind, and expectations. There is no doubt that fear, stress, and tension produce greater pain—physiologically. Still, one cannot legislate happy, calm feelings. Some people simply are more prone to difficult feelings, regardless of techniques. The life situations of others—a berating or beating husband, for example—produce more stress and fear.

Then, too, there are some few women who have a good personal situation, a fearless approach, excellent prebaby training, who still have terrible pain during childbirth. For any one of dozens of reasons the physical aspects of the birth may be difficult. The baby may be very large, the position may be breech (the baby's position is *not* head first), the labor may be very lengthy. While such circumstances are not usual, they do occur with enough frequency that parents-to-be should realize that an anesthetic or analgesic sometimes seems to be vital to relieve the pain.

The most important thing to recognize, if you find yourself in such a situation, is that you have done nothing wrong in wanting pain relief. Nature—glorious, wondrous nature—sometimes plays a trick or two. And if you feel far more pain than you can take, be thankful that there *are* pain relievers which are usually safe.

Will you have such pain? The chances are small that you will have unendurable pain. The chances are good that you will be uncomfortable, achy, hurting some, and feeling totally absorbed in dealing with the next contraction, and the next, and the next.

I agree with Dr. Dick-Read, who believed that the word *pain* should not be used; instead, he advocated *contraction*. But it is a word still common in our culture to describe childbirth—unfortunately.

My best suggestions are as follows:

Make arrangements with your doctor or midwife early on about what you will want done, and what he/she can do, should the strength of the contractions or the birth process become too difficult for you.

Then forget it. Banish the word *pain* from your vocabulary. Do not talk to anyone who

uses the word. Talk only to those people who had no or few problems. Believe that you will be one of them—and you will greatly increase your chances of doing so! Toward the end of your pregnancy, remember to remind your doctor or midwife about the arrangement you've made with her or him. Then forget it again.

With this method, you have recognized a possibility realistically—and still given yourself every benefit of the doubt. You have also, if the possibility occurs, given yourself the permission to be human, to be *unable*, without guilt later on.

From the Pioneer Who First Questioned Pain in Labor

In labor . . . *autosuggestion* does play a definite part in pain production. . . .

Quite apart from pain sensations recalled from the memory centers is the suggestion of pain consciously or unconsciously conveyed to the woman in labor by people and things about her. Every clinician knows that pain can be produced by suggestion; it is indeed easy to convey strong suggestion to a woman who believes in the necessity for pain.

Thus, suggestions of pain are conveyed by the atmosphere of the labor room; it emanates from doctors, nurses and relatives. They believe in pain; subconsciously or consciously they suggest, expect and even presume pain. (Grantly Dick-Read, *Childbirth Without Fear*, 1944)

No Suffering Is Necessary

The point of education for birth is that childbirth becomes not something that simply happens *to* one, but a process in which the labouring woman actively and gladly participates. And it is here that the great distinction between incidental pain—which is common to most labours—and suffering lies. For suffering in childbirth is unnecessary and a complete anachronism nowadays. With adequate preparation beforehand and support at the time, and with the additional aid of modern obstetric analgesics or anaesthesia if necessary, no woman need suffer in labour. Instead it becomes an exciting adventure of the first magnitude, and brings with it a sense of deep satisfaction, of thrilling achievement and triumph. (Sheila Kitzinger, *Giving Birth*, 1971)

◇ ◇ ◇

On Queen Victoria and Anesthetics

In 1853, while being delivered of her eighth child, [Queen Victoria] took chloroform to ease the pain. She was so delighted with the result that she told everyone about it, and for the first time it became quite proper for decent people to talk about such matters and even to write about them. The use of anesthetics was no longer considered "unnatural." Indeed, anyone who dared call it so would have been guilty of treason. (William and Joanna Woolfolk, *The Great American Birth Rite*, 1975.

◇ ◇ ◇

DO NOT TAKE THIS PAIN QUESTIONNAIRE —IF YOU HAVE DECIDED ON A NATURAL CHILDBIRTH

This questionnaire is designed only for those people who are worried about themselves and their reaction to the birth itself. If you are *not* worried or concerned, then remain so. *Don't* answer this questionnaire.

For those of you who are concerned, the questionnaire may help. When you've answered it, a pattern may emerge. You may find that your previous reactions to pain have been less important than you thought—and you may then elect the nonanesthetic, natural childbirth route. But, while the author of this book believes very strongly in natural childbirth and all of its concomitants, not every one of us can march to the same drummer all the time. You have every right to choose your best way—and to make your peace with your way versus the way of others.

You may, of course, elect the anesthetic route—and still attend natural-childbirth classes, both for the value of the exercises and the preparation for baby caring involved.

◇ ◇ ◇

Too Much Sympathy?

The modern obstetrician's attitude toward birth is cautious to the extreme. When he looks at birth he is waiting for something

YOUR OWN PAIN REACTION SURVEY*

Yes	No	
☐	☐	Do I react strongly to injections, cut fingers, bumps?
☐	☐	Do I tend to ignore most pain?
☐	☐	Do I remember specific pain?
☐	☐	When I compare myself with others, do I seem to react more strongly to pain?
☐	☐	Does my family make a big issue about pain?
☐	☐	Were my bumps and cuts kissed away as a child?
☐	☐	Do menstrual cramps bother me a great deal?
☐	☐	Am I afraid of pain?
☐	☐	Have my associations with childbirth been dominated by the concept of pain—instead of achievement or joy?
☐	☐	Does my partner/husband worry about my reaction to pain?
☐	☐	Is my doctor or midwife confident that I won't need painkillers?
☐	☐	Do I believe that pain is necessary to childbirth?
☐	☐	Am I very fearful about going to the dentist?
☐	☐	Do I tend to frighten easily?
☐	☐	Do I consider many difficult life situations as inevitable?
☐	☐	Is my state of being the most important factor to me?
☐	☐	Does the word *pain* automatically recall actual pain?
☐	☐	Do I worry about my ability to live through tough and painful situations?

*With the exceptions of Yes answers to Questions 2, 6, and 11, more Yes than No answers seem to me to indicate greater sensitivity to the issue of pain.

to go wrong. Pain is the assumption from which he works, for the obstetrician not only believes in the truth of pain in labor, he subconsciously or consciously suggests this pain to the woman he assists. His image of woman is that of a fragile, emotional creature not meant to endure strenuous work or pain. He likens her to a child, and through excessive and misplaced sympathy, he seeks to spare this grown-up little girl any suffering in the course of birth. (Suzanne Arms, *Immaculate Deception*, 1975)

◇ ◇ ◇

How It Used to Be

One would almost fancy that, since chloroform has come into use, the process of labour has acquired an intensity of suffering which, before, it was never thought to possess. I can only account for this by the supposition, that the magnitude of the evil has been unconsciously exaggerated, in the effort to make the virtues of the remedy the more conspicuous. I fear the diffusion of erroneous estimates of the suffering endured may cause a great amount, in this *natural* process, of unnecessary mental distress.

Thomas Bull, M.D., *Hints to Mothers*, 1853

THE DIFFERENT KINDS OF ANESTHETICS

There is much controversy today concerning the use of anesthetics during childbirth. The controversy is actually three-sided. In one corner stands the medical profession (most obstetricians, all anesthesiologists, most general practitioners, some pediatricians) defending anesthetics and analgesics in childbirth. Mothers-to-be, their thinking goes, are spared enormous and unnecessary pain, the birth is easier and less potentially damaging to babies. Anesthetics represent a tremendous advance in medicine.

In a second corner is the entire movement of nonestablishment medicine. This is represented by the advocates of natural childbirth, rooming-in, home births, birthing centers, and by consumer advocates and social investigators in general. It also includes some obstetricians and pediatricians as well as those young women and men who believe that having a baby does not need to be painful, that mothers are deprived of this crucial life experience if they are anesthetized, that there are harmful later effects of missing one's own child's birth.

In the third corner stands the government—which is, at this writing, investigating the question of whether giving anesthetics or analgesics to women in labor can produce harmful effects on the babies.

There really should be a fourth group composed of those people who believe pain can be handled in nonmedicated ways—but who may be more traditionalist on other issues.

The outcome on this issue is still undecided for our society as a whole—but in case you, as an individual, are confronted with an anesthetic or analgesic, the following information may be useful to you.

Medication given the mother *does* pass from her bloodstream through the placenta to the baby and may depress the sections of the infant's brain which govern behavior. Therefore, the doctor has to consider carefully whether to use anything—and, if so, which type of analgesic or anesthetic to give, in what dosage and when. He has two patients to consider—the mother and her baby.

Analgesics are a category of pain reliever. This category includes sedatives such as tranquilizers which lighten anxiety and tension, barbiturates to sedate and produce sleep but which don't relieve pain, and amnesiacs which do nothing for pain but erase the memory of it. These latter are rarely used anymore.

In the early stages of labor, gases can be

used for an analgesic effect in smaller doses than the dose for general anesthesia. Medical opinion is that inhalation medication has no clinical side effects and doesn't depress the fetus. There is a large body of opinion opposed to this view.

Anesthetics can be general or regional. General anesthesia is only used very close to delivery and seldom in normal birth situations. It produces deep sleep; the patient is not conscious while under its effect. Regional anesthetics are preferred for mother and child; they allow the mother to be conscious at birth. They can be administered in various ways:

Caudal. This is an injection at the tail of the spine. It does not mix with spinal fluid and can be administered as a drip. It blocks sensation but doesn't have much effect on motor nerves, so a woman can still move.

Epidural. This is similar to a caudal except it goes into the tissues surrounding the spinal fluid. The mother may continue to feel pressure though she feels no pain.

Spinal. The anesthetic is injected directly into the spinal fluid. It is sometimes used for a mother who is so tired she can no longer push. If she is anesthetized, the doctor can use forceps.

Saddle Block. This injection is made into the spinal fluid at a lower point in the spine than the above spinal. It deadens that part of the body which would be in contact with a saddle were the mother on horseback, which gives it its name. It is administered closer to delivery.

There are other areas which can be injected to interrupt pain from uterus and cervix, numb the vaginal and perineal areas (good for forceps delivery), and anesthetize the perineum before an episiotomy.

AN ANESTHESIOLOGIST'S VIEW: THE PAIN OF CHILD-BIRTH—AND RELIEVING IT

Dr. John J. Bonica is the founder of the World Congress on Pain and president of the International Association for the Study of Pain. He is also an anesthesiologist of long experience. In a conversation with him, he gave the following views:

"The basic facts are these: Notwithstand-ing the claim by Lamaze and company, childbirth is normally and physiologically a painful process. Nature made it that way.

"You will find that the proponents of 'natural' childbirth say that the pain is a product of civilization and civilized societies. The fact of the matter is that these are theoretical assumptions. Based on facts produced by a large number of investigators who went to Africa and Asia and studied the most primitive tribes—childbirth is indeed painful, and in many instances was much more painful because the woman had a narrow pelvis. . . .

"Having said that, one must add that the human experience that we call pain is influenced obviously by many, many factors, and culture is one—upbringing, personality, the meaning of the pain. There's no question that an informed mother will have less pain. Why does she have less pain? Positive mental activity provided to the mother through information, instilling motivation, suggestion and so forth. These mental activities can assimilate the newly found antipain system.

"The evidence is indirect, but we now know that this system exists in all mammals including man, and, when it is stimulated electrically, produces profound analgesia by liberating morphinelike substances. I think that what happens in childbirth to a woman who is fearful is that she inhibits the production of this system to fight off pain. . . . I have shown, and others have shown, that if you relieve the pain, all of these effects are relieved. Hyperventilation is eliminated so that ventilation is normal, carbon dioxide elimination remains normal. Assuming that the individual who's giving the anesthetic has the experience, expertise and knowledge, the risk is less than the risk the mother incurs in having the baby itself—whether it is with or without anesthesia. Good anesthesia is better for the baby and the mother than no anesthesia. Only 15 percent of patients are susceptible to hypnosis. The problem with hypnosis is that it does take a little bit of time and it does take a skillful hypnotist, and most doctors are not interested in devoting the time and effort."

PAST AND PRESENT ANESTHETICS

At the Second World Congress on Pain in Montreal, Dr. Elie Cass was another person

I interviewed. He is an M.D. in family practice who delivers babies in Toronto. His view on anesthetics is different from Dr. Bonica's. Dr. Cass described anesthetics as follows:

"The methods used in the past include general anesthetic, gas, like nitrous oxide, cyclopropane, even chloroform and ether. In China I understand they use open ether anesthetic and chloroform ether because they don't have the machines or the skill to administer our modern anesthetics. We don't use open ether, or chloroform, anymore because of the toxic effect on the liver for mother and baby. It's a great anesthetic other than that. It destroys the liver completely in many cases.

"Halothane is beginning to get the same reputation. It's the most widely used anesthetic in the world and we've had a number of deaths we've investigated in the coroner's office in Toronto and we've come to the conclusion that halothane can be a dangerous anesthetic. Halothane can sensitize the body, so it's dangerous to have two consecutive anesthetics using halothane if the time interval's too short. And some people should never have it. But it is such a fantastic anesthetic—like chloroform—it's so great that you're tempted to use it and use it and use it and take your chances.

". . . Aside from the gas anesthetics and the short-acting ones, like pentathol and other barbiturates, and the analgesics like Demerol and the tranquilizers like Valium, you come to spinal anesthetics—epidurals, anesthetics using Xylocaine or Novocain or a total spinal, where you're paralyzed from the waist down.

"You're injecting Xylocaine, mostly, and there are problems. For example, some people are allergic to it, they die from it. A person who's never been allergic can suddenly develop an acute sensitivity and it causes depression of the total vital functions like breathing and heart rate. . . .

"Although you can knock a person out, you don't get rid of their doubts, anxieties, and uneasiness; and by knocking a woman out she doesn't participate in the birth process. . . . despite an anesthetic a person can still receive messages to the brain through the ear. What is said in the delivery room [is] still going into the brain, and [is] being processed uncritically, which can cause terrible situations. Having worked in operating rooms for years, I know what goes on. It 'ain't' good for the patient. They tell dirty jokes; they make remarks about the patient. That's why I favor the Lamaze method or any method in which encouraging, pleasant things are being said or done to the patient."

Studies on Medication During Childbirth: The Effect on Babies

Dr. Yvonne Brackbill is a graduate research professor at the University of Florida, Department of Psychology, and Department of Obstetrics and Gynecology. Her statement, which was submitted April 17, 1978, to the Senate Subcommittee on Health and Scientific Research, describes long-term research:

The newborn human being is an organism poorly positioned for dealing with drugs. They cross the placenta rapidly. They lodge in brain structures that are still developing and are therefore at high risk to damage. They are not readily transformed to nontoxic compounds since the necessary liver functions are immature. And they are not readily excreted because of inefficient kidney function.

From all these considerations, it would be small wonder if obstetrical medication agents did not inflict some mischief on the infant. . . . The 35 investigators I have mentioned have studied healthy, full term babies who came from low-risk pregnancies and whose deliveries were normal and uneventful. Most of the studies have been done on newborns, though a few have been older babies. The most important study is NIH's Collaborative Perinatal Project, a longitudinal study of over 50,000 children which Congress authorized in the 1950's. Dr. Sally Broman and I have finished analyzing the results of this study for 3500 of its most healthy babies tested at 4 months, 8 months, and 12 months. . . .

Looking at the results of all 35 studies, almost all have found statistically significant behavioral effects of obstetric medication. NO study has ever demonstrated or even suggested that obstetric medication improves normal functioning.

. . . During the first year of life, the strongest effects can be seen in the development of gross motor abilities—e.g. the ability to sit, to stand, and to locomote. They can also be seen in certain emerging cognitive functions, principally the ability to *stop*

. . . crying when comforted, to *stop* responding to distracting stimuli. During later years, the strongest effects can be seen in the development of language and associated cognitive skills. At all ages, the effects are more clearly visible when tasks are difficult, i.e. when they require the child to exert itself, to make an effort, to cope with problems. . . . It now appears that obstetric medication has adverse effects on language ability. . . .

. . . Stronger drugs and larger doses of a single drug produce stronger behavioral effects. For example, general anesthetics have stronger effects than local anesthetics, and local anesthetics have stronger effects than no anesthetic at all. . . .

. . . The most important general finding is that the behavioral effects of obstetric medication are not transient. They persist. Within the age range for which we have data—1 day to 7 years—there is some evidence of decrease for a few drugs. But for other drugs, most notably inhalant anesthetics, the adverse effects are as strong at 4 years as they are at one year. It is difficult to avoid concluding that the damage is permanent.

. . . There seems to be a widespread misconception among the medical and nonmedical community alike that the number of drugs administered during labor and delivery is decreasing. This is not true. In point of fact, it is increasing. . . . On the whole, I estimate that 95% of births in United States hospitals nowadays are medicated. This means 3,500,000 medicated births out of 3,700,000* total births per year. If the average IQ loss per medicated birth is four points, this means 14,060,000 IQ points lost to new U.S. citizens every year. Cumulatively, that figure should put the problem of obstetric medication at the head of the class of national health priorities.

. . . The United States does not monitor these or other adverse drug reactions, as Senator Kennedy pointed out last year. Neither does it effectively control the use of drugs commonly used in obstetric medication but never scientifically evaluated for that purpose. The drugs I'm talking about have all been cleared for clinical use by the FDA. However, the research that served as a basis for FDA clearance was carried out on adults.

None has been done using infant subjects.

. . . [the data indicates] that mothers do not receive adequate information on adverse drug reactions, on differences among drug risks, or on alternatives to drugs for relief from pain. They also indicate that women have little voice in deciding which if any drugs they will consume.

. . . For many illnesses today, drug therapy is the only effective therapy. Under these circumstances, there's very little real decision-making involved. But pregnancy is not an illness. Childbirth is not an illness.

. . . Not all behavioral abnormalities are apparent immediately after birth. Many behaviors do not develop until later.

◇ ◇ ◇

THE TIP OF THE ICEBERG?

Doris Haire is the co-founder and co-president with her husband, John, of the American Association for Maternal and Child Health, which encourages better birth practices in hospitals. She believes that the findings of Drs. Brackbill and Broman represent "only the *tip* of the iceberg." For example, she points out, *a lot* of babies were not tested. Left out of the studies were babies who were born after induced labor. Also left out were babies whose mothers had hypertension, long labor, very rapid labor, any big change in heart rate, shock, or oxygen deprivation, among other conditions. Doris Haire believes, however, that such conditions can be brought about or increased by predelivery drugs like tranquilizers, narcotics, uterine stimulants, and regional block anesthesia.

She has also brought to the attention of the United States Senate Subcommittee on Health and Scientific Research the effect of regional block anesthesia on infants. Such anesthesia has seemed relatively harmless, yet there was a drop in the fetal heart rate in almost half of one group of mothers after they had a spinal block. Newborn infants were also less active and less capable of managing well without help.

Doris Haire is the author of *The Cultural Warping of Childbirth*, put out by the International Childbirth Education Association (ICEA) in 1972. She has traveled to and ex-

*I presume that Dr. Brackbill is using 1970 figures because 3,730,000 million U.S. babies were born in that year. In 1980, 3,580,000 babies were born; in 1981—3,647,000.

amined childbirth practices in many countries all over the world.

Other researchers have noted that some newborn babies are so affected by childbirth drugs—even spinal injections—that they are dazed in their first days. Harvard University professor and noted pediatrician T. Berry Brazelton described how these infants couldn't suck well and didn't gain weight as they should—in contrast to another group of babies whose mothers did not have medication. This situation may affect the close physical and emotional tie—called bonding—between infant and parent.

There Is No Safe Dose

Few women realize when they accept a drug prescribed for or administered to them during pregnancy and childbirth that most of the drugs used in obstetrics have never been specifically reviewed and approved by the FDA for use during labor and birth; therefore, no safe dose has been determined by the FDA for the parturient and her unborn baby. There is nothing in the present or proposed FDA regulations which will prevent another DES-like disaster from occurring. (Doris Haire, statement before the U.S. Senate Subcommittee on Health and Scientific Research, April 17, 1978)

Your Legal Right

Consider the "pricetag"of drugs before you take any. There can be a domino effect in which one drug necessitates using another—often an epidural "knocks out" contractions and Oxytocin has to be used.

You have a legal right to refuse all medication. Some doctors have standing orders for routine medication of their patients in labor.

Wait before accepting drugs. A few encouraging words and some physical contact with your mate can get you past a tough time. . . . Try to wait 15 minutes to half an hour after you think you want drugs before taking them—you may make considerable progress during that time or you may find you can manage without them.

Alertness is impaired by any drug. Even a minimal amount of Demerol, for example, offered to "take the edge off contractions," can affect your childbirth techniques.

There are times when drugs can be helpful during labor. The foremost reason for accepting drugs is if you become very tense and cannot relax with the techniques you were taught. If tension mounts it not only increases your perception of pain but it can even slow down labor, which can cause fetal distress. In a case like this drugs to reduce tension may be beneficial. (Tracy Hotchner, *Pregnancy and Childbirth*, 1979)

Does Hypnosis Work?

Most obstetricians who have employed hypnosis in childbirth endorse the method heartily. It is particularly valuable in a difficult labor that may go on for many hours and even days. In prolonged labor chemical analgesics and anesthetics have a toxic potential for both mother and child. When administered during the second stage of labor, they may also depress uterine contractions as well as impair the respirations of the infant. In an article in the *Journal of the American Medical Association*, Dr. Frank Moya and L. Stanley James reported that controlled clinical studies during the first hour of life have shown "a significantly greater ability of the hypnosis group of babies to recover from the asphyxia of birth, as compared to the non-hypnosis infants including a non-medicated regional anesthesia group." The group of mothers who used hypnosis were calm, relatively comfortable, and co-operative. They demonstrated an unusual degree of rapport with and confidence in their doctor, in contrast with the other mothers, who were experiencing moderate to severe pain. While Dr. Moya and Dr. James endorse hypnosis as a valuable aid in obstetrics, they stress the need for competent administration and careful observation because of the time factor in training preparturient patients. (Lewis R. Wolberg, M.D., *Hypnosis: Is It For You?*, 1972)

A HYPNOTIST'S VIEW

Dr. Elie Cass is a hypnotist, as well as an acupuncturist, a writer, the coroner for the province of Ontario—and a ritual circumciser. His views on hypnosis in childbirth, stated in an interview with me, are presented here.

Q. In your experience, what seems to work best in terms of pain?

A. I think hypnosis. If the patient is prepared in advance, if the woman receives training in hypnosis, especially autohypnosis, and if she learns relaxation techniques and how to cope with pain abatement through hypnosis. Hypnosis can make [things] so simple, you can do anything with it. You can do cesarean sections. It's being done all the time. But, then you see, it may take a little more time for the doctor to adapt to this technique. In fact, all the delivery room personnel have to adapt to it. They're adapting to all kinds of other techniques, so why can't they adapt to this?

Medical Procedures and Childbirth

American Life-Style
Creates Serious Health Problems

Childbirth—the very word evokes a sense of joy and wonder; the true miracle of life renewing itself. No parent will ever forget the mixture of hope and fear that accompanies the onset of labor: hope that the baby will be well; fear that it will not. And no parent will ever forget the exhilaration of a normal birth.

Pregnancy and childbirth are very vulnerable times in parents' lives. They are unusually dependent on their physician to guide them through the strange mixture of emotional and physical changes. And it is a very vulnerable time for the fetus as well, for what the mother does or does not do— the medicines she takes, the cigarettes she smokes, the alcohol she drinks—may have a profound effect on its health and development. And . . . what the obstetrician does or does not do—whether ultrasound is used, X-rays are taken, fetal monitoring is employed, inhalation anesthesia is used, or labor is induced—may have an equally profound effect on the health of the newborn infant.

Modern obstetrics has significantly reduced the risk of childbirth to both the mother and child. . . .

Yet problems remain. The United States has only the 12th lowest infant mortality rate in the world. And the American lifestyle, combined with the modern practice of obstetrics, has created serious additional health questions and problems for the mother and baby. (Senator Edward M. Kennedy, chairman, U.S. Senate Subcommittee on Health and Scientific Research of the Committee on Human Resources, reprinted in *Obstetrical Practices in the United States*, 1978)

Routine Standard Birth
Practices—What Price Science?

There is virtually no scientific support for almost any obstetric procedure carried out for a healthy woman.

There is no scientific support for separating the mother from her family during labor and birth.

There is no scientific support for routine medication and . . . the American Academy of Pediatrics Committee on Drugs has stated that "there is no drug that has been proven safe for the unborn child."

There is no scientific support for shaving the perineum . . . it actually increases the incidence of infection.

There is no scientific support for the routine electronic monitoring of the fetus. It has not been shown to reduce neurologic impairment in children.

Ultrasound. No one has done a scientifically controlled study.

X-rays. . . . What are we doing exposing millions of American children, unborn children, to procedures for which no one knows the long term effects?

There is no scientific support for rupturing the amniotic membranes . . . it creates stress for the fetal head.

There is no scientific justification for routine episiotomy . . . *there is no scientific support* in any country of the world or from any health agency in the world that shows any health advantage to routine episiotomy. . . .

Stirrups. I dream of the day when putting a woman's legs in stirrups when there is no medical indication will be considered malpractice.

It is likely that most American women would not be so quick to demand pharmacologic relief from their discomfort if they were advised of the potential dangers of the drugs to the integrity of their baby's brain and its future intellectual functioning. There is no doubt in my mind that obstetric drugs contribute to the skyrocketing incidence of learning disabilities in the United States and that alternatives to our present system would reduce this incidence. (Doris Haire, "Maternity Practices Around the World: How Do We Measure Up?" *Safe Alternatives in Childbirth*, 1976)

DRUGS AND DEVICES AND PROCEDURES

Medical innovations never cease to amaze me. For almost every itch you or I may have, the medical fraternity provides a scratch. And practically every problem that can arise during the course of having a baby has one or more medical techniques and interventions. These drugs and devices save lives. There is no question about that.

There are many other questions, however, about the proliferating medical technology. For example:

• Do some medical techniques also cause deaths? And if so, how many? And when?
• Do the babies saved have lifelong problems? And if so, what kind? And how many?
• Are some problems—cerebral palsy for one—prevented or created by intervention?
• How much intervention is needed, and by whom, and when?
• Should the usual problem-free pregnancy and delivery be accompanied by the newer techniques, just in case. . . ?
• Is the cost of medical technology for better births so skewed that most of our maternity dollars are spent on devices and

doctors rather than on methods that would prevent much of their "need"?
• Should you, the about-to-be parents, have the knowledge to decide—and the choice—concerning what drugs and devices are to be used before, during, and after your baby's birth?

Some of these questions cannot be completely answered until a large controlled nationwide study is undertaken on behalf of our babies of the future. But since you can't wait for that, you should have the benefit of knowing what the more common of these techniques consist of, and what different factions believe about them. Here is a brief rundown:

Amniocentesis, mentioned earlier, is considered a preventive of birth defects—because you can have an early-on abortion if any are found. There are risks of miscarriage and fetal injury. Ultrasound, which may have risks to the baby, is used with amniocentesis. (See earlier "Genetics" section.)

Various ways to voluntarily induce or speed up labor. These range from the doctor breaking the amniotic sac to the administration of such "natural" drugs as Oxytocin (Oxytocin is the hormonal substance released to allow the mother's milk to flow) or prostaglandins. It has been quite customary for a woman to make an appointment to have a baby. Labor has been started through Oxytocin injections, usually if the baby seems to be overdue. In addition, under natural circumstances some women have a long labor with shallow contractions which is enervating and worrisome. Oxytocin injections have been used routinely in these circumstances. Speeding up labor with Oxytocin increases the strength of the contractions. Does this aid the baby's birth? Many doctors think so.

The problem, however, is that the kind of contractions generated by Oxytocin (which is Pitocin as a synthetic hormone) are different in intensity from those normally experienced—and are sometimes very hard on the baby because of oxygen deprivation. Overdoses of Oxytocin can be given by mistake and may result in hemorrhage and uterine rupture for the mother.

As a result, the U.S. Food and Drug Administration has withdrawn labeling approval for the use of Oxytocin for *elective inductions* (on January 31, 1978). This is a very mild action for a drug that is potentially very harmful and used very frequently. The routine "breaking of the waters" to induce or speed up labor also produces much harder contractions—which probably, like the use of Oxytocin, causes the mother to resort to anesthetics and may harm the baby. The whole question of whether women with apparently full-term babies should undergo *any* induction— whether to start labor or to speed it up—is now very much under dispute.

Different drugs and techniques to prevent pain during labor and delivery. (See page 126 for a fuller discussion of these.) There presently exists a controversy surrounding the use of *any* anesthetics or sedatives which are potentially harmful to the baby. Some people feel they all have some ill effects on the newborn. Others consider the judicious use of anesthetics to be a blessing. Various methods to avoid anesthetics range from breathing techniques and exercises (Lamaze and Dick-Read) to full hypnosis. Anesthetics presently used range from those that totally block out consciousness to local drugs to numb the delivery area alone. Sedatives are also used in the delivery room to calm the mother's fears and discomfort, and these, too, have been accused of causing distress to babies. Both anesthetics and other drugs are blamed for breathing problems in the newborn. In difficult labor and delivery situations anesthetics and analgesics are claimed to be essential, however.

Devices which provide continuous nutrition. Intravenous feeding devices (IVs) are now often used as a substitute for women's taking in conventional nourishment during the early part of labor. IVs are defended by some doctors because the mother may have to have anesthetics later, and eating might be dangerous. Doris Haire and other family-centered-care advocates feel they are unnecessary, uncomfortable, and contribute to the woman's feeling of being ill rather than giving birth. It is also not possible to move around when you have an injection device strapped to your arm. Actually, eating at the beginning of labor is considered (by some alternative birth center staff) to be positively helpful. They believe that, as a result of eating, the uterus functions much better, and the blood sugar level is kept up.

Electronic fetal monitoring (EFM). This technique involves the use of ultrasound and other techniques to determine the fetal heart rate and the strength of the uterine contractions. Midwives and doctors have traditionally listened to the fetal heartbeat through the stethoscope but in the last few years the EFM machinery, which has largely replaced human monitoring, has become standard in many hospitals, particularly in big city or teaching institutions. For instance, Beth Israel Hospital in Boston now monitors eighty-five percent of its patients.

EFM is an ultrasound device involving the use of external and internal monitors—the external ones for the first part of labor. One electrode is strapped with belts onto the mother's abdomen, to keep a continuous record of the baby's heartbeat, and another records the progress and intensity of the contractions. This type of equipment prevents women from moving around during labor. But new fetal monitoring devices are now being marketed. These allow the mother to move around freely while she carries a small device that transmits the fetal heart signal.

Once labor progresses and the amniotic sac has broken (this may be done artificially to enable the monitor to be used), very fine electrodes are inserted through the cervix. One is attached to the baby's head and the other placed between the baby and the uterine wall. A monitoring recording screen watched by the hospital staff indicates the contractions and the baby's breathing and heartbeat. Changes can be seen on the screen. As each contraction rises, the baby's heart rate naturally drops. If the baby is in distress during labor, the heart rate is slow to return to a normal level between contractions.

A recent article in the journal of the American College of Obstetricians and Gynecologists (ACOG) described the reactions of two groups of women to EFM. The high-risk mothers were delighted with it; the others were not at all happy with the use of fetal monitoring. Some were uncomfortable; some complained that the staff watched it and not them and felt that the monitor created an intrusion on their privacy. Others were distressed that their husbands were utterly fascinated with the machine rather than with the baby's actual arrival.

Fetal monitoring is being used more and more routinely. The doctors who favor it point out that babies' lives are saved as a result of their knowing precisely when the infant is having difficulty. Tracy Hotchner, in *Pregnancy and Childbirth*, mentions a study of pregnancies initially regarded as low risk, one third of which turned out to be complicated childbirths. Another study in Australia indicated fewer babies with postbirth problems among those whose birth had been monitored.

Doctors have explained, frankly, that they are afraid of parents suing them over a brain-damaged child delivered without a monitor, and as lawsuits and malpractice insurance rates rise, they increasingly feel pressure to use it. The "con" group counters that the monitoring devices may themselves create future problems for the infant and certainly do lead to a much higher rate of cesarean births (see page 269), thereby engendering more risk for mothers, and on some levels for babies. Also, ultrasound is considered by some to be potentially risky to the infant. We now know that X rays and the drug DES should not be used during pregnancy; how do we know that ultrasound (also used in amniocentesis) may not have ill effects?

The mother's birth position. This is also subject to much discussion and is one basis for objections to EFM, during which women usually must lie down, and often cannot move around. In some countries, like Sweden and Russia, the birth table can be raised at the back so that a mother is half sitting during birth, and stirrups are not routinely used. There is a growing movement here to question our traditional birth position, and an attempt to encourage mothers to walk around during early labor. The flat-on-the-back position is under attack because it may impede contractions, therefore lengthening labor and leading to unnecessary episiotomies. (The latter is a surgical incision of the perineum, to provide a larger opening for the baby.) Incidentally, Dr. Robert Bradley (*Husband-Coached Childbirth*) believes that the only animal that gives birth on its back is a dead one!

At the 1979 ACOG convention in New York I saw two new and very interesting products which may help to change birthing positions in the United States. One is a real bed in two pieces. The back can be raised to a sitting position and the bed ends just after the buttocks. The second piece is very much like an oversize hassock that wheels up to or away from the rest of the bed as needed. The other item is a modern version of a birthing chair. Sleek and Eames-like, the chair can be tipped backward and forward, raised and lowered.

Ways to ease the baby out. Most of the methods used have been controversial ever since the invention of forceps in the eighteenth century. Standard medical techniques now are: episiotomies, forceps, and the use of a hand inside the birth canal or even in the uterus. Accompanying these methods—but preliminary to them—are shaving the pubic hair, enemas, and local anesthetics for the pubic area. All of these methods have their supporters (largely the medical profession) and detractors (largely the midwifery groups, childbirth educators, and home birth advocates). Regarding shaving, the feeling among detractors (based upon studies) is that the rate of infection is actually higher *without* pubic hair, and that simply clipping the hair is more efficacious and much less demeaning. Enemas are given to ease the pelvic area and to create space for the baby, but may sometimes adversely increase the strength of contractions.

Episiotomies are attacked as unnecessary, since prior exercises and before- and during-birth massage of the perineum area plus the use of more comfortable birth positions should prevent the need for an episiotomy. In addition, some believe that tearing, which may occur naturally during childbirth, can either be repaired or will heal of itself. Episiotomies can cause pain and sexual problems in the period just after childbirth.

Forceps, or at least low-forceps, are still commonly used, although cesareans are taking the place of forceps in the more dangerous deliveries. Forceps deliveries have been blamed for injuries to the baby's face, hemorrhage, and possible minimal brain damage. Obstetricians have been accused of resorting to them far too frequently. Many childbirth experts believe that the necessity for forceps (or indeed for cesareans) could be avoided by better management of labor, and by avoiding any medication.

(The use of the doctor's hand to turn a baby or to provide an easier birth seems to be more accepted.)

Doctors defend all of these techniques in terms of the needs of the particular and individual situation.

Procedures after the baby arrives. These are almost universally used but now disputed,

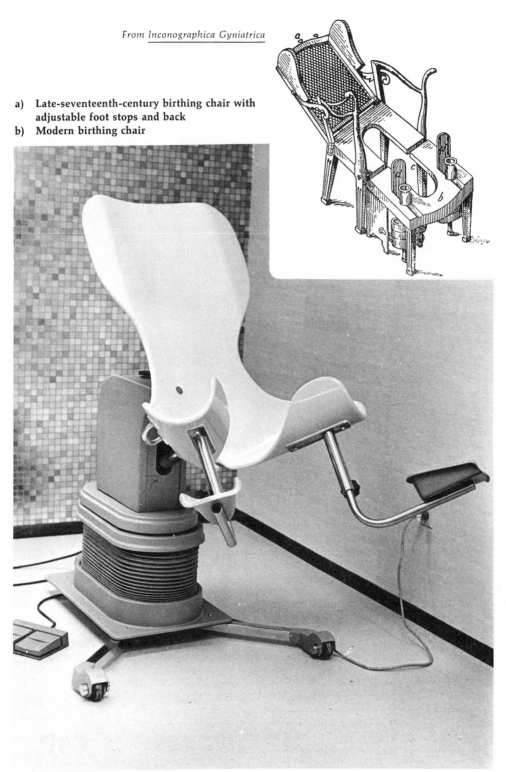

From *Inconographica Gyniatrica*

a) Late-seventeenth-century birthing chair with adjustable foot stops and back
b) Modern birthing chair

Courtesy Century Manufacturing Co.

too. Silver nitrate is put in the infant's eyes, and the mucus from the newborn's mouth and nostrils is suctioned out. The clamping and cutting of the umbilical cord is done immediately, and the baby, after a very short time with the mother, is taken off to the newborn's nursery and not brought back to the mother for a number of hours. The baby is usually separated from the mother and father during the hospital stay, although rooming-in is becoming more accepted. The newborn is generally not nourished for the initial 24 hours, and a bottle of water (often sweetened) is still the first liquid given instead of the baby being put to the breast immediately after birth, as is done in many other countries.

Silver nitrate in the baby's eyes is thought by most people to be mandated by law. It prevents eye problems that can result from a venereal infection of the mother. It also prevents babies from seeing clearly for some hours. Some charge that the use of silver nitrate seriously interferes with the bonding process, which takes place very strongly during those first hours. It has been suggested that nurses should wait a few hours before putting silver nitrate in the baby's eyes. Actually, parents who object to it can prevent the process by saying so in advance.

Suctioning is also considered not good for the infant by birth-educated consumers—unless there is real trouble breathing. The mucus may actually be of value to the newborn. Many doctors, however, feel that suctioning some of the mucus helps the baby to breathe.

Cutting or "clamping" the cord before it stops pulsating (which naturally happens in 3 or 4 minutes) is done routinely in American hospitals. The timing of this procedure has been questioned on the grounds that a quick cutting is harmful to the baby—and the mother. The opponents of this procedure, including Dr. Leboyer and his followers, believe that the baby needs the extra oxygen; and the third stage of labor, the expulsion of the placenta, is said to be lengthened and possibly complicated by early clamping of the cord.

Since the baby receives an additional 25 percent of his or her blood supply through a placental transfusion if the cord is not immediately cut, the American practice has been deplored as simply a convenience for the hospital staff—certainly not an action

with the best interest of the baby in mind. Doris Haire has cited research to show that the red cell volume in late-clamped babies increases by 47 percent.

On the other hand, the brochure of the Alternative Birth Center of the San Francisco General Hospital indicates that "clamping is done immediately after the baby is placed on the mother's abdomen to *avoid* too much blood given to the baby which may cause drowsiness, jaundice or a need for partial exchange transfusion."

Separating the baby from the mother and father without an opportunity for full bonding (see page 242) because of the fear of contaminating the newborn is attacked as one important cause of emotional distance in the family and of later child abuse and neglect. A great deal of recent, fascinating research has been done on the importance of bonding to future family relationships, for both mothers *and* fathers. There is now much more interest in "rooming-in" as a routine practice in hospitals, and encouragement, in some hospitals, of "sibling bonding," by allowing small children to visit.

The lack of breast feeding (with the colostrum) in the hospital immediately after birth is considered a major reason why women do not choose to breast-feed, as is the hospital use of bottles with infants. Colostrum has recently been found to contain a very important growth hormone.

In general, these practices and drugs, devices and medical methods have both advantages and disadvantages. You should consider whether any of these procedures or practices should or could be avoided in your own case. Discuss the issues at your childbirth classes.

There are fascinating literature and studies available on the subject of medical devices and procedures in childbirth, particularly in *The Cultural Warping of Childbirth* by Doris Haire. The Committee on Human Resources of the United States Senate, chaired by Senator Edward Kennedy, held hearings in 1978 on the value of such routine practices as EFM and the use of drugs. Doctors and other experts testified both for and against EFM, increased use of cesareans, and elective induction of labor. The proceedings of these hearings are available to the public. Call your local congressman's office or write to Senator Kennedy.

◇ ◇ ◇

Relief and Risks

No drug has been discovered that will give 100 percent relief from pain without the risk faced by mother or child. Under normal labor and delivery (without any medication), infants are subjected to varying degrees of oxygen deprivation. Usually the child tolerates this brief "hypoxia" without difficulty. But a significant reduction of the oxygen supply during labor may reduce the infant's ability to breathe. . . .

Oxytocic agents—drugs which stimulate the uterus to contract—have been used for many years to induce labor and to reduce bleeding after delivery. There are instances in which induction of labor is necessary for the safety of the fetus and mother, such as when a woman has diabetes or hypertension. The effect of drug-induced labor is similar to that of natural labor except that the uterine contractions caused by the drug can be stronger and more frequent. During contractions, the blood vessels which bring the blood supply to the placenta are compressed, reducing the amount of oxygen going to the fetus. It is possible that the fetus can suffer from prolonged lack of oxygen resulting in damage to the brain and other organs.

FDA's (Food and Drug Administration) Obstetrics and Gynecology Advisory Committee has concluded that drugs should not be recommended for use to induce labor except when it is medically necessary for the safety of the mother or baby. (Pauline Postotnik, "Drugs and Pregnancy," *FDA Consumer*, 1978)

◇ ◇ ◇

Should Obstetricians Have a Nine-to-Five Job?

It is also easy to think of a variety of reasons why physicians would prefer to have scheduled deliveries. One obstetrician told me that he induced 40 percent of his patients. When asked why, he said that he preferred to have weekends with his family—something we can all understand. Another obstetrician told me that he preferred scheduled deliveries because they did not interfere with his office schedule. Another reported that with an induced labor, he was able to devote full attention to his patient. Another said that the nurses were best during the Monday to Friday day shift.

It is also easy to understand why obstetricians would want predictability in their lives. What I cannot understand is why a person desiring a predictable daily and weekly schedule would become an obstetrician. (Ronald R. Rindfuss, M.D., *Obstetrical Practices in the United States*, 1978)

◇ ◇ ◇

Fetal Monitoring—Ultrasound

FDA Commissioner Kennedy testified before the Senate Subcommittee on Health and Scientific Research April 17, 1978, about the use of drugs and devices in obstetrical practice. Media interest in his testimony about the use of ultrasound for fetal monitoring has resulted in continuing inquiries. The following summarizes FDA's position on diagnostic ultrasound.

Diagnostic ultrasound was introduced to the medical community around 1970 and was used in 16 percent of the general and maternity hospitals by 1974. It is expected to be available for use in virtually all pregnancies in the U.S. by the 1980s. . . . Sales of ultrasound equipment are growing by about 20 percent each year.

There have been no reports of injury or adverse effects from ultrasound, and it is generally assumed to be safe. FDA (Food and Drug Administration) is concerned, however, about the increasing use during pregnancy because there is no conclusive evidence to support the current assumption of safety. It will probably be several years before such evidence can be gathered.

In the interim, FDA does not see the need to restrict ultrasound use but suggests that it be used cautiously. Commissioner Kennedy has emphasized in public testimony that there is no justification for the claims made by one manufacturer that ultrasound "can be safely employed at any time during pregnancy." (Food and Drug Administration, *FDA Talk Paper*, 1978)

◇   ◇   ◇

The Value of Monitoring

Some small part of the current increase [in cesareans] is certainly due to the use of monitoring, and this is as it should be. Monitoring allows us for the first time to recognize early signs of fetal distress before the baby is permanently damaged. If vaginal delivery is not feasible, the only other form of intervention is cesarean section. (George Ryan, M.D., on behalf of ACOG, *Obstetrical Practices in the United States*, 1978)

◇   ◇   ◇

Benefits Outweigh Risks

My first experiences with clinical fetal monitoring occurred in 1968 when this type of instrument became available at Yale New Haven Hospital. The selective use of this tool led to a 75 percent reduction in cesarean sections done for "fetal distress." . . .

We have seen a halving of perinatal mortality over these years and I believe fetal monitoring has been an important factor in this benefit.

The occurrence of death during labor has

decreased dramatically. The survival of very premature infants is significantly better when they have been monitored during labor.

The incidence of cesarean section in our hospital has not risen over the past 7 or 8 years even though the incidence of monitoring has more than doubled. Cesarean sections done for fetal distress have decreased with the ability to better interpret fetal condition as seen through the fetal heart rate. . . .

. . . The trend in my hospital and across the country is toward the lesser use of analgesic drugs and a more natural birth due in part to fetal monitoring.

In cases where anesthesia or drugs must be used, fetal monitoring is an invaluable tool. The first signs of an adverse reaction in the mother may be reflected by the fetal heart rate. Corrective measures may then be instituted to benefit both mother and fetus. . . .

. . . Monitoring, in my opinion, benefits both mother and fetus. (Richard Paul, M.D., on behalf of ACOG, *Obstetrical Practices in the United States*, 1978)

◇   ◇   ◇

Fetal Monitoring: Risks and Costs

The following material is extremely significant because of the prominence of the two doctors who wrote it. They are H. David Banta, M.D., M.P.H., who is the Health Program Manager of the Office of Technology Assessment, which is a Bureau of the United States Congress (Washington, D.C. 20500), and Stephen B. Thacker, M.D., who is Chief of the Consolidated Surveillance and Communications Activity, which is part of the Bureau of Epidemiology of the U.S. Center for Disease Control (Atlanta, Georgia 30333). These two government agencies are very solid, very prestigious—and their reports must be given most respectful attention. This particular report, from which I have taken a few excerpts, was issued in 1978. It is called *The Premature Delivery of Medical Technology: A Case Report*.

It is our thesis . . . that EFM has little if any proven benefit not given by regular auscultation, and . . . it is a costly and dangerous procedure. . . .

In terms of cost, we have estimated that EFM costs the United States about $411 million each year. This cost includes $80 million for the direct cost of EFM. In addition, EFM apparently helps induce inappropriate cesarean sections because of its lack of specificity as a diagnostic tool. We estimate the cost of these added cesarean sections to be $222 million.

EFM also has risks for mother and child. The newborn is at risk of hemorrhage and infection at the site of the electrode . . . and is also at risk of respiratory distress syndrome in relation to cesarean section. We have estimated the cost of these risks to be about $50 million. The mother is at risk of death from cesarean section . . . and is at risk of pelvic infection from both EFM and cesarean section. We have estimated the cost of these risks to be about $58 million. . . .

. . . The diffusion of EFM is a case of a widely-used technology of uncertain benefit associated with definite risks and financial costs. This case suggests the need for changes in public and private policies toward evaluation and control of other medical technologies.

◇ ◇ ◇

The Red Flag of Monitoring

Monitoring, for the mother, increases not only the cost of her delivery, but decreases the naturalness of that delivery; decreases her mobility while in labor; requires that she receive care in a rather large hospital complex thereby limiting her choice of a place in which to have her baby; and significantly increases the probability that she will have major surgery (cesarean section) during delivery.

I feel that fetal monitoring gives the doctor and nurse information. More information doesn't necessarily give a better outcome. It seems that in the OB patient, the more information you receive the more anxious you become about its significance and the more aggressive to ameliorate the problem so every piece of information that looks irregular problematically is like a red flag to a conscientious physician to get in there and do something. C-sections are done by conscientious people who are nervous, not knife-happy. (Albert D. Haverkamp, M.D., *Obstetrical Practices in the United States*, 1978)

◇ ◇ ◇

Le Voyeur Accoucher

Another "breakthrough" that transferred woman's authority in childbirth to the doctor had occurred a few years earlier, when Louis XIV replaced the birthing stool with a flat horizontal table. The king, it seemed, had a royal perversion. He liked to watch his various mistresses giving birth and took great sexual pleasure in hiding behind a nearby curtain. When the woman sat on the birthing stool he could see little, especially as she was dressed to her toes and her genitals were hidden from view by the extended sheet. So Louis called in a male physician who gently convinced the ladies of court that childbirth would be easier and simpler if they reclined on a high table. Of course the supine position was easier for *him*, as it gave him a closer view and better leverage in delivery, and it was better for Louis, who could see everything he wanted

How It Used to Be

The obstetric chair or birth stool was fashioned as a substitute for the lap; it was made of wood with a slanting back, arm rests, and a cut-out seat. It was in common usage with the Greeks and Romans and was carried by the midwife from house to house. There was much to commend the chair in that the position assumed by its occupant provided comfort and favoured the expelling powers of the mother in labour. Not only did the Greeks and Romans adopt the chair, but all Europe employed it almost with no exception until the early part of the eighteenth century, when it was replaced by the couch.

Dr. Palmer Findley, *The Story of Childbirth*, 1933

to see, but it was disastrous for the woman, who no longer had the force of gravity working to her advantage and labored longer and harder in an effort to push the baby out. Gradually, however, all women of the court, and later their lesser counterparts throughout the country, copied the royal fashion of lying down at birth so that a male midwife or physician could deliver the baby and, in effect, take care of everything. (Suzanne Arms, *Immaculate Deception*, 1975)

The Thanksgiving Turkey

The introduction of routine episiotomy and outlet forceps led to the dehumanization of the American obstetrical delivery. Routine episiotomy and outlet forceps led to the routine lithotomy position, led to routine knee stirrups, shackled legs and strapped wrists—the mother spread-eagled or trussed-up like a Thanksgiving turkey— led to routine anesthesia, led to postpartum incapacity and distress from anesthesia and episiotomy. (Herbert A. Ratner, M.D., "The History of the Dehumanization of American Obstetrical Practice," *21st Century Obstetrics, Now!*, 1977)

Position Is Everything

Dr. Caldeyro-Barcia and others have determined that uterine activity is influenced by the position of the mother. The characteristics and quality of the contractions are weak, irregular, and *frequent* when the laboring woman is supine, but contractions are stronger, more regular and *less* frequent when the woman is on her side, sitting, squatting, or standing. Squatting is the best position for actual birth since the diameter of the pelvic outlet increases by 1.5 centimeters when the legs are flexed and with the gravitational forces, the baby is delivered. (Frederic M. Ettner, M.D., ". . . A Working Physician's Home OB Service," *Safe Alternatives in Childbirth*, 1976)

To Avoid an Episiotomy

It would appear callous indeed for a physician or nurse-midwife to perform an episiotomy without first making an effort to avoid the need for an episiotomy by removing the mother's legs from the stirrups and

bringing her up into a semi-sitting position in order to relieve tension on her perineum and enable her to push more effectively. (Doris Haire, *The Cultural Warping of Childbirth*, 1978)

The Dangers of Too Much Medicine

An infant born in Japan or in the Netherlands is 3 times more likely to survive the first day of life than is an infant born in the U.S., despite the fact that in Japan and the Netherlands there is no strong inclination, as opposed to the U.S., to save infants who cannot be expected to participate in society to a reasonably normal degree.

One out of every 35 American children will eventually be diagnosed as retarded (in 75 percent of these cases there is no genetic or sociological predisposing factor).

One out of every 8 American children has some form of minimal brain dysfunction or significant learning disability. Learning disability appears to be primarily an American problem.

Forceps may have formerly unrecognized long-term deleterious effects that do not manifest until young adulthood. The incidence of initial grand mal seizures [epileptic seizures] in young adults between the ages of 20–25 is apparently on the increase in the United States. . . . As the glia cells (scar tissue) [from some forceps delivery] continues to accumulate over the years eventually the glia cells thicken to the point where they interfere with the normal functioning of the brain.

One out of every 4 American graduates from high school is functionally illiterate, unable to read beyond the fifth grade reading level.

We are producing a generation of subnormal Americans. The statistical disasters described above are not limited to the poor but cut across the entire socioeconomic and ethnic strata of the United States. . . .

. . . Commonly employed obstetric procedures and drugs which interfere with the normal progress of labor and birth . . . *contribute* to the skyrocketing incidence of mental retardation and learning disability in the United States [italics added]. . . .

. . . Diagnostic levels of ultrasound have been shown in animal studies to disrupt the spleen's ability to produce antibodies, the body's primary defense mechanism against infection. *No one knows the delayed, long-*

range effects of electronic or ultrasonic fetal monitoring on the offspring exposed to these procedures in utero.

Will ultrasound be the DES of the next generation? What will be the long-range consequences of routinely irradiating, with ultrasound, the delicate, vulnerable ovum of the female fetus? It will take at least a generation to find out. (Doris Haire, "The Cultural Unwarping of Childbirth: How Can It Be Accomplished?" *21st Century Obstetrics, Now!*, 1977)

◇   ◇   ◇

DHEW

Nursing

When my first child was about to be born, and I was in labor, I felt a separation anxiety. A definite sense of loss. Breast feeding was a way of getting me adjusted to the fact that this was a separate person but someone still dependent upon my body. I feel that breast feeding, from the mother's point of view, is a gradual weaning away of all the feelings you have when the baby is actually physically part of you, and then isn't.

HELEN REDDY

WHY SHOULD YOU? OR WHY SHOULDN'T YOU?

Why Nurse

It's one of life's great experiences, the continual giving of basic sustenance from your own body to your very own child.

It's fun and cozy to hold and feed a nuzzling newborn.

It protects the baby from various ailments in the first months of life. The mother's antibodies get passed along in her milk to her child.

It gives both mother and baby a close emotional bond.

It probably saves money.

It brings better physical well-being to you, the mother. Your uterus gets back into shape quicker and there is some evidence that it may protect against cancer of the breast in later years.

It provides daily islands of peace and quiet and restfulness for mother and child—and for fathers, too.

It is quick and easy and totally sanitary.

Why Not Nurse

You *must* work full time and cannot bring the baby to the office or go home once or twice daily, cannot take a maternity leave for a few months, and don't want to nurse just at night. (See later pages on working while nursing.)

You can't stand the idea at all.

You are not well enough, for whatever reason.

Your nipples will not behave properly—no matter what you have done.

Your baby develops jaundice which does not go away for a long period.

Your life is too involved for you to sustain your milk supply (illness, tensions, or whatever in your family).

You have carefully considered the alternatives, without pressure from anyone, and have decided that you and your particular family will be better off overall without nursing.

146

MYTHS ABOUT NURSING

Myth: Nursing will ruin your breasts.

Fact: Nonsense! Wearing a good bra and limiting nursing to a year or so will prevent this, unless you are constitutionally prone to pendulism—in which case nursing will not have any effects.

Myth: Nursing hurts your nipples.

Fact: Again only a little for a short time *and* if you don't toughen them up. (See page 153)

Myth: Nursing ties you down.

Fact: There is a kernel of truth here. Nursing is like sex: if you don't use it, you'll lose it—to quote the vernacular. Or in other words, the use of the breast and its milk stimulates the flow. *But* no one ever legislated against relief bottles which could give any mother at least six to eight hours out and away.

Myth: Nursing is not important: millions have grown up on a bottle in fine shape.

Fact: A higher proportion of nonnursed babies develop infections and other ailments; psychological distance, emotional problems, child neglect, and abuse run rampant—and lack of nursing is believed to increase the risks of these.

Myth: Nursing is a bother: time-consuming and complicated.

Fact: Just the opposite! Preparing a formula is usually more bothersome. You must be prepared with milk and supplies, be sure of sterilization, get the nipple holes just right and so on. Without preparations, after the first few weeks, breast milk is portable, sanitary, ever-present.

Myth: Nursing prevents working.

Fact: Many women take a maternity leave, go part time, take a hiatus for some months between jobs. Some lucky ones can bring the baby to work. (*Ms.* magazine is marvelous to its staff in this respect!) Even full-time working mothers nurse their babies part time. It may be harder to work, but not impossible.

Myth: You'll gain a lot of weight from all that food you must eat to nurse.

Fact: While you must eat well and nutritiously, you do not need to eat excessively. You do need to add extra calories, but breast feeding burns them up.

Myth: Nursing is antiwoman, and is used by men to keep women down.

Fact: The ability to nurse is a great gift of nature, almost comparable to the ability to make a child. While it is true that only women can nurse, it is essentially outside the realm of sex and sexism—as all creative, life-making gifts initially are. And while it is also true that men have distorted the capacities and values of being a woman, you don't *have* to let this happen to you. Besides, nowadays it is only very socially backward and ignorant men who would try to use nursing to "keep a woman in her place," that is, pregnant and barefoot.

Myth: Your husband will resent your closeness with your baby, and his inability to feed the baby.

Fact: If your husband resents this fact, he's likely to resent other areas of closeness just as much—and he needs some help in accepting the presence of the baby. He can feed the baby relief bottles after the milk flow has been established. (For more on this subject, see page 151.)

A PERSONAL VIEW

I have become a fanatic about breast feeding. I believed in breast feeding when I was a new mother, but I gave my babies supplementary bottles and baby foods, too, when they were days old.

Now, through reading the research, I take my stand with the most doctrinaire advocates of breast feeding. Bottle-fed babies can do fine, too. But almost all the evidence I have seen points to the likelihood of a far better beginning in life for breast-fed babies.

And almost all of the experts agree on this.

So strongly do I feel about the breast-feeding situation that I urge a rewrite of the government's *Infant Care* booklet last published in 1973. This booklet advises that other than an allergy to cow's milk, "there is really no strong medical, psychological or economic reason for choosing either breast-feeding or bottle feeding." This statement is untrue and outrageous.

There are practicalities in life that may go beyond breast feeding: the need to hold a job too far away, the need to travel for the job, the physical inability to breast-feed. But it is my conviction that many of these "practicalities" can be solved in favor of breast feeding if there is a thorough understanding of the possibilities.

Professional help can make all the difference. In one hospital, instruction about breast feeding enabled ninety-six percent of the mothers to breast-feed successfully.

Other hospitals could help increase nursing by changing some of their practices. For example, they could (1) decrease sedation and anesthesia during childbirth, (2) keep mother and baby together, (3) use an "on demand" feeding schedule, (4) help their staff encourage new mothers in breast feeding.

If you are still undecided, or think—as I did—that supplementary bottles are just fine, please read on.

THE HEALTH FACTOR

Just *why* is it healthier for your baby to be nursed? For those of you who are undecided or even if you'd just like to know the specific details, here they are.

Your unborn and just-born child has little bodily capability to fight infection. The gastrointestinal tract of any infant is sterile, contains no bacteria which resist disease. In the uterus the fetus is protected by the mother's immunities which come to the unborn baby through the placenta and the umbilical cord.

Once born, the newborn baby is much more vulnerable than you or I to almost any disease; there has been no gradual exposure and no chance for immunities to build up. Therefore, an ailment that an infant develops can be far more serious than the same ailment in an older child or adult.

This is, of course, the main reason for keeping things as clean as possible around babies, and for avoiding contact with people who have colds or other sicknesses.

Babies who are breast-fed sometimes catch something, sometimes get sick. But if you breast-feed for the first four months, the chances are far better that your baby will *not* come down with any one of a variety of ailments. Mother's milk protects against colds, lymphatitis, pneumonia, gastrointestinal and urinary ailments, diphtheria, scarlet fever, measles, necrotizing enterocolitis, eczema, diaper rash, colic, and constipation, among other conditions.

Some authorities even believe that breast feeding helps bring about good facial structure! "Persons bottle-fed from birth are more

likely to have poorly-developed dental arches, palates and other facial structure in adulthood," according to La Leche League. Dentists agree, and make another claim. They believe that dental caries are more prevalent in bottle-fed babies.

Two recent studies concerning both the physical and intellectual development of breast-fed babies are especially significant. The National Academy of Sciences reported in late 1978 that breast milk contains a special substance which stimulates growth. Colostrum has the greatest concentration of this substance—about 15 times more than milk of a later time period. But even in later months the strength of this growth factor is 5 times that of those found in the blood.

There was some other rather spectacular news reported in the July 1978 issue of *Pediatrics:* the evidence of recent scientific studies in Boston shows that breast feeding may help prevent some types of severe mental and physical retardation! A congenital metabolic defect called hypothyroidism (not at all uncommon) leads to physical and neurological impairment in infants. Breast feeding seems to deliver enough thyroid hormone to reduce the severity of this condition—to the extent that breast-fed babies with this thyroid problem turned out to be just about normal in physical and intellectual development, in contrast to many who were not breast-fed.

There is additional evidence concerning the cholesterol factor in the blood of babies. While babies who are formula fed have lower cholesterol levels than breast-fed babies, the advantage does not lie with bottle-fed babies—as might at first appear. Cholesterol is very important in healthy cell and nerve growth. And a high cholesterol level in infancy may help *prevent* damage to heart and arteries later on. The Harvard School of Public Health has conducted a long-term study of a group of people from infancy to their middle years and concluded that those subjects who had been breast-fed were much better able to withstand the effects of a high-fat diet. There is evidence from animal studies, too, since low cholesterol levels in young animals is linked with a much higher level at maturity. Remember that for a baby to be fully protected, human milk has to be given alone, without additional cow's milk.

As far as the nursing mother herself is concerned, there may be some decided health advantages. C. D. Haagensen, M.D.,

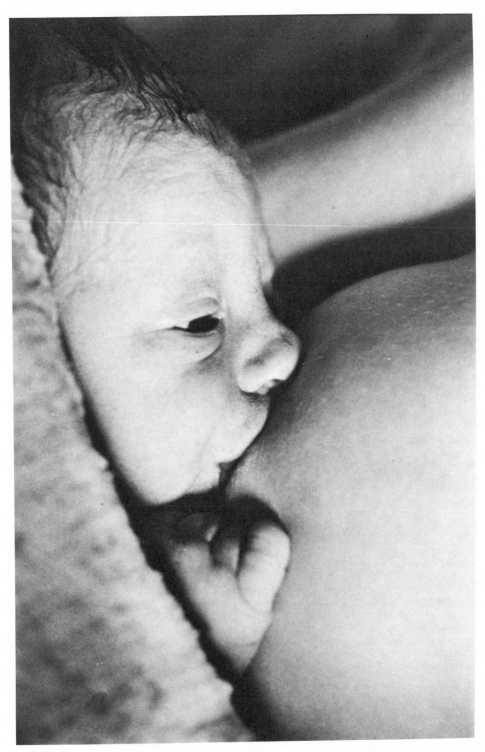

Daniel Kaufman

the world-renowned authority on the breast, is very familiar with all of the breast cancer studies. He believes that the bulk of the evidence shows lower breast cancer rates for women who have nursed, and particularly over long periods. Dr. Haagensen also believes that having a baby does not change the shape of the mother's breasts, although he says that the breasts of mothers are "softer and slightly more dependent." He feels these changes happen naturally as a result of pregnancy and have nothing to do with breast feeding.

Meanwhile, for the sake of yourself and your baby, if you're still undecided, do think about breast feeding seriously. Read the literature, talk to the people who know, and you'll probably realize, as I have, that breast feeding is the *only* alternative—and that in most instances the objections you may have can be worked out. In other words, become a breast-feeding "fanatic" for your baby's sake!

Advantages of Breast Milk: A Summary

Although both cow's milk and human milk contain little iron, iron deficiency anemia is uncommon in breastfed babies during the first six months of life. A healthy, term baby will have received enough iron during pregnancy that no iron supplement will be needed initially. Iron is needed after about six months of life, the time when solid foods containing iron should be introduced.* Vitamin D is required by all babies who are not exposed to sunlight, for the prevention of rickets. For this reason it has been customary to add it to formulas and to provide supplementation for breastfed infants.

There seems to be better development of appetite control in breastfed babies. The reason is unknown, but it may be that the thick, rich hind milk may act as a signal to the breastfed baby that the feeding is over. Many bottle-fed babies are overweight. The reason again is unknown, but it may be that with a bottle one cannot tell when the baby is full. The risk of obesity for babies is that once fat has developed, the fat cells remain for life. Obesity with all its attendant physical and psychological problems can then remain a lifelong problem even with no organic, genetic, or other predisposition.

Lactation infertility has been used as a form of contraception. It does result in decreased population growth, but is unreliable on an individual basis, especially if supplementary feedings are given. It is relatively easier for the lactating mother to control her weight, as extra calories are used for milk production. Some authorities feel that there is a decreased incidence of breast cancer in women who breastfeed. (Merilyn Salomon, M.A., Victoria Schauf, M.D., and Anne Seiden, M.D., "Breastfeeding, 'Natural Mothering,' and Working Outside the Home," *21st Century Obstetrics, Now!*, 1977)

How It Used to Be

Attitudes toward breast feeding were profoundly influenced in the mid-eighteenth century, especially in France, by the Swiss philosopher and author Jean Jacques Rousseau (1712–1778), whose views, highly respected by the aristocracy of his adopted country, exerted their impact far beyond its borders. Rousseau's *Emile* (1762), reflecting his advocacy of maternal nursing, appealed to the womanly emotions of his female readers. Almost overnight nursing became fashionable, and mothers began to suckle their infants even at social gatherings.

Harold Speert, M.D. *Iconographia Gyniatrica:*
A Pictorial History of Gynecology and Obstetrics, 1973

---

*The American Academy of Pediatrics, which is solidly behind breast feeding, says that human milk supplies enough iron for babies until the birth weight has tripled.

On Breast Feeding and Cancer

The Chinese Tanka (boat people) live on the coastal waters and rivers of southern China, and their women breast-feed with only the right breast, probably for convenience, the opening of the clothing being on the right side.

In comparing the laterality of breast cancer in Tanka and other Chinese patients in Hong Kong, we found a significantly increased incidence of breast cancer in the unused breast in women who had breast-fed unilaterally.

Of 73 patients with a history of exclusively one-sided breast-feeding, 27 of 34 patients aged 55 or over (79.4%) and 19 of 39 patients under age 55 (48.7%) had a carcinoma in the unsuckled breast.

The study indicates that in post-menopausal women who have breast-fed unilaterally, the risk of cancer is significantly higher in the unsuckled breast and that breast-feeding may help to protect the suckled breast against cancer. (Roy Ing, J.H.C. Ho, and Nicholas L. L. Petrakis, "Unilateral Breast-Feeding and Breast Cancer," *Lancet*, July 16, 1977)

◇ ◇ ◇

The Advantages of Breast Feeding for Fathers

Your opinions on breast-feeding are important to your wife, and your encouragement is vital to her success.

Breast feeding definitely has its advantages for a father. You don't have to get up in the middle of the night and run for the bottle, a duty that many men feel they should shoulder. You don't have to worry about running out of formula at an inopportune time and having to dash around trying to find a store that's open. You can save money on baby-sitters, since it's very easy to take a nursing infant out with you—to friends' houses, drive-in movies, even on trips. When you do go places with a breast-fed baby, there is less to lug—no bottles, cans of formula, sterilizing equipment, etc.

You can support your wife most effectively if you are really convinced that breast feeding is best for baby and mother. But even if you are not 100% convinced, you can appreciate the fact that *she* is and try to help her in all the ways you can.

One of the most important ways you can boost your wife's morale is to keep showing your interest in her as your wife. She needs to know that you still consider her interesting and attractive. . . . A woman's ability to be a successful breast-feeder is closely related to her state of mind. (Marvin S. Eiger, M.D., and Sally Wendkos Olds, *The Complete Book of Breastfeeding*, 1972)

◇ ◇ ◇

A COUNTERNOTE

Unfortunately, there is one serious negative consideration about breast feeding today.

Environmental and industrial public health researchers have discovered pesticides and other chemicals in mothers' milk. The Environmental Protection Agency in both 1977 and 1978 analyzed milk samples of large numbers of women (well over a thousand each year) in most states of the Union.

The overwhelming majority of these women had detectable levels of pesticides in their milk (dieldrin and oxychlordane primarily) and of the toxic compound PCB (polychlorinated biphenyl). The amounts of the pesticides were very low, and health authorities did not believe there was any immediate hazard to mothers or their babies. The use of these pesticides has been curbed by the EPA because they are suspected to be human cancer agents.

PCB, an industrial chemical used mainly in insulating fluids in heavy-duty electrical equipment, has caused tumors, birth defects and liver problems in laboratory animals at low levels of exposure. Again, health experts were uncertain whether the levels of PCB found in the women studied posed health problems. They did not advise any women to stop breast feeding.

Cow's milk also contains pesticides—*unless* the cows have been fed only on organically grown feed, a rare situation today. But cow's milk has far lower levels of pesticides than does human milk.

The American Academy of Pediatrics Committee on Nutrition says that "the problem of pollutants . . . in breast milk, which might be toxic to the nursing infant, has not yet been resolved."

This author, however, believes that there is no question of toxicity; there is only a question of how much—and when and how it will show up. There are ongoing studies. It is not unreasonable to suppose that there *will* be harmful effects later on.

Your own effort should be toward finding ways to reduce your own pesticide level. (If you lost weight *before* your pregnancy, you lost some pesticides, too.) There are some things you can do. Although the experts disagree, it seems reasonable to:

Avoid fresh fish altogether. Pesticide levels are higher in these fish.

Monitor your meat eating. According to the U.S. Department of Agriculture, chicken, beef, veal, and turkey have high pesticide levels; lamb and pork are much lower. Remove all fat before eating, and cook any meats well to reduce fatty content.

Eat low-fat dairy products—particularly cut out butter and high-fat cheese.

Eat organic vegetables, if possible. You may be able to raise some of your own food yourself by organic methods.)

Wash and peel all store-bought vegetables and fruits.

The best way of all is to change to a vegetarian diet. Such a diet has been shown to have far less pesticides. You would have to start before breast feeding, though, and of course be extremely careful about your protein intake during pregnancy and breast feeding.

You may be able to have your milk analyzed. Ask your doctor, write to the Environmental Protection Agency in Washington, D.C., or contact your local public health department to find out how to do this.

In addition, if you happen to work in a company that manufactures batteries or in a chemical plant, for example, you should not continue to work there during pregnancy and nursing. The levels of substances potentially harmful to you and your baby are much higher in some plants. Check with the Occupational Safety and Health Administration in Washington, D.C.

However, after taking whatever precautions you can, I still believe with Merilyn Salomon and Drs. Victoria Schauf and Anne Seiden writing in *21st Century Obstetrics, Now!* that *"a woman should not give up the known benefits of breastfeeding for the potential hazards of pollutants. (However, political action should be taken to control introduction of toxic substances into the environment.)"* (Italics are mine.)

How to Work and Nurse

Because working women are often encouraged to feel a destructive kind of guilt about both working and having children, breastfeeding provides an important source of confidence in her mothering which the working mother needs.

A working woman who expects to be separated from her infant will need some means of manually expressing milk to maintain milk supply, to feed the baby while she is absent, and to take care of breast engorgement when she is away from the baby for an extended period of time.

Good beginnings are the key to the initiation and success of the nursing relationship.

One theme emerges from conversations with mothers who nurse and work: *Continued breastfeeding success upon return to work seems to be associated with how well breastfeeding is initially established.*

A mother, especially the first-time mother, ideally should plan to take a minimum of four weeks away from full-time work, and preferably six weeks. The nursing relationship is rarely fully established (that is, with a well-conditioned letdown reflex and adequate milk supply) before one month, and it can take as long as two and one half months for the mother to fully "learn" to nurse. Nevertheless, the mother who cannot make these arrangements should not abandon the idea of breastfeeding. If she is strongly motivated and has immediate access to good breastfeeding advice—and good luck—there is still a very high probability of success.

For working mothers, rest and relaxation pose particularly important issues. The early weeks of nursing are a time when a mother has a legitimate right to think of nothing but her own and her baby's pleasure. *Care that leads to successful nursing is a well-deserved indulgence.*

The working mother should understand that she may get different kinds of rewards from nursing from those she will get from her job. Breastfeeding is not a rational, predictable process which can be organized and controlled as some jobs are. It is emotional, intuitive, sensual, and enjoyable, and responsive to the baby's needs. . . .

It is advisable for the baby to be fed its mother's milk during the substitute feedings, either from refrigerated milk expressed the day before or from supplies stored in the freezer. If this is not possible, a formula may be substituted. Unmodified cow's milk should not be used in infants under six months of age, as it is very hard to digest.

Fresh milk or milk refrigerated overnight is best for the baby. However, having a supply of frozen milk on hand is desirable as this is next best.

There is no substitute for nursing an infant to maintain lactation. Although hand expression stimulates about one third as much milk production as a suckling infant, the mother *must* allow the baby to nurse when she is home. Most nursing pairs do well if they maintain roughly four feedings a day. Both psychologically and physiologically, it is important to maintain a continuity of feeding at critical times: morning, evening after return from work, and bedtime.

The chances of carrying through breastfeeding successfully are excellent, once breastfeeding is established. There will be days when the milk supply is down, and the mother should expect these days. Usually, some minimal curtailment of activity (postponing the return of one evening's phone call, having the husband or other family member take care of an older child for a couple of hours, or reducing other demands) will solve the problem.

Some infants will gradually lose interest in the mother's breast and milk as they reach a year of age. Others may continue nursing until 18 months or even two years. The duration of nursing is a continuum. There is no arbitrary point at which the working mother should stop giving milk.

Any amount of breastfeeding is important. A little bit helps; a mother should not consider her nursing a failure if she nurses for six weeks, then returns to work and discontinues breastfeeding. She has provided her infant with the best nutrition it could have in those early weeks of life. There are no arbitrary definitions of successful nursing for the working mother; if the nursing relationship with the infant brings them joy and satisfaction, she has succeeded. (Merilyn Salomon, M.A., Victoria Schauf, M.D.,

and Anne Seiden, M.D., "Breastfeeding, 'Natural Mothering,' and Working Outside the Home," *21st Century Obstetrics, Now!*, 1977)

THE HOW-TOS

AN OUTLINE OF SIMPLE FIRST STEPS

Before the Baby Comes

One important physical step is to *toughen up your nipples*. Different authorities recommend different methods, as you will discover if you dip into the books. There are several ways which seem to me to make the most sense:

Spend five to ten minutes each morning and night pulling your nipples out with a *rough* Turkish towel.

Leave your nipples open to the air as much as possible. Air *and sun* toughen up tender skin.

Let your nipples rub against clothing, the rough kind.

Ask your husband to help you get your nipples in shape. He will love it!

Another important before-the-baby step is summed up best by one word: *prepare*. Here is how to do so:

Most important, get in touch with a La Leche League group early on (see page 156) and see them regularly to work out any problems in advance.

Buy several top-quality nursing bras that will be easy to use under any circumstance.

Buy nursing bra pads in case of leakage.

Be sure that you have enough zippered or button-down-the-front shirts and blouses and dresses for full wardrobe convenience when you are nursing.

Buy a rocking chair (with padded bottom and back) or other chair that best fits your height and back and comfort. *Do not* consider anyone else's back or arms to be more important in this purchase than yours.

Place the chair on a rug in a quiet corner next to a large end table with a soft light nearby.

Buy a few bottles for use with your own milk or for juice later on.

Conduct a *formal interview with your doctor* or nurse-midwife, with any hospital nursing personnel you can see, and especially with your baby-to-be's doctor, concerning their approach to and experience in nursing. What you want to know is:

Do(es) he/she/they firmly believe in the value and importance of nursing?

What is her/his/their experience regarding nursing? Are all or almost all the patients in their practice who want to nurse able to do so? What conditions prevent nursing?

If the baby is premature, cesarean, jaundiced, twins, or triplets, or even adopted does he/she/they believe you can still nurse? (You can, you know!)

What is done about possible problems: sore or cracked or inverted nipples, for instance?

If any of these people waffle about nursing, don't think it's very important, or make you feel childish for wanting to nurse—*walk out. Change.* Find doctors or nurses who believe wholeheartedly in the value of breast feeding, and the fact that you *can* do it if you want to, with help.

Plan ahead for your work situation. Arrange for a leave, try to go part time, see if you can work at home for the nursing months, and/or try to bring your baby to work with you. If necessary or possible, make your boss feel guilty for forcing you to decide between job and nursing. All of these possibilities may seem like pie-in-the-sky to you. And perhaps they are. But a woman determined to nurse often can move heaven and earth to make it possible. *Try.* And if you don't succeed, at least you'll have the satisfaction of knowing that you did make every effort to start your baby off in the best way. (See page 152 for more information.)

Since nursing is a totally female-and-baby occupation, *fathers can and do feel left out,* unnecessary, useless, jealous, and unhappy. Here are some before-baby steps to consider:

Talk about it. Bring out in the open how men feel. Talk together a lot. *And* talk to other people—each of you. Ask questions of men and women friends and relatives: Did they have any of these feelings? What did they do about them? What helped?

Prepare for ways to alleviate these kinds of feelings. Set up another chair for reading or whatever for the new father, near the nursing chair. Figure out pleasant things he can do in advance during the nursing times—particularly if nursing periods become extensive. If he wants this, decide on areas where he can be the main person to give primary care. Perhaps he will want to take the baby out or give the baths every weekend?

Figure out in advance who either or both of you can turn to for talk or help should the situation become too difficult after the baby arrives.

Read the books about nursing together.

How It Used to Be

Flannels or any thick covering that is ordinarily worn immediately over the nipples must be laid aside. Daily, upon rising and going to rest, each nipple must be washed, either with green tea, or the infusion of oak or pomegranate bark and, having been carefully dried, must be exposed to the air for eight or ten minutes, and rubbed gently during this time with a piece of soft flannel.

Thomas Bull, M.D., *Hints to Mothers,* 1853

All of these purchases and preparations will help you with the last step: *Believe that you can and will nurse,* and do not listen to any contrary opinions or negative perspectives. Given determination and a belief in the solution of most problems, nursing a baby is quite possible for almost everyone.

◇ ◇ ◇

Colostrum Before the Baby

It is sometimes recommended that you hand-express a few drops of colostrum from each breast every day during the last six weeks of pregnancy, and you may want to do this, with your doctor's approval. Colostrum is the fluid secreted before the milk comes in, which doctors say is so important for the newborn baby and one good reason (there are others) why you should nurse your baby as soon after delivery as possible. The reason for expressing the colostrum daily for a few weeks before the baby is born is to open the milk ducts, thereby reducing the engorgement which sometimes occurs when the milk first comes in and which some mothers find quite uncomfortable. (*The Womanly Art of Breastfeeding,* La Leche League International, 1963)

◇ ◇ ◇

THE DOULA SYSTEM: MOTHERS NEED MOTHERING

Dana Raphael of the Human Lactation Center, author of *The Tender Gift: Breastfeeding,* proposes a novel and most valuable plan to help new mothers breast-feed. She says, "The common denominator for success in breastfeeding is the assurance of some degree of help from some specific person for a definite period of time after childbirth."

Mrs. Raphael recommends a support system that she calls the *Doula.* In essence this is a person other than the new mother who can *mother the mother* in one or more of a variety of ways. The Doula and the new mother make a friendly compact (written down) concerning what shall be done (or not done)—all to help the mother establish the milk supply and the nursing situation. The Doula, who is most likely to be a woman relative, can also be a father, another woman soon to have a baby—or even, very rarely, a nonperson in the form of books, journals, and television (for information and help).

Read the book for the details of the plan.

THE POLITICS OF BREAST FEEDING—OR, OTHER COUNTRIES DO IT BETTER

The value of breast feeding *is* established. Every expert in the field of baby care agrees on this one fact: Breast feeding is almost always physically better for infants—and for mothers. It is also emotionally better for both.

But there is another incontrovertible fact which tends to prevent breast feeding. More and more women work, must work, work too far from home, cannot afford the time off necessary to be able to nurse. This trend will continue and grow. The clock does not go backward very often.

Further, office and job realities today mean that the woman who tries to juggle nursing and work is likely to lose her work—or her milk.

Oh, there are some lucky ones among us: writers and artists who can work at home, doctors and lawyers who can shift their patients and clients, and some who work a block or a walk away from home. There are even a few politicians who go to work *with* their nursing babies. An outstanding example is State Representative Susan Catania, mother of five, who nursed her infant in the building of the Illinois state legislature in Springfield.

Why is it so difficult to breast-feed on the job? For a very good reason. The men who make the laws and the men who run the companies do not know or care about nursing babies. Question any legislator, any company owner or manager about breast feeding. He will be in favor of it. Ask him to arrange for you and other pregnant women to take a long maternity leave, *with income* and your job guaranteed when you get back—and he will claim inability to arrange for it. Even ask for a part-time or flexible schedule, and you will probably find the same inflexibility.

This is a political situation.

Mothers who *want* to nurse, who *need* to work, should be able to do so with the full support of the society. The men who run the businesses should put their money where their mouths are. And if they don't, you should start your own breast-feeding lobby. Other countries do it better, with maternity leave and other benefits.

Last point. Even on a dollars-and-cents basis, it may turn out to be economical for our society to encourage nursing much more than we do. Healthier babies are less expensive for everyone, need social and health services far less, are later able to contribute more to society! If the protection against hypothyroidism from breast milk is a reality, as seems likely, then the prevention of mental and physical impairment of an infant can save at least twenty thousand dollars a year for institutional care or other societal support systems later in life. Compare this to six months' or a year's nursing leave at full pay for any working mother—and it's apparent that on a hard-money approach alone, we as a society are being penny-wise and pound-foolish.

Actually, the dollars and cents perspective may be the best way to look at breast feeding today from any angle. Let's get some social economists and statisticians involved in working out comparative figures in many different areas.

Preserving Our Natural Resources

Breast milk is one of the world's greatest natural resources. We call on the world's governments and industries to protect this food source by taking better care of the breast-feeder. As a beginning we say consider the working woman. Long postpartum leaves should become standard practice as should lengthened midday breaks which permit the mother to return home. A whole new creative attitude at the workplace is wanted. (Dana Raphael, "Mothers Need Mothering," editorial, *The Lactation Review*, 1976)

Malpractice?

It should be considered medical malpractice if a physician does not encourage a mother to breastfeed. It is rare that a mother is allowed or encouraged to breastfeed her child in the delivery room. (David A. Birnbaum, "The Iatrogenesis of Damaged Mothers and Newborns," *21st Century Obstetrics, Now!*, 1977)

THE LA LECHE LEAGUE

If ever there can be said to be "breast-feeding fanatics," this organization would fit. But that's precisely why it is such a good and important organization. La Leche literature is totally single-minded and one-sided, as indeed it should be. With the worldwide drop in breast feeding, we badly need organizations which will speak up and out, loud and clear, *for* breast feeding. And even though breast feeding in the United States is coming back into style with the majority of mothers (over 50 percent in a 1981 study) starting out nursing, there are still an enormous number of babies—about one and a half million (!)—who are not getting any mother's milk—and many more who are being breast-fed for only a short while.

La Leche League was formed in the fall of 1956 by a group of seven mothers to help others breast-feed. The league issues a variety of publications, including a regular newsletter, and holds local meetings and international conventions. It is a membership organization and some chapters even hold meetings for fathers! There are now (as of this writing at the end of 1981) over 4,335 groups in 42 countries, with 12,665 La Leche League leaders and 37 medical advisers. You can get the literature, or join, or find your local group by contacting La Leche League International, 9616 Minneapolis Avenue, Franklin Park, Illinois 60131. Their telephone is (312) 455-7730.

What Is the Breast?

In films and photographs and the half-veiled renderings of the advertisements, the female breasts have become almost exclusively a symbol of sex rather than maternal love. Instead of accepting these responses as natural or desirable, we should take a look at what breasts are really for and why they are important to the human race.

For thousands of years babies were fed from their mothers' breasts or sometimes, in unusual circumstances, from the breasts of a wet nurse. Nursing was an uncomplicated and invariably successful process for healthy mothers. As a result, an anthropologist examining the symbolic meaning of the breast in primitive society found that it almost always stood for motherhood. (Alice Gerard, *Please Breast-Feed Your Baby*, 1970)

TIPS AND HINTS: NIPPLE PROBLEMS?

One of the common reasons why women do not nurse involves problems with nipples. In *The Womanly Art of Breastfeeding*, the La Leche League International gives some very useful suggestions about nipple care.

If you suspect that you may have an inverted nipple, pinch the areola between the forefinger and thumb just behind the base of the nipple (as in hand expression) and see what happens. If it reacts by coming out, even a little, this is not a true inverted nipple. Even though you may not be able to get it out very far now, the baby will later on.

If the nipples react to this pressure by retreating (exceptional, but it sometimes happens), then you do have inverted nipples,

and you will have to work a little harder to get them in condition for nursing. . . .

The best treatment for bringing out truly inverted nipples is the use of breast shields designed for this purpose, worn during pregnancy before the baby is born. These breast shields should not be confused with nipple shields, which have rubber nipples that go over the real nipples and are sometimes used for a different purpose, while the baby is nursing.

The special breast shields may be useful at this (nursing) time, too, worn between feedings. If it's simply engorgement, just the times between two feedings may do the trick. In more severe cases it may be necessary to wear them for a day or two or even for two or three weeks.

Sometimes, even though there is no problem of inverted nipples or engorgement, a mother may have quite soft, small nipples, and the young baby may open his or her mouth and shake the head back and forth at the breast trying to locate the nipple. Placing a cold, wet cloth on the nipple for a few seconds, causing the areola to shrivel and the nipple to protrude and become firm, is usually all that is needed.

Bottle Feeding

SOMETHING TO AVOID

If you decide to bottle-feed your baby, for whatever reason, it will be far better for you and for the baby to avoid feeling guilty. Whatever the realities in your life, they are *your* realities—and guilt feelings are seldom helpful.

One major disadvantage of using bottles can be easily avoided. You may be tempted to prop the bottle, rather than hold the baby at times of rush and hurry and mix-up. Parents of twins who are bottle-fed are particularly subject to this tendency. There are *many* reasons to avoid bottle propping—Dr. Spock notwithstanding (he doesn't seem to feel it's so bad). These reasons range from the physical to the emotional. And just to give you the points you should pass on to baby-sitters, here is a little list:

Babies can choke on the milk from a propped bottle.

Babies can develop digestive upsets from milk flowing too fast, from not burping enough.

The contours of the baby's face and jaw may be adversely affected.

The experience of being held while feeding is important to a baby's feeling of emotional security. (It most closely parallels the womb situation.)

The bonding between parent and child is closely tied to the giving and receiving of life's basic sustenance: food.

It is far easier to tell if the baby is having *any* problem if the baby is held during feedings.

Bottled Breast Milk

If you cannot nurse your baby, consider purchasing breast milk for him, especially if he has been born prematurely or is unhealthy in any way. Even one bottle of breast milk daily will stimulate the growth of valuable intestinal bacteria and supply human antibodies (gamma globulin), thus tremendously increasing his resistance to infections. The more breast milk you give him and the longer you give it, the healthier he will be. Though seemingly expensive, breast milk usually proves to be economical because money is saved later on antibiotics, drugs and often hospitalization. (Adelle Davis, *Let's Have Healthy Children,* 1972)

Author's Note: Call La Leche League in your community to learn where to obtain this milk.

WHAT IS A FORMULA?

Most baby formulas are mixtures of cow's milk, water, and sugar. The water is to dilute the protein and fat in cow's milk which is much more concentrated than in mother's milk. The sugar is to sweeten cow's milk which is less sweet than mother's milk. You can mix your own or buy one of several prepared commercial formulas. Your baby's doctor will advise you on which formula to use.

Prepared formulas are either *ready-to-use*

or *concentrated*. The latter must be diluted with equal amounts of water.

The ready-to-use, already sterilized, come in thirty-two-ounce cans and can be poured directly into the day's supply of bottles. The convenience is great but so is the cost. Generally, the ready-to-use formula in the thirty-two-ounce (one quart) can costs *half again as much* as the concentrate to which you must add water and *three times as much* as the formula you mix from scratch.

There is also a ready-to-use formula packaged in six-pack disposable bottles. These don't require refrigeration and are even more convenient to use. But at this writing, the disposable-bottle formula is priced at *half again as much* as a prepared ready-to-use formula in a thirty-two-ounce can, which, as noted above, is already the most expensive of the commercial products.

In figuring the amount your infant will need, remember that he or she may feed for twenty minutes every three hours (or thereabouts), totaling eight eight-ounce bottles in twenty-four hours or fifty-six bottles per week.

For the most complete available breakdown of formulas—homemade and commercial—and information on ingredients and/or preparation methods, see Dr. Spock's book *Baby and Child Care,* the 1976 edition.

SUPPLIES

Bottles come in eight-ounce and four-ounce sizes and, if you are not using the disposable bottles, you will need both. (See page 171, on buying.) It's a good idea to start out with at least ten large bottles. The baby will use at most eight or nine bottles daily, but there will be breakage. Heat-resistant bottles last longest but cost more. Wide-mouthed bottles are easiest to clean. A few of the four-ounce size for water, orange juice, and first feedings will come in handy.

The nipples you purchase will depend on the bottles you use. Obviously a wide-mouthed bottle takes a different size from a small-mouthed bottle. If you buy a large enough supply, you will be able to replace worn-out ones instantly. Also, you will have a fresh nipple for each feeding and need boil them only once a day.

Holes in the nipples sometimes have to be enlarged. The baby may have become used to the soft, well-used hospital nipples. Enlarging a nipple hole is easy. Force the eye of a needle into a cork or pencil eraser. Hold the cork or eraser and put the sharp end of the needle in the flame of a match until it is red hot. Then pass the hot tip through one or more holes in the nipple. Be careful, though, not to make the hole too large. If you do, the milk may come out too fast and the baby could choke on it.

Your regular kitchen accessories will do for most of your specialized needs. For instance, a pot for boiling the bottling equipment. You may want to buy a pot made specially for this purpose, with a rack to hold the bottles and a tight-fitting lid. But this is not necessary. You can substitute for the rack an upside-down pie tin with holes punched into it or a grill such as you would use to keep a roast off the bottom of a dutch oven. If you do buy the rack, though, keep it; you can use it as an asparagus cooker after your baby outgrows bottles!

As for the rest—do you already have a set of standard measuring spoons? a boilable funnel? a measuring cup marked in ounces? a long-handled spoon? a can opener that punches holes (in case you use canned milk)? a pair of tongs? different-size saucepans (if you're mixing your own)? It is fairly likely that you do have these supplies on hand. The only items you probably won't have are a long-handled, stiff-bristled bottle brush and covers for the nipples. The covers can be purchased in glass, plastic, aluminum, or paper, or you can make your own from brown or waxed paper. If you use bottles with their own covers, though, you won't need any others. As for the brush, get one which is already bent at the tip or bend it yourself so the bristles can reach the edge of the bottom of the bottles.

Sterilizing

Sterilizing bottles is essentially the same as steaming or boiling potatoes. You merely put the potatoes (bottles, nipples, spoons, tongs, etc.) in water or steam, and let them cook for a given time before taking them out. You usually avoid handling hot potatoes; thus they remain sterile. Sterilizing bottles is as simple as that.

If your pediatrician wishes you to sterilize food and equipment, be sure to ask him when to stop sterilizing; the time varies depending on how healthy a baby is. (Adelle Davis, *Let's Have Healthy Children*, 1972)

How It Used to Be

Artificial feeding of infants was initially accomplished from pottery, later metal, and ultimately glass nursing vessels, each equipped with a nipple or spout of the same material, or of parchment, sponge, wood, cork, or ivory. Rubber nipples were introduced in 1868. In frontier America nursing bottles were also fashioned from wood, gourds, and bovine horns. Some of the extant nursers date back to about 500 B.C.

These feeding vessels were used for both milk and pap, a thick gruel of flour or bread cooked with water or milk. Fed from a boat or a spoon, pap came into use in the mid sixteenth century first as a supplementary food for infants, later as their sole nutriment, even from birth, as a substitute for mother's milk.

Harold Speert, M.D., *Iconographia Gyniatrica:*
A Pictorial History of Gynecology and Obstetrics, 1973

OTHER DOS AND DON'TS
ABOUT BOTTLE FEEDING

DO:

Wash and sterilize all equipment before you use it. When your baby is able to get around, there's no longer any point in sterilizing—but you still need to keep things clean.

Buy more nipples than bottles, so extras will be on hand.

Fix eight bottles (a full day's supply) at a time. (If you're living in cramped quarters and need more refrigerator space, use preprepared bottles from a service or buy a small wall-installed refrigerator.)

Be sure the bottle nipple has holes that are neither too large nor too small. You'll have to experiment to find the right size for your baby. Just remember, he or she needs to be fed steadily without swallowing air, but the holes should be small enough so your baby has to work at it a bit in order to get enough sucking. The nipple should simulate the human nipple as closely as possible.

If you are using a particular formula, follow the directions on the can exactly—unless your doctor advises differently. There has been a lot of research recently into baby formulas and the manufacturer's directions are usually sound.

To warm the formula, stand the bottle in a saucepan of hot water. Test its temperature by shaking out a drop onto the back of your hand. That drop should feel luke-warm.

Once the baby is finished feeding, dispose of whatever is left in the bottle.

Hold your baby in your arms in the sitting position, as if you were breast-feeding. Feeding time is the time of greatest happiness for your baby! It should be associated with loving contact with you and the baby should have a good view of your face.

Halfway through a feeding, burp the baby. Put the baby over your knees or shoulder, stomach side down, and pat or rub gently.

DON'T:

Don't leave a bottle warming for any length of time. Bacteria present can start to multiply if the bottle is kept warm too long.

Do not save what's left in the old bottle.

Don't refrigerate.

Never try to make your baby finish the bottle. The baby knows when she or he has had enough. Fat babies can and do grow into fat adults.

Don't *ever* add more formula than the instructions specify. Your baby's kidneys may be strained by an overconcentrated formula. If you lose count while measuring, throw it all out and start over.

Avoid changing the quantity of the formula by packing it down or heaping it. Instead, scoop it out and scrape off any extra amount.

For a new baby, don't use cow's milk that is undiluted or unboiled.

Don't feed the baby while she or he is lying flat. This makes swallowing difficult.

Never leave the baby unattended with a propped bottle. A baby may swallow air or, worse still, choke or gag.

Never tease a hungry baby by withholding the bottle.

On the other hand, do not shove the nipple into the baby's mouth rapidly and angrily.

PREPARING FORMULAS

There are two basic methods of preparing the formula: aseptic sterilization, or presterilization; and terminal sterilization.

In presterilization the formula is mixed, then boiled and finally put into already sterilized bottles.

In terminal sterilization the formula is mixed in clean utensils and poured into clean bottles. The filled bottles are then heated, thus sterilizing both bottles and contents simultaneously. This is the quickest, easiest, and probably most widely used method.

There are variations on both:

For instance, if you are short on refrigerator space, you can store formula in a sterilized quart jar and fill one clean bottle at a time as needed. Or you can store the water-sugar mixture in sterilized bottles and add boiled milk at feeding time. You can prepare a day's worth of bottles each morning and store them in the refrigerator, taking them out one at a time. Or you can utilize the old-fashioned, most time-consuming way of preparing one bottle at a time as needed.

HOT VERSUS COLD

Contrary to popular opinion, babies don't have to have their formula at room or warm temperature. The idea that bottles must be warmed arose from the fact that mother's milk is warm. To my mind, this is still preferable. But in fact, all that the baby seems to need is consistency. However you start out—warmed up, room temperature, or straight out of the refrigerator—that is the temperature at which you should give all subsequent feedings.

An average bottle feeding takes about 20 minutes. Adjust the tightness of the bottle cap and the size of the hole in the nipple to the sucking power of your child to arrive at this time span. Don't expect the baby to drink the same amount each time. The quantity will vary with the time of day, the baby's sleepiness, et cetera. There's no rule that says the bottle must be emptied. Just remember to throw away what the baby leaves.

◇ ◇ ◇

More What-Not-to-Dos

Don't feed formula that has been left standing at room temperature in a nursing bottle or open can for more than 30 or 40 minutes. Germs grow rapidly in warm milk and can become a problem whenever milk from open cans stands for more than an hour at room temperature or stays in the refrigerator for more than three days.

Don't feed any formula unless you have read the instructions on the can or bottle. Some formulas are sold ready to feed and should not have water added to them. Powdered formulas are mixed one tablespoon of formula for each 2 oz. of water. Most con-

---

How It Used to Be

A new kind of bottle has recently been introduced . . . which is represented as possessing peculiar advantages. This bottle is of oval form, made of strong green glass; the mouth has a thin ring of cork fitted inside, into which a glass stopper is fixed when the bottle is not in use. The feeding appliance consists of a tube of pure tin, which cannot affect the food, and which may be kept bright by merely washing: to this the nipple is attached. The advantages of this feeder are, that by the use of the tube the fluid is drawn from the bottom of the bottle; consequently, air cannot be imbibed; it is also simple, clean and durable.

The Mother's Resource Book for the
Management of Children, 187?

centrated liquid formulas are mixed half and half.

Don't give added vitamins or iron if you are using a prepared infant formula unless these are specifically prescribed by a physician who knows that you are feeding a vitamin-and-iron-containing formula.

Don't expect much change in bowel habits, spitting up, or other symptoms by changing from one brand or type of formula to another. (Children's Bureau, Department of Health, Education and Welfare, *Infant Care*, 1973)

◇   ◇   ◇

TIPS AND HINTS

If you are not going to wash the finished bottle immediately after each feeding, it's a good idea to fill it with water and let it stand until washing-up time. That way, the residue of the formula won't harden and stick.

Nipples tend to harden with repeated boiling. Therefore, an old nipple may have a hole that needs enlarging (see page 160). By the same token, if a new nipple has too large an opening, it should be boiled a few times.

Very small and premature babies need special, or "premie," nipples which are softer and smaller. The nipple should not be so long that it can touch the back of the baby's throat and cause gagging.

A good way to tell if the milk flow is proper is to watch for the appearance of bubbles in the formula still in the bottle.

In addition to sitting upright while bottle-feeding your baby, you should also alternate sides, as a breast-feeding mother does. Thus, the baby develops the ability to focus equally to the left and to the right.

The position of the bottle is important. It should be held upright so the nipple is full of milk, not air.

Choosing the Baby's Doctor

WHAT ARE THE OPTIONS?

Most of us choose our baby's doctor on the same trial-and-error basis that we use to select doctors for our other needs. Usually we wait until the need is upon us. Then we ask friends or relatives to recommend doctors whom they have heard about or know themselves. We try the recommended doctors and, if they prove unsatisfactory, we try another recommended doctor. Many times this method works out very well. That is, we are lucky! Or we have lucky friends and relatives, and happen to find a fine doctor. Other times we must visit two or more physicians before finding one who is just right for what ails us.

To make a bad choice of a doctor can be upsetting and in some situations quite harmful. But to make a bad choice of a first doctor for a new baby can affect our entire early relationship with the infant. As parents, particularly first-time parents, we tend to rely heavily on the advice of the doctor who is caring for our precious newborn. Often, especially during the baby's first months, we depend on the baby's doctor to teach us how to parent. This is a new experience for us and the feeling of responsibility can be overwhelming at times.

How distressing, then, if we come to dislike, distrust, or be disturbed by the pediatrician! How much difficulty we would have been spared had our first choice of a doctor been the right one!

While it is not possible to eliminate all poor choices, you can make *informed* choices by a little advance planning. Here are some guidelines and considerations to ease the process of choosing your baby's doctor, and to help you select the kind of doctor who will fulfill your needs.

First of all, there are two categories of doctors to consider, a pediatric specialist and a family-practice generalist. If you have been using a general practitioner for yourselves and have confidence in that person's medical skill, then you will probably continue with this doctor for your new baby. But if you are undecided between pediatrician and general practitioner, and live in an area where both are easily available, I believe that the specialist's training and experience, especially geared to the unique needs of very young patients, is a big plus. If an unusual problem develops, the special training of the pediatrician can be of great value.

If you live in an area where you do not have the option of a specialist, you can still expect good care. Doctors going into general or family practice are aware of their responsibilities to the entire population they serve. There is even an Academy of Family Physicians* today—an organization which was not in existence a dozen years ago. (You can ask your doctor if he or she is a member—membership may indicate a progressive attitude toward learning and developing.) Family doctors, in general, try to keep in touch not only with latest medical developments, but also with the nearest specialists, full-service hospitals, and medical schools. By means of computerized communications

*at 1740 West 92nd Street
Kansas City, Missouri 64114
(816) 333-9700

164

systems even doctors in the most isolated areas can consult with experienced specialists and obtain up-to-the-minute advice in an emergency. So—if you choose the most knowledgeable and responsible person available to you, there's no need to worry.

And as Dr. Arthur Levin points out in *Talk Back to Your Doctor:*

There are also other "options." . . .

Prepaid group practice plans have been shown to deliver a high level of primary child health care. One study showed a prepaid plan provided at least as good care as that given by medical school hospital OPD's [outpatient departments]. The federal government's *Neighborhood Health Centers* have also been shown to provide a high level of care—again as high as (actually somewhat higher than) the medical school hospital.

Some local health departments operate child health clinics. In New York City, for instance, there is an extensive network of well-child stations, which, by and large, provide decent preventive care.

That said, how does one locate a pediatrician? Pretty much in the same way you located an obstetrician. (See page 92.) For starters, ask. Ask these sources:

Your obstetrician (or nurse-midwife) and any other doctors you know and have confidence in. *Particularly, ask them which doctor they use for their own children.*

Your hospital, for a list of pediatricians on its staff. Find out at the same time which of these doctors are in group practice. (Doctors in group practice are often better for you, since someone is usually on call and available.)

Parents of young children in your neighborhood. They are as close to the situation as you will be very shortly. Ask for the names of their doctors, whether they are pleased with the care given their children, and the personal treatment they receive.

Your county medical society, only to find out the specific credentials—medical schools, training hospitals, and present affiliations—of the doctors on your list.

The directory of the American Academy of Pediatrics (see page 321 for address).

If your investigation has produced several names of physicians who sound like good possibilities, you should telephone and meet each one, so you can make a choice on the basis of your own personal reaction. It is definitely *not* a good idea to wait until the time for the baby's first checkup and walk in!

Plan to meet and select a pediatrician well before the baby is born. The baby should be examined shortly after birth—immediately, if possible—by the person who will have responsibility for the baby's medical care. Your obstetrician or nurse-midwife will, of course, examine the baby immediately after delivery. And if you're in the hospital, a pediatrician will do so also if you have not made arrangements for a baby doctor.

It's a good idea to start looking for a pediatrician early on. Although pediatricians are as busy as any other specialists, they should understand your request for an appointment in advance. And if any of them do not understand—well, perhaps he or she is not the person for you anyway.

During your first meeting try to find out what the child-rearing philosophy of the doctor is. Child care is both an art and a science. While every child is a unique individual, he or she will have certain needs that all babies share. Your baby's doctor should be sensitive to both aspects. Further, personal interaction counts for a lot—and that includes your family's interaction with the baby's doctor. You will be learning from your doctor, and what you learn can affect not only your baby, but your family as a whole. Then, too, you certainly need a doctor who understands your point of view and respects your opinions. You don't need a doctor who will be the real autocrat of the nursery. After all, the doctor's patient will be *your child.*

It is important also for you to know that the doctor will be available when needed, *including as soon as the baby is born.* In the case of a low-birth-weight baby, or if there are any other problems, there should be a second pediatric examination before you and the baby leave the hospital, or no later than one week after birth. In any case, the pediatrician who will be responsible for the child's medical care should take charge from the beginning.

Consider also the hospital affiliation of the doctors you are interviewing. You want someone attached to a reputable hospital or clinic.

The most important factor of all is what kind of *person* your baby's doctor is. The characteristics recommended earlier to help you choose your own doctor also apply to the doctor you will choose for your child.

QUESTIONS TO ASK A BABY DOCTOR

What is your fee?

The pediatrician's fee should be within the range of that of others in the community. You can ask the county medical society for the suggested fee schedule. You might also be able to find out from your local Medicaid office. Be sure you know what the fee covers and what extras you are expected to pay for. One common arrangement calls for payment of an annual fee, covering one in-hospital examination, and periodic in-office examinations, plus the first year's inoculations. House calls and special medical care would be extras.

Do you make house calls?
Under what circumstances?

Most doctors these days only visit the home in an emergency. The medical fraternity gives two reasons for this. They are: first, traveling about consumes a lot of time that could better be spent seeing patients; second, essential equipment and supplies are in the pediatric office, not in the automobile. Nevertheless, most new parents feel there is nothing like home visiting at times of sickness. Besides, special problems occasionally *do* come up, and a very sick child should not be taken out or subjected to the added stress of a journey, if it can be avoided. Diagnosis by telephone led to my own daughter's *unnecessary* case of scarlet fever. Naturally, you can expect to pay a little more for the special service of a home visit.

What is your policy about nonemergency phone calls?

Many doctors have specific hours when telephone queries of a more or less routine nature are encouraged. Try to picture how free you would feel about telephoning at two in the morning about a screaming baby if you have already called earlier in the day. Naturally, you have a responsibility not to impose on anyone's life at the twitch of the baby's eyebrow. But some doctors have a sympathetic—if somewhat humorous—understanding of a new parent's need to telephone even about inconsequential matters (although they hope not at unreasonable hours)! On the other hand, there are doctors who go so far as to charge for each phone call!

Who is available when you cannot be?

If the doctor is part of a group, you can be sure that there will always be someone on call, even in the middle of the night. A doctor in individual practice should have mutual-coverage arrangements with a number of colleagues, preferably all affiliated with the same hospital and practicing in the same neighborhood, so that an emergency never finds a patient unable to locate medical help. The doctor should also subscribe to a medical answering service, which forwards phone calls and messages regularly and follows through until an emergency call reaches the doctor or a colleague.

What is your recommendation about breast feeding?

If you are sitting on a fence on this subject, you need clear explanations and support while you come to a decision. The doctor who will give you straight answers now is the one who will answer your questions later on, too, whether about nursing or toilet training or whatever. A doctor can try to talk you out of your decision *not* to nurse, for example, without making you feel guilty about it. In any case, he or she has a medical obligation and responsibility to explain to you the benefits of nursing for you and your baby. Your baby's doctor should let you know what the sides of the issue are clearly and fully.

What kind of schedule do you recommend for the baby's feeding?

Choose a doctor who tends to have a flexible attitude on this subject. The rigid every-four-hours approach is as dated as bathtub gin.

How do you feel about allowing a baby to cry?

Your doctor should *not* take a let-'em-cry-it-out approach. He or she should help you figure out what your baby's cry means. Sometimes crying means hunger. Sometimes it is a problem signal. Sometimes it just calls for a little cuddling. Sometimes a baby will cry on and off for a few minutes before dropping off to sleep. And sometimes . . . Well, you can see already there are many kinds of crying.

How do you feel about working mothers?

If you are planning to work, for *whatever* reason, the last thing in the world you need is a doctor who will make you feel guilty about it. Try to find one who understands the special needs—and anxieties—of a working mother, and especially of the baby under his or her care. A sensitive doctor will try to see if he or she can help you in this decision, since many aspects of the baby's care and health will be involved. A baby doctor should also know about many resources to assist you.

THINGS YOU SHOULD NOTICE ABOUT THE BABY DOCTOR

By the time you have asked these and other questions, you'll have a fairly good idea of the doctor's method of communicating with parents. But there are other factors to pay attention to:

Does the doctor listen to what *you* are saying? If you get a strong sense of a too-abrupt or hasty approach, or of too much technical information that is not to the point or not translated, you might well decide that this is not the doctor for you.

What is the condition of the waiting room? Is it crowded with fretting babies and parents who have obviously been kept waiting far too long? Is it cluttered with diaper bags and stacks of overcoats? Or is it tidy, with just a few patients waiting?* Is there a coat rack, a sofa, or table for baby changing? Are there child-oriented pictures on the walls, playthings and books in the room?

How does the doctor greet the babies and the toddlers and their parents? Cordially, in a clipped way, or not at all? By name? Tak-

ing just a second to make personal contact, or hurrying by?

How does the doctor's staff respond to children and patients? With warmth and concern? Or with a brusque efficiency, a don't-bother-me-can't-you-see-I'm-busy air?

How does the doctor handle phone calls that come in while you're there? What if you were the parent on the phone—would you be satisfied with the answer?

Do older children (toddler age perhaps) seem comfortable in the office? Do they greet the doctor as a friend, or are they crying and hiding in their mothers' laps even before it's their turn? Children know when they're being treated humanely, and even though they've had inoculations that may have hurt and throat cultures taken that were uncomfortable, they should feel confidence, not fear or panic, in their doctor's office—most of the time. Of course, every doctor's office has its share of criers, under the best of circumstances. In most instances, however, how the doctor (and the staff) handles this is more a key to the type of care your child will have than the actual crying or shyness itself.

CHOOSING A CLINIC FOR YOUR BABY

Choosing a clinic for your baby's care usually involves much less of a choice for you, because of geography. Most areas do not have more than one clinic, and even in well-populated cities there are not enough clinics or clinic personnel to care for everyone in a reasonable time period. The quality of clinic care varies enormously. I have been to well-baby clinics which are cheerful, efficient, and excellent in services. One in Houston has carpeting throughout, and colorful, small-size dental chairs plus large-size toys in the dental department—even though this clinic is under the auspices of the State Public Welfare Department of Texas. At least in appearance, it was marvelous to find such visible concern for children on the part of a welfare department. I have been to others (Charity Hospital in New Orleans, for one) in which everyone sits in grim surround-

---

*Sometimes the too-neat office indicates a rather rigid, close-minded approach to life's problems—while clutter and waiting patients, which may appear out of keeping, actually can indicate a warm heart, a busy practice, and a doctor who spends a lot of time with patients.

ings, waiting and waiting and waiting. In between are clinics like that of Michael Reese Hospital in Chicago or Columbia Presbyterian Medical Center's Babies Hospital in New York where attempts have been made to use color and paint in the waiting areas for a more cheerful effect. Families with babies and small children often wait a long time for medical attention at these clinics—the medical care, insufficient in quantity, is supposed to be excellent in quality.

If you *do* have a choice of a clinic, then watch for:

Pleasant physical surroundings

How many people are waiting for how long

The medical reputation of the hospital or clinic

Whether the staff consists of one intern and one student nurse or one or more full doctors

Whether there will be a chance for you and your baby to be seen most of the time by the same staff members

Whether there is adequate emergency coverage (Who can you call or see late at night or on a weekend?)

Whether the hospital and/or clinic has the best accreditations available

Whether the clinic routinely supplies *useful* printed or typed materials in both English and Spanish, if there are Spanish-speaking people in your area or if you are Spanish-speaking

Whether there are multilingual people on the staff to help translate in emergencies

There are many other criteria to check, *if* you do have a choice—but perhaps the most important of all from the point of view of any consumer is how well or poorly other parents speak about their treatment at the clinic.

One of the most useful prebaby trips you can make is a visit to your local clinic to sit and question the parents who are already there. Don't hesitate to try it!

Part Four

GETTING READY FOR
THE NEW ARRIVAL

*My wife and I began our family while I was still a
struggling performer. The pain of financial insecurity
was a heavy weight to bear . . . the responsibilities of
the family came at me full blast. . . . Today all my
personal happiness emanates from my family. I'm a
very lucky man and owe so much to the firm foundation
that is the family.*

BEN VEREEN

The Fun of Buying for a Baby: Clothes, Equipment, Toys

DOWN WITH THE OLD LAYETTE LIST!

Childcare theories, medical opinions, lifestyles, and available equipment have all changed drastically during the last ten years. Mothers and babies simply do not use the same kinds of baby clothing that they used years ago. And they do use or want some things that didn't even exist in the not-too-distant past.

The following list has been derived by culling from many sources and much experience. You can expect to spend at least one thousand dollars for your baby's clothing, supplies, and equipment. (1980 prices)

YOUR NEW-BABY SHOPPING LIST

Wardrobe

At-home clothing

Diapers	80–100 per week from diaper services: 6 dozen if laundering your own; *or* 8 dozen disposables *plus* 2 dozen cloth diapers
Diaper pins*	6 plastic-capped, double-lock, large
Waterproof pants*	6
Undershirts	6–8
Socks	2–3 pairs (optional)
Bootees	1–2 pairs (optional)
Outerwear	6–8 garments (perhaps 3 kimonos, and 3 coveralls to start off with; you're sure to get gifts of some of these to fill in)
Kimonos	
Nightgowns	
Sleeping bags	
Terry cloth stretch coveralls	

Outdoor clothing (2–3 outfits)

Sweater-and-hat sets	1–2 each, light and medium weight

Nursery Furnishings

A place to sleep

Bassinet	1 (optional) large but very convenient with handles for carrying around

*Not needed if only disposables are used.

Cradle	a small-size solution
Portable crib	(optional)
Standard crib	1; absolutely necessary by the time baby is four or five months or perhaps earlier

Bedding

Firm, waterproof mattress	1
Zippered mattress cover	1 (optional)
Waterproof pads or sheets	2–3
Fitted sheets	4–6
Receiving blankets	3–4
Crib blankets	2 (buy 1 to start; you'll probably get at least 1 more as a gift)

Additional needs

Dressing table *with* straps for holding baby firmly, or	
Countertop with straps also	
Chest of drawers or other storage unit for clothing	
Gates for stairways	
Storage for supplies	
Waterproof covered pail	1 (preferably with step-on opening mechanism, and deodorant container in lid)
Lamp	1–2 (not overhead or near baby's eyes, and not a standing one)
Night light	1
Clock	1 (on wall or table or counter, just as long as it's easy to read)
Cushioned floor covering	a must—carpet, or foam-padded vinyl
Rocking chair for mother/father	1 (a must for easy feeding and lots of comfort)
Other comfortable seating	
Thermometer for room temperature	(optional)

Bath Equipment

Baby-size bathtub	(optional)
Soft cloth towels	3
Old bath towels	2 (these can *really* be old; they are used to cover the drying and dressing area)
Cotton knit or soft terry washcloths	3
Bath thermometer	(if you're edgy about judging water temperature)
Soft apron	1
Mild soap	1 cake (to start)
Covered soap dish	1 (traveling soap container is fine for this)
Baby lotion	1 container
Cornstarch or baby powder	1 package or can
Round-tipped nail scissors	a must; do *not* use emery boards or adult nail scissors for baby
Baby comb and brush set	(bristles of brush should be very soft; teeth of comb should be thin and close together)
Dressing table tray	1

Shallow pan	(alternative choice)
Covered containers	2–4 (glass or plastic; used to hold cotton, diaper pins, miscellaneous toiletries)
Box of tissues	large (pop-up kind is most useful in a nursery)
Sterile absorbent cotton	1 package of either (the latter are very
Cotton balls	convenient)

Feeding Equipment

If breast-feeding

8-ounce bottles, complete	2–3 (for relief feeding or emergency)*
4-ounce bottles, complete	4–6 (for saving breast milk, and for juice later)
Extra nipples	2
Nipple covers	2

If formula-feeding

8-ounce nursing bottles, complete	8–10 glass or plastic (complete means with nipple assembly)
4-ounce bottles, complete	4–6
Extra nipples	4
Nipple covers	4

For sterilizing

Complete sterilizer set *or*	1 (electric or top-of-stove, highly
Large pressure cooker *or*	recommended; otherwise, 1 each of the
Large pot with cover	items listed at left)
Rack to hold bottles	
Tongs	
Covered jar to store sterile nipples	
Bottle brush	
Nipple brush	
Strainer	
Funnel	
8-ounce measuring cup	
2-quart measuring cup	

For warming and serving

Small enamel saucepan	1 (preferred by many mothers)
Bottle warmer, electric	1 (optional)
Baby teaspoon	1 silver, stainless or plastic; should have small bowl and long handle for baby's first feedings

For Going Places

Baby carriage	1
Carriage mattress	(waterproof)
Carriage sheets	2
Carriage blanket, robe or throw	1 (of course, you may use a crib blanket instead)
Infant carrier	1 (optional)

*Breast-feeding advocates do not believe in relief feedings by bottle unless essential—and then only with mother's milk.

Travel bed/cradle	1 (optional; many carriage bodies lift out to convert—good for plane or train)
Infant car seat	1 (*not* optional—see page 204 for safety items)
Harness	1–2 (use in carriage and other baby-holders; it's a good idea to keep a spare handy—sooner or later you'll need it)
Carriage and travel toys	several (small rattles and chewable things)
Bottle warmer	1 (the kind that plugs into a car lighter is practical)
Carryall or diaper bag	1–2 (ideally, of wipe-clean material, with a thermal pocket to keep milk cold until needed; second one useful for long trip and to keep bottles separate from diapers)

Additional Toiletries and First-aid Supplies

Rectal thermometer for baby*	2 (an extra will sooner or later be needed)
Petroleum jelly	jar or tube
Fever-lowering medication for infants	rubbing alcohol
Ointment for skin irritation	tube
Adhesive bandages	box of assorted sizes (should be a standard item in every home)
Vaporizer or humidifier	(cold steam type)

Later-On Needs

For feeding

Warming dish	1
Plastic cup	1–2
Feeding spoon	1–2
Blender	1
Baby food grinder (especially the Nurtury, by Water-Pik)	To make your own baby food!
Feeding table	1 (recommended), *or*
High chair	1

For play and movement

Playpen	1–2 (extra for travel)
Walker	1 (optional)
Cupboard or open shelves for toys	As many as you have space for

*A new-style thermometer may soon be available.

ALL ABOUT CLOTHES, CRIBS, CARRIAGES, AND OTHER BABY ITEMS

KIMONOS

Four to six of these were a standard old-layette-list requirement. A baby kimono is, simply, a little, loose-fitting long shirt, usu-ally of cotton knit, usually with a snap-opening front. A newborn baby in a warm room really need wear nothing more than a kimono and a diaper. Don't stock up on them; buy only the six-month size.

SACQUES

A sacque is a loose-fitting lightweight sweater for a baby. Like a bed jacket, it opens in front and usually fastens with a tie. But mostly your baby will be wearing one-piece coveralls. If necessary, a lightweight sweater or any little top could be slipped on over that to serve the same purpose as a sacque.

UNDERSHIRTS

Usually cotton knit, sometimes cotton-and-polyester: snap-front, tie-front, or over-the-head; long sleeves, short sleeves, or sleeveless. Short-sleeve, snap-front models are best for young babies. The pullover style may prove more convenient at the toddler stage. Buy the six-month, up to 12-pound size, to start.

DIAPERS

Cloth diapers come in various fabrics and styles: (1) a large, hemmed square of bird's-eye cotton, which must be folded in half or thirds lengthwise and folded down again before being put on a baby; (2) a rectangle made of layers of cotton gauze, stitched in a few places to hold together; (3) contoured, narrowed in the center to fit between a baby's legs.

All cloth diapers should be laundered, with fabric softener, and machine-dried, *before being used*, to soften and preshrink the fabric. If you order from a diaper service, (becoming rare these days) be sure to order *new, prewashed* diapers.

Disposable diapers come in sizes to fit growing babies. Buy the newborn size for newborns, and babies up to 12 pounds or so. Daytime size is for babies in approximately the 12- to 22-pound range; overnights, which have greater absorbency, are also for the 12- to 22-pound babies; and toddler size is generally for babies 22 pounds and over. At least one brand is available in a toddler overnight size as well.

It has been estimated that the cost of using disposables is at least *four times greater* than the cost of buying and laundering cloth diapers at home. And cloth diapers are certainly kinder to the environment.

But disposables *are* convenient. And the self-adhering tapes, which make diaper pins unnecessary, add to the convenience.

WATERPROOF PANTS

It's a good idea to put protective pants over the baby's diaper. If you use disposable diapers, however, add waterproof pants only when necessary, at night, or when the baby gets older.

SOCKS

Not really necessary, unless the room is drafty and baby is not wearing a coverall with feet. You really won't need them until your baby is ready for shoes, probably a year away.

TWO SIZE CHARTS FOR BABY CLOTHING

An Infant Size Chart*

Age (months)	Weight (pounds)	Height (inches)	Size
0–3	to 14	to 24	Newborn
6–9	15–20	24½–28	Small
12–18	21–26	28½–32	Medium
—	27–32	32½–36	Large
—	33–36	36½–38	X-large

A Toddler Size Chart (Walking Child)*

Weight (pounds)	Height (inches)	Size
23–27	29½–32	1T
28–31	32½–35	2T
32–36	35½–38	3T
37–40	38½–41	4T

*The various baby-clothing companies and stores have their own size charts. They are comparable to these.

BABY BUYING DOS AND DON'TS

DO:

Make sure *everything* you buy is washable—and that means everything!

Make sure you understand the fabric content information and laundering instructions attached to each garment.

Be certain that all zipper tops are covered by a fabric tab that snaps in place.

Make sure everything goes on and off quickly and easily—snaps and zippers are generally the most practical fastenings for baby garments.

Look for clothing with built-in growth and comfort features—two rows of snaps for attaching matched tops and bottoms, raglan sleeves, strong seams, easy elastics.

Check safety features in clothing: no loose strings or ribbons, no buttons for tots and toddlers, no zippers locked tightly at the throat, no flowing sleeves.

DON'T:

Buy just because something looks cute; infants' clothing must be comfortable, and stiff frilly ruffles are not.

Feel you must be up-to-the-minute and buy every new gewgaw and gadget.

Overdress any child. How often I've seen mothers in summer sundresses carrying infants bundled into sweaters, knit hats and blankets! Dress your baby for the weather, as you dress yourself.

Believe that any old piece of hand-me-down equipment or clothing is fine for your new baby. Some hand-me-downs are not fit for anyone's infant, and some are such heirlooms that they should be museum-housed, not hampering that wetting, spitting-up, wriggling baby of yours.

Try to get an extra month's wear out of a garment your baby has outgrown. Clothing for babies and children must give their bodies space to move about in.

BOOTEES

Well, they *are* cute, although they sometimes get kicked off and lost! But baby-having can't be all practical. So do try knitting some, if you like to knit.

NIGHTGOWNS

I don't recommend them. First of all, there's an unsettling controversy over flame-retardant treatments of children's nightwear. Second, nightgowns are really not practical items, not even for sleeping. They hamper movement. There are better choices—stretch terry jumpsuits, for example. Or diaper, kimono (shorter than nightgown), and receiving blanket for a newborn.

The law says that all children's sleepwear must be flame-retardant, but a problem developed in 1977 over a chemical called TRIS used to make such nightwear nonflammable. The National Cancer Institute had been testing the flame-retardant chemical which was then used to treat children's nightwear. The Environmental Defense Fund claimed that TRIS is a cancer-causing chemical. All TRIS-treated clothes were banned and removed from the stores by the Consumer Product Safety Commission, but that agency reported some firms still selling TRIS-treated garments in June 1981.

Other flame-retardant substances are used but have not been tested.

Well, I'm not Solomon—but until we know more, use regular untreated daytime clothing for nighttime sleep! Close-fitting shirts and pants and diapers!

Furthermore, be excessively cautious. Do not let *anyone* with lighted cigarette, cigar, pipe, or joint near your baby. And keep the baby far from stove or oven or space heater.

SLEEPING BAGS

These are available in different weights—for cold or warm weather—to be worn over an undershirt and diaper, depending upon climate. The front closes with a zipper.

TERRY CLOTH STRETCH COVERALLS

A baby-size jumpsuit to grow in is the best thing to happen in baby fashion since swaddling went out of style! Lightweight, stretchable, easy-to-launder terry cloth, in a one-piece, long-sleeved, long-legged, enclosed-foot coverall—that is the "stretchie." It usually snaps down the front and part of the way down each leg for easy dressing and diaper changes, and the stretch grows to fit a baby for several months. It looks absolutely adorable in any color, on any baby. And it is so practical! Especially good for crawlers and creepers. In a survey taken by a manufacturer of baby clothing, 82 percent of the mothers questioned preferred one-piece coveralls to two-piece outfits for their four-to-eight-month-old babies to sleep in.

SWEATERS

It's not a bad idea to have one or two sweaters in each of several different weights. If you knit or crochet, you'll find lots of patterns; buy extra yarn so you can add a few rows to sleeves and sweater bottoms as your baby grows. For some reason, many patterns make the sleeves too long, and the sweaters too short; adjust as you work if possible.

HATS

Outdoors, your baby should wear a hat—usually. Naturally, you won't put on a sun-bonnet in February (unless you are in our southernmost states) or a knitted cap in July. But protection is needed from wind, dust, and especially sun and cold. The biggest problem about a hat for a baby, especially for a newborn, is the fit.

Try all hats on the baby; if they are loose, take a couple of stitches at either side in the back to make them fit. Hats that fasten with Velcro tabs or with snaps are better choices.

OUTDOOR CLOTHING

A bunting is a sort of sleeping bag for daytime outings, a kind of zippered blanket, usually with attached hood. It is great—

warm and snuggly—and will be useful if you are going to be taking out a young baby frequently, especially without a carriage. But a bunting will not do past four or five months of age.

CRIBS

Good news! A leading consumer-oriented organization has surveyed cribs on the market nationwide, and found a number of sturdy, safe models in a moderate price range. The area of a standard crib is about 53 inches long by 30 inches wide. The distance from floor to top of the crib side is about 45 inches; from a safety point of view, the higher the better. Most are equipped with casters. They have either one or two drop sides. The side should be at least 22 at its highest and at least 5 inches at its lowest. Most drop sides are activated by a foot-release mechanism, which is preferable to hand-operated releases. There are springs under the crib sides to cushion the impact, and stabilizing bars across for extra support. Some cribs also have knobs which can be tightened, reducing rattling and shaking.

In one recent year there were 9,100 estimated injuries involving cribs reported to hospital emergency rooms nationwide; this does not include injuries referred to private physicians, which escalates the number to 40,000. Mostly, tiny feet wiggled between the crib slats until the body became wedged in. Federal safety standards for cribs became effective on February 1, 1974: the spacing between crib slats should be *no greater than 2⅜ inches*. There is not necessarily a label to indicate whether a crib conforms, so bring your own ruler to check; three adult fingers occupy about the same space. Other safety features to look for: Metal hardware should be smooth-surfaced. There should be a plastic covering or teething rail on top of the crib sides. There should be no rough edges or exposed bolts. The drop mechanism should be proof against accidental release; it should be well under the rail so your leg doesn't set it off unintentionally.

Some cribs have adjustable mattress levels; this is an advantage, raising the mattress so you do less bending to take care of the very young baby, lowering it for safety with a larger and more active older child. Mattresses should fit the crib tightly with no room for a tiny face or nose to get caught between mattress and crib. If you can get two fingers between mattress and crib side, the mattress is too small.

OTHER SLEEPING PLACES

A baby needs his or her own sleeping place. A baby should *never* sleep in the same bed as any other person, not even a parent or young child, for safety reasons. But a crib is not the only sleeping place for a new, young baby. A newborn can really sleep almost anywhere, and there are many who believe that a small container such as a bassinet or cradle is a more secure environment for this recent arrival from the confining security of the womb. (I do *not* recommend such makeshifts as a bureau drawer, laundry basket, or even a sturdy box.) You won't be able to continue using one of these substitutes, though, much after baby gets to be about four months old, or earlier.

Your baby's first bed must:

Be well padded completely around all sides.

Be placed off the floor, well away from drafts and where it cannot be accidentally bumped into, pushed or tipped over.

Have a firm, waterproof mattress or mattress substitute that fits tightly.

If your life-style will include a good deal of traveling, a portable folding crib might be a good investment. It serves as a fine playpen for a traveling tot, too. The average size of a portable crib is about thirty-nine inches long by twenty-five inches wide. Accessories are all available in this size. Check safety factors, however.

SHEETS

A crib is made up with only a bottom sheet. I recommend cotton knit fitted. Sizes to fit carriage and bassinet mattresses are also available.

BLANKETS

There are, first of all, three basic kinds:

Receiving blankets. A receiving blanket is a large square of lightweight flannelette to wrap an infant in a cozy, easy-carry way. They can later be used as lightweight coverings in crib or carriage. They are also useful to pad a dressing table or on your lap while you're feeding the baby.

Crib blankets. A crib blanket is of heavier weight, is rectangular, and is made of synthetic or wool, woven or fleece covering.

Carriage throws. A carriage throw is made of wool or synthetic, often plaid, usually fringed, and is a warm outdoor blanket (not unlike a stadium robe, only smaller).

Carriage covers. A carriage cover is simply a blanket, carriage size, washable, lighter in weight than a carriage robe, and prettier, too. This is a popular gift or make-it-yourself item if you or another relative knit or crochet.

PILLOW (Don't use.)

You don't *need* them and shouldn't use them for the crib or the carriage. Some parents use a small one for the carriage to serve as a sort of bumper in the rear. I do not recommend this at all—and certainly *never put a baby's head on a pillow!* Pillows increase the possibility of suffocation.

WATERPROOF PADS OR SHEETS

Never use sheets of thin plastic to cover a mattress, or for anything to do with a baby or child. Use only the soft, almost fleecy-surfaced waterproof sheets with a rubberized inner layer (they are available in mattress size, and a large one can be trimmed to fit, or cut into several pads for travel, carriage, bassinet, and so on).

CRIB BUMPER

This is a washable, plastic-covered pad that fits completely around the inside of the crib. It is a safety and comfort item. The bumper protects a baby from drafts, from bumping into the hard wood of the crib, and from getting caught between the crib slats or in the gap between the mattress and the side of the crib. Some have an extension that fits under the mattress and helps to hold the bumper more securely in place—a good extra safety feature.

CRIB GUARDS

Better than bumper pads is a crib guard of see-through white nylon mesh. The crib guard snaps over the top and bottom rails of each crib side without interfering with the drop mechanism while it covers the spaces between the slats. It keeps a baby's arms and legs well within the crib.

CRIB MOBILE

Lying in one place for a long time with nothing to do or look at is not good for an infant. A crib mobile has colorful, interesting shapes to catch your baby's eye. Some mobiles also have music boxes. Some of these are operated by pulling on a plastic ring. Be sure that the mobile hangs well out of reach of your baby's hand, and never behind a baby's head; be sure that it is se-

curely attached; that the clamping device is in good working condition and that the construction is firm and contains nothing harmful to a baby.

DIAPER BAGS

There is a wide choice here, and in many cases a sturdy tote or beach bag will do. Things to look for are:

Washable lining
Convenient opening, easy to open with one hand
Adjustable shoulder strap
At least one zippered section inside
At least one zippered section outside
Insulated pocket for keeping bottles cold

DIAPER PAILS

Washable polyethylene plastic is the material of choice for a diaper pail. I prefer the kind with a step-on mechanism, so your hands can concentrate on holding things, but these are hard to find. The pail lid should have a container to hold a deodorant cake. Use with two removable nylon net or mesh laundry bags. (Diaper services usually provide both pails and laundry bags.)

DRESSING TABLES

Where you dress the baby is a matter of importance. For the sake of your back, use a dressing table that brings the whole process up to a comfortable height. Different types of tables offer different clothing storage features. The main thing to watch for is a strap to buckle around the baby. It should be of sturdy canvas or plastic, long enough to reach over a growing child, securely attached to the *table* (not just to the pad or mattress). *Never* leave a baby alone on a dressing table, not even for a second. Whatever else is happening, take the baby with you or put the baby on the floor.

One variation on the dressing-table theme is the old-fashioned Bathinette. It folds compactly when not needed and stands firmly on wide-based legs when ready for use. The tub part is soft and flexible, with a hose that attaches to any water faucet. Hinged at the back is a firm padded lid which folds down over the top of the tub to form a dressing table. This item is safe, convenient, and great for new families and small nursery spaces.

How It Used to Be

The daily ablution of an infant is no more natural or necessary than to take a fish out of water and cover it with dirt once a day that it may thrive better in its natural environment.

Mary Baker Eddy, *Science and Health*, 1875

DRESSING-TABLE TRAYS

A tray is useful; it will hold the lotions and such together in one place. Any pan with low sides will help you carry bath supplies from one room to another. Try decorating a baking pan with a piece of wallpaper or Con-Tact as a covering.

COVERED CONTAINERS

Small glass apothecary jars are fine for storing cotton balls, safety pins, and other small items. But plastic containers are useful too—especially if they are boilproof. Before using, sterilize jars and lids by immersing in gently boiling water for ten minutes.

BATHTUBS

A small plastic bathtub that can be placed inside your regular bathtub or on a kitchen counter is fine, and far easier than the kitchen sink. But if you use the sink, be sure it is well cleaned—and line it with a towel, or with a pad of sponge or foam rubber so that your baby won't feel any chill against

New York Public Library Picture Collection

his or her skin, and to avoid slipping and sliding. Don't forget a plastic-backed apron.

FACE MASKS

These come three to a box and should be on hand and ready to use at the first hint of sore throat or sniffles on your part. They are also useful for any visitor.

CARRIAGES

There are many choices: nonfolding or folding, single-purpose or convertible models. Then there are hard bodies, canvas, or other woven-fabric bodies, and vinyl bodies. Purpose, convenience, and, most of all, safety are the key factors in choosing.

Folding carriages can be stored in a closet or the trunk of a car. Some of them are convertible—that is, they consist of a folding frame and two interchangeable bodies, one a bassinet or carriage body, the other a stroller body. Most convertible and other carriage bodies lift off to become carrying bassinets, which can also be used instead of a crib during your baby's first months.

No carriage is completely safe. All can be tipped over, and sometimes by the baby leaning out. And babies can fall from them, or be injured by some protruding or clamping part. Here are carriage safety features to look for:

Four-wheel brakes are best; two-wheel brakes are satisfactory, and one-wheel brakes should be avoided.

The carriage should have an easy-to-operate brake release. Carriages that have to be given an upward tilt to release or apply brakes should be avoided.

Courtesy Gerico, Inc.

Avoid scissor-type folding mechanisms in which your baby's fingers or yours might get caught.

Latching mechanisms should lock in the open position to prevent accidental folding. The safest have slip rings as well as a safety bar or catch. Spring-loaded snap latches are moderately safe even without an additional safety catch, but slip rings alone should be avoided.

All latches and adjustments should *not*

be "so simple a child can do it." Rather, they should require adult strength.

The wheel base should be wide enough to support the body without tipping.

The wheels themselves should be large enough for stability and a comfortable ride.

The shopping basket should be low, under the carriage body, and centered so that it doesn't contribute to tipping.

The latches or bolts holding the carriage bed or bassinet in place on the frame should be of metal, rather than fabric or plastic. A simple fabric snap-tab is of little use, and will soon be torn off.

There should be a harness, or harness anchors at either side.

STROLLERS

A stroller backrest should be firm and nearly vertical, not forward-slanting, when in the upright position. The canopy should be high enough so that a growing baby will have enough room to sit under it.

The shopping cart in a stroller should be low on the back and either centered or over the rear wheel axle, again under the body. Any other position will throw the stroller off balance; numerous accidents have been caused by imbalance due to loaded shopping baskets in the front of strollers. The stroller should have a wide base and large wheels, and no sharp edges or scissorlike mechanism.*

Before setting out with your baby in carriage *or* stroller, always make sure that:

Latching devices are securely fastened.
Brake is operating properly and locks tightly (a two-wheel brake is best).
Child is secured by seat belt or harness.

And here are some vital *nevers*!

- *Never* allow another child to stand on any part of a carriage or stroller.
- *Never* allow a small child to push a carriage or stroller; because the handle is beyond reach, the child is likely to pull down on it, and have it fall on him or her.
- *Never* hang anything—not a shopping basket, not a coat—on the handle.
- *Never* leave a child in a carriage or

stroller untended even for a minute, even within your sight. It is all too easy for an accident to happen as a result of the brakes giving way or the carriage/stroller being thrown off balance.

INFANT SEATS

These are handy for feeding and carrying very young babies. The typical seat consists of a plastic shell with a snap-in metal support that adjusts to several positions. A wide, sturdy base and a safety belt are vital. Always make sure the support is securely in position and the safety belt in use. Always stay within arm's reach of the baby when the seat is on a table, counter, chair, or sofa. Never place an infant seat on a slippery surface such as a wet countertop or a glass-topped table. Never use an infant seat instead of a car seat. To make the bottom of an infant seat skidproof, attach rough-surfaced adhesive-backed safety tape strips.

BABY CARRIERS

There are basically two types. The soft carrier of fabric, which has no frame, is a sack-type sling seat suspended from straps that cross around the parent's shoulders and body. It can be worn either in front or back, with the baby's face toward the parent in either case. This carrier is useful until the baby can sit without help, and should be used only for young babies. Soft carriers may be somewhat difficult to adjust for a comfortable and secure fit. Most have holes for the baby's legs to go through, but at least one model snaps diaper fashion around the baby. The result is that the sides are open and a small baby could slide right on through. Avoid this type of carrier. The other type of carrier has its seat part attached to and supported by a lightweight metal frame. This frame carrier is easier to take off or put on (especially the kind that has a stand to steady it while you lift the child in and out). To fit properly, the top of the carrier should be level with the parent's shoulders when in position, and the bottom back band should be comfortable against the hip.

Since you must not use a frame-type carrier until the baby is about five months old, or able to sit up alone, you can take the baby with you when you shop for one, and try it on. Bear in mind, however, that the load will

*Even as recently as July 1981, a baby's finger was severed in a stroller.

get heavier during the months ahead! Be sure the frame is secure when being worn, and that no parts can accidentally close. Be sure there are no sharp points, edges, or rough surfaces. There should be some padding over the part of the frame that comes close to the baby's head and face.

Some models have a double seat, one inside the other, at different levels. This is an excellent feature, since it positions the growing child at the correct level according to size.

The shoulder straps of all carriers should be cushioned for your comfort. Avoid any seat that has a band or strap that is supported to protect your baby's head but instead will rub against that precious head and ears. Make sure leg openings are small enough so your baby can't slip out, and yet roomy enough not to chafe the baby's legs.

Seats should be deep enough to provide support for your baby's neck, *including* the neck and head of a young baby. All should have a safety strap to restrain children who may try to stand or climb; a child's movements may throw the parent off balance. All carriers should be made of sturdy material, such as canvas or nylon webbing, and have strong stitching, or large, heavy snaps to prevent slipping out. No metal parts should be near the baby's face; any parts of the frame that may come in contact with the baby should be padded. When wearing a baby carrier, always bend from the knees; never stoop over to pick something up. Your baby could fall out. Better yet, don't bend.

CAR SAFETY SEATS

The type of safety seat required depends on the size of the child. For the smallest, an infant carrier is necessary. This is a molded-plastic cradle type of restraint with straps that go over the baby's shoulders and around the body. In this carrier the baby lies down, but not completely horizontally. The infant carriers can be used until the baby can sit up alone, or weighs about 16 pounds, or is somewhere between six to nine months. Some infant carrier models convert to seats for older babies, and some can be used as infant seats out of the automobile as well as in it. The baby must ride facing backward.

A baby who has outgrown an infant carrier should have a car seat with a harness and/or an impact shield. The impact shield is usually of molded plastic, curving to fit loosely over the child's lap, tilting away somewhat from the chest. The shield is cushioned. This is considered the safest type of car seat for a baby by many people.

No matter what car restraint is used, the child should ride in the center of the rear seat, since this is the safest position in a car.

How It Used to Be

Traveling with Baby—

All long journeys should be avoided for young children. When they are necessary, this rule should be followed:

Hold the child in your arms, and allow the elasticity of your muscles to counteract the jolting of the car.

If this is not clear to your mind, try this experiment the next time you get on a train: Fill a glass of water and put it on the floor of the car. You will see the water splash over.

As that water is shaken, so your baby's brain and liver are shaken when you lay it down on a seat. Hold the glass of water in your hand, counteracting the jolting with your muscles, and you can keep the water smooth and quiet.

That will show you how to hold your baby, saving its liver, brain, and health at the expense of your own big, muscular energy. Don't forget this advice if you want your baby to stand the railroad trip well.

Motherhood: A Magazine for Young Wives
and Mothers, 1901

Every child car seat should have a high back. The safest also have a special strap or tether that anchors the back to the shelf behind the rear seat. Follow directions to install this type of seat.

All safety seats for infants and children must also be fastened with adult safety belts. If you use a safety seat plus harness, be sure the harness is fitted properly to the child. Many harnesses slip off very slim children, or children wearing bulky winter clothing. Buy the correct type of seat for your child's size, and *use it all the time.*

An infant, tot, or toddler who is used to a steady routine or restraint in a car will accept it more readily in later years.

Buy a seat now, and use it on your baby's very first trip—home from the hospital, or out on a visit.

Since accidents to even tiny children in automobiles are *very* common, it is vital to get and use the best safety seats available. Two organizations can help you greatly. They are Physicians for Automotive Safety, 14 Rye Ridge Plaza, Rye, New York 10580 and Action for Child Transportation Safety (ACTS), P.O. Box 266, Bothell, Washington 98011.

BABY WALKERS

I'm not very fond of baby walkers, and don't really see much necessity for their use. But if you do want one or get one as a gift, always remember that a walker gives your baby an exciting sense of mobility without any sense of danger. This means increased responsibility for you. You *must* watch your small tot at all times. Further, you should anticipate the kinds of hazards that could contribute to injuries, such as carpet edges, sidewalks, stairs, and pinch points.

If you are buying an X-frame baby walker, look for one with protective covers over accessible coil springs, spacers between scissoring components, and locking devices to prevent the X-frame from collapsing. Be sure that the walker has a wheel base wider and longer than the frame of the walker itself, so that it will be as stable as possible. Stability is important to prevent tipping.

Keep your infant and the baby walker on flat, smooth surfaces—away from carpets, door thresholds, and other obstructions. Place gates at the tops of all stairways to prevent children and their baby walkers from falling down the stairs. (Gates should be there anyway.) Also, remember to keep doors closed so that your baby cannot slide the baby walker toward the stairs.

PLAYPENS

Would that we could do without the playpen! Babies who are free to roll and tumble and play on a clean, warm, safe floor are much better off, in my opinion, than in the confines of a barred space. *But* playpens are often safer than the floor, and sometimes even useful. The main thing to remember is to keep your baby's playpen visits short and pleasant and usually within your view.

When you buy a playpen, look for one with wooden slats no more than 2⅜ inches apart so no part of the baby can possibly become wedged, or for one with very closely woven mesh netting.

Remember that it is possible for a child, unseen, to climb out of a playpen by standing on a large toy or box or by using a toy or mobile tied across the top of the playpen as a climbing device. So look carefully at the kind of playthings your baby uses in the playpen. If you want to secure toys to prevent them from being thrown out, make the cord short enough so there is *no* danger of a child being strangled.

HIGH CHAIRS

Sooner or later a high chair or feeding table becomes essential. The advantage of a high chair is that it allows your young baby to sit up at the dinner table with the rest of the family and enjoy your company. However, it is very important to look for stability and safety in the model you choose. A wide base to prevent tipping is your first consideration. Making sure the baby will not come in contact with sharp edges is next.

Make absolutely sure that the tray is properly latched to both sides and that the baby is securely fastened in by the safety straps, which should *not* be attached to the tray. Keep an eye on the baby at all times and prevent other children using the chair as a climbing device. Keep it out of major traffic areas and doorways. And since a high chair is usually in regular use in the kitchen, think carefully before you position it. It should not be close to the refrigerator, stove, or kitchen cabinets. Babies can do some very unexpected things, very fast.

A nice variation on the high chair is the feeding/play table. A Formica-topped table

From the U.S. Consumer Product Safety Commission's *Buyer's Guide,*
some tips for selecting and using nursery equipment.

Selecting Nursery Equipment	Using Nursery Equipment
Check for sturdy construction and a broad base for stability.	Supervise children—nothing can substitute for constant supervision as a safety measure.
Examine latching devices to make sure they operate properly.	Use equipment only in the way it is intended.
A safety strap is a must.	Use protective straps.
Test restraining straps.	
Make sure edges are smooth and rounded.	Make sure latching devices are securely in place.
Make sure there are no exposed screws or bolts with sharp edges or points.	Always help a baby into a stroller, walker, or high chair.
Check the distance between slats on cribs and playpens. It should be no more than 2⅜ inches.	Teach older children not to climb on high chairs; teach your baby not to stand up or climb out of the high chair without help.
Avoid scissor-sharp mechanisms.	Remove throw rugs when walkers are in use.
Be suspicious of so-called safety products and doctors' endorsements. *Just because a product is advertised as safe does not mean that it is.* [The italics are mine.]	Help the child using a walker to move across thresholds, carpet edges, and raised flooring that could cause tipping.
	Place guards at stairways and keep doors leading to stairways closed.

surface provides much more room for baby's toys and dinner and sloppiness than the usual high chair tray. A guard rail along the perimeter of the table top prevents toys and dishes from being pushed overboard. The legs are on wheels, which allows for great maneuverability. A padded seat with wipe-clean vinyl upholstery, a strap to buckle around baby, and a footrest are built in.

TOY BOXES

The most important thing to consider is the probability of your child climbing into the box along with the toys. Be sure that the lid cannot be totally closed from the inside and that it cannot be locked from the outside. In addition, make sure that there are ventilation holes in the top and side. When a toy box lid is the hinged kind, check that it is lightweight and has a device to hold it open in a raised position. If you are at all doubtful on any of these points, remove the lid en-

tirely. Choose rounded edges or pad them yourself to cut down on injuries and try to keep the box out of heavily traveled areas.

WHAT YOU NEED TO KNOW ABOUT TOYS

To your baby a toy is not a toy. For at that mysterious point when we are able to call a toy a toy, to recognize it for what it is, we have left babyhood forever. To the soft bundle that is or shortly will be yours, a toy (as far as anyone can tell) is simply part of the bundle. An extension of the self. Other fingers and toes. Colorful bits and parts of the baby whole. The fine distinctions we as adults make are simply not part of a baby's perspective.

A baby's eyes focus on and follow a bright something—perhaps a mobile—when that object moves. A new thing often creates a look on a baby's face of puzzlement, wonder, or excitement. And often a tiny body will quiver at the sight of something new. But if that object is your baby's hand or face in the mirror, the reaction may be the same. Tiny feet, too, can bring just as strong responses. One baby I know went into paroxysms of laughter at three months when he "found" his toes.

For babies, too, all objects are part of the "mouth-use or mouth-test syndrome." All small enough objects or parts of any object with hardly an exception land in a baby's mouth. This reaction pattern, as far as I have been able to tell, is universal and pervasive. There are scholarly treatises on the subject, of course. But regardless of studies there are some clearly observable facts of universal experience to which all of us bear witness. The salmon swim upstream to spawn. The squirrels gather their nuts in tree holes. The bears sleep all winter through. And the human babies put everything in their mouths.

Is the infant mouth full of extrasensory sensitivities? Is the baby's reaction related to the constant need to suck? Are all objects comparable to the life-giving breast?

The whys of this reaction can only be speculated upon, guessed at from our adult frame of reference. But in watching a baby, we see that, along with toys, fingers, toes, nose, and anything that fits, all land in that mouth sooner or later, more or less.

The hand is equally involved with the eyes and mouth in the baby's relation to objects. All babies have what we call an "involuntary grasp reaction." In other words, a baby's hand seems to grasp anything and everything automatically and often holds on like iron. This reaction, too, is usually undis-

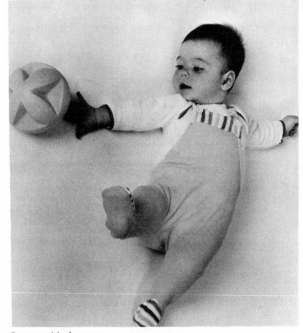

Courtesy Mothercare

criminating: a baby will hold fingers, toes, noses, and toys equally.

When a baby is able to move arms and body—which often happens much sooner than is traditionally believed—the reaction to objects is similar. There are few distinctions between types and classes of objects to try to get and hold and roll around. Those few, of course, are very important. Babies do react—from the moment of birth on—in a more intense way to brightness, movement, foods, nipples—and to the sight of a mother/father.

Every baby reacts to sound: with crying or a fearlike reaction to sudden loud sounds; with a nodding, sleepy response to soft sing-y sounds; with laughter to laughter; with tense, tight body reactions to yelling, scoldings, or strange rough sounds.

How It Used to Be

But as to rocking children, the custom is altogether absurd. He was an ingenious man who invented a mouse trap, though none but a fool first thought of a cradle; it was certainly invented to save the attendants trouble, for which, bye the bye, they suffer more in return: I never permitted a cradle to disgrace my nursery. Infants, if well, sleep without this lullaby-labour, and such forced dosings generally render them peevish and watchful in the night; which is the most proper time both for them and their nurses to enjoy their rest.

The Female Instructor; or, Young Woman's Companion, 1811

And toys, many toys, can and do bring sound to your baby's ears. Such sounds can please and soothe and puzzle. They can also create an environment in which a baby grows with pleasant, learning reactions—or the reverse.

Despite my belief that the type of toys matters greatly to infant and child, in all objectivity it is we as adults who believe that a *particular* object itself can make a difference in our baby's development. In reality, it may be we who are reacting to the toys, and the baby who is reacting more to us or more to us-cum-toy. In fact, the history of infant-stimulation programs is replete with examples of engaging the parent in a relatedness to toy-with-baby; in other words, to ways of helping parents play *with* their babies— and the toy, whatever toy it is, is a tool used between them.

Still, even if this is so, a clear necessity exists for safe and interesting objects of play to be present in every baby's life. Just as a carpenter needs a plane and a typist needs a typewriter, so too a baby needs things to play with. Play is any baby's "work." And *whatever* we may call toys, they are important to babies.

At the very least, toys are part of your baby's environment. In their presence, or in their absence. Their significance for your baby's development *may* be primarily physiological. That is, they may aid in helping the gross motor reflexes become more refined, or stronger. A baby who spends time grasping and holding different-size balls *may* develop a stronger grip in later years, or may hold smaller and larger objects in a better or quicker way.

A baby who is encouraged by the presence of a swaying mobile to move his or her eyes frequently *may* develop stronger eye muscles earlier.

But beyond physiology and body development, toys—whatever we call toys—are a crucial part of an infant's life. They represent, in fact, an active involvement in the continuing adventure and drama of world discovery that each of us, each of our babies, has repeated from time immemorial.

Infant's Mouth Can Stretch

When you shop for a rattle, *keep in mind that no part or end should be small enough to* *fit in your baby's mouth.* An infant's mouth is extremely flexible and can stretch to hold larger shapes than you might expect. To date, the largest rattle known to have lodged in a baby's throat had an end 1-3/8" in diameter. (U.S. Consumer Product Safety Commission, *Product Safety Fact Sheet No. 86: Baby Rattles,* 1978)

BASIC POINTERS ABOUT TOYS*

Toys are a necessity, not a luxury. Budget toys *in*.

Any object can represent a toy to baby or child. Look around you just where you are now. And remember that whether the object your eyes rest upon is a book, glass—or gun—it will mean *play*.

Common household or job implements may make excellent toys. But you need to find out some things about them.

Homemade or handmade toys may also be of great value. You need to know something about parts and finishes. Do watch out for thin, cheap plastic, parts that come off, paints that are leaded, or objects that are small enough to get into a baby's mouth.

An environment rich in play objects is preferable to one that is too sparse. Don't be afraid of having too many toys, *but don't give your baby too many at one time.* Three or four are enough until it's time to change them.

Take toys seriously—at least as seriously as you take your job or career; they *can mean* life or death, or a child with enriched capabilities.

In buying, making or converting objects to toys, *always* think safety first. (See safety lists in this section.)

If a relative or friend—or even husband or wife or other child—gives a toy gift which is dangerous or otherwise bad for an infant, *do not use it.* Return it, throw it away, lock it up for later years. Try to spare feelings, but *not* at the expense of your baby.

In giving a toy gift to a baby, remember the wrappings and the package; they can be fun to use—or lethal. Plastic wrap is dangerous.

*These are based upon the collective experiences of many specialists.

Great big enormous toys may be decorative and impressive for adults—but overwhelming to a baby.

Tiny bitty toys should *never* be given to babies.

Records, cloth books, clocks, maps, globes, scales, calendars may not seem appropriate for your new baby—but if they are there, ready to use at a later time, you'll find yourself and your baby making use of them.

Toys and play objects need good, safe, sturdy containers. Open shelves and shelves in closed cupboards with latches too strong for small fingers are probably best.

Be sure to have a locked closet with a high shelf where you can store things for future use.

Never leave toys scattered on the floor—or even *one* toy. Too easy to trip.

Never leave a toy in your infant's bassinet, crib, or carriage when the baby is sleeping.

Always think of toys as appropriate for either sex.

Never use a toy as punishment or reward.

Even with a tiny infant, don't just grab a toy away suddenly (unless something dangerous is happening)—remove it slowly. Try distracting the baby away from the toy first.

Use the new toy to play *with* your baby. Don't just dump it and forget it. Try a little buildup.

Read toy and child experts. And question them in your own mind, too. Don't believe all you read—but if many of them agree, perhaps you should think twice about whatever advice is given, even if your point of view is different.

THE MANY USES OF TOYS

Toys help children to grow emotionally. Mastery through play gives children that sense of pleasure and accomplishment so important to the development of a positive self-image. Toys provide props and models for role-playing. Toys enable children to try on the world, to test what they think and feel about themselves and others. (Multi-racial toys, for example, provide children with a background for feeling at ease in a multi-ethnic society.) Toys also provide a means for interaction among children and between children and parents. Toys are a way for children to explore and understand their fantasies as well as the adult world. (Public Action Coalition on Toys, *Guidelines on Choosing Toys for Children*, 1976)

A PAEAN TO A SMALL GROUP, OR WHY TOYS ARE BETTER TODAY

Your baby is luckier than those born in the early 1970s. Toys *are* better today—safer, at the least. There have been various forces at work to make them better, including the existence of the Consumer Product Safety Commission and, of course, the mass media. The commission could and should be a *lot* better, and the media could pay much more non-Christmastime attention. But they do exist—and any attention helps.

Still, the most potent force for better toys has been a small group of volunteers (including myself) who have no axe to grind, no personal stake in trying to improve the toy market. This group, Public Action Coalition on Toys or PACT, was started as an offshoot of a Ralph Nader activity.

Quiet and not-so-quiet pressure on the toy industry has brought about a sharp recognition that safety in toys is *not* an accident.

PACT now has produced a booklet that you can send for. Write to (include $1 for postage and handling) Victoria Reiss, PACT, 222 E. 19th Street, New York, New York 10003.

You may, for your baby's sake, want to get involved with PACT, which is greatly concerned about sexism in toys and about toys of violence, too. It is my conviction that violent toys are to be avoided at all times. The Swedish government has banned all war toys. Would that all other governments did so! In my opinion toys that promote sexism are almost as bad.

◇ ◇ ◇

**Something That
Is Something Else**

The toy that can "become" will stimulate more creative activity and hold a child's interest much longer than the plaything that simply is-what-it-is. (*Today's Child*, April 1977)

◇ ◇ ◇

How It Used to Be

Baby rattles have been known from prehistory and whether in wood, ivory, precious metals, wicker, celluloid, tin or plastics will continue to the end of time, puzzling and charming the animal or human young. It can soothe or alarm, be rhythmic or sound at random, a truly wonderful thing. Rattles of surprisingly modern design have been found at Pompei, and Roman rattles of terra-cotta, shaped like a bird or piglet, would delight the child of today.

Arnold Haskell and Min Lewis, *Infantilia*, 1971)

Spaces and Places for a New Baby

A BIGGER FAMILY MEANS S-P-A-C-E

Where will you put the baby?

If that seems like a silly question, stop and think. A baby doesn't take up much space—but the supplies and equipment you must have certainly do. And as the baby grows to crawler and then toddler stages (how quickly this happens is unbelievable!), more space is needed. So it is important to figure out how a baby will fit into your present home, or if you will need more space, and when.

To analyze your space needs for the foreseeable future, consider the following:

A new baby may stay for a while in the parents' room, but a separate room is preferable toward the end of the breast-feeding period.

Every child has a right to privacy, even at a very young age. A small area of private territory—even partitioned, or just a personal storage or thinking space—is better than a large area that must be shared.

Children need safe crawl and stretch space, safe toddling and walking space, safe playing and exploring space.

There must be adequate room for storage of essentials. Otherwise, every member of the family will constantly be tripping over things, moving things about, and not able to locate precisely what is needed—resulting in constant chaos. Where *will* you keep diapers, toiletries, travel supplies, the carriage when it is not in use . . . and all the other things you will buy or receive?

Where will you feed the baby? Is there room for a feeding table? Where could a high chair go? Remember that room is needed for *you and your chairs* as well as for baby's chair at mealtime!

Where will you bathe the baby? Will you use the kitchen sink? Is there room on the kitchen counter to dress the baby, or will you be carrying a wet child through the house to get to a convenient dressing area? (This is to be avoided, obviously, unless you like a stream of water dripping over your floors and a baby in and out of drafts.) Is there room in the bathroom for a portable Bathinette (if you can find one)? Will you use a plastic bathtub in the regular tub and bend awkwardly to bathe the baby? Is there room in the bathroom for baby's toiletries?

Where will your baby play? Where can the baby crawl safely, without restrictions? Where will you set up the playpen and, later, other play equipment? Where can a tower of blocks or a nest of stuffed animals be left overnight?

You need privacy, too! Think of where you can be alone or together, make love without inhibitions, read in peace, or even watch TV!

Is there separate space for the possessions of each of your present children, or children to come? It's important that each child's belongings be kept separate, unless you want a constant job as a referee. It's important, too, for each child to be able to have friends visit without interference from brothers and sisters.

MOVING? NOW?

In general, it's easier to move during pregnancy than it will be later on, with a baby or toddler. And it's best to plan this upheaval for the middle three months of pregnancy, instead of during the first and last trimesters. But—there might be special circumstances to consider. Certainly, if a move would depend on a new job opportunity that will not be available for several months, moving must wait. If finances are uncertain, this is not the time to undertake the high initial expenses of moving plus the probably greater expense of maintaining a larger house or apartment. It might be better to postpone a move until you can see more clearly where you're headed financially, even if the baby would be several months or a year old. Or if a pregnancy is under close medical observation for complications, a move is probably out of the question. So weigh carefully the factors that apply in your own particular situation.

MAKING DECISIONS ABOUT MOVING

Consider the importance to you of these factors; balance them carefully:

Need for More Space
 A separate room for the baby
 A room for each child
 More play space
 More storage space
 More space for adult needs and activities
  (entertaining, office in the home,
  hobbies)

Closeness to Friends and Relatives
 Close to other family members
 Close friends in the neighborhood
 Other families with young children in
  the neighborhood

Job Opportunities
 New or better job for father
 New or better job for mother
 Part-time work opportunities
 Continuing educational opportunities

Safety Factors in the Neighborhood
 Many unfenced swimming pools
 Waterways without signs or people

 Broken sidewalk and street pavements
 Dark streets, dim streetlights
 Unleashed dogs
 Pollution heavy in air or water
 High crime rates
 A lot of traffic without traffic lights

Community Resources for Child Rearing
 Many other families with babies
 Mixed age groups
 Active community recreational programs
 Good community social agencies (family
  counseling, mental health, child
  welfare)
 Good medical services and health
  facilities
 Excellent emergency services
  (ambulances, twenty-four-hour hot
  lines, poison control center, and
  others)
 Homemaker service if needed
 Day-care services
 Nursery schools
 Other schools and colleges
 Playgrounds (safe ones)
 Libraries, museums, and other cultural
  institutions
 Income support services if needed
 Houses of worship nearby

SOME EASY GUIDES TO HELP DECIDE ABOUT MOVING

Use the following pro-con checklist. It will help you both think through the values of moving—and to decide whether to do so during pregnancy. You can and should add your own particular pros and cons to get a full picture. If you find many checks in the pro column, the decision will probably be weighted toward moving. However, even one factor—such as being close to family and friends where you now are—may be the strongest element and prevent you from moving during pregnancy.

ABOUT NEIGHBORHOODS FOR BABY GROWING

There are several key factors about good neighborhoods for times of pregnancy, delivery, and child care that do not easily fit

PRO–CON CHECKLIST

Pro Moving Now	**Con Moving Now**
—— Too crowded now	—— Enough make-do space
—— Want to be closer to sources of help, family, and friends	—— Close to family and friends now
—— Have a great new place	—— Housing is adequate
—— Present place is dark, damp, and inconvenient	—— Present space is light, airy, relatively convenient
—— Air and/or water are heavily polluted	—— Pollution rate is low
—— Enough money for a move and more costly housing	—— Strapped for funds now anyhow
	—— New housing too expensive
—— Present environment is unsafe or depressing	—— Environment is relatively safe and friendly
—— Few facilities or programs for young families here	—— Many programs for young families
—— Better medical care elsewhere	—— Have a great doctor now
—— Few friends here	—— More friendship opportunities
—— Better jobs elsewhere	—— Have a fine job situation

into ways of checking off on a list. These all relate to that most intangible of factors: quality of life.

Actually, some aspects are not so intangible. You can tell by just walking or driving through the streets if a neighborhood is deteriorating or already has. Is there much litter by the curbs? Have the dogs taken over the public walkways? Does the housing look tacky or greatly in need of paint and repairs?

Unless you are into helping a community reverse a downward trend—and if you are, three cheers for you!—you would do better for yourselves and your new baby to move into a more upbeat community. That doesn't mean a move to the antiseptic unreality of a beautiful suburb.

Isolation is one vital intangible to look at. Will you be physically or socially isolated? You may adore peace and quiet and communing with nature. But baby-time is the time for thinking more about close-by sources of aids, close-by easy sociability. Look at any new community with this factor uppermost in your minds. Try to estimate a *neighborhood's sociability quotient.*

In a *non*-isolated living circumstance, there are easy sources of learning about having a baby and about baby care. There are nearby sources of help in emergencies. There are health and medical aids within short distances. There are potential baby-sitters or child-care exchange possibilities. There are companions and learning sources for your child.

More, and less obvious—isolation can make every problem loom larger. It affects the rate of postpartum depression in communities where young families are all new, and alone. It affects the rate of child neglect and abuse. It affects the rates of alcoholism and other social indicators of problem living situations.

There are not many Thoreaus in the world. Living in a non-isolated neighborhood can be much better for you and yours.

Another intangible factor you should consider in where you move is the *mixed* nature of the community. Not all of us have that choice anymore. Age- and class- and race-segregated communities seem more the rule than the exception. However, if you do have a choice, consider the benefits to you and your family—and to our entire society, in fact—if you opt for the mixed neighborhood.

Age variations where you live means an easier way for you to develop friendships and to learn from people who are older than you, and whose experiences are different from yours. As your child grows, he or she will see and be familiar with people who can represent grandparents, who can bring more interest and a varied coloration to growing up. In the opinion of experts in the field, the child who knows intimately that living includes aging will be far less likely to reject his or her parents at a later stage of life, too. It is my own opinion that a bonding situation occurs between the very young and the old, which means greater empathy of the young for the old throughout life.

Economics, religion, and race still divide us enormously. But if you care about how your child grows, whether he or she becomes helpful to others who are different— or mistrustful of them, you will care about your child's leading a life that is rich in its dimensions. You will want your baby to grow into an understanding person who believes in and lives according to the basics of our democracy: equality, opportunity, freedom of choice, fairness. All of these child-growing assets are harder to achieve in single-class, single-race, segregated neighborhoods.

There is something about the mix of peoples, under decent living conditions and in circumstances of tolerance, that tends to produce people who *are* understanding. Of course, many a leader in peaceful race relations was born into a very segregated community. But the averages are the other way. Familiarity sometimes breeds contempt; more often it can breed a sense of humanness.

Neighborhoods that care about the handicapped matter, too. Watch for easy-access situations, preschool and school programs, work opportunities. Neighborhoods that include instead of exclude truly grow better people of all sizes.

But Will *You* Move?

The probability of migrating is greatest for women at age 22. . . . young married women (14 to 19 years old) are more likely than young married men to move between states. Married women under 45 are more mobile than single women of this age probably because of moves associated with setting up a new household, the birth of a child, or a husband's job transfer. After age 30, divorced, widowed, and separated women are more likely than married or single persons of the same age to change their place of residence. (Bureau of the Census, *A Statistical Portrait of Women in the United States*, April 1976)

IF YOU DECIDE TO MOVE WHILE PREGNANT

Decide on the most comfortable way to get to your destination—auto, train, plane.

Consult your doctor or nurse-midwife about the amount of physical exertion you're planning. Limitations on activities are highly individual and no blanket restrictions can be given. There may be valid reasons for not hanging wallpaper or heavy draperies at this time.

Arrange for a new doctor, birthing center, or hospital, or a new midwife, in advance if you can.

Even if you get a medical go-ahead, *take it easy*. If you get exhausted or are under physical and mental strain, you cannot provide support for your unborn child as well as when you are mentally and physically at your best.

Avoid overexertion by being organized, getting whatever help is needed, and planning and doing one thing at a time.

If you're moving to another country, join Intermedic, Inc., at 777 Third Avenue, New York, New York 10017, or the International Association for Medical Assistance to Travelers, Empire State Building, 350 Fifth Avenue, Suite 5620, New York, New York 10001, which gives a list of participating physicians in foreign countries.

ENVIRONMENTAL SAFETY

There is one other large-scale factor which is usually invisible to everyone moving into a new neighborhood. This is the quality of safety in the environment. Today—and for the foreseeable future—this type of safety is crucial for all of us, but particularly for young families with pregnant women and new babies and small children. We don't know the causes of most birth defects, of most mental retardation, even of many at-birth physical anomalies and serious later-in-life diseases.* But almost daily we find out more

*I have heard several scientists estimate that 50 to 80 percent of birth defects are caused by environmental pollutants and hazards!

and more about the effects of one pollutant or supposedly "safe" substance after another.

In various areas of the world during the 1970s industrial waste products poisoned local communities, creating illness and anxiety and apparently engendering a higher rate of genetic defects—some of which will endanger future generations or show up as later-in-life ailments. In Japan, the late Eugene Smith, the noted photographer, documented the effects of industrial mercury poisoning. In Seveso, Italy, a whole area was poisoned by Dioxin.

In Niagara Falls, New York, in the Love Canal area, 80 different chemicals became the waste material that posed a real threat to children and families. The threat was so serious that the government is paying for the necessary relocations of families. I have heard a recent (1980) report that 80 percent of the Love Canal women who were or became pregnant had either stillbirths or babies with birth defects. There has also been a state-sponsored study denying that there were *any* ill effects.

In 1973 virtually all the meat, poultry, and dairy products produced in the entire state of Michigan were, in essence, contaminated by a fire-retardant chemical called PBB. This occurred when Michigan Chemical Company packaged the material in the wrong bags and the Michigan Farm Bureau mixed it with cattle feed.

As Stephanie G. Harris and Joseph H. Highland have pointed out in *Birthright Denied: The Risks and Benefits of Breast Feeding,* "Some symptoms of PBB's poisoning are: weight loss, fatigue, loss of hair, and aching of joints." In addition, these researchers note that "PBB's are linked to liver degeneration and birth defects . . . [and] can cross the placental barrier and accumulate in the liver and fat of the fetus." Since babies may not readily metabolize PBBs but rather store them in the body fat, the effect of small doses over time may pose a highly significant risk.

In the spring of 1979 the entire world was mesmerized by an accident at the Three Mile Island nuclear plant near Harrisburg, Pennsylvania. Pregnant women and small children were evacuated from the immediate area. Small amounts of radiation did escape from the plant. In addition to the fear that the entire state might become severely contaminated, grave concern was expressed about the effects of low-level nuclear radiation on unborn babies and small children. We still don't know what these effects have been or might be.

These have been the spectacular events. There are many, many others—often unnoticed problems of environmental safety, ranging from trucks carrying dangerous materials through neighborhood streets to gas pipes badly connected under those same streets to nuclear or other nearby plants, creating hazards for you and yours.

Actually, there are midnight movers who dispose of toxic chemicals under cover of darkness. According to Marc Leepson in *Editorial Research Reports News Brief:* "Midnight movers operate in nearly every state of the union. They have dumped toxic substances in sewers, streams, lakes, rivers, oceans, old quarries, forests, fields, trenches and even along roads." With an estimated 70,000 chemicals manufactured and another 1,000 new chemical compounds introduced each year, midnight movers may well continue to flourish.

One of the well-known, well-documented but least visible hazards is the existence of lead paint on interior walls and doors and banisters. Very little is done about this problem despite common knowledge. And few among us, finding a charming apartment or house of an older vintage, think to question the nature of the paint on the windowsills. Yet that paint, even covered by another coat, is a potential danger to a new baby. Mental retardation, behavior problems, physical ailments of all kinds can be caused by lead paint chewed on, ingested, burned, breathed in.

Do you know if your new neighborhood's water is coming to you in old, decaying, and hazardous lead pipes? This was happening in Bennington, Vermont, for a number of years before the condition was corrected. The city of Boston is now faced with this problem, and Miami may be. The overwhelming majority of cities and towns haven't even looked at their water pipe situation.

Since the hazards are so pervasive, what any parent wants to know is: How can I protect my baby, unborn or born? Before you move to a particular community, you can only ask questions. You might, however, visit city hall, talk to officials and workers and storekeepers, call local agencies, check out a few plants and a few organizations, read the local newspapers very closely, and listen to the local radio and television news.

You might avoid becoming another family in the stream of the new refugees—the refugees from environmental contamination.

◇ ◇ ◇

Low Radiation Affects Babies Most*

A detailed study of cancer statistics in Connecticut and nearby New England indicates that cancer mortality increased sharply around two large nuclear reactors in southeastern Connecticut in direct relation to the measured pattern of accumulated levels of strontium-90 in the local milk. Cancer rates increased most strongly closest to the Millstone Nuclear Power Station located in Waterford where the measured strontium-90 levels reached their highest values, with lesser rises being observed for areas with lower values of strontium-90 in the milk located at increasingly greater distances in every direction away from the Millstone Plant, [the plant] known to have released the largest amount of radioactive gases ever officially reported for any nuclear plant in the United States. . . .

Thus, the range of sensitivity can easily vary by a factor of 100 to 1000, depending on the age and the intensity of the radiation, the effect per unit absorbed dose being most serious for very low-level, protracted environmental exposures to the developing fetus and the individual with reduced immune resistance over 65 years of age, in agreement with the observations of Bross.

This means that the most serious of all radiation exposures are not brief medical x-rays and diagnostic isotope tests for the adult, but prolonged environmental exposures to fallout accumulating in the body from nuclear bomb-testing and releases from nuclear facilities acting slowly on the infant in utero, the young child and the oldest individuals in our society. . . .

. . . Each year that we persist in closing our eyes to the new data, we will increase the total amount of Sr-90 accumulated in the soil and thus the biological damage to our newborn and the cancer risk for our older

population. But if we should be able to accept these disturbing findings, then the evidence for the declining cancer rates in the least polluted areas of our country clearly points the way to the possibility of greatly reducing the risk of cancer and chronic disease in the years to come as we learn how to prevent the subtle damage from what we once believed were harmless levels of man-made and natural background radiation. (Dr. Ernest J. Sternglass, University of Pittsburgh, testimony presented at a congressional seminar on low-level radiation, February 10, 1978)

◇ ◇ ◇

TIPS ABOUT HOME FIXING-UP

Painting, papering, floor sanding, carpentry, electrical work, linoleum and carpet layings should all be done *before* you move in—if possible. Smoke alarms installed, too.

Tub or shower floor grips (or a good stay-down bath mat) are a necessity to prevent slipping and falling while you're baby-carrying. They should be there the day you move in.

Carpeting or rubberized stair treads can also be an important security item before and after the baby comes. Polished floors and stairs are very dangerous.

Lightproof window shades or curtains may help you both get a little more sleep when you most need it—immediately after the move, and during baby's nap times later on.

Be sure to check the number and places of electrical outlets in advance—and get a licensed electrician to add new ones or cover old ones. (You should not have a lot of extra plugs on one outlet, or extra cords to trip over when you're planning for a small child—or while you're pregnant.) Be sure to get outlet covers for all those not in use—for the protection of tiny exploring fingers.

---

*There are some scientists who question the validity of Dr. Sternglass's methodology and findings. However, I have never heard the value of this particular piece of research questioned. And, even more significant, *no one* has ever claimed that strontium-90 is *good* for babies.

Furnishings for the Nursery

SOME ELEMENTS EVERY NURSERY SHOULD HAVE

Soft and pleasant lighting. Most babies' eyes are sensitive to harsh lights, so you must give this thought and time.

Way to control the lighting. Again, think naps, nighttime, getting around in the dark.

Soft or bright primary colors. Avoid depressing or dark shades.

Soft floors. To ease noise and tumbles.

Airiness without draftiness. Chilliness should be avoided.

Sunlight. Sunlight carries vitamin D, which helps prevent rickets. Also, sunlight has obvious psychological and health benefits.

A safe and secure baby sleeping place. Bassinet, cradle, or crib.

A comfortable place for adult sitting. Best bet: rocking chair.

A comfortable place for adult lying down. Best bet: couch, cot, single bed.

Good storage for supplies. Cupboards, open shelves, drawers, closet space—actually all are needed.

A changing area. With supplies conveniently right there.

Wall decorations and toys. These are really *essential* for best baby development!

Bathing equipment and supplies. In or out of the nursery itself.

Step-on can and/or wastebasket. For disposal of waste materials.

Table for small convenience items. A few diapers, a box of pop-up tissues, a pacifier, and so on. Could be a shelf also.

Equipment for transporting baby. Carryall, carriage, car seat, or whatever.

Safe play space for baby. This can be the floor (cover all outlets!—and keep it clean) which is the best place in one way. Or a playpen. Or a sling seat. Or a play table.

Special eating place and equipment for later on. Eating table or high chair, plus dish, spoon, and baby foods. (If you make your own, the equipment to do so.) Not necessarily in nursery.

A way of laundering. Not in the nursery room itself, of course. But equipment in the house is easiest—if possible.

ALL ABOUT A NURSERY

SPACE STRETCHERS

Most people, at the beginning of both their families and their careers, simply do not live in roomy homes. Yet a baby coming means space is necessary. You must make room for your baby. What can you do?

Quite a lot, really. If you're not moving, you can use many ingenious tricks to stretch the space available to you now. Here are some ideas:

Baby's Room

Partition off a portion of another room. If the area to be given to your baby does not contain a window, use a partition only two-thirds floor-to-ceiling height. A dining alcove is usually about eight by ten feet, and windowed. A partition can be louvered panels, hinged to fold like shutters. Place storage units alongside the partition wall for sound insulation—floor-to-ceiling shelves

197

containing diapers, blankets, and clothing will be remarkably good insulation. Where to eat? That's easy—move your dining right into the living room.

If your home includes a bedroom you could give a corner of it to your newborn. Screens also make a useful partition for a smaller space. Even in a corner, the arrangement can certainly work for the bassinet.

Some new parents move out of their bedroom and give it over to their baby while they convert the living room into a nighttime bedroom. This arrangement usually makes for a longer postbaby period in the prebaby housing.

Some couples have put two large back-to-back closets together—and *voilà!* a divider for a baby's room.

Balconies and porches have been enclosed for baby space, and parts of kitchens have been given over to supplies and equipment—*never* for sleeping! Just make sure your arrangements are healthy and safe!

DECORATING THE NURSERY

Are you decorating for a baby, or are you decorating for a baby who will grow into a child? Pink and blue and fluffy lambs and white eyelet cotton are lovely for a newborn. But an infant doesn't stay an infant for very long, and such dainty decor doesn't suit the perpetual-motion style of a two-year-old or three-year-old. If you've always wanted an ethereal-looking, quintessentially delicate nursery, go right ahead and have one—it's your baby.

But if you want to be practical, think ahead: the nursery you prepare now is the room your growing child may have to live in for the next eighteen years! Plan it as carefully as you plan any other room in the house. Consider colors to be lived with, not just looked at. Consider quality in furnishings. Consider sturdiness, and ease of maintenance. Consider the effect that a room's appearance can have on the person who inhabits it.

Color

Pink and blue represent sexist and other problems. If you have decorated everything in pink in advance, you're sure to have a boy. Some parents use both pink and blue in an equal mix, which is a lovely solution. Or you can avoid the hassle completely and pick a cheerful color anyone can live with—

sunny yellow, cherry orange, apple green, restful mauve.

Floor Coverings

Don't have a bare floor! Crawling babies need a warm, soft floor; playing toddlers need a surface that can support block fantasies and zooming cars. Just-walking tots need a nonslip surface—*and* a soft, bounce-proof floor to take spills on. All children need a splinter-free floor.

There are partisans of carpeting, and advocates of cushioned vinyl. Each has its merits, and its disadvantages. The qualities to look for in any floor covering are as follows:

Is it easy to clean and mop up spills? No question, vinyl has the edge here, although the new miracle-fiber kitchen-type carpets are treated to be spill-resistant.

Does it give protective cushioning against falls? Carpeting wins out on this count, although many vinyls nowadays have an underlayer of foam rubber that is somewhat protective.

Is it easy to put down (and perhaps pick up when you move)? There are do-it-yourself versions of both vinyls and carpets, and some versions of each are available in easy-to-manage tiles or squares. Wall-to-wall carpeting usually requires professional installation.

Walls

Washable wallpaper provides color, pattern, and practicality, and would be a fine choice if you own your own home. However, in most apartment leases, there is a clause stating that any wall coverings added by the tenant must be removed by the tenant at moving-out time. If you can't see the expenses of wallpapering rented quarters, a washable semigloss paint might be your best choice.

In deciding on a color for painted walls, bear in mind that dark colors and bright ones make a room seem smaller; light colors give an illusion of spaciousness.

WARNING ABOUT LEAD-BASED PAINT

Lead paint has caused poisoning in babies and children—resulting in abdominal pain, vomiting, joint pains, mental retardation, and eye and other problems. But lead-based paint is no longer being manufactured. Some firms, unfortunately, do try to get away with things—and occasionally, against the law, lead paint for interiors will be made and sold. You can check with your local health department and with the Consumer Product Safety Commission.

Use only recently purchased paint. *Do not use old paint.* When refinishing old furniture, *strip off all the old paint.* Babies and toddlers may scratch and nibble their way through several layers of painted finishes, getting into paints of dubious composition on the way. And the new finish will adhere better and look best if you get down to the bare wood before applying it. Do not burn off old paint, even outside. The fumes create poisoning.

Furniture

Your choices are limitless. First, there is traditional baby furniture available in everything from ready-to-finish to Italian Provincial. Then there is baby furniture that converts for later use: a crib that becomes a bench, a changing table that converts to a desk. One couple furnished the baby's room with most of the items that would be needed later on. Here's what they bought:

A crib
A daybed
A wall unit, consisting of two three-drawer chests, a two-door cabinet, and a large hutch-type bookcase
A matching night table
A ready-to-finish hinged-lid "stereo cabinet" to serve as a toy chest, enameled white

The crib, wall unit, and night table were of walnut and clean-lined. The daybed was used by the mother when the baby was ill or wakeful, and sometimes just for naps. It substituted for a changing table, turning dressing time into play time for mother and baby alike, and was a comfortable nursing seat also. (The armrest was the right height, the seat firm.) The crib and toy chest were later handed down to a baby sister.

Window Treatments

For privacy and room darkening at nap time, something must cover the windows. It must be easy to clean, and should fit in with the color scheme of the room. Shades, curtains, or blinds are all usually fine—but avoid shutters, for tiny fingers could get caught in the hinged joints. Curtains can be standard tie-back, crisscross, or draw draperies, but café style is well suited to a growing child's room. Draw draperies are very convenient, however, for a parent with a babe in arms. (Be sure that the cord is *securely* anchored and not hanging loose.) Also, such draperies can be lined with a lightproof material for daytime room darkness. Draperies also can be converted to curtains later, with the addition of contrasting materials.

Wall Hangings

What you hang on the nursery walls is important! Your baby's surroundings now and in the future can stimulate future interests.* It is not just decoration—it serves many purposes related to a baby's development. First of all, wall items aid in encouraging baby's eyes to focus, and also encourage eye-mind coordination. Second, whatever is on the wall enhances the mood of the room—bright, gay, alert (and the mood of a room *may* influence personality development to some extent!). Third, wall decor is a learning experience in itself, perhaps developing your child's taste for color and design, perhaps teaching object recognition.

Nothing needs to be permanent. Think of the walls as your baby's own private gallery, and change the "exhibit" frequently. Be sure to leave space for your child's own found objects or artwork; toddlers are prolific creators.

A PAEAN TO THE ROCKING CHAIR

The old-fashioned rocking chair is back in style, thank heaven! You can forget the hurly-burly outside your door and create an

---

*One of my now-grown-up babies adored a painting (a copy) of Van Gogh's, remembered it years later, and on a trip to France happily found the original, Van Gogh's room at Arles.

island of rest and peace in your home—for you and your baby. If you spend a little while each day rocking yourself and your new diaper-clad bundle, you'll see the difference it makes, and why.

Your new baby may soon get the notion that a little play at three in the morning is a fine diversion. And that's where the rocking chair comes in. There's nothing like that gentle, swaying motion to put a baby back in dreamland.

Perhaps you're afraid that your baby will become too dependent upon the rocking chair to put him or her to sleep? It's better than walking the floor! And this, too, will provide a soothing interlude during your baby's stimulating day—and will lead to better sleep at night.

Years ago the cradle was standard equipment. And for very good reasons. By an attached rope or pedal, a mother could rock her baby to sleep—and all without getting out of bed herself! The cradle is also back in vogue to some extent but the rocking chair makes a grand substitute.

Little babies are used to a rocking motion. Before birth, in their mother's womb, they are constantly being rocked. Then they are born and life suddenly becomes quite stationary. Is it any wonder that babies miss the continual motion? Often, unexplainable crankiness, sleeplessness, and the need to be carried around a lot will vanish with a little regular rocking. An attack of colic can sometimes be relieved when baby is held against mother's shoulder and rocked and sung to softly.

And this brings to mind another of the fine results which come about through the use of a rocking chair—singing! For some mysterious (and, I'm sure, quite mystical) reason, mothers (and fathers) tend to break into song while rocking their baby. Singing in itself is relaxing—and babies, of course, adore the combination of songs and rocking. (Incidentally, they may soon begin to burble a few tunes themselves.)

You'll find the rocking chair a fine place to nurse. Your baby's head will fit easily into the crook of your elbow as it rests on the arm of the chair.

Another important feature of a rocking chair is the pleasure that it can bring to *you*, by providing change of pace at odd mo-

ments during your busy day/night. You'll be thankful for the warmth of feeling, the renewal of energy that rocking will bring to you—with or without your baby on your lap.

The chair you buy should be comfortable for you. The back should be high enough so that you can easily rest your head against it. The arms should be low. And the seat should be the right distance from the floor for your length of leg. A sturdy, comfortable chair will be a boon and a pleasure to both your baby and you—and the rest of your family, too.

A GROWING-UP NURSERY

There are several items in the marketplace which have been designed to grow up with a baby. Others can be found in catalogs and stores, or made yourself. The concept to keep in mind is that almost anything can have more than one use. A bassinet can become a travel bed; a couch can be a trundle bed; storage drawers can fit under a bottom bunk bed; tables can grow in height and width with additions; storage bins, cupboards, and shelves adapt to many different room styles as wall units, room dividers, bedside and end tables. One of the few baby items that does not seem to have a change-and-grow use is the Bathinette—and now someone will probably let me know how they have used it later as a planter or a fish tank!

Family raising and working and general complications of living leave little shopping time in many of our lives. Looking ahead now to what can be adapted for a growing child could save time and money later.

WHAT'S GOOD FOR THE KITCHEN CAN BE GOOD FOR THE BABY

The following items, all made by Rubbermaid* of that company's usual sturdy, easy-to-clean plastics, can be extremely useful for keeping baby's equipment organized and ready at hand:

Turntable and twin turntable: can serve as a dressing table tray for baby oils, cot-

---

*I happen to be familiar with that company's products. If you prefer other firms which make similar items, don't hesitate to use them.

ton balls, and the like in the nursery. In kitchen or dining area, use it to store baby feeding equipment.

Storage bins, in different sizes: hang on the wall in nursery or bathroom or on doors; choice of 11 inches wide by 3¾ inches deep by 2 inches high, or 11 by 4¼ by 4¼.

Stacking modular shelves are a convenient size: 9¼ by 12¼ by 6. They interlock to stack securely on a counter or table top, or they can be used side by side on narrow bookcase shelves to organize baby clothing.

Clean-up caddy: a partitioned bin with a carrying handle, 11 by 5½ by 14¾. Keep baby supplies in it on the dressing table in the nursery, and carry it to any room where baby is being tended. Good to fill with toys, too. And easy to manage for visits to neighbors' or grandparents' or a day at the beach.

Needless to say, when your baby is past the nursery age, all of these items will come in handy in the kitchen, laundry, and cleaning closet.

THINGS FOR THE BABY'S MEDICINE CHEST

While there are very few items that are absolutely essential to have on hand for a new baby, there are some that can be very useful. Your doctor may add to this suggested list.

Cotton balls (2 or 3 boxes). These are very useful for wiping off a tiny bottom.

Baby oil. A lightweight oil is considered best.

Rectal thermometer. Two, since one is bound to be lost or break in the middle of the night. (There's a new thermometer, a 3-inch plastic strip to be held on the forehead, that takes 15 seconds(!) to register the temperature. It's called the Fever Scan.)

Baby nail-scissors with ball tops

Hand tissues (lots of them). Pop-up type is most convenient.

Some cloth diapers, even if you use only the other kind, because cloth diapers are marvelous for spitting up and wiping up and general baby cleanup.

Ipecac syrup. A lifesaver in many cases of poisonings. It should not be used in some situations; *read the label.*

Vitamins or supplements. Any kind that are necessary *and* recommended by your baby's doctor.

Pure soap bars (several; for bath time)

Baby comb and brush

Cornstarch (instead of or in addition to powder)

Soft baby-size washcloths (several)

Bandages (for comfort later in the year)

Petroleum jelly

Rubbing alcohol (to bring down a fever)

I have deliberately excluded from the above list: baby aspirin, paregoric, Kaopectate, and numerous other common products because I am uncertain about their safety. Do check with your doctor.

Making Your Home Safe for the Baby

HOME ACCIDENTS ARE NO ACCIDENT

You, like all parents-to-be or new parents, are concerned about your baby's health, well-being, *and* safety. You will take various precautions to try to ensure that your baby will be protected from harm. On these pages there are enormous aids to help you. One great help will be your own alertness and attitude about prevention and safety.

Do you feel and understand that safety for your child goes into every room of your home, indeed every area where your baby will be? If so, a crucial aspect of preventing accidents is already part of your psychology.

Because accidents represent one of the major public health problems we face—and because so *very* many happen to children (see below), I have included some beyond-the-nursery material. Just to alert you. Also, check the Bibliography and the Resource List for further information.

And remember that the so-called inevitable is often *not* that at all. Accidents usually don't *have* to happen.

SAFETY IS *NOT* AN ACCIDENT

Here is a short list of common opinions:

- What will be, will be.
- No matter what you do, children get hurt.
- Children *need* to get hurt in order to learn to avoid some things.
  If you get worried about safety, you'll be overprotective.
- Children have to fit in with the way their parents live.
  If you make everything in the environment safe, children will have no challenges.
- You can't safetyproof everything just because you have a child.
- Children are resilient like cats and drunks and never get hurt.

All of these points have a *faint* element of truth in them. But if you believe and follow them in practice, you will not give your child a fair chance to *avoid* getting hurt.

Largely, these opinions are canards which will lead your child into accidents.

There were over 22 million *significant* accidents to children under 17 in 1980 in the United States, of a child population of 58 million. That means that almost every other child has a more-than-skinned-knee injury each year. Automobile accidents are *very* high in number. So are playground accidents. But ordinary home-style accidents and injuries are also extremely high, with falls and fires causing enormous havoc in millions of people's lives.

You can do a lot about this—*without* becoming a too-hovering, too-fearful parent. (Although frankly, better to be overprotective and to have a living child than vice versa.)

The kind of environment you provide for your child and family will make a very basic and vital difference. Take safety seriously.

Every baby, every child needs and deserves a better, safer environment to grow in.

CHILDPROOF YOUR HOME—NOW!

Childproofing is a continual process, not a onetime, forget-it-forever-after affair. As your child's size and motor skills change, you must go through the whole house again and yet again, keeping at least a few jumps ahead of that tiny Marco Polo in your household.

Childproofing progresses from the ground up—literally. As soon as you've childproofed at the floor-crawl level, you will have a cabinet-opening toddler to contend with, and pretty soon that curious little head and bunched fists reaches coffee table and chair-seat level. As you may imagine, knick-knacks displayed at toddler eye level are an open invitation to disaster.

Now, before your baby arrives, is the time to look over your entire home, top to bottom, inside and out, to analyze everything you live with from the points of view of safety, ease of maintenance, and convenience of use.

In general, I do not recommend such keep-out devices as gates (although they are essential for preventing access to real danger areas such as stairwells). It is far preferable to plan ahead and adjust your furnishings to the stage of your child's development than to hinder curiosity and activity and to have to be on constant alert and no-no duty. Here's how to go about it:

With pencil and pad in hand go through your home room by room. Start at the floor and work your way up to your eye level. Get down on your hands and knees and look at the world the way your baby will. Crawl completely around each room while you take your infant's-eye view of things. Make note of every potential hazard.

Watch out especially for:

- Area or scatter rugs (get rid of these for the duration)
- Fringed rugs (ditto)
- Fringed floor-length draperies
- Too-long venetian blind or drapery pull cords (very important to avoid these)
- Dangling electric cords (babies chew on them)

- Electrical outlets *not* concealed by heavy furniture, or behind table or chairs, under which a tiny child could crawl
- Floor-standing planters
- Low shelves (as on an étagère or coffee table) holding audio components or bric-a-brac
- Floor lamps (better avoid them completely unless placed behind a heavy couch with no access)
- Furniture legs with protruding metal or wooden parts
- Low tables with sharp projecting corners
- Ashtrays (give up smoking, anyhow—our *best* advice!)
- Table lamps and their electrical cords

Analyze all of your furnishings with an eye to how well they will stand up to baby and child use. Look, for example, at your chairs and sofas. Have they button-tufted backs? All young children are absolutely unable to resist pulling at these buttons! Either divest yourself of such an item—or order or make attractive slipcovers now so they will be ready when your baby reaches the button-pulling stage.

Slipcovers may be the answer to other babyproofing problems as well, because they are easily removed for cleaning if accidentally smudged by sticky fingers.

Vinyl upholstery may be easy to keep clean, but it is cold and unappealing to the touch—and easily scratched or torn, too.

Instead, you can have all upholstered furnishings Scotchgarded, which will help prevent stains and stickiness. (The Consumer Product Safety Commission assures me that Scotchgarding is safe.)

Clear plastic and glass furnishings are potential hazards, too. The plastic is lightweight and easily unbalanced; furthermore, it scratches and loses the gleaming appearance that attracted you to it in the first place. And glass, of course, can be too easily shattered. Also, glass tables and other items are usually constructed with a framework of metal, which may jut out to create additional hazards.

All storage units, tables, chests, and other cabinet pieces must be *sturdy*. Wobbly legs, precariously balanced bookcases, poorly fitted shelves and drawers are, quite simply, unsafe. Unbalanced and poorly constructed pieces of furniture also endanger the items placed in or on them. You do not want to fear for the life of your hi-fi components if a toddler bumps into a cabinet or grabs a door pull.

So—be sure all of your old furniture is sturdy; repair hinges, table legs, catches, and whatever else needs fixing. If you are buying new items, choose storage units that will protect your turntable, records, books, knickknacks, and bric-a-brac.

And try a *good lock* on cupboards that store items you care a lot about. For instance, the *Whole House Catalog* (Simon and Schuster, 1976) recommends Kindergard latches, which are invisible and require adult-strength finger pressure to open. You can order it through the Mothercare catalog.

Also in the Mothercare catalog are two other safety items I particularly liked.

A safety medicine cabinet of molded polyethylene that hangs on the wall. The drop front door opens from the top and becomes a safety shelf with a spillproof edge for holding medicines and toiletries being used. A safety catch at the top of the door can only be opened by adult fingers. The top of the cabinet slopes forward, making it impossible to leave medicines there instead of inside the cabinet.

A range guard of nickel-plated steel, adjustable to fit stovetops from 16 to 23¾ inches wide and 14⅛ to 22 inches long. This safety device is simple to install and easy to remove for cleaning.

FOR BETTER NURSERY AND HOME SAFETY

Below is a list of items which you should consider buying now while your nursery decorating is in progress. Later on you may forget. But if they seem insignificant, try to digest a few fire statistics.

In the United States in 1980 there were an estimated 757,500 fires in residences plus an additional 300,000 in related structures. An estimated 300,000 persons were injured, according to the United States Fire Administration. Although fire deaths are a third less than they were ten years ago, still, almost 8,000 lives were lost—and one third of these, children. Whether the figures are larger or smaller, they are still enormous. Also, if your family is involved, the figures don't matter at all. Home protections are truly vital!

Smoke Alarm

As Mel Mandell, author of *Being Safe*, says, this has become an essential item for every home and has saved many lives. Several companies manufacture them: they vary in size and price but the principle is very much the same. Whichever type you get, *make sure the alarm is working*. Install in the ceiling of your most central room or near bedrooms. My own preference is the use of several smoke alarms in different locations. Also, periodically, check on whether the alarm is still working. Check with the U.S. Consumer Product Safety Commission on which type of detector (battery-operated, plug-in, or photoelectric-operated) would be best for you. Also check them periodically.

Fire Extinguisher

If you read the instructions carefully and remember them, if you know how and when to use the extinguisher—then it can be a lifesaver. This is particularly so when the fire is small, the use of water takes too long, or your fire department is too far away. *But fire is too dangerous to take chances with*. Therefore, rather than deal with an unfamiliar implement, get the help of your local fire department to show you how to use an extinguisher and what else to do in case of fire. *Learn how and when*.

Intercom

For use from the baby's room to your bedroom and kitchen. The intercom should not be used *instead* of looking in, but rather in addition. Be sure, too, that this is an item which fits your life and home. Some people recommend against an intercom because the sounds of the baby can produce anxiety. But some homes are very large—and some mothers are reassured by being able to hear a baby wake up in the nursery while they are half a house away in the kitchen.

Burglar Alarms

There is an explosion occurring in this field, with more and different types coming on the market all the time. Such an alarm can be a protection for you and your baby, either by scaring an intruder away with a loud noise, or through a silent telephone dial which calls the police. You can buy an inexpensive alarm in a hardware store, or you can get a specialist in security to install a more elaborate alarm system, perhaps tied in with your smoke alarm.

Guards for Electrical Outlets

Why not just install these in advance, before your baby is crawling around and investigating everything in sight? They are inexpensive, easily available, and provide complete protection. Almost any hardware store or five-and-ten carries them.

Locked Cabinets

Every home with a baby should have at least two locked cabinets: one in the bathroom for supplies and medications, the other in the kitchen for household cleaners. If you have a garage or basement, you need a third locked cabinet for tools or other potentially harmful supplies. The rate of early childhood poisonings is still very high, as is the accident rate. And *prevention* is the key word. Install or have installed a combination lock, because it is the easiest for you to use, and will be the hardest for your baby. Also, if you do it now, it will become second nature to use the lock by the time your tyke is toddling.

Window Guards

If you live in an upstairs apartment, or even in a house, window guards can be a major protection. There is a conflict about their value between proponents of ease of exit during a fire, and those more concerned about preventing a baby or child from falling out. In New York City alone at least 150 children fall out of high apartment windows every year. My own preference is for window guards on all windows, with the key to them heavily taped on the inside windowsill. *And* with every adult or baby-sitter trained in how to open a guard in case of fire. You may want to check with your fire department about this situation, too.

Ladders

An emergency ladder for each upper story of your home is a good idea. One volunteer fireman told me that he kept a hose attached to a water faucet in an upstairs closet of his rural home.

Nonskid Rugs

Although area rugs are beautiful and sometimes valuable, you would do well to put them away for the duration. The possibility of tripping is strong, even with adhesive backing. Far better to go to wall-to-wall carpeting or cushioned tile. If you do need to use your great-aunt Agatha's Orientals, then take every precaution to make them skidproof. Be especially careful about edges where tiny feet, or indeed your feet, can catch. Never use them on landings.

Stair Treads or Carpeting

Wide and shallow stairs usually represent the least problem for tots and parents who carry them to navigate. But all stairs are easier with carpeting (not too smooth in type) and/or with rubberized stair treads. Steep stairways (which are truly difficult for young families) should always have these treads and a sturdy railing. Don't pooh-pooh this bit of advice: home falls are high on the accident list.

Extension Gate for Stairs

There is some controversy concerning the use of gates for stairways. The pro-gate people believe it prevents crawlers and toddlers from trying to use the stairs before they are able to do so safely. The con-gate people believe the gate prevents such crawlers and toddlers from learning how to get up and down the stairs under their own steam. Learning how to do things with confidence *is* important. But so is preventing falls! Actually, since children learn stair climbing sooner or later anyhow, you should protect them during the crawling-toddler years. A gate does seem advisable to me, especially when baby-sitters are there. But do put in the money to get the more expensive, better kind—the high permanent small-mesh expansion gates.

Baby-sitter Instruction List or Booklet

Many of these are available from the U.S. Government Printing Office, from commercial companies, and from books. You can also make up your own list of instructions. As your baby grows, you will want to change the list somewhat. The list or booklet should be next to the main telephone. A copy should be given to grandparents, too.

Telephone-Numbers List

Make a list of important numbers to have near your telephone (doctor, police, fire department, poison control center, hospital, emergency ambulance service).

What-to-Do-If Books

There is a wealth of books on the market which give instructions on how to handle problems or emergencies.

Small Items like Covers for Doorknobs

Lights that glow in the dark and plastic covers for table corners can be a safety help. Check your five-and-ten or hardware store, as well as the safety literature.

A Special File on Safety Courses, Training Programs, Special Items, and Lectures

You may not have the time or ability to become a safety and health specialist right now. However, if you both get in the habit of keeping a file of things to look into for the future, you will better orient yourselves toward accident prevention and health issues.

You can obtain a catalog of safety devices by writing to: Safety Now
P.O. Box 567
202 York Road
Jenkintown, Pennsylvania
19046

Protecting the Infant of Four to Seven Months from Accidents

Play Areas. When you are busy, put the baby in a safe place near you. Without supervision the floor, the full-sized bed, and the yard are unsafe.

Bath. Don't leave the baby alone in the bath for any reason. It takes only seconds to drown. Keep the faucets out of reach. Check the temperature of the bath water with your elbow.

Protecting the Infant of Seven to Twelve Months from Accidents

The Kitchen. Hot liquids, hot foods, and electric cords on irons, toasters, and coffee pots should be kept out of the child's reach. The tablecloth should not hang within his reach. (Vincent J. Fontana, M.D., *A Parents' Guide to Child Safety*, 1973)

Potentially Dangerous Objects

Balloons	Coins
Beads	Peanut shells
Beans	Peanuts
Bobby pins	Popcorn
Bones	Screws
Buttons	Straight pins
Carrots	Tacks
Safety pins	Hard candy

Some Unhappy Statistics— and Facts You Should Know

Half of the newborn babies (or 1,750,000 babies a year) have at least one bad fall before they are 1 year old, according to a study by Dr. Harvey Kravitz of Northwestern University. Such falls can result in skull fracture, permanent brain injury, nerve damage. In another study by the National Commission on Product Safety, in *two-thirds* of the injuries reported from infant furniture, the product itself was judged to be at fault. Sixty percent of the injuries were to the head and face. (Shirley Camper Soman, *Let's Stop Destroying Our Children*, 1974)

Window Falls

Windows are an attraction to a young child. The natural curiosity of children impel them to see the outside world. Because falls are so fast and can be so deadly, *you must never have an opened or openable upper story window accessible to a young child.* What can you do to develop a safety reflex that is faster than falls? Do one or more of the following:

- Keep upper story windows locked. If fresh air is needed, heed the following:
- Open only top window.
- Keep bottom window closed or opened to only four or five inches by using:
    Window burglar lock or ventilation lock.
    Upright wooden pole fastened above bottom window.
    Jam bar (adjustable spring type) across the top.
    Jam blocks above.
- For windows that swing outward or inward:
    Remove turning handle and keep away from child.
    Install window burglar lock or adjust-

able chain fastener and either keep windows closed or allow opened only four or five inches.

- If windows must be opened wide, then use special removable window bar grills or a portable safety expansion gate similar to type used on doorways. Make gate releases as inaccessible as possible to child.
- *Don't seal off fire escape routes;* window inhibitors should be quickly releasable by an older person.

- Avoid placing furniture, baby or otherwise, near windows, and prevent assisting climbing out windows.
- Don't depend upon window screens, "securely fastened," to restrain child. A variety of child falls involving screens attest to the need for this precaution. (Murl Harmon, *A New Vaccine for Child Safety,* 1976)

FIRE SAFETY PRECAUTIONS

To Prevent Fire

Don't smoke. Don't let guests smoke. Never smoke in bed.

If you or visitors *must* smoke, wet down and empty all ashtrays into a metal-covered garbage can before bedtime.

Keep matches up high in metal tins with hard-to-open covers.

Don't wear flowing anything (gown, blouse, hair, ribbons) near the stove.

Never hold a baby near the stove, or smoke while holding a baby.

Fix all wires with electrical tape.

Make an exit plan and practice it. Home fire drills should be a regular routine.

Avoid space heaters, if possible. If not, use only the highest quality.

Check the Underwriters Laboratories (UL) label on all electrical appliances and electric wires. (But realize that UL is *not* a regulatory agency and that the label is *not* a complete guarantee.)

Make friends with your local fire department personnel—and ask for a home visit, analysis, and advice. Ask to have your home wiring and boiler checked.

If you're not too high up, keep a rope ladder near your bedroom window and another near the baby's window.

Get the best education you can on fire prevention: read the literature, ask questions.

To Deal with Fire

Take your baby and get out right away. Don't stop for anything—cat, dog, or antiques.

Call the fire department from a neighbor's home or call box.

Before opening a door, feel it. If it's hot, don't open—fire is on the other side.

If smoke is heavy, use wet towels around nose and mouth.

If possible, use stairs instead of elevator.

Don't go back into a house on fire.

If exits are blocked, call your fire department from home; with your baby stay near a window opened only a little from the bottom, use wet towels.

Unless it's a very small wastebasket blaze, don't try to put the fire out yourself.

Don't open oven door if there's a grease fire inside.

Do *not* jump from a window, or throw the baby out unless there is someone there to catch the baby or a way to break the fall.

If you wake at night to the smell of smoke, break the nearest window for air. Do not try to feel your way out in dense smoke.

If your baby is in another room, and the smoke is heavy, try to find a window entranceway to that room.

When you get out, do not stand around watching. You're in shock; so is your baby. You need warm blankets, warm liquids, and comforting people around you.

An Antipoisoning Safety Checklist

1. Use safety packaging when available.
2. Properly re-secure the cap and keep the product in the original container. Never put any medicine or chemical in a cup or soft drink bottle.
3. Keep household products and medicines out of reach and out of sight.
4. Store internal medicines away from other household substances.
5. Read the label on all products and heed warnings and cautions.
6. Always turn on the light when giving medicines. Never take medicines in the dark.
7. Avoid taking medicines in your child's presence. The child may learn to imitate your action.
8. If you have a crawling infant, keep household products stored above the floor level, not beneath the kitchen sink.
9. If you are using a product when called to the door or telephone, take it with you; otherwise your child could get into it.
10. Have handy the phone number of your nearest doctor, poison control center, hospital, and police.

(U.S. Department of Health, Education and Welfare, *Preventing Childhood Poisonings*, pamphlet)

Making Arrangements for Help

You will need help, believe me. Even if you are the most energetic new mother, with the most cooperative new father at your side. For one thing, the two of you will need time off to be by yourselves, to get out and celebrate, and do a few of the things you used to do together. You'll need someone to stay with the baby so you can get away!

Second, childbirth is physically demanding, and it takes the mother's body a while to get caught up. If she must be scrubbing floors and washing windows before she gets physically back to par, it will take her longer to recover. (We've all heard of women in primitive societies who drop the baby and go back to the fields the same day. But who wants to look the way they do only a few years later, or have the ailments that give them short life spans in many of those parts of the world?) You'll need help at least with the housework, so you can spare your body.

Then, if you're both working on jobs outside the home, you'll need help with the baby and with the housework. This kind of help is a tall order—particularly full time.

All of these situations are discussed in the following pages, with special attention to baby-sitters and the child-care help needed by working parents. The suggestions given are quick guides to dealing with baby-sitters and child-care help. They really apply to *any* child-care helper *any* parent might need for *any* period of time.

HOUSEWORK HELP OR BABY NURSE: A CHOICE

In the first weeks after your baby is born, help with the housework is much more im-portant than help with the baby. Conventional wisdom always called for a baby nurse to spend at least a week, and better two, in the home with the new baby. But caring for a newborn is much less time-consuming and physically demanding than keeping a house or apartment clean, especially at a time when a stream of packages and visitors may be daily descending upon you.

What you really need more than anything else is *daytime* housecleaning help. The baby's father probably will help out at night with baby-tending chores—unless his job is very demanding or he is traveling. But daytime help of some sort is essential. Even help for two days a week during the first month or so will take an enormous burden off you.

If you opt for a baby nurse, you will get help only with sterilizing bottles, baby changing and bathings and perhaps with the baby's laundry. And you'll have to provide the meals, see that the shopping and cooking are done, and probably have to watch a well-paid helper sitting idle while the baby sleeps contentedly and you scurry around trying to get caught up with all you have to do. With breast feeding, there's even less for a baby nurse to do.

But there are times when a caring baby nurse can be great:

- If this is a first baby and you have not had *any* baby-care training, you can learn some of what you need to know from her.
- If you've had twins or even more babies. Several hungry mouths and soiled diapers at a time can be overwhelming until you get into a routine of baby care.
- If there have been complications and

you and/or the baby need special medical care.

• If you want to be as free as possible to pay extra attention to other young children.

So if you *do* need a baby nurse, by all means hire one. But if your budget for help is limited, spend it where it will do you the most good—taking care of your home, so you can get some rest, get back to yourself, and take care of your baby.

If you do get a nurse, before she leaves, be sure that:

• You know how to give a bath, shampoo, and manicure to your baby.
• She has left behind a full supply (two days) of sterilized bottles and formula, if needed.
• She has not left behind any personal belongings. (One couple I know once had to mail a lipstick, two brassieres, and a girdle to a nurse they had dismissed because she was slovenly—in addition to having to clean up after her!)

HELP FROM GRANDPARENTS

Naturally, everyone wants to see the baby, and some offer to help, too. What should you do?

First of all, help from grandparents and other relatives can be an enormous plus—if they are available. Who could love a baby as much as a grandmother—or grandfather? Who ever has as much patience? Then, too, grandparents often don't mind being asked in case of emergency, or at the last minute. They can be a precious resource—and should be treated as such.

But—help from relatives can be a problem, too. If you don't get along well with them in the first place . . . if they are the kind of people who insist that their way is the only way or else . . . if they feel they're doing you a favor and therefore expect favors in return . . . if they are fifty years behind the times in everything . . . if they haven't looked at a baby since you were born—then you'd be better off with nonrelated, paid assistance.

So, if you are considering assistance from a relative, be sure that he or she:

• Is willing to help, no strings attached.
• Is competent, and not disorganized.
• Has the emotional readiness to help.
• Has the physical stamina to do the job.
• Has had baby-care experience.
• Is up-to-date on child-care practices.
• Respects you, your home, and your opinions.
• Is easy to get along with, and is not a total take-over type.

In particular, older relatives may not be up-to-the-minute on theories of child rear-

---

How it Used to Be

[A baby nurse] must be very cleanly in her person, and guilty of no idiosyncrasies in dress or manner; of gentle voice, quiet and subdued, clean of speech, and self-conscious enough to know her ability and prove it. She must have a strong individuality, and an authority second to none save the physician's. She must not wear squeaky shoes, or rustling dresses, or bright colors, or jewelry or fancy trimmings of any sort. Quietness, unobtrusiveness, ladylikeness, and simplicity should characterize all her dress and manner and habits. She need not be pretty, but she must have the attractiveness of a good face, and a kindly eye. . . .

Finally, she must not be a talker; she can read to you, converse with you, but never gossip. The more she knows of books and people, the pleasanter her companionship.

Mrs. Emma F. Angell Drake, M.D., *What a Young Wife Ought to Know*, 1901

---

ing; they still may be fixed on the every-four-hours schedule, or on not picking up a crying baby (although it would be a stern grandparent who could resist!), or on early toilet-training, or some other hangover from the past. You may have to explain current attitudes in some detail, quoting at length from your pediatrician, the courses you have taken, and the magazines and books (including this one) you are reading. Try to be informative, not argumentative or abrasive, so that the generation gap will not become a chasm!

If the helpful relatives in your family try to change *you* instead of trying to adapt themselves to your ideas, perhaps making you feel guilty for not following their advice, you'd do better not to rely on them. A conflict with your parents or in-laws over your children is the last thing you need. And I have seen instances where grandparent fussiness led to feeding and other problems, and the parents felt helpless because they were dependent on the free baby-sitting services being provided while they were at work. The resulting tensions between all three generations created additional pressures on every member of the family, and all in all the problems that occurred were definitely not worth the dollars saved. Sometimes "free" baby-sitting can be a false economy, and paid help can be a wise investment.

But I have also seen tremendous love and sharing and giving among grandparents, their children, and grandchildren. All in all, my own feeling is that willing grandparents are worth their weight in gold—and paid help is paid help. That's why I would try my best to work things out with a grandparent, if it is possible to do so. They need to be needed! But of course you—your baby's parents—must make the decision.

When grandparents or other relatives serve as baby-sitters, you have certain obligations to them:

• Do not take their assistance for granted; treat them with consideration.
• Let them know exactly when their services will be needed, as far in advance as possible, so they can schedule the rest of their time.
• Return home when you said you would, if you go out. Relatives are prone to worry.
• Let them know how much you appreciate what they do for you and your child;

invite them for a special dinner, perhaps, or take them out, or buy a special gift.
• Compliment them in the presence of other people. Grandparents are a little like the babies they care for: they need tender loving care, too!

HOUSEHOLD AND BABY-SITTING HELP

Whenever you leave your children in someone else's care—for occasional evenings or during each workday—you need to be certain that you have selected a reliable and warm person. This, as every parent knows, is not easy! With the higher pay possible in other fields, it has become increasingly difficult to find a reliable housekeeper, nursemaid, or baby-sitter. Well-qualified full-time workers in this field are in great demand, and usually request a bigger salary than most working mothers (who often work out of necessity themselves) can afford to pay.

There are, nevertheless, certain steps to take in selecting baby-sitting or household help that will reduce the hazards and help provide a relatively good standard of care for your child(ren) while you're away. Before you start looking for help, be clear in your own mind about:

• The number of hours you will want the person to work;
• Exactly what her tasks will be;
• The salary you will be able to pay;
• And most important, the major principles you will want her to follow in caring for your child(ren), as well as the vital things she should *not* do.

If you plan to return to work quickly, select a housekeeper or baby-sitter *before* you start working, or during a vacation period, so that you will be able to supervise for a week or two.

Ask friends and relatives for recommendations. This is generally the best way to get a person you can count on. Trustworthy, pleasant people tend to have friends like themselves, and some of the best household helpers ever located were referred by women who worked for friends.

Look in the Situations Wanted ads of the local newspaper, as well as the ads of the weekly neighborhood newspaper. Place a Help Wanted ad yourself. Call a reliable agency (one that has been recommended by a friend) and specify that you would prefer someone from your own neighborhood.

Try a local church, college or university, particularly departments of social work or family relations. These students often care about babies and children a great deal and will pay special attention.

It is often marvelous if you can get someone who has had children herself. A woman who has had children herself will generally not expect angelic behavior from yours, will not be thrown for a loss at a tantrum, and will be on the lookout for all of the dangerous unexpected things children are apt to get into or do.

Most important of all is whether the person you hire really likes babies and children and likes to be with them. To find this out may take some doing because a lot of people like children when they are clean and sweet—but when the tears or complaining start, they become impatient or harsh. The person who is able to respond to your baby or talk to a youngster *naturally*, without attempting to force interest or impress you, is your best bet. If you have an older child, it would be helpful for this child to be present for the first interview. A child's reactions can be most valuable.

Insist on two or three references and check them carefully. In questioning references, talk about your family situation in detail. Explain that you need to know a lot about the person you hire because that person's judgment and stability may well involve your child's health and safety. Most references will be honest with you.

Insist that any person you expect to spend substantial time with your infant get a physical examination, including a tuberculin test, before starting to work. Be prepared to pay for this, or perhaps send her to your own physician. If she has recently been examined, call her doctor.

Don't expect a shining, spotless house *and* good child care from one person. In fact, if your house is too consistently shining, you can be fairly certain that your baby has not been getting the extra attention s/he will need while you're away.

Do expect patience, and some special qualities—tenderness, affection, good nature, a sense of humor, a sense of proportion. You want someone who will sing and gurgle and talk and play with your baby during waking hours, rather than someone who reads a magazine and leaves your small bundle to his or her own baby-style preoccupations. Maybe yours will be a quiet, nondemanding tyke. But even so, your baby caretaker should be ready and able to give a lot of input to your baby. Full-time child caring is a tall order. It is really good substitute-parenting on a full-time basis; it goes way beyond merely baby-sitting.

Don't give contradictory instructions. Do be sure your instructions are clear and consistent. If you want your employee to tend to the baby as soon as crying begins, don't tell her on another occasion to let the baby cry for a few minutes first.

Don't hire anyone who does not meet your minimum standards, not even on a temporary basis. It's not fair to your child, nor to the employee, nor to you. If someone makes you feel uncomfortable, do *not* take a chance. And if the person you employ proves to be unreliable, don't hesitate to dismiss her right away.

Do tell your friends and neighbors that you have hired someone, and ask them to give any needed assistance. Also ask them to let you have the benefit of observations of how your employee interacts with your child. Too often mothers observing a child being unfairly treated, or even neglected, by a neighbor's housekeeper choose to "mind their own business" instead of constructively criticizing for the child's benefit.

Always leave the telephone number where you can be reached and the numbers of close neighbors and the doctor.

If you have an older child, or as your baby grows, be sure that s/he is as well-satisfied as you are—or that the complaints are minor ones. Know the difference between "Mary's mean, she wouldn't let me have a cookie" and a *real* problem.

Remember that no one can replace you. No one can do exactly what you would in every situation. Be reasonable in your expectations of others. Be realistic, too.

PRACTICAL POINTERS CONCERNING BABY-SITTERS

Always give the baby-sitter a phone number where you can be reached and a list of emergency phone numbers.

How It Used to Be

Patience and good temper are indispensable qualities [for a nursemaid]; truthfulness, purity of manners, minute cleanliness, and docility and obedience, almost equally so. She ought also to be acquainted with the art of ironing and trimming little caps, and be handy with her needle.

Mrs. Isabella Beeton, ed., *Beeton's Book of Household Management*, 1861

Show the sitter the entire house, the location of the phone, the exits, and where the baby's things are kept.

Emphasize that the sitter must never leave the baby alone in the house.

Instruct the baby-sitter never to let anyone into the house.

Never leave your baby asleep before he or she has met the sitter.

Do not permit smoking.

In case of fire, instruct the baby-sitter to grab the baby and leave the house immediately.

Selecting a Name for the Baby

To a very large extent, our self-images throughout life depend on our names and attitudes toward them. All children should be told, as early as they can understand, the reasons for their names. Whether family tradition, pleasant sound, or significant meaning, the reason for a particular name will become part of the way that children think of themselves. It is important for children to like their names, and be proud of them.

NAMING TIPS

Choose a name you—and your child—*will* be proud of.

Watch out for a hidden meaning—particularly in slang.

Be careful of first initials—your son will not be happy with Charles Robert Andrew Petersen, nor will your daughter enjoy Tatania Indira Thomas.

On similar grounds, try to avoid name combinations that produce childish laughter, or that are an anomaly—Blossom Rabinovitz or Percival Charlamanski.

If possible, avoid very popular names. Try to find out from your birth records department or at your house of worship which are the very much used names of this year or last.

Try to choose names which can have a shortened version—Andrew-Andy, Virginia-Ginny, Daniel-Danny—unless you object to this proclivity for the diminutive and the familiar.

Try for meanings which are part of family history. Some Jewish people follow the custom of using either the name or the first initial of some no-longer-living family member who was loved and respected. This recalls the relative and provides a feeling of continuity. The Spanish Jews name for the living, as do most Christians.

Do use a middle name or initial. If your child doesn't like the first name, at least there is a reasonable choice. Archibald Carl Rogers can become A. Carl Rogers.

If you use a historical personage's name, be sure you don't burden your child with grandiose expectations just because—your own Alexander may *not* become Great in any area, and may not want to be!

Names which are part of a group's identity are often marvelous—if they are not out of keeping with the place and culture and people with whom your child will grow up. Try for a name that is easy to remember, and that sounds good.

If possible, the names should sound well together, especially if said quickly or in a slurred way. To this end avoid three three-syllable names in a row.

Try to avoid a very common first name if the last name is also very common. Instead of John Smith, what about Joshua or Jason Smith? Or Maria or Mariette Brown instead of Mary?

Try to avoid unique names of infamy: Benito and Adolf, for example.

Use several guides to name meanings (see list of reference books on page 334) to help you choose appropriate names. If you are pacifists, you won't want a name that means spear thrower.

214

Do not let grandparents or other relatives override your own clear wishes about a name. After all, the baby will be yours, *not* your mother's or father's. (Some families actually get into long feuds over a baby's name. Do try to avoid this, too.)

Use one or more pleasant (*not* demeaning) nicknames in calling or referring to your child. In that way children who do not like their main name will have some choice later.

Take your time, take care in naming your baby. A name *is* important. But if you both disagree, try to reach an amicable compromise with the use of middle names. One couple decided that the choice of the first name of their first child would be the wife's and the middle name, the husband's. For the second child, they just reversed the process.

Write down the reasons why—try to include details—you chose your baby's particular name. He or she will *love* to know this at a later age. Just remember that a child may feel that "as his name is, so is he" (I Samuel 25:25, circa 500 B.C.).

Eccentricities in Naming

Nothing so advertises the ignorance or mental eccentricities of a parent as queer or awkward names given to children. One large family is said to have named a baby Finis supposing and wishing it to be their last. But they were equal to the occasion later when a daughter and two sons came who were called Addenda, Appendix and Supplement. Then another daughter was born, to be named Errata. (Elsdon C. Smith, *Naming Your Baby*, 1943)

NAMES AROUND THE WORLD

Names are like the language. They are ancient; they are new. They are beautiful; they are strange. Some are filled with meaning; others mean nothing. Contrast the names Sarah and Harrice.

Sarah is biblical, probably prebiblical. It signifies "Princess" and "One Who Laughs." It was my great-grandmother's name (after whom I was named) and it is my great-niece's name. Its popularity has varied through the centuries, but quite probably the name will continue into infinity.

Harrice, on the other hand, is brand-new. It belongs to one young woman whom I met recently. The name has no meaning and may never belong to anyone else again. The name was created by Harrice's mother. Both of the new baby's grandfathers were named Harris. Her mother, searching for a way to name her girl child after these two gentlemen, hit upon Harrice. The name bothered the child—but the young woman is happy with the distinction and named her own baby girl an unusual name, Sloan.

The living language is like Sarah and Harrice: the same and changing all the time. In every culture some names have lasted through time and remain popular. One of the names that has been most eternal and that has spread across the world is John. John has an incredible number of male *and* female variations. They all derive from Yehokhanan, the Hebrew for "God is Gracious."

Consider the way the name has been adapted in different societies and languages. There is Ivan in Russia, Johann in Germany, Shane (and Eoin and Seann) in Gaelic, Giovanni in Italian, Juan in Spanish, Jean in French, Johan in Swedish, among others.

In the feminine version we have Jane, Joan, Jeanne, Johanna, Juanita, Sheena (Irish), Janet, Jeanette, Janice, Gianina, Giovanna, Sine, Seonaid (Scots)—again among others.

In every culture certain trends in naming dominate. In some societies (American Indians, for example) natural phenomena and plants and animals are the source of many names. Numbers have great meaning in Japanese society, where order of birth and number names for children are often used (Man for 10,000 or Ichi for 1, for instance). The Japanese are superstitious about numbers, believing that they can change a person's destiny. Girls' names in Japan, however, frequently evoke virtuous qualities: Setsu means "Fidelity" and Sumi means "Refined." Round numbers are believed to be good omens!

Many other societies did or do believe in the magic of names. The names of children are supposed to endow them with the qualities that the name denotes. The once warlike Scandinavians, for instance, used to favor the name Lars (a symbol of victory, "Crowned with Laurel"), but are turning more to names like Frederick, which means "Peace."

Many Africans, Hindus, and Chinese believe that an ugly name will keep away evil spirits. These demons will think a child so named is beneath their notice.

The Chinese also like names that go together well—both internally and in the family. Therefore, one child named after a jewel might have a sister or two named after others. Or the descriptive adjective might be the same for several names. A lovely custom.

Some names are combinations of different cultures, as the children are. Such a lovely mix is a man I know named Ricardo da Silveira Lobo O'Reilly Steinberg. Originally from Brazil, he has one difficulty in America: in the United States there is only space for three names on forms!

In one sense all societies believe in the magic of names. We want to endow our children with the quality of the person for whom they are named. Of course, parents don't always realize the meaning of their child's name and it can still turn out to be remarkably appropriate. One child named Jessica was thrilled to find out that her name meant her life's ambition: wealthy one! Often we want to carry on a tradition and a heritage through our baby's name. And sometimes we go to extremes, like Eugene Jerome Dupuis of Tampa, Florida, a born-again evangelist who, in 1978, became a father for the sixth time. All his children—three boys and three girls—are named Eugene Jerome Dupuis! His wife, Katherine, minds not at all being so ignored. But will his children mind later on either their given names or their nickname numbers, 1 through 6?

This can be called passing on his Eugenes!

Do *not* name your baby with a punning name; you would never be forgiven if your child became, for example, Warren Pease!

MOST POPULAR NAMES

The New York City Health Department has made a little list for a number of years. Why they have kept track of popular names is a mystery. But since they have, here are four of the lists for your comparative enjoyment!

1980

Boys	Girls
Michael*	Jennifer*
David	Jessica
Jason	Melissa
Joseph	Nicole
Christopher	Michelle
Anthony	Elizabeth
John	Lisa
Daniel	Christine
Robert	Tiffany
James	Maria

1948

Boys	Girls
Robert	Linda
John	Mary
James	Barbara
Michael	Patricia
William	Susan
Richard	Kathleen
Joseph	Carol
Thomas	Nancy
Stephen	Margaret
David	Diane

1928

Boys	Girls
John	Mary
William	Marie
Joseph	Annie
James	Margaret
Richard	Catherine
Edward	Gloria
Robert	Helen
Thomas	Teresa
George	Joan
Louis	Barbara

1898

Boys	Girls
John	Mary
William	Catherine
Charles	Margaret
George	Annie
Joseph	Rose
Edward	Marie
James	Esther
Louis	Sarah
Francis	Frances
Samuel	Ida

*Michael and Jennifer have been most popular for the past nine years, while John and Mary have not been there since 1928!

Part Five

THE BIRTH ITSELF

*The most emotional moment came when de Watteville
brought an instrument that allowed me to listen to the
baby's heartbeat. Suddenly, there it was. A miracle of
sound. The steady, rhythmic, beautiful music of my
baby's beating heart. I cried with joy.*

SOPHIA LOREN

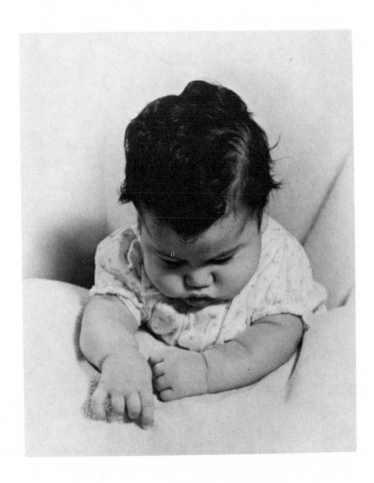

First Minutes, First Hours, First Days

GETTING READY

You, of course, are eager to know the signs and signals of your baby's imminent arrival.

I have searched the many books on childbirth—and found very little to help you. The last month, the last week, have been largely ignored! But you will be living through it. And you should have some notion of what your body will be experiencing. Here are some common observations.

Your "baby" in the ninth month has usually turned and settled so that the position is head down. Arms and legs still have room and account for the moving bulges in your abdomen. But generally, the space has become so cramped for the baby that movement has lessened.

At the beginning of the month your organs—intestines, stomach, liver—are all crowded together. And as a result, your diaphragm has been pushed upward. This causes breathlessness and a very cramped feeling. You will feel very full—stretched tight—and something like a conveyance for a "foreign" body.

Your breasts will be much enlarged and tender. Their veins will be dilated and there will be a darkening around the nipples—especially in brunettes. The breasts contain fluid (colostrum) which may leak out, and can certainly be expressed.

You may find other kinds of markings on your skin—stretch marks (light, tiny lines) on the stomach, pigmentation on the abdomen or forehead.

During this last month of waiting, your baby's position drops visibly by some inches. This usually occurs about two weeks before the birth. This is a gradual drop. The entire waistline becomes lower, although you may not notice it at first. You can now breathe much more easily, and you no longer feel uncomfortably full after meals. The uterus has actually sunk about two inches.

This is called "lightening" or "dropping." The baby's head is now wedged tightly in the birth position, and the baby stops growing about a week before the delivery.

You are feeling many effects; there is much pressure to urinate, but at the same time, you may be constipated and your legs probably ache—especially if you stand a lot. Your movements are much more circumscribed and careful.

You are becoming weary of the whole business. You may feel as though time is crawling along in agonizing slowness. At the same time, there is a strong desire to HURRY UP! You may also be somewhat apprehensive.

During the last days of your pregnancy, you may have trouble sleeping. But since childbirth is a very physical activity, your body needs to be in top shape. Try to get enough rest and avoid fatigue and exhaustion.

Just before your baby-time arrives, you may find your appetite changing, either increasing or decreasing. Weight loss of 2 to 3 pounds is not unusual. Neither is diarrhea. Many women experience a great spurt in energy, and tackle all sorts of housecleaning jobs. This is known as "the nesting urge," which some people think represents a subconscious need to get everything shipshape now because there may not be much time for anything but baby care after the infant comes. If you feel like washing windows and vacuuming draperies, only clean and putter in fairly short periods with *plenty* of rest in between.

The man in your life may be going through a lot right now, too. Sex has become more difficult—awkward at the very least. And he may feel even more impatient than you are. Perhaps more apprehensive, as well.

You both feel as though you're in limbo, but actually you are moving toward that glorious time when the single cell and single sperm you started with, now multiplied to about five *trillion* cells, start the descent into a new life. This will be *the beginning of the end of your pregnancy*.

THE COUNTDOWN

What happens on the eve of having a baby? Here are two typical experiences of first-time parents.

"I raced-lumbered around the house, cleaning everything up. An out-of-town guest was coming for dinner. During the meal this friend could hardly refuse our request that he become our baby's godfather. Lovely evening.

"The next morning, I just knew. I rushed to wash my hair, to make the bed, to call my husband. Then the backache began. I started to have contractions, called the doctor's office and was laughed at by the nurse. 'Oh, you're many hours away,' she said, knowing that the baby was two weeks late.

"I remembered something terribly important, not yet done. Was there time? There was. But as I completed a letter to my unborn baby, it was very obvious to me—if not to the doctor's nurse—that the trip to the hospital should be made immediately. My husband came flying through the door at that instant, and we decided to take off. The letter was left in the bassinet as a gift!"

"The baby was by now two days over the due date. That morning, a beautiful spring day, I went out to finish shopping for dinner—we had invited two friends over.

"Throughout the afternoon of cleaning and cooking I *did* feel something . . . indigestion, maybe? But not until five o'clock did I realize that these funny feelings were contractions and they were now coming quite close together.

"Very hurriedly, I put a suitcase together—of course I hadn't done it before—turned off the beef casserole and out we went, looking frantically for a taxi.

"When we got to the hospital I went almost straight into the delivery room and my very annoyed doctor was quickly summoned. He asked me, would I please give him more notice next time.

"That evening my husband met the guests on his way back from the hospital; and together they finished cooking the dinner and toasted the baby."

FOR HOSPITAL OR BIRTH CENTER—CHECK YOUR PACKED SUITCASES

Your suitcases were probably packed around the seventh month. If you're having the baby at home, you may not have packed anything. It is a good idea, however, to have a suitcase ready just in case the hospital turns out to be the place for you for any reason.

When you're getting ready to leave for the hospital, you may want to add a dress or skirt to your suitcase at the last minute. Otherwise, your cases probably contain everything you'll need—and a lot more than that! You'll only take one case with you now. The baby's suitcase comes along on the day you're going home.

While there are some individual variations in terms of climate and other variables, such as the expected birth of twins, the basic suitcase necessities for hospital or birthing center are on these pages.

THE SUITCASE FOR A NEW MOTHER

Two nightgowns. Most convenient are shortie gowns that button down the front, because of nursing. You don't have to have nightgowns in a hospital; you will be supplied with white cotton gowns. However, most new mothers like the idea of wearing their own nightgowns.

A bed jacket. For receiving visitors at bedside.

A wraparound robe. Choose a robe that is easy to get in and out of and that you find comfortable—and pretty!

A pair of flat or low-heeled slippers. Your balance will feel different right after the baby is born, and those slippers that give you a secure footing are best.

A going-home dress. Pants or a skirt may not fit you too well still, whereas a loose dress (definitely *not* a maternity dress) will fit you *and* lift your spirits at your new figure.

Two nursing bras and pads, or a size-larger regular bra. If you're not nursing, you will still be fairly engorged with milk when you leave the hospital and you may need to wear a bra that's larger than your usual size, or one that can accommodate a somewhat larger breast. Nursing pads, of course, are adjustable and are useful to wear both in the hospital and traveling home afterward.

Underwear: pantyhose and slip. These should also be a size larger than usual, too. You might consider wearing panties, girdle, and stockings rather than pantyhose, in case there's a problem in fitting.

A pair of shoes. Obviously, the kind of shoes that you have worn before pregnancy may not be the best type to wear on your return from the hospital simply because you should have as firm a footing as possible. The shoes should not be the spike-heel type.

Outerwear. Whatever coat, sweater, or rainwear the kind of weather in your area may dictate.

One or two sanitary belts. The hospital will supply the sanitary napkins.

Your hospital insurance cards.

Any *inexpensive* jewelry you may wear home.

NONCLOTHING ITEMS

Notepaper and pens for making lists and/or for writing thank-you notes

Your new baby's book for those first descriptions

Envelopes, stamps, and address book

Announcement cards

Comb, brush, mirror, hair supplies

Toothbrush and toothpaste

A cosmetic case and cosmetics

One or two baby reference books

Materials about breast feeding

Camera, film, tape recorder, tapes, batteries, video camera

Telephone numbers of your own doctor, your baby's doctor, your husband, parents, friends. Be sure to include the phone number of the person who is going to help after you're home.

THE BABY'S SUITCASE

Two diapers. If you are using the traditional cloth diapers with safety pins, you must, of course, include the pins.

A pair of waterproof pants, or a pair of soakers, unless you are using disposables.

A small shirt, the smallest size you have that ties in the middle.

A flannel gown (to go over the shirt and diapers) that ties down the middle.

A receiving blanket. This is a cotton blanket in which you will wrap your baby.

A wool blanket. If the weather is cold, to use over the receiving blanket.

A cap or bonnet. The kind that covers the head and ties under the chin is ideal.

A safe car seat for infants.

WHAT IS FALSE LABOR?

"False labor" is the popular phrase for something that may occur throughout your life. It isn't painful, and often isn't even noticeable until some point during your pregnancy.

The uterus, like so many muscles, contracts and relaxes regularly without your even knowing it. About the middle of your pregnancy, you may notice a knot in your lower abdomen which lasts for 30 seconds or so, disappears, and then returns 10 or 15 minutes later. That is called a Braxton-Hicks contraction. It rarely hurts but sometimes, especially in the final weeks of pregnancy, these contractions can be quite intense and many mothers-to-be think they are actually going into labor. They're not. Hence the familiar term "false labor."

There are some distinctions between the false and the real thing:

- True labor contractions usually start in the back and radiate to the front. Braxton-Hicks contractions are usually in the abdomen.
- False labor often starts at night. A

change in position, a warm bath or a glass of sherry can stop it.
• False labor contractions occur at irregular intervals. They maintain the same degree of intensity and the intervals between them don't change.
• Walking around intensifies true labor. It often stops false labor altogether.

If you're having twins, false labor is more likely, according to the late Dr. Alan Guttmacher, noted obstetrician and author, former president of Planned Parenthood Association.

WHEN THE BABY IS READY

Rule of Thumb

If you *think* you are in labor, call your doctor or midwife.

Evidence?

• Low-back ache
• Regular pains, fifteen minutes apart
• Any strong contraction
• Appearance of the "show," a blood-tinged mucus plug
• Rupture of the membranes, no pain necessary
• A rush of fluid or very heavy discharge
• Any of these may mean labor

Doubtful?

Better to call and describe and ask.

THE NUMBERS OF CHILDBIRTH*

HOW TO FIGURE LABOR

All of these figures are for *the average;* you may have experiences totally removed from the average, and still have a perfectly normal delivery and baby. The reason to give averages is to alert you to what happens most frequently. The *averages* in hospital births are:

13 hours of labor for a first baby
8 hours of labor for a second baby

There are about:

135–150 contractions for a first baby
68–75 contractions for a second and third baby
50 contractions for a fourth and fifth baby

Fifty pounds of force are put out by the uterus, the strongest muscle in the body, during a contraction.

In the *three stages of labor:*
the first lasts up to *10 hours*
the second stage lasts *1–3 hours* for a first child, *30–60 minutes* for a second child or more
the third stage lasts *10 minutes–1 hour*

Contractions are:

15–45 seconds long and *10–30 minutes apart* during the first stage
40–60 seconds long and *less than 5 minutes apart* during the second stage
50–90 seconds long and *2–3 minutes apart* during the third stage

COUNTING UP YOUR BABY FIGURES

The average newborn baby is *18–21 inches long, 7–8 pounds* in weight.
The baby's head is *one fourth of the length of the body.*
The baby loses *10 percent of birth weight* during the first *2–3 days*, under current hospital practices.

Birth Experiences Recreated
[T]here is a fact of which we are becoming aware: that the fears or difficulties that woman is experiencing in childbirth actually are the difficulties or the fear she experienced when she was born. This is how the cycle goes from one generation to the next to the next. . . .
It is something we cannot account for. (Dr. Leboyer)

---

*Numbers *never* give the true picture of childbirth. And whatever you do during your own baby's birth, do *not* think about numbers or averages. Realize, too, that definitions of just what is a stage vary from one source to another.

THE EVENTS OF GIVING BIRTH

For nine months you have been waiting for the first day of your first baby's life. Now your waiting time is over. Your body and your baby are signaling that imminent arrival. The birth process can be compared to a passage or an immigration, with varieties of happenings occurring en route and at the destination.

The stages of labor are progressing; the cervix (the neck of the uterus) is opening wider, stretched by your baby's push to be born.

The series of events during the birth process requires time and work—involuntary work by the uterine muscle during the first stage, deliberate work by the mother during the second stage, and work by the doctor or midwife throughout in making sure that everything is going along well. The time required for your baby to travel the short distance from the uterus (in the pelvic cavity) to the great world outside can take a few hours or 24 hours. First babies usually take longer in getting born than subsequent ones. (Sometimes, though, even first babies are born *very* fast—within an hour or two. And other times, a baby will linger for a longer time than 24 hours.) Here is a quick description of the way childbirth happens.

The first stage: From the onset of labor until the cervix is completely dilated—10 centimeters, or about 4 inches wide, or the width of the baby's head. *Time:* the longest stage.

The second stage: The actual birth—from the time the cervix is completely dilated until your baby is born. *Time:* an hour or two.

The third stage: From the time the baby is born until the placenta (or afterbirth) is expelled, with practically no discomfort. *Time:* very quick, usually 10–15 minutes to an hour.

The Life Forces

The very best births are very, very simple. There is little to do but attend. There is a great spiritual energy in the room—you can feel the life forces. Respect them. The woman needs to feel safe, nurtured, and supported, has to have inner resources, and must not be afraid of working hard. She needs to em-brace the contractions and will herself to open. *Good should not be equated with easy, a common error in our culture.* (Ruth T. Wilf, C.N.M., Ph.D., "Fulfilling the Needs of Families in a Hospital Setting: Can It Be Done?" *21st Century Obstetrics, Now!,* 1977)

A Midwife's Description of Giving Birth

It's a flow and you're in the middle of that flow and it happens and you don't try to control it and if you're somebody attending the birth and you see the flow going off, you can be there as a guide to direct it back, but you don't try to alter it or to interfere, you just try to be there and go with it. It takes its own form and occupies its own space and you become part of that.

There are no ideas to be imposed on it.

Laboring women are Mother Earth. Your body is working totally. So you become Mother Earth. You become part of the whole. You are no longer disconnected in any way. You are total when you give birth. (In a conversation with Karen Pardini, a midwife of Kingston, New York)

Mothers and Mothers-in-law During Delivery

The husband should always be present. But historically the husband has never been the person who gives the major support to the laboring woman. He needs support as well as the laboring woman. When couples come to us, we encourage over and over again that they talk either to their mother or mother-in-law and ask them to be with them at the time of birth.

We have to start strengthening the family. We have been doing this for a year and a half. The majority of women have had either their mother or mother-in-law with them. I have never, never had a bad experience with a mother or a mother-in-law there. They have always greatly supported the laboring woman, greatly supported their son or son-in-law, and always made the birth experience really one of elation.

One thing we have to learn is *not* to split families. We have to learn not to be independent. We have to learn to be dependent. Life is so hard, and we should try to seek as many people as we can to help us.

Equally as important at a birth is to have a close friend or relative, either a cousin, aunt or uncle, preferably a woman who has had a baby before, preferably a woman who has had her baby at home. (Gregory White, M.D., and Mayer Eisenstein, M.D., "ACHO: Philosophy and Practice of Physicians in Homebirth," *21st Century Obstetrics, Now!*, 1977)

◇ ◇ ◇

THE ANATOMY OF LABOR

The most important anatomical part of your body during labor is the cervix, the bottom, necklike part of the uterus. It usually extends about two inches into the vagina. In order for the baby and the placenta to be pushed out of the uterus, the cervix must *efface* and *dilate* (effacing means that the cervix softens and thins until it becomes a part of the lower segment of the uterus; dilating means widening). The cervix starts to efface before it starts to dilate, and it continues to dilate after effacement is completed. The contractions of the uterus pull up the cervix and at the same time press the baby downward against it, which forces it farther open.

Normally contractions get progressively stronger and progressively closer together, allowing mother and baby to adapt to the increasing strength of the uterine contractions. No two women seem to experience these contractions the same way, but everyone agrees that when a contraction occurs, you can't concentrate on anything else! You know it's there. (Understanding what is happening helps reduce fears and tension and this, in turn, goes a long way toward making the baby-birthing experience dramatic and fulfilling, rather than frightening or upsetting.)

As labor progresses, the contractions get longer, harder, and closer together. The time between them is calculated from the beginning of one contraction to the beginning of the next. Each contraction's length is timed from beginning to end of the same contraction. (Contractions, for example, might be 10 minutes apart and 45 seconds in length.) It is most common for a contraction to start, build to a peak, and then recede. During the last part of labor a contraction may have two or even three peaks.

The uterus, like the heart, is an involuntary muscle. If someone tells you she managed to control the contractions, the likelihood is that what she really did was control *everything else*. She relaxed the rest of her body during a contraction, thus allowing the uterus to act most efficiently. If you tighten up, muscle tension will spread and intensify the discomfort caused by the contractions. The interval between contractions is best used to rest, breathe deeply, practice relaxation techniques, and prepare for the next one. Otherwise, as one writer put it, the peaks "can curl your toes." But if you're prepared, contractions are much easier to handle.

◇ ◇ ◇

A Man Goes Through Labor

With each contraction I hooked her left leg over my left arm and supported the back of her head in my right, going grunt for grunt with her although not realising it at the time.

I felt that I was the only one in physical contact, the only one with a grip, and that it all depended on me and on me alone. Despite this, however, there was a moment when I thought I might faint with the effort and quickly turned to a sink behind me for a drink of water, forcing myself not to give way.

I cannot remember feeling so utterly full of anything in my life. (Sheila Kitzinger, *Giving Birth*, 1971)

◇ ◇ ◇

Walking Around While Having a Baby

In virtually all countries except the United States a woman in labor is routinely encouraged to walk about during labor. Such activity during labor is considered to facilitate labor by distracting the mother's attention from the discomfort or pain of her contractions and to encourage a more rapid engagement of the fetal head. (Lewis E. Mehl, M.D., "Research on Alternatives in Childbirth: What Can It Tell Us About Hospital Practice?" *21st Century Obstetrics, Now!*, 1977)

◇ ◇ ◇

BIRTHING POSITIONS

Birth positions are almost as various as sex positions. But those most comfortable for most women are least popular with American doctors. You may want to discuss the whole matter with your own doctor. Here are a few of the possibilities.

Lithotomy. This is the most common position. You are flat on your back, your legs are up and apart in stirrups. It is the same position used in doctors' offices for a pelvic examination. Its main advantage is the convenience for the physician. It is *not* the most helpful for the mother since her ability to push effectively is lessened. Her circulation and blood pressure are altered because she is flat on her back and her contractions are less intense.

Dorsal. You lie on your back here, too, but your feet are flat on the delivery table instead of in stirrups. This is more comfortable for most women and allows more freedom—but it has the same inhibiting effect on circulation, blood pressure, and pushing.

Lying on the left side. Someone holds your right leg up during pushing contractions, or the leg can be supported in a stirrup. Most women seem to find this most comfortable during the first stage of labor and choose to retain it during the second stage. It doesn't reduce contractions or pushing but the raised leg blocks a view of the baby being born.

Semisitting. The upper torso is propped at a 45-to-50-degree angle; knees are flexed; feet are flat on the delivery table. This is physiologically good. Sitting helps a woman push, and the force of gravity helps the descent and arrival of the baby.

Squatting. This is the position most commonly used around the world. Gravity has the best advantage here. And the pelvic outlet apparently is changed advantageously by squatting.

Hands and knees. The main advantage of this position is that it relieves pressure on the mother's spine. It is a hard position to maintain on the narrow delivery table and difficult for the attending doctor to manage.

GRAVITY AND POSITION

Though most doctors still prefer the mother-to-be to lie in the lithotomy position, recognition is growing that you may well be more comfortable sitting or semisitting; and what's more, in such a propped-up position you have gravity working for you. Consequently this semisitting position is coming into greater use. In addition to the new birthing bed and chair there are even delivery tables structured to accommodate a semisitting delivery. They have a hinged drop-leaf which can be let down at the moment of birth so the doctor or midwife can receive the baby from below as s/he emerges into the world.

THE BEGINNING OF THE END OF YOUR PREGNANCY: THE PROGRESSION OF LABOR

Although there are many times when I have wished that another, pleasanter word could be substituted for "labor," the term actually does have some validity. You are in a state of great exertion at times while your infant is getting born. Here is what is happening.

There are three classic indications that labor has begun and all of them often are preceded by a lower-back ache for twenty-four hours or more ahead of time. Or you may wake up with a backache—and just know the baby is arriving soon. The three signs of labor are:

Powerful, regular long contractions

Rupturing of the membranes or amniotic sac which encloses the baby along with the amniotic fluid. This is often called "the bag of waters." This may not produce the gushing sensation many people expect, but you'll feel it.

A "show," sometimes called "bloody show," which is the passage of a small plug of bloodstained mucus that has been blocking the opening of the cervix all these

months and is discharged as the cervix begins to dilate. Any one of these may signal labor.

Dilation begins slowly. During the first 4 to 8 hours, the cervix dilates to 4 to 7 centimeters, or from 1½ to almost 3 inches. Contractions can be between 15 and 45 seconds long and 10 to 20 minutes apart. Most first-time mothers go to the hospital sometime during this first stage of labor—usually when the contractions are 5 to 10 minutes apart—depending upon distance from the hospital—and as a rule, they are taken directly to the labor room.

When you first arrive, your medical history will be taken. You will be given various examinations. Urine and blood samples will be taken. (Blood must be cross-matched in the unlikely event that you might need a transfusion so they can have a supply of your blood type ready.) In all probability, you will be shaved in your pubic area and be given an enema—unless you and your doctor have agreed beforehand on different arrangements. The enema is supposed to ensure that there is no waste remaining in your lower intestine to be accidentally forced out during labor when the baby presses against the thin wall separating the vagina from the rectum. (See page 138 for a contrary opinion.)

Most women time the duration of labor from the moment they enter the hospital. This means that the longer you wait at home before checking in, the shorter the labor seems.

Effacement (the softening and thinning of the cervix) may be completed before this phase starts or the process may finish up during this period. After effacement is completed, dilation (widening) proceeds more rapidly.

Contractions now are usually 40 to 60 seconds long and occur less than 5 minutes apart. At this point, in most hospitals, the mother is now put to bed. Sometimes dilation slows down and seems to stop. This is called reaching a plateau. It may seem discouraging, but once dilation resumes, it is usually quite rapid.

You may have a backache at this stage because the baby may be pressing on your spine. A back rub or counterpressure applied to the lower back during contractions helps. If your husband is present and working with you, he can do this for you.

As the second stage of labor starts, the

cervix completely dilates and is stretched up over the baby's head. Contractions are at their most intense, 50 to 90 seconds long and occurring every 2 to 3 minutes. There is little time to rest between them. This is toe-curling time, the moment toward which all your training, exercises, and practice breathing have been targeted. Aside from back rubbing, this is also the time when your husband's supportive presence is most valuable.

At this point labor is called "transition," and fortunately this part of the birth process is the shortest, averaging between 30 and 60 minutes, or 20 to 30 contractions. A woman who has had a previous baby may have a short transition; with a first baby it may take an hour or more. But often it is less. It can be as short as one contraction or as long as two hours.

During "transition," you may experience a few symptoms such as nausea, dizziness, muscle cramps, a splotchy face, cold feet, or you may have none of these. You may also become anxious. Your husband can ease this considerably through massage or even just touching you a lot.

All this time your doctor or midwife is checking you periodically, either rectally or vaginally, to see how dilation is progressing.

Toward the end of the "transition" you may have the urge to push. You'll be told not to do so then. If dilation isn't complete, you could cause the cervix to swell and lacerate. If you ever practiced breathing exercises, now is definitely the time to use them. If you have *not* been trained in breathing exercises, do *not* try them now. You might overbreathe and experience hyperventilation of your bloodstream. This may result in dizziness, numbness, and tingling of your extremities. Also, by flushing out too much carbon dioxide, you could cut down the baby's oxygen supply. But if you *are* well trained, breathing exercises of the panting type could help you over the strong contractions. Your husband or partner can help you breathe out *and* in at an even rate. He can assist any problem with his cupped hands over your nose and mouth.

The Transition Phase of Labor

Transition—when the cervix dilates from about 7 cm. to 10 cm.—is generally con-

sidered the most difficult phase of labor and it is at this time that the couple who have learned a psychoprophylactic technique, such as the Lamaze method, face their most stringent test. Control can be precarious.

The concentration required in breathing and relaxing takes the edge off pain and enables the woman to cope with it, but the contractions are nonetheless intense. Couples are told not to expect as much relief from the method as they had obtained earlier in the labor. A woman will continue breathing and relaxing automatically because of her conditioning, or because her husband demands it. It is stressed that the woman is trying to stay in control, not to set a record or impress the doctor, but to benefit from the pain relief made available by that effort. Therefore, in transition she must follow instructions despite the difficulty otherwise, the pain will increase. (Barbara A. Smith, et al., "The Transition Phase of Labor," *American Journal of Nursing*, March 1973)

THE SECOND STAGE: DELIVERY

Once the cervix is fully dilated, the second stage of labor actually becomes delivery. In a traditional hospital this is the point at which they put you on a wheeled table and bring you into the delivery room. This is a sterile, functional room with lots of instruments and equipment in evidence. You have been swabbed, sterilized, gowned, and prepared for your baby's arrival.

The actual delivery usually takes 1 to 3 hours for first-time mothers, 30 to 60 minutes if you've had babies before. By this time the character of your contractions changes. Most women feel relief when this expulsion stage starts, and a lot of their discomfort is eased.

At the height of each contraction, you will spontaneously take a deep breath, hold it, and press downward as if you are about to open your bowels. Though the impetus is similar, you are really using a different set of muscles. You may be asked not to push. Gradually, the baby's head is pushed through the fully dilated cervix and begins to inch down the vagina.

During the last weeks of pregnancy the vagina has become quite elastic and can stretch easily to accommodate a baby. As the

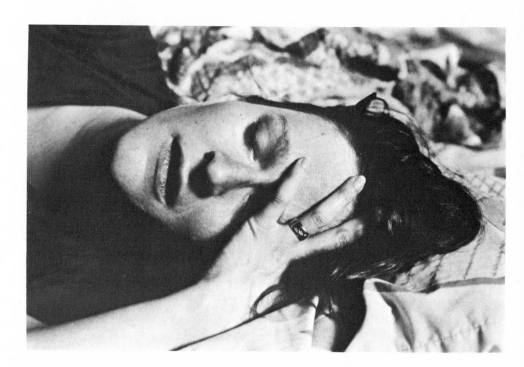

A birth at home

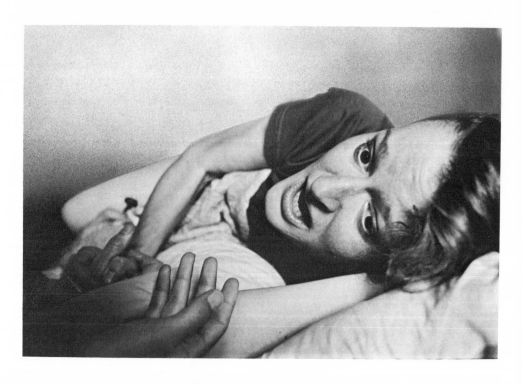

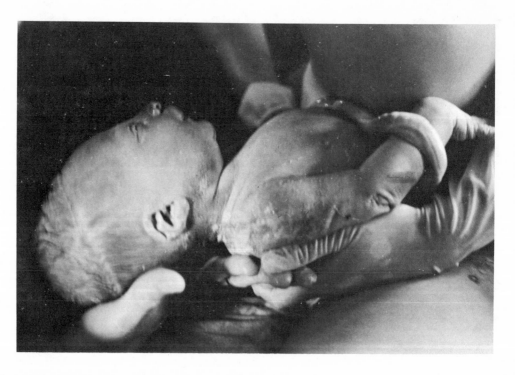

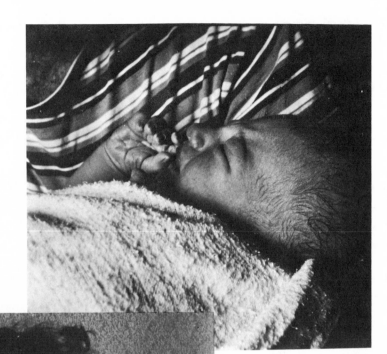

Daniel Kaufman

baby's head comes closer and closer to the exit from the vagina, you will feel it and also feel an even greater desire to push down. If your doctor holds a mirror, you can see the top of the baby's head appearing through the vagina. The incredible sight of your very own baby's head just beginning to show has a medical term: it is called crowning.

Your doctor may perform an episiotomy—under local anesthetic—to make the vaginal opening bigger. They have been routinely performed on several generations of women; it would be hard to find a study which confirmed any contrary position. But there are experienced people who are opposed to this so-called routine procedure. Stephen B. Thacker, M.D., H. David Banta, M.D. and M.P.H., recently reviewed the benefits and risks of episiotomy recorded in 35 books for the last 120 years. Thacker is chief of one department in the Center for Disease Control in Atlanta; Banta is Health Program Manager of the U.S. Office of Technology Assessment. Their conclusions? No clearly defined benefit for routine use; postpartum pain and discomfort; and some serious complications, including death. The operation is performed in over sixty percent of all United States deliveries.

◇ ◇ ◇

Without Episiotomies

The midwives practiced perineal massage to prevent tearing, while the physicians typically did not. This was optimally done by the mother and father for the month prior to delivery and was done by the midwife during the last half of the second stage. This was not done consistently by all parents or all midwives, but it was felt by the midwives that it helped prevent lacerations during delivery. (Lewis E. Mehl, "Statistical Outcomes of Homebirths in the U.S.: Current Status," *Safe Alternatives in Childbirth,* 1976)

◇ ◇ ◇

FORCEPS DELIVERY

Your doctor may also use forceps, if there is a delay in the second stage of labor, perhaps after two hours. Forceps are used when there is fetal distress, such as a lack of oxygen (which shows up when the baby's heartbeat slows), or maternal distress, such

as the inability to bear down. A forceps delivery occurs only if the cervix is fully dilated, the membranes ruptured, and the baby's head is right down in the pelvis.

Forceps are metal tips with ends shaped to fit snugly around the baby's head. In a forceps delivery you are anesthetized. Then each blade is eased separately into the vagina and up to its position cradling the baby's head. The two tongs are then locked together. It is quick and easy to extract the baby, and, according to many generations of doctors, harmless. In the case of premature babies, doctors sometimes prefer a forceps delivery because they believe it spares the still-soft skull from too much pressure from the vaginal walls.

Today there is considerable controversy about the use of forceps. Some people have claimed that their babies have suffered minimal (or maximal) brain damage through their use. Lawsuits have been brought, and doctors have become frightened. Perhaps in response, the rate of cesarean sections keeps increasing; doctors do not want to risk lawsuits and heavier fees for malpractice insurance.

DURING DELIVERY

During the ordinary delivery without forceps, the baby tilts the head upward so the first part to be delivered is the brow, followed by the nose and face, and then mouth and chin. At this point the doctor wipes the eyes, cleans the mouth, and runs a finger around the baby's neck to make sure it is free of the umbilical cord. He or she will probably ask you to pant and not bear down. At the next contraction, with little effort on your part, the shoulders and the rest of the baby will slip out. Seeing this actually happen (through a mirror or sitting up) is an incredible experience for mothers *and* fathers.

At last here is your baby. The first thing you will want to do is hold this tiny new bit of humanity you have helped create. You may be able to. In some births the baby is placed on the mother's stomach before the cord is cut. More often, the doctor cuts the cord, checks the baby, wraps her or him in a blanket and places your infant in your arms. Completion.

Your closeness is the most comforting thing your baby can feel, especially if you hold him or her next to your heart where s/he can hear the heartbeat so familiar after nine months within your body. Try to avoid noise. The hearing of a newborn is acute, and the baby is easily startled. Any movement of yours should be slow and firm. The baby has been floating gently on a cushion of water and is not used to sudden movements.

THE THIRD STAGE

Frequently, doctors give an injection of a drug called *ergometrine* when the baby's head comes out. This causes the womb to contract again about 4 minutes after the baby is delivered. The doctor may then pull gently on the umbilical cord (which in most cases has been cut away from the baby by this time), at the same time pressing your abdomen upward and backward. After the cord is cut, the placenta enters the vagina. You will again feel a desire to push, and the placenta will ease out.*

After delivery the episiotomy is sewed up. This takes about 10 minutes. The stitches will be absorbed in a week's time. By now you will have lost at least 10 pounds—the baby and all the fluid. It will take a month or two to get back to your prepregnancy weight.

THE FOURTH STAGE

Some doctors refer to the immediate postpartum period as the fourth stage of childbirth.

After your child is born, cuddled, and transferred to the nursery, or to your room, you will be cleaned up and probably moved to the recovery room for an hour or so. You'll be carefully watched for signs of hemorrhage or other complications. Once the staff is assured that you're fine, you'll be wheeled either to a postpartum floor as an interim stop or directly back to your own room—which you may not even have seen!

There you may want to sleep—an ordinary reaction in view of what your body has gone through. Or you may find yourself thoroughly exhilarated, lightened, raring to talk to everyone, anxious to move around. Either way, you should do what you prefer to do.

Some experts advise you to limit your visitors, for a day or two, to your husband and the immediate members of your family while you regain your strength. Exerting yourself now is not advisable; you will run the risk of excessive tiredness and less milk later on. Do beam, talk, walk—but rest, too. A lot.

COMMON PRACTICES SHOULD BE UNCOMMON

I have on these pages tried to describe what is usual. And, indeed, these are very common practices in hospitals around the country. For example, Tracy Hotchner estimates that 85 percent of women are medicated during childbirth, with some drugs being given in the IV fluids without the mother's knowledge.

I do want to make it clear, however, that I, as a knowledgeable researcher, am very much opposed to many of the standard practices. I am against the use of drugs in 95 percent of deliveries. I am opposed to shaving the pubic area, to routine enemas, and routine episiotomies. I am very much against the use of forceps, unless their use is crucial to save the baby's life. I am not in favor of cesareans, unless mother or baby is in great danger. And I do not believe doctors should help the placenta get born by pulling on the cord, however gently.

I wish doctors and hospitals would change their practices drastically. Some changes—fathers in the delivery room, babies given to parents right after birth—have been taking place. But it's all *too slow* for my taste. This next generation may need to save the world, and birth practices can hinder them or help

*It has been demonstrated that if a mother can hold her baby immediately after birth, the expulsion of the placenta (or afterbirth) is more readily completed! Further, if a mother must wait longer than two hours after birth to hold and nurse her infant, she is less likely to nurse her baby or make frequent physical contact—and when she does breast-feed, she may not hold him or her so they make face-to-face contact. In later years she may be less loving and could be more likely to respond to her child's behavior with physical punishment rather than sympathy, discussion, or other nonviolent methods. A father's ability to feel and hold his baby, and to establish eye contact, can be just as important as a mother's. (See more on "Bonding" on page 242.)

them begin life in an enabling, humanistic way.

◇ ◇ ◇

When Fathers Are Present

I was beside myself with joy. I had given birth along with my wife. I was exhausted. It was glorious, just glorious.

Whoever said that a joint endeavour of husband and wife in natural childbirth was extremely fulfilling did not come anywhere near describing the ecstasy I experienced. We are so very happy. This experience has made a bond between us that no ordinary birth, nor in fact any other experience, could have done . . .

I couldn't have done it without any analgesics if he had not been with me. His help, encouragement and love were constantly present, and the joy of all three of us being together immediately is indescribable. (Sheila Kitzinger, *Giving Birth*, 1971)

◇ ◇ ◇

MY OWN EXPERIENCES

The First Time

I was crying tears of ecstasy. Here was this amazingly tiny, totally charming, familiar stranger with the quizzical, puzzled expression and a full head of hair—my baby! I could hardly contain myself. As I gazed raptly at him, his lips parted—they move, he moves! I thought—and he gave a long contented sigh. "So this is where I am," said the sigh to me, "interesting, interesting." He was a real person already. I had never been so gloriously thrilled in my life.

The Second Time

"A girl, a girl?" I couldn't believe it until the doctor showed me the first view of my baby, bottom side up. Quickly, too quickly, she was whisked into a small bassinet without clothes on. Immediately, my tears, my joy, my wonder at having a girl unexpectedly gave way to concern. She would be cold! Why didn't they cover her? As soon as they found time to tell me that the bassinet was heated, I relaxed. . . . I watched . . . I listened. Her arms and legs were waving around. And—was it possible?—she was gurgling! Cooing and gurgling. And a dim-

ple showed. A beautiful baby girl with flyaway hair and dimples who gurgled right away! I had never been so gloriously thrilled in my life—except the first time.

◇ ◇ ◇

The Night of My Baby's Birth

I specifically remember the night of my baby's birth, standing out in a corridor of the hospital, looking in through a glass wall at the little newborn babies, knowing that in there was my little girl and from now on it was a good feeling to know that we would be together for the rest of my life, hopefully, even when her road may go separate ways from mine, and most importantly, that I no longer was the center of my universe. (Liv Ullmann)

◇ ◇ ◇

WHAT HAPPENS TO YOUR BABY RIGHT AFTER BIRTH

The traditional hospital procedures for newborn infants are currently under serious question by many birth consumers. Routine matters like suctioning the baby are being challenged as unnecessary and possibly harmful. And evidence now shows that separation of parents from the baby and the standard use of infant nurseries, though quite common, may be unnatural.

Your baby has just completed the most strenuous journey of anyone's life, yet in most hospitals there is no rest! In the first moments in this world, s/he is usually subjected to a rapid series of examinations and procedures.

It used to be the practice to hold the baby by the heels, head down. Current thinking is that gravity can help clear the nasal and oral passages of mucus and blood accumulated during the birth passage. The old-fashioned spank to produce the baby's first cry is quite obsolete, too. Suctioning still is prevalent. Using a rubber tube or bulb, the doctor sucks any blood or mucus from the infant's mouth and nose. The naval cord is clamped about 3 inches from the abdomen and cut. For the first time in nine months, the zygote which became an embryo which became a fetus who became a just-born infant is an independent being.

At one minute after birth, and again at 5

minutes, your baby is rated on a 5-point scale devised by the late pediatrician, Dr. Virginia Apgar. As you can see from the chart of the Apgar Score, p. 237, the rating determines how well your baby is doing.

If your child requires resuscitation, a trained assistant takes over. Modern delivery rooms are equipped with a machine which provides for suction, positive pressure to inflate the lungs, and a mask with constant oxygen to be put over the infant's face until his or her own respiration has taken over.

Without the machine it *is* possible to resuscitate the infant. But this must be done by someone with the proper training and experience. Some doctors advocate an injection of one of several drugs; others immerse the baby for a moment in ice water; still others continue to favor the time-honored spank. But today more and more doctors believe that, short of the need for resuscitation equipment, patience, gentleness and calmness save more babies than all of yesterday's methods combined.

Once the baby is breathing satisfactorily, a gadget resembling a bobby pin is substituted for the clamp on the 3-inch stump of the umbilical cord. This remains until the cord dries up and drops off, usually within a week. Dressings are seldom applied. The cord dries better if exposed to the air.

Next, a drop of silver nitrate or a penicillin ointment is put in the infant's eyes. This is done to eliminate any possibility, no matter how remote, of eye infection as a result of gonorrhea. Since this procedure prevents a baby from clearly seeing the faces of his/her parents right after birth, some parents are asking that the procedure be eliminated or at least postponed as long as possible. A vitamin K injection is also routinely given, but can be avoided by asking the doctor in advance not to give the injection.

Your baby is then tagged with your name. Hospitals vary in the ways they identify the newborn, but generally they provide identical wrist or ankle bands for mother and child, and take footprints of the babies. Your tagged baby is usually snuggled temporarily in a heated crib. The doctor returns to you for immediate postdelivery care. After the placenta is expelled (which may take a short time), the doctor repairs the episiotomy, checks the consistency of the uterus. If it hasn't firmed up, it must be massaged through the abdominal wall. Some people believe in massaging the fundus in any case. Nursing helps the uterus contract, even immediately. Blood pressure, pulse, and respiration are checked, as well as any evidence of vaginal bleeding.

Back to your new baby.

First, the doctor examines the baby to see if there are any congenital defects. With minor ones immediate corrective action can be taken.

The skull is checked to determine the size of the "soft spot." (If it is too wide, that indicates pressure usually caused by a condition known as water on the brain.) Heart and lungs are listened to in order to check that the sounds indicate proper heart structure and lung expansion. The doctor feels the infant's abdomen for tumors, turns the baby over to examine the spine.

Next, genitals and rectum are checked. In boys, especially those born prematurely, both testicles may not be descended. There is a procedure to rectify this. Should the anus be closed over, which sometimes happens, a surgical procedure to open it will be performed by a specialist within a few hours.

The fingers and toes are counted and examined and the whole bone structure is felt, just in case there is an unsuspected fracture.

After the checking procedures your baby is wrapped in a receiving blanket and brought to you for an introductory visit before being transferred to the nursery, and before you enter the recovery room. In some hospitals your baby may already be with you. More and more, parents are asking that their new infant be placed on the mother's stomach right after birth. As a result, more of today's hospitals are giving the baby to the mother's arms right away. The Leboyer method is spreading and influencing traditionalists!

To Protect the Eyes

In 1884, a great German obstetrician, Karl Crede, discovered that a drop or two of a weak silver-nitrate solution dropped into each immediately after birth assured healthy eyes. This was one of the most beneficent contributions ever made to medicine, for its employment has almost eliminated this cruel scourge [blindness caused by maternal gonococcus infection]. It is now a law in most states that the doctor must instill some kind

Abbie Soroka photographed by her father

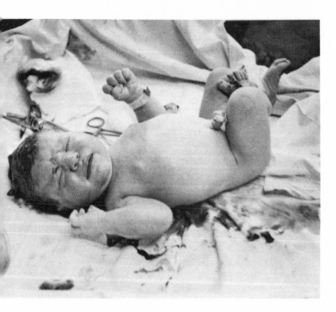

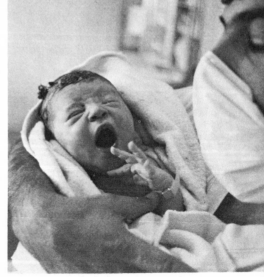

Father and daughter

of silver solution into the eyes of every baby shortly after birth. The antiseptic solution itself may occasionally cause mild irritation for a day or two; accordingly, if your baby develops some redness of its eyelids, along with a small amount of secretion, do not think that this portends a cold or an infection, but understand that it is merely a slight chemical irritation which is invariably harmless and of brief duration. (Nicholson J. Eastman, M.D., *Expectant Motherhood*, 1947)

◇   ◇   ◇

The Herculean Task: Breathing

According to Stanley James of Babies Hospital in New York City . . . pressure changes [in the chest cavity] may play a major part in causing the infant to take his first breath. While the baby is still in the womb, his lungs are crumpled up and deflated, although they contain some fluid. When the baby passes through the birth canal, his chest cavity is subjected to considerable pressure. This forces the fluid out through the nostrils and mouth. Immediately after birth, when the constriction has been removed, the chest expands the way a sponge does after being squeezed, and air rushes into the lungs to fill the vacuum. The baby's first sound may not be the traditional cry, but a cough, designed to expel the last remaining fluid in the lungs.

If Dr. James is correct, the baby's first intake of air is a passive process. Thereafter, he must actively breathe for himself. And the effort this involves is sometimes Herculean. The first independent breath may take as much as 10 times the inhalation force required of an adult. The first few breaths expand the baby's lungs up to three quarters of their total capacity, but the healthy newborn does not seem to find this too much of a strain. His lungs expand this much every time he cries in anger. (J. M. Tanner and G. R. Taylor, *Growth*, 1965)

Method of Scoring for Apgar Score

Sixty seconds and again at five minutes after the complete birth of the infant (disregarding the cord and placenta) the following five objective signs are evaluated and each given a score of 0, 1, or 2. A score of 10 indicates an infant is in the best possible condition. Infants with scores of 5 to 10 usually need no immediate treatment. A score of 4 or below indicates the need for prompt diagnosis and treatment.

Sign	0	1	2	1 Min. Score	5 Min. Score
Heart Rate	Absent	Slow (Below 100)	Over 100		
Respiratory Effort	Absent	Slow Irregular	Good Crying		
Muscle Tone	Limp	Some Flexion of Extremities	Active Motion		
Reflex irritability: Response to Catheter in Nostril	No Response	Grimace	Cough or Sneeze		
Color	Blue, Pale	Body Pink, Extremities Blue	Completely Pink*		

Doris Haire, *The Cultural Warping of Childbirth*, 1972

*American professionals are frequently amazed to see the consistency with which Scandinavian and Dutch newborn infants "pink up" to the very tips of their fingers and toes a few seconds after being born.

◇ ◇ ◇

Dr. Leboyer on Newborn Breathing

The danger the child faces during birth has quite properly been stressed. This danger is anoxia: a deficiency of the precious oxygen to which the nervous system is so acutely sensitive.

If it happens that the child fails to receive oxygen, the result is irreparable damage to the brain: a person maimed for life. So at all costs, the child must not lack oxygen at birth, not even for an instant. As the experts tell us. As Nature has always known.

She has arranged it so that during the dangerous passage of birth, the child is receiving oxygen from two sources rather than one; from the lungs and from the umbilicus.

Two systems functioning simultaneously, one relieving the other: the old one, the umbilicus, continues to supply oxygen to the baby until the new one, the lungs, has fully taken its place.

However, once the infant has been born and delivered from the mother, it remains bound to her by this umbilicus, which continues to beat for several long minutes: four . . . five . . . sometimes more.

Oxygenated by the umbilicus, sheltered from anoxia, the baby can settle into breathing without danger and without shock. At leisure. Without rush.

In addition, the blood has plenty of time to abandon its old route (which leads to the placenta) and progressively to fill the pulmonary circulatory system.

During this time, in parallel fashion, an orifice closes in the heart, which seals off the old route forever.

In short, for an average of four or five minutes, the newborn infant straddles two worlds. Drawing oxygen from two sources, it switches gradually from the one to the other, without a brutal transition. One scarcely hears a cry. (Dr. Frederick Leboyer, *Birth Without Violence*, 1975)

◇ ◇ ◇

A CONVERSATION WITH DR. LEBOYER

When the great French birth specialist was in New York, he made the following remarks to me and others who came to meet him.

They Are One

"There should be a feeling, ultimately in the child (which is never going to be there when there is forceps or anything)—this feeling [that] it's 'my' experience. She or he earns it, and this is one of the main points against all the techniques which are depriving the child of this feeling—and from this deep, close, total relationship between the child and the mother, because all along during the process, they are not two, they are one."

Talking to the Newborn

"The only thing which matters is that whatever you do, you first tell the child, 'I'm going to put drops in your eyes. I hope you don't mind.' Continuously. You are not manipulating a passive object. You are talking to someone and you are relating to someone. For each and everything you are doing with this baby, first you should say, 'I'm going to do that and I hope you don't mind.' And the reaction or the attitude of the child will be totally different."

Baby and Mother

"Usually, with a normal birth, and when there's no difficulties, keep the baby on the mother's stomach for three minutes, two or three minutes and put a blanket on both of them."

The Baby's Bath

"The warm water bath is just nearby, close to the mother so that she can be in the picture, not in the next room. Otherwise she has a feeling that the child is taken away and, as it were, the magic circle is broken and the people are there.

"After the bath, the child is given back to the mother, of course, and the bath should be given close to the mother. She should even be able to touch the baby's feet or hand. It must be within reach."

A Love Story

"I'm sure you understand that this is a love story, no more, no less. The love between mother and child."

THE NORMAL NEWBORN

To give you some clues to how your new baby will look and behave, the following is a list from the American Institute of Family Relations of Los Angeles, California.

I. Initial Behavior
  A. First cry
    1. physician usually removes mucus from throat as head emerges
    2. after this, infant begins active respiration, as chest emerges
    3. if infant does not breathe spontaneously, he may need stimulation, e.g., stroking of back or gentle patting of buttocks
  B. Further crying when restrained or manipulated. For example:
    1. when silver nitrate is put in eyes
    2. when cord is clamped
    3. when bathed
    4. when dressed
  C. Sneezing
    1. common in newborns
    2. clears upper respiratory tract
  D. Reaction to light
    1. eyes don't focus perfectly, but infants attempt this
    2. baby squints, blinks, or frowns when there is bright light
    3. eyes will follow bright object if it moves slowly
  E. Reaction to sound
    1. infant startles when loud noise occurs nearby
    2. arms and legs flail wildly, often in circles
  F. Breathing is irregular. This is usual
    1. sometimes gasping
    2. sometimes holding their breath
    3. sometimes panting
    4. some long, slow breaths
  G. Coughing helps newborns get rid of mucus
  H. Grasp reflex strong
    1. fingers will grasp what is put in the hand
    2. especially strong in the premature infant
    3. arms and legs grasp, seeking to cling
  I. Little need for nourishment at first
  J. Sucking and swallowing reflexes are present in the full-term baby

II. Initial Appearance
  A. Head
    1. is likely to be molded, especially if second stage was long (bones of skull overlap to permit passage through pelvis)
    2. black hair or very little hair are common
    3. nose usually flattened
    4. eyes blue
    5. eyes may be puffy from silver nitrate for a day or two after birth
    6. pulse shows through fontanels (soft spots)
    7. if forceps were used there may be bruises on the cheeks
    8. ears may be distorted due to position in the uterus
  B. Body
    1. skin wrinkled and loose if baby weighs 6 or 7 pounds
    2. skin likely to be smooth and firm if baby weighs 8 or 9 pounds
    3. skin may be yellowish when four or five days old
      a. breakdown of extra red blood corpuscles
      b. called physiologic jaundice
      c. shows most in the white of the eye
    4. greasy, white material is called vernix, nature's cold cream
    5. lanugo is fine hair which remains on the ears, back, shoulders, and other parts of the newborn, but disappears shortly
    6. color is likely to be bluish at first, then purplish-pink, then quite red and finally settles down to pink
  C. Limbs
    1. legs may be bowed
    2. feet may turn different ways due to position in uterus
    3. limbs may wave about in random movement

III. Functioning
  A. Temperature-regulating mechanism not well developed
    1. infant is easily chilled
    2. feet may be bluish and feel cold for many weeks
    3. infant does not sweat; care should be taken not to overdress
  B. Sleep
    1. newborn likely to sleep most of the time for a day or two
    2. when he drowses during a feeding, jiggling his body will arouse him without upsetting him

C. There is likely to be some weight loss. This is normal in the first few days
D. Scaling and peeling at the creases is normal and to be expected

IV. Mother's Feelings
    A. If not heavily medicated, she may be alert, quite excited, and may have trouble settling down to rest and sleep
    B. Concern for her baby is generally first for his sex and then for his healthy normalcy
    C. Most mothers do not feel their infant is immediately good looking
    D. She may wonder if she will ever feel at ease with her new baby
    E. She may worry whether his stores of water, fat, and sugar will be enough to last him until her milk comes in
    F. She is sometimes weepy, as glandular changes are rather drastic
    G. She may be irritable at times and quick to fatigue

WHAT WILL YOUR BABY LOOK LIKE?

Most babies just born look perfectly wonderful to their parents. New mothers and fathers often cry with happiness at the sight of this incredible part of themselves who has come to life as a separate person. And even to an objective outsider, many newborn infants look enchantingly tiny, deliciously whole and human with all their parts functioning.

Still . . . some babies are born less than perfect. And many new parents do not have any experience in what a newborn looks like. The fact is that a newborn baby often looks rather odd and can be a disappointment even to a prepared parent.

One father I know, who participated in the birth experience from start to finish and had read extensively, still confidently expected that he would have a round, pink and white, curly-headed cuddly baby to hold the minute his child was born. Not so!

His baby had a bald pointed head, a squashed-in nose, a blotchy red skin, and seemed totally out of proportion. All of this, while quite normal, was a shock to him. As he was busy adjusting himself to this strange

apparition and reassuring his wife, the baby's appearance gradually changed over a few days to the more expected kind.

To help you realize that all is not pink and white and soft and smooth, here is a rundown of what many parents see when the baby is born.

Compared to adult proportions, the face of a newborn is much smaller than its head size. Some babies' heads are more egg-shaped than round as a result of the passage through that narrow birth canal. If your baby's head looks like this, don't worry! It will round out spontaneously in three or four days.

Many children are born with a thick, softish swelling of one part of the scalp. This may be caused simply by the birth process. The part of the head that first appeared before the cervix was completely dilated is the part that has swollen. Sometimes the swelling is caused by a superficial blood clot, or cephalhematoma. This sounds frightening—but is not at all. The first kind of swelling disappears in a few days. The cephalhematoma may grow for a while and be present for a few weeks. Medically, it has no meaning. There are two slightly depressed parts of the top and back of your baby's head. These are called the fontanels—and the area will remain soft (and should be protected) for a good part of the first year.

Some babies have a squashed look: their noses resemble that of a battered prizefighter! Since the nose is only malleable cartilage at first, and since during birth your baby slides out of the birth passage on the nose, it is easy to understand how it might become spread and flattened. But rest easy! A couple of weeks later there is scarcely any resemblance between the nose at birth and the nose now.

In a forceps delivery a facial nerve on one side may be temporarily paralyzed from the pressure of the instrument. The face of the baby is then lopsided. This, too, clears up—as a rule within 24 hours. There may also be a little bruising, which will clear up.

Your baby's arms will seem out of proportion to the legs. They *are* longer.

Your new arrival may be keeping his or her eyes shut most of the time. (Sleepy babies whose mothers have had an anesthetic tend to do so.) If you lift the infant to a sitting position, the eyes will snap open like a doll's. The eyes will be blue, usually, and will change some months or a year later—if they are to be dark. In dark-skinned babies, the blue may be a darker shade or colorless.

Some infants are born with hemorrhages—red blotches—within the whites of their eyes. These usually disappear in 10 days. Some babies react to silver-nitrate drops, if these are used, by developing a secretion in one or both eyes. This goes away of its own accord in a few days.

The most common characteristic of the eyes of a newborn baby is that they don't focus: they look crossed. When this seems to be the case, it usually is not so at all. Focusing will develop gradually.

At birth a baby's skin is covered with a soft, greasy white material called *vernix*, or *vernix caseosa*. This coating has helped the infant slide easily through the birth canal—but it *does* make a newborn slippery to hold! The vernix washes off, but if it is left on, it will absorb gradually and lessen the chances of rashes for a few days. At birth the skin may have tiny cracks in the folds. A baby's skin is incredibly sensitive and subject to such irritations as prickly heat, diaper rash, and infections such as impetigo. Skin protection is desirable.

Infections do happen and if your baby is hospital born, s/he may receive antibiotics and be transferred to an isolation nursery. Don't worry about sneezing, however. Newborn babies sneeze a lot. It doesn't mean they are catching cold. It is almost unheard of for a baby under two weeks old to catch a cold. Hiccups and snorts are quite common, too. Gurgles may also be present immediately—a most delightful situation which is a blessing for a new parent.

Lots of babies have small strawberry marks on the forehead, the nape of the neck, the eyelids or the bridge of the nose. These usually disappear. If not, they can be faded by specific medication. A couple of days after birth your baby may develop a touch of jaundice which shows up for about a week.

(About one third of the babies develop this.) Nursing mothers sometimes stop for a few days until the jaundice clears up. Or at the base of your baby's spine there can be a bluish-gray spot, called the Mongolian spot. It is more frequent among non-white babies than among white ones. In the former cases it blends into the natural skin color; in white babies it fades.

Your baby may be covered with down (or hair) known as lanugo, even on the face, which will shed in a week or so. For a couple of weeks thereafter the skin will scale off. Some babies have a head of black hair growing low on the forehead. This "first hair" comes out. When the new, permanent hair grows in, it may be quite different in all respects. Many a blond started out that way!

A new infant is tiny and barrel-chested. By comparison with the chest the hips and belly seem flat and small. You may wonder how you will ever be able to secure a diaper on this tiny frame!

Hands and feet often seem enormous compared to the size of the arms and legs. (Some parents are also amazed at the disproportionate size of a baby girl's genitalia, which seem quite large.) The baby's legs curl up in the fetal position and are bowed. If you had a breech birth, your baby's legs may turn inward. Your baby's tiny hands are typically clenched into fists. Both hands and feet may be darker than the rest of the body, sometimes as dark as crimson to bluish purple. Toes, too, can be deeply colored. The color also disappears shortly. There may be mottling, as well. This coloration disappears after a few hours.

In any case, despite your first impressions, it is likely that in a few weeks you, too, will have a pink (or brown), plump and cuddly—if not curly-haired—baby simulating the traditional artists' conception of how a baby should look. Believe it or not, babies do look like the most sentimental rendition of them once those first days or weeks are past!

Bonding

SNUGGLING BENEFITS BABIES

Can you and your baby look at each other right away? Will you be able to touch your baby and feel his or her skin? Will you hold your newborn infant?

These may seem like questions of slight significance. Yet they are momentous—according to recent research. How you react to your baby and how the baby responds to you are greatly influenced by simple matters like touching and holding right after the birth.

Studies in this field are called bonding studies, and among the pioneers of the field are Drs. Marshall Klaus and John Kennell.

These doctors have compared babies separated from their mothers for some hours after delivery with newborn babies who immediately spent 45 minutes with their mothers in a private room with both lying down and cuddling skin to skin. The latter group, when checked a number of months later, had had fewer illnesses and had gained more weight. The mothers of this group were also more likely to breast-feed, and were more loving with their babies.

These and other studies do indicate definite long-term benefits over the years: early and continued touching between parents and child seems to produce healthier, brighter children, happier families, less child neglect and abuse.

How It Used to Be

The father transmits to the daughters the form of the head, the framework of the chest and of the superior extremities, while the conformation of the lower portion of the body and the inferior extremities is transmitted by the mother. With the sons this is reversed. They derive from the mother the shape of the head and of the superior extremities, and resemble the father in the trunk and inferior extremities. From this it therefore results, that boys procreated by intelligent women will be intelligent, and that girls procreated by fathers of talent will inherit their mental capacity.

George H. Napheys, M.D., *The Physical Life of Women: Advice to the Maiden, Wife and Mother,* 1889.

Strokes

One of our basic needs is a need for stimulation from outside ourselves. *The most effective way of meeting our need for stimulation is physical contact from another human being.* Eric Berne . . . defined "strokes" as the basic unit of recognition between persons. . . . Rene Spitz's studies . . . demonstrated that infants who are not stimulated fail to thrive and often die. Stroke-deprived grownups may have at least temporary mental disturbances. Lack of stimulation is a frequent cause of the rapid decline in elderly persons who live isolated lives.

Physical stroking is a particularly important component in the survival of all infants. Quantity of stroking is not the only factor; the ways in which babies are stroked help to define their world: rough, gentle, secure, indifferent. Adequate physical stroking when we were infants forms a base from which we all expanded to a more active approach to the world. As we grew we also came to accept other strokes: a smile, a frown, words of praise or punishment. (Dorothy E. Babcock, R.N., M.S., and Terry D. Keepers, Ph.D., *Raising Kids O.K.*, 1977)

Exploring the Baby

One of the things you notice if you put a nude baby next to the mother is a specific "getting acquainted" sequence shown in motion pictures we have taken. First she begins to touch the infant's toes and fingers and within eight minutes proceeds to massaging his entire trunk, eventually exploring much of the body. This might also be compared with the nuzzling and licking of her newborn by an animal mother. It's an identification, examining process. However, in humans during this period there's increasing eye-to-eye contact. And if you cover the eyes, the mother is upset. If the baby's eyes are closed because he's asleep, it will often be a day or two before the mother fully believes that the baby is hers. (Dr. Marshall H. Klaus, quoted by Elliott H. McCleary, in *New Miracles of Childbirth*, 1974)

Babies Move in Time to Speech

Recent exciting observations by Condon and Sander (1974) reveal that newborns also move in time with the structure of adult speech . . . as the speaker pauses for breath or accents a syllable, the infant almost imperceptibly raises an eyebrow or lowers a foot. The investigators demonstrated that live speech in particular is effective in entraining infant movement. Neither tapping noises nor disconnected vowel sounds showed the degree of correspondence with neonate movement as did natural, rhythmic speech. (Marshall H. Klaus and John H. Kennell, *Maternal-Infant Bonding*, 1976)

Gentle Handling

It is a handicap to the parent-child bond if the couple does not share with each other the first meeting with their child. The baby belongs to the couple, not to the hospital, the grandparents, or the in-laws. . . . The baby is awake for a while after birth and needs the physical contact of being held before being wheeled down to be added to the row of cribs in the nursery. Gentle handling helps to stimulate his breathing and circulation. (Constance A. Bean, *Methods of Childbirth*, 1974)

That Most Important Hour

In an interesting and significant observation of fathers, Lind (1973) noted that paternal caregiving in the first three months of life was greatly increased when the father was asked to undress his infant twice and to establish eye-to-eye contact with him for 1 hour during the first three days of life. On the basis of this evidence, we strongly believe that an essential principle of attachment is that there is a *sensitive period* in the first minutes and hours after an infant's birth which is optimal for parent-infant attachment. . . .

. . . Wolff (1959) described for the first time six separate states of consciousness in the infant, ranging from deep sleep to screaming. The state with which we are most concerned is state 4, the quiet, alert state. In this state the infant's eyes are wide open, and he is able to respond to his environment. . . . Desmond and co-workers (1966) observed that the infant is in state 4 for a period of 45 to 60 minutes during the first hour after birth. After this discovery it was possible to demonstrate that an infant can see, he has visual preferences, and he will turn his head to the spoken word, all in the first hour of life. After this hour, however, he goes into a deep sleep for 3 to 4 hours. Thus for 1 hour after birth he is ideally equipped for the important first meeting with his parents. (Marshall H. Klaus and John H. Kennell, *Maternal-Infant Bonding*, 1976)

Baby Caring

HOW TO NURSE AS SOON AS THE BABY ARRIVES

Ask to have the baby at your breast right away. You won't have any milk yet; you will have colostrum—but your newborn will nuzzle and suck and will benefit from nursing right away.

Whatever your baby's birthplace, be sure that he or she is with you, and starting to nurse many times for short periods during the first days after birth. Avoid long hours or a day of separation. The sooner you both begin, the easier it will be.

In the first days nurse the baby sitting up in bed, with the baby's head resting in the crook of your arm, and your arm resting on pillows for support. (Some people suggest a lying down position—but I believe that this is risky. New mothers sometimes doze during nursing, and a sitting-up position will prevent rolling on the baby or other difficulties.) Your sitting position in bed or chair should be comfortable with support for both of your arms. Be sure to support your baby's head and back at all times.

Stroke your baby's cheek with your nipple so that she/he will turn to the breast. Squeeze your breast horizontally, so that the full nipple, including most of the areola (the dark surrounding area) enters your baby's mouth.

Use a finger of your other hand to depress your breast slightly next to your baby's nose, so that there will be plenty of breathing space.

Prevent your baby from clamping his/her gums on your nipple at all times. Remove your nipple from the baby's mouth and wait a minute or two before resuming nursing.

For the first days, give your baby 5 min-

How It Used to Be

It was believed at this time [the eighteenth century] that babies were born hungry, so various concoctions were poured down newborns' throats immediately upon arrival: pap of bread and water, or a blend of flour and sugar, or oil of almonds, or a syrup of violets or a spoonful of sugar or butter, or sugar and butter combined. It was also customary to feed newborns ten or twelve times a day.

Joan Bel Geddes
Small World: A History of Baby Care from the Stone Age to the Spock Age, 1964

utes of nursing time on one breast and then 5 minutes on the other. (After this time, put a finger on the side of the baby's mouth to loosen the hold on your nipple.) Keep the time limited to help prevent soreness. The next nursing time, start on the second breast first.

In between nursings, as much as you can, keep your nipples open to the air, and the sun, too, if possible.

Nurse *often*—every 2, 2½ or 3 hours—to help increase your milk supply. Some experts recommend waking a sleeping baby in order to establish a good quantity of milk during the first weeks.

Keep your general routine, and your life, calm and even. Avoid tension-producing situations, arguments, hectic rushes, worries, and problems as much as you can. The two most common causes of insufficient milk, or the drying up of the milk supply, are insufficient nursing—and tensions, worries, rushing around.

After each nursing period, manually express from each breast whatever milk remains. There will always be a little milk left, but the more the breasts are emptied, the more likely the supply will continue.

Use some of the time to *start a dialogue* with this brand-new human being you both have produced. Hum or sing softly to your baby. Talk or sing baby-talk. (There is absolutely nothing wrong with baby-talking to an infant.) Make up your own songs and words.

Enjoy it! Think of nursing as a fun—together time for you and your baby. It's important, even vital, for you and very serious business. But—it is also just plain lovely. An activity of love and giving; one of the great natural gifts of life.

TIME—AND NURSING: QUESTIONS AND ANSWERS

Here is a simple question-and-answer list gleaned from many sources, which should help you during those first weeks.

Q. Suppose my baby wants to nurse much longer than the recommended five minutes on each breast?

A. Unless your nipples are too tender, give your baby as much nursing time as s/he wants. The need to suck is almost as strong as the need to be fed, and varies in strength from baby to baby. Try a breast shield for *very* sore nipples.

Q. How many times at night should I nurse?

A. At least once during the eight-hour period. Twice if your baby seems to need it. Some babies may need a *lot* of night nursing (or sucking) at first.

Q. If my baby wants to stay at my breast for an hour or two at a time, what do I do?

A. Try to put your baby down in crib or bassinet after a reasonable nursing-and-play period—and see if the baby's crying lasts too long, or subsides after burping. If it continues for 7 or 8 minutes, try rocking the baby to sleep. Also try a pacifier, if necessary.

Q. How long should I nurse my baby for the sake of antibody protection?

A. Four months is the recommended time, in terms of protection against infection and other ailments.

Q. If I'm able to nurse longer, when is a good time to start weaning my baby from the breast?

A. Any time up to a year or 15-16 months, or even longer if you like. Your baby may still need a bottle for another year or two (or more), but will also drink from a cup.

Q. Can I use a relief bottle every day from the beginning?

A. Yes, if your milk supply is *very* good and you really need and want the time off. But most specialists in the field of breast feeding do *not* recommend it in the early weeks, however, even using your own milk. A breast-feeding baby's sucking strength is weakened by bottle feeding.

Q. Will nursing delay my baby's eating solid foods and drinking other liquids?

A. It certainly should! Breast milk is the ideal food and is all that is usually needed by infants, even in liquids, for a long period of time.

Q. What if the baby's doctor wants to start solids early?

A. Maybe there is a good reason why—but be sure to read the literature and to question the doctor closely before you agree. For four to six months, I am *very* doubtful about this procedure, and think it is probably harmful to babies, who could run a greater risk of allergies.

Q. What should I eat and drink?

A. Eat a balanced diet. Drink water (juice or milk) for two. Avoid Coke, coffee, and lo-cal drinks most of the time. Also, avoid chocolate. The *Journal of Pediatrics* reported (in 1979) on research which found negative infant reactions—diarrhea, eczema, irritability—when mothers ate chocolate.

Tips and Hints from La Leche

It has been our experience that alcohol, tincture of benzoin and similar drying agents, and soap tend to be irritating, so avoid using any of these things. Avoid plastic-coated pads in your bras; they can cause trouble, especially in hot weather.

Some mothers think that nursing less often—say every four hours instead of two or three—will help sore nipples. The opposite is more often true. Easy-going, leisurely nursing every two or three hours is actually easier on nipples that are tender, because then the breasts don't become overfull, and the baby doesn't get so ravenously hungry that he nurses over-vigorously.

There is possibly a relation between apprehension on the part of the mother and sore nipples. Slightly tender nipples may cause enough tension to hold back the letdown reflex. The delay in the milk may make the baby angry so that he pulls and tugs at the nipple, making it even sorer—and creating greater concern on your part. What can you do about this? You can hand-express a little milk to start the flow.

Make a deliberate effort to relax before nursing. Try a warm tub or shower, or quicker and sometimes even more effective, lean over a washbowl with breasts immersed in comfortably hot water. (*Nipple Care*, July 1978, adapted from *The Womanly Art of Breastfeeding*, 1974)

If it is difficult for baby to grasp the nipple because of engorgement, express some of the milk first by hand.

How to hand-express your milk: cup the breast in your hand, placing your thumb above and forefinger below the nipple, on the edge of the dark area (areola). Press inward toward the chest wall, squeeze thumb and finger together gently, release, and repeat. (Don't slide the finger and thumb out toward the nipple.) Rotate your hand to reach all the milk ducts, which radiate out from the nipple at all points of the clock. Alternate sides every few minutes. Don't worry if nothing comes out the first few times you try it; you'll get the knack of it soon.

If baby has lots of wet diapers, the baby is getting enough to eat. What comes out must have gone in. Your completely breast-fed baby doesn't need water. Even in hot weather, increased nursing will usually take care of baby's need for fluids. Again, judge by the diapers.

Some breast-fed babies never need burping. Others need it only in the early months.

Do not worry about bowel movements. The completely breast-fed baby does not get constipated. The stool is usually quite loose, sometimes just a stain on the diaper, and varies in color. Your baby may have six or more bowel movements a day, or only one

---

How It Used to Be

The Board of Health yesterday issued the following circular in relation to the care and feeding of infants during the hot weather:

In nursing, over-feeding does more harm than anything else; nurse an infant a month or two old every two or three hours. Nurse an infant of 6 months and over five times in 24 hours, and no more. If an infant is thirsty, give it pure water, or barley-water, no sugar. On the hottest days, a few drops of whisky may be added to either water or food, the whisky not to exceed a teaspoonful in 24 hours.*

"How to Save Infants," *The New York Times*, July 18, 1876

*Author's Note: Even the Board of Health can err—Whiskey for babies, alas!

every five or six days. This is all normal and no cause for worry.

Most important to successful breast-feeding is having confidence in yourself. As the weeks go by your confidence will grow, and you will take even more pride and pleasure in nursing your baby. Happy mothering! (La Leche League International, *When You Breastfeed Your Baby*, 1974)

◇   ◇   ◇

Nursing After Separation

Sometimes a mother and baby are separated for a few days, and the mother finds it difficult to dispense with formula feeding when she rejoins her baby. If this situation arises, you can rebuild your milk supply and decrease the formula gradually by nursing before you give the bottle. Each day dilute the formula a little more with boiled water. The baby will nurse more often in response to the weaker formula, and your milk will usually increase after a few days to the point where the supplemental feeding is no longer necessary. (Alice Gerard, *Please Breast-feed Your Baby*, 1970)

◇   ◇   ◇

Mother Caring: Rest and Exercise

And Sixty Years Later

The first day after delivery you will probably do a lot of sleeping. Labor is hard work and you are tired. Depending on how you feel and if you had a normal delivery, you will be allowed out of bed as soon as you feel you want to get up. Actually, getting out of bed and moving around helps speed up your recovery. (U.S. Department of Health, Education and Welfare, *Prenatal Care,* 1973)

YOU'RE BACK TO YOU

You have been the vehicle. And in many ways you still are, especially if you're nurs-ing. But there is a *you* underneath all of the concentration upon your baby. Quite apart from your new progeny, you still need care and loving.

What kind of care?

Well, you need to know about your body first of all.

You will have a floppy belly. No use kidding yourself. The skin simply is hanging in folds. It is *extra* skin. But take heart. It will not stay that way. And if you exercise, a week or two will see the folds disappear.

You will also have an enlarged abdomen. No one ever has the same flat prebaby belly postbaby. Your uterus is keeping your abdomen enlarged. In about 6 weeks, the uterus is back to normal. Your stomach should be, too, *if* you exercise.

*The first landmark publication of the great U.S. Children's Bureau helped reduce infant and maternal mortality. Its approach is antiquated only by today's knowledge and standards.

What about exercise? How soon should you start? Within a few days or even almost right away. You can do them on your bed at first. Follow your doctor's instructions. But do exercise to get back into shape. Even if you don't do specific exercises, you should walk around and move. Nothing strenuous, but definitely be active. An excellent book with instructions for postpartum exercises is *Essential Exercises for the Childbearing Years* by Elizabeth Noble. Also excellent is Elisabeth Bing's *Moving Through Pregnancy*.

You may have some afterpains in your abdomen for some days. These are like menstrual cramps and occur because your uterus keeps on contracting. For some unknown reason, these pains cause more discomfort after a second baby.

Another hurting area may be your bottom. The episiotomy stitches may pull. A heat lamp, a pain-relieving spray or sitz bath (just sitting in warm water) may be used to help.

There are some other possible problems, usually quite minor. For example, you probably will be perspiring more than usual. Or you may be constipated. (Eat a lot of fresh fruits and vegetables; do *not* take a harsh laxative; check with your doctor about it.) Or you may have some problem urinating. If so, you will need assistance and do tell the nurse or doctor about it.

There will be some bleeding. This will be bright red (it is called lochia) and will diminish as well as change color to a brownish discharge after a week. After that, the discharge is usually yellow-white—and it disappears by the end of the third week.

Your regular menstruation will usually begin 6 to 8 weeks after childbirth—if you're not nursing. But you may not menstruate for 5 or 6 months, if you are.

Sex after childbirth varies from couple to couple. Nowadays, 3 to 6 weeks is the suggested waiting time. But some couples do not want to wait—and a lot depends upon the healing of the vagina, and the individual feelings of each of you.

After about 4 weeks (sometimes 6) you will have the official postpartum examination. The standard work-up will be given (an internal, your weight, blood pressure, hemoglobin checked and probably a Pap smear taken). This is also the time to ask questions.

Of course, you will be caring for your body in other ways—by sleeping and resting as much as you can, by keeping clean with showers or sponge baths at first, by brushing your hair (or otherwise stimulating your scalp). You'll be getting back to your old clothes, which will seem new all over again.

But *you* also need another type of care: emotional self-care. For your emotions influence your body—and vice versa. See a later section for more about your emotional well-being.

How It Used to Be

The mother should maintain rigidly the recumbent position for the first few days, not raising her shoulders from the pillow for any purpose, and should abstain from receiving visitors, and from any social conversation for the first twenty-four hours.

After the third or fourth day *the dress should be changed.* The dress worn during labor, if our directions have been carried out, will not have been soiled. The clothing should be changed without uncovering the person, and without raising the head from the pillow.

A mother should remain in bed for at least two weeks after the birth of the child, and should not return to her household duties under a month.

George H. Napheys, M.D., *The Physical
Life of Women: Advice to the Maiden, Wife and Mother,* 1889

Part Six

NOT–SO–USUAL BIRTH SITUATIONS

A baby is God's opinion that life should go on.

CARL SANDBURG

Columbia Presbyterian Hospital

To Know Is Better

Your pregnancy and baby's birth may seem extraordinary. But the likelihood is that the process of growing and birthing your child will be quite *ordinary*. "Ordinary? This miracle?" you may well ask with rising inflection.

Oh, but you must, should, ought to be nothing but grateful for the "ordinariness," for the "normalcy" of your becoming a mother (or father). Otherwise, you will be one of those select and often not-too-happy few who experience a complication. This can range from the lovely but somewhat overwhelming prospect of having twins or triplets, to the dreadful, but very infrequent, possibility of losing your baby. Yes, complications, out-of-the-ordinary situations you can do without.

Nonetheless, they *do* occur. And with enough frequency so that you should at least be informed about the more common situations. There may be complications with the birth itself, or complications with the baby after birth. The discussions that follow are by no means complete, and other literature has fuller information. Whether this is the time to acquire it is a decision that no one else can make for you. Personally, however, I favor the route of some knowledge. For it is only with knowledge that we are somewhat armed against the unexpected. Further, early knowledge often helps prevent complications and/or alleviates their effect.

The High-Risk Numbers are Estimates

Each year in the United States, approximately 3,300,000 women give birth. An estimated half-million cases—almost one of every seven—are deemed to be at high risk. *A precise estimate of the number* of pregnancies at high risk in the U.S. is elusive. Many obstetricians estimate about 15%. But definitions vary, the range of opinion is vast—from less than 5% to more than half. (Robert Wood Johnson Foundation, *Special Report No. 2*, 1978)

Multiple Births

WHO WILL HAVE A MULTIPLE BIRTH?

TWINS

You have the greatest chance of bearing twins if you are black, aged 35 to 40 and already have 6 children. On the other hand, if you are an Oriental teen-ager and pregnant for the first time, you have the least possible likelihood of having twins!

White women in their teens have twins once in 167 births.

If you are between 35 and 50 years of age and this is your first pregnancy, the chances for twins are one in 74. But you have increased your chances considerably—to one in 45 births—if this is your seventh pregnancy!

After age 40 the chances go back down to those for teen-agers.

If you already have twins, your chances of having twins are 5 times the national average.

Twins are relatively commonplace: one in approximately 85 births are twins.

TRIPLETS

Until the development of fertility pills (designed to help women with sluggish or inactive ovaries produce a monthly *ovum*, or egg), the chances of having triplets were 1 in 10,000–17,000, depending on whose statistics you use.

. . . AND QUADRUPLETS

Before fertility pills, the chances for quadruplets were 1 in 5–8 million, and for quin-

tuplets 1 in 15–20 million. The odds against sextuplets weren't even computed! It was rare for any such infants to survive. When the Dionne quintuplets were born in rural Canada on May 28, 1934, news headlines flashed around the world, and the local doctor who delivered them, Dr. Allan Roy Defoe, became an international folk hero. Tests by a group of Canadian scientists indicated that the Dionne quintuplets derived from a single egg. They were *identical* quintuplets.

Today, fertility drugs have increased the chances of multiple birth. The fertility drugs stimulate the ovary, and may prompt an ovary to produce more than one egg. Sometimes there are many more eggs produced at one time, which results in multiple fertilizations—and a multiple birth of the *fraternal* (that is, nonidentical) type.

THE "TWIN" TYPES OF TWINS

Identical twins come from one fertilized egg which, for an unknown reason, splits down the center, usually within the first week after conception, and forms two identical or mirror-image embryos.

Fraternal twins result from two ova being fertilized simultaneously. They have separate—and different—genetic makeups. They may or may not be of the same sex, and may or may not even resemble each other any more than other brothers and sisters do.

The identical twins from a single ovum and spermatozoa have an identical germ plasm. They *must* be the same sex (since sex is determined at conception) and will either be carbon copies down to finger and sole prints of each other or mirror images. If they are the latter, one twin will be right-handed, the other left-handed; dental irregularities appear on opposite sides of their mouths; one twin's hair spirals clockwise, the other counterclockwise, on into other fantastic *Through the Looking Glass* detail.

ARE YOU GOING TO HAVE TWINS?

The certainty of twins or a multiple birth is often discovered (7 out of 10 times) in the sixth month. Twins *can* be discovered at 6 weeks, but unless some defect is suspected, there is no need to find out early on. Occasionally, even today, the second baby is as much of a surprise to the doctor as to the mother!

Still, there are a lot of signals a mother-to-be may notice; and there are signs that only a doctor will notice.

Carrying twins usually is considerably more uncomfortable than carrying a single fetus. Breathlessness, varicose veins, hemorrhoids, insomnia, swelling of the legs, morning sickness can all be doubled in intensity. In fact, if you've been pregnant before without experiencing morning sickness, and now have it, that *may* be the tipoff. Also

if you are watching your weight and your diet, and still gain more than you wish, that's another clue.

For your doctor the proof is in the size of your uterus. If you are visiting your doctor regularly (which you should be), she or he can gauge the rate of enlargement. If your womb is enlarging too rapidly, your doctor will suspect twins.

Normally the doctor can confirm this guess by listening for the heartbeats with a stethoscope. When there are two beats at different spots on your abdomen at rates differing by 10 beats or more per minute, then it's twins. If the doctor can feel two heads or two breeches on abdominal examination, it's twins.

Ultrasonography, electrocardiography, and X ray have all been used to find out if twins are on the way. But unless there is some compelling medical reason to know, why risk any iota of safety just for prior knowledge.

There are some possible complications in carrying more than one baby. You may, for example, be more subject to anemia. But any kind of complications should be checked and rechecked with not only your doctor, but a second doctor—a specialist, if you wish—and the latest literature in the field.

Charles Richardson

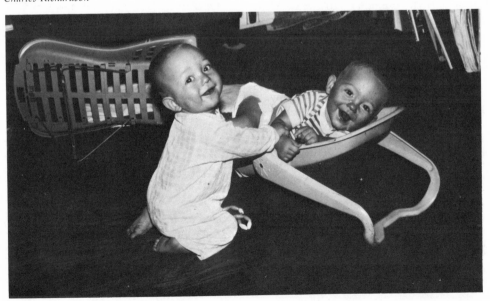

DELIVERING TWINS

Delivering twins is seldom a problem. In fact, labor may be easier and it's usually shorter than for a single child. Twins are smaller. Pressure from their combined weight in utero often causes the cervix to begin to open prematurely so it is partially dilated before labor even starts. You may find yourself spending the last 6 to 8 weeks of your pregnancy in bed to forestall a premature delivery. And bedridden or not, during your last trimester if you are carrying twins, the usual lovemaking is not a good idea because the cervix may become dilated prematurely and labor may begin.

Most twins are born 3 to 4 weeks ahead of schedule, but, unlike single early births, twins are fully developed although small. False labor (see page 221), however, is more frequent in multiple births than in single pregnancies. There is also a higher rate of sluggish labor due to a higher incidence of uterine inertia and inadequate contractions, probably owing to overdistension of the uterus. Sometimes, a doctor will believe it is necessary to use drugs to stimulate the uterus.

Because twin babies are so small, labor and delivery is conducted, even by firm believers in anesthetics, with as little analgesia as possible. The babies' tiny respiratory systems are easily depressed by drugs.

The least interference with natural processes is best for mother and twins. If the first child appears head first or breech, it is delivered as if it were a single birth. If the vagina is relaxed and the infant small, an episiotomy is not done.

After the birth of the first twin, the doctor waits 4 to 15 minutes to see if the second twin will be born spontaneously. If by 20 minutes there is no evidence of a forthcoming twin, she or he manually extracts the second child. So don't be surprised if one hand is inserted inside your uterus while the other is pressed downward on your abdomen. This may be necessary to urge the second twin out into the world.

In multiple births the uterus has a tendency to relax and bleed excessively. Mothers of twins must be watched carefully for the first few hours. Otherwise, if you are a twin mother, your postnatal care and lactation will be quite the same as in single births.

WHAT DO THEY LOOK LIKE?

The average birth weight of twins is 5 pounds 5 ounces compared with seven and a half pounds for a single baby. (Twins grow more slowly in utero.) Sometimes (one twin pregnancy in 20) twin birth produces an infant who weighs from 14 ounces to 2 pounds. But a 2-pound twin has a better chance of surviving than a 2-pound single baby—the twin is further along in development despite weight.

Your twins may weigh in with as much as a 2-pound difference. This difference is greater between identical than fraternal twins, largely because of their positions in the womb and the placental blood circulation. Once home, environmental factors take over and even identical twins may not develop at the same rate or in the same way.

Of course, you should realize that twins have a lower rate of survival than single babies. And triplets and other multiple babies have still less ability to live. But, with today's expertise, there are cases of some quintuple and sextuple babies surviving.

TWIN BABIES: TWIN HANDS NEEDED

You *may* have had double discomfort during pregnancy. You'll certainly have double duty when you get your twins home! In almost all cases someone to help around the house is absolutely essential. The more competent the help, the better. Don't trust your twins or your house with twins in it, to your inexperienced preteener. Get the best twin hands you can.

WHAT IF SOMETHING GOES WRONG?

Sometimes one twin survives and the other dies. If this happens, your emotions are bound to be difficult and too complicated to sort out by yourselves. Your feelings about your living baby may be particularly conflicted. It's important to talk things over, either with a therapist or with other parents who have had a similar experience—or with both. Talking about it may make it easier, and certainly should help you care for your baby in better ways.

Suppose you are among the precious few who have given birth to *more* than twins. Quadruplets, quintuplets, sextuplets. Perhaps you had advance warning: perhaps you knew there was more than one but you didn't know for sure how many. You weren't prepared for *four*! But they don't all survive. Only two make it. You have the joy of two healthy babies, the sorrow of the loss of the others, the relief at being spared the incredible work load and financial expense of four more children all at once, the guilt at feeling relief. Your mind and heart are spinning like a top. You need all the physical and emotional help your family and friends can supply. And certainly, you need some expert therapy, as well. You have gone through a huge crisis situation, and you are continuing to be in one. At the very least, a therapist is an emotional safety valve—the one person you can always cry to, always express rage and fear to.

THE REASON WHY IS A MYSTERY

In Finland 1 person in about 60 will have a multiple birth. But in Japan, which is at the opposite end of the scale, 1 woman in 154 has a multiple birth.

NURSING IF YOU HAVE TWINS OR MORE!

Yes, you can! It's more complicated, but then so is everything else with a multiple birth.

Sixteen bottles a day? Yes, that's about the number of formula bottles you'll need to prepare if you decide *not* to nurse your twins. It *still* may be easier than breast-feeding two at a time for *you*. If so, don't grieve—and *don't* read on! Just consult page 158 on bottle feeding.

For those of you who want to nurse, your course of action is likely to be far better for you—and your babies—in the short *and* long run. Since twins are usually smaller than single babies, they derive special benefits from their mother's milk. And breast-feeding twins may be much easier than you think: you *can* feed them both at the same time!

But most mothers of twins do tend to feed one at a time. One twin may be ravenous—and the other just too sleepy. Although I am a devotee of nursing on the baby's demand, you may need to take some action of your own. If your twin babies set their own nursing schedule and they set different ones, you'll be almost completely rocker-bound! Better to let the hungriest twin set the schedule and when he or she starts hollering for food, wake the other twin up. The not-so-hungry baby still won't refuse a full breast.

It actually can be more fun to feed just one at a time, however. You'll be able to give more cuddling, more undivided attention—a happy situation for all of you.

How It Used to Be

If there should happen to be twins, the mother must, if possible, be kept in ignorance of the fact till both children are born. This is an established practice with medical men, as mischief might ensue from the apprehension with which the patient might contemplate the second labour. Unfortunately, however, the attendants in a lying-in room, taken by surprise (when informed by the medical man, after the birth of the first, of the existence of another child), often, by their incautious conduct, discover the fact prematurely to the patient. This, be it remembered, should ever be carefully guarded against.

Thomas Bull, M.D., *Hints to Mothers*, 1853

Some experts recommend alternating breasts so one twin doesn't get all of his or her sustenance from the same source every time. On the other hand, twins often develop a preference for one side or the other!

If your twins have to stay in the hospital longer than you, or if they are too small to nurse satisfactorily at first, you can establish your breast-milk supply by hand or pump. But once they start to nurse, the satisfaction may compensate for those days or weeks of "nonnursing" nursing.

If you have triplets, do *not* believe that you must bottle feed. It will certainly be easier if you have some help and feeding relief (with a bottle now and then)—but nursing is still the best method to choose. There is even a mother of quintuplets in Japan who is breast-feeding all five of her babies!

A TWIN CHECKLIST FOR TWIN CARE

What do you need to know in caring for twins? Here is a short dos and don'ts checklist.

THE BASIC DOS AND DON'TS OF TWIN CARE

DO:	DON'T:
Dress them a little or a lot differently, even at first.	Expect them to entertain each other more than any two children.
Notice distinctions between them.	Lump them together in your speech.
Avoid unfavorable comparisons.	Expect one to develop at the same pace as the other.
Use their individual names as much as possible.	Blame either or both of them for your extra work or life situation.
Play down the fact of the twin birth.	Expect peace and harmony between them, even if they're identical.
Give more attention to the one who needs it most.	Neglect the quieter twin because you must pay more attention to the fussier one.
Carry one at a time, unless there's an emergency.	Leave them alone together in crib or playpen once they can do more than lie quietly.
Compliment both equally, even as infants.	Show preference for one over the other, even if you feel it.
Try to switch care equally between the two of you. Maybe an every-other-day method will help.	Compare them in conversation with other people, even if you think they won't hear you.
Take pictures of one without the other— and also together.	Give them the same toy to share.

Late Births

Fairly often a baby is late, carried three or four weeks beyond the due date. That is, assuming the due date was accurately figured in the first place.

There are mixed opinions as to whether a prolonged uterine life does or does not affect the fetus. Some European physicians think it is harmful. In America doctors tend to see no damage.

The main thing to remember is: Don't panic. The greatest problem you're likely to face is your own impatience! But even so, it is better to let nature take its own sweet time than to pressure your doctor into taking action if he or she doesn't think it imperative.

Sometimes your doctor *will* think it important to induce labor. If the cervix is ready for birth and there is no question of the accuracy of the menstrual history (on which the estimated due date is based), then the doctor may induce labor.

If the baby seems to be growing very slowly near or after term, the doctor may resort to a cesarean section. A cesarean is also sometimes done if the baby is unusually large and, as a result, there is a question about the safety of normal delivery.

A fetus carried beyond forty-two weeks is called postmature. Very occasionally, such an infant will develop *placental insufficiency* which causes fetus and placenta to lose weight and results in a decrease in the amount of amniotic fluid. When born, these babies show signs of malnutrition and are given the mouth-filling name, *dysmature postmature infants.*

This baby's skin sags as if fat once there has been melted off too fast. Other differences are the absence of the usual fine hair of the newborn and the thin fatty layer at the crown of the head. There may be other temporary problems in establishing normal breathing and normal blood sugar level. Some nervous functions may be slightly awry. Probably some malfunction of the placenta has caused this. All these factors get straightened out.

The late baby who has no physical problems cannot be distinguished from a full-term baby except that he or she seems to be unusually wide-eyed and alert.

No one yet knows why!

Premature Births

What is Prematurity?

More than 200,000 infants of low birth weight are born alive in the United States each year. Low birth weight—2,500 grams or less—is one of the greatest hazards to infant survival. The risk of death in the first 28 days of life to infants who weigh 2,500 grams or less at birth has been about 30 times the risk among infants weighing more than 2,500 grams at birth. (Metropolitan Life Insurance Company, *Statistical Bulletin*, 1976)

WHO IS PREMATURE?

Until recently our description of a premature baby has related either to weight or to length of in utero life. (Prematurity, by the way, is often called preterm today.) Babies who are born earlier than the usual 40 weeks, (give or take two weeks) of gestation, or who weigh under 5½ pounds at birth, have been labeled premature. Often there has been a correlation between these two statistics. Still, a full-term (38 to 42 weeks' gestation) baby can be a 5-pounder, and once in a while a baby born before the dividing line of 37 weeks (some doctors put it as early as 33 weeks) checks in at more than 5½ pounds.

Recently, however, a more important criterion has gradually been replacing weight as a measure. *How developed* is the newborn infant? For premature babies are not simply small babies; they are *immature* babies who may or may not be small at birth.

Prematurity is related to the infant's true age. Physical age is judged by weight, length, size of the head, development of nipples, genitals, and earlobes. Neurological age is determined by a number of responses, including the infant's ability to grasp.

Today, owing partly to the enormous increase (40 percent in the last decade) in pregnancies among teen-agers, premature births are increasing. Many young people are not well-nourished enough or physically mature enough to meet the demands of pregnancy. Although it is mentioned only slightly in the literature, it is possible that later-in-life pregnancies may also produce more prematurity. But despite steadily increasing scientific knowledge, the medical profession still doesn't know what causes over 50 percent of premature births. In many cases premature births occur quite unexpectedly with no prior warning.

Currently, 5 to 15 percent of all pregnancies end in premature deliveries. About seven to nine percent of pregnancies in white women in the United States end this way. Among black women, the rate is 10 to 12 percent, undoubtedly because of the effects of poorer socioeconomic conditions.

WHY BABIES ARE BORN PREMATURELY

One reason for premature births is that some babies suffer undernourishment in the womb. This happens most often among poor people. Too often the mother-to-be, especially if she is a teen-ager, doesn't seek medical advice and doesn't eat well enough.

Sometimes, too, the mother may have an undetected flaw in the placenta which deprives the fetus of sufficient nourishment. Perhaps she has had German measles, which affects a baby's growth in utero, or perhaps the baby has a congenital defect which causes inadequate nutrition.

Whatever the reason, an undernourished fetus will be an underweight baby, even if carried a full nine months. These babies are referred to as *dysmature* rather than *premature*. They resemble premature babies in many ways and are given the same postnatal care, but they do have one problem which most preterm infants don't—hypoglycemia, or low blood sugar.

Because doctors know so little about the causes, they are comparatively helpless in preventing prematurity—but they try. A woman threatened with an imminent premature delivery is often ordered to bed in an attempt to gain a few more days or weeks before birth for the fetus. At that point, every day can count. (Actress Sophia Loren spent a good part of her pregnancies in bed.) Occasionally doctors take more extreme measures such as administering a muscle relaxant or an alcohol drip, given intravenously, both of which have been known to prevent the onset of contractions.

In cases where the mother had *diabetes* or the child *erythroblastosis fetalis* (which is the Rh factor), prematurity is often deliberately brought about by cesarean section at about the thirty-sixth week. In such cases the chances of the fetus being stillborn are greater than the risk to the baby of coming into the world too soon.

Premature birth is the eighth-greatest cause of death in the United States today. The survival rate for premature babies varies from 20 percent to over 90 percent, depending on a variety of factors. The first few days are the most critical. The longer a child lives the greater are his or her chances to keep on living. Only a dozen or so years ago, prematurity was an even higher risk. This was before the development of neonatology, the specialty of caring for infants.

There are many theories concerning the causes of prematurity, ranging from the Freudian to the purely physical. There are some indications that a baby's birth is influenced by the mother's size and weight, whether she smokes, lives at a high altitude, or has had an undetected infection of the urinary tract.

But regardless of whether the cause can be traced to the mother or not, it's a rare mother of a premature baby who doesn't feel in some way responsible. Most parents who have had a premature baby feel that they have failed or that they did something wrong during the pregnancy. Some blame it on drinking or working too long or on a metabolic deficiency. The mother (and father) may look on the premature birth as their "punishment." The mother may doubt her qualifications to care for the infant, or may be excessively angry at the baby who "caused" such problems. These feelings should be dealt with early on.

Some hospitals have social workers, as well as psychiatrists, on staff. If they are not burdened with too much work, these professionals often are excellent listeners and therapists. Other parents of premature babies may also be enormously helpful. If you find yourself upset or feeling guilty after having a premature child, do seek out these people to talk to.

CAUSES OF PREMATURITY

- An undernourished or physically immature mother
- Multiple birth
- High blood pressure with kidney or liver complications, known as *toxemia of pregnancy*
- Improper positioning of the placenta
- Premature separation of the placenta from the lining of the womb
- Maternal illness with severe infection such as pneumonia
- Maternal diabetes or a fetal disease called erythroblastosis fetalis in which the mother has antibodies in her blood to the fetus's blood type
- *But mostly, no identifiable reason at all*

WHAT HAPPENS TO THE PREMATURE BABY?

To some babies prematurity doesn't seem to make any difference at all. To others it is literally a matter of life or death.

The more immature the baby, the greater its chances of not surviving. According to Boston Children's Medical Center, a baby weighing in at 5 to 5½ pounds has a better than nine-to-one chance of living, whereas only 30 percent of those under 3 pounds will make it.

The crucial factor is still the degree of maturity of the baby.

What can the doctor do to help the baby over the threshold of life? Quite a lot, actually, and more all the time.

The too-early babies are much more sensitive than full-term babies to painkillers given the mother during labor. Such drugs make their way from the mother's bloodstream through the placenta to the baby's blood. They depress the baby's nervous and respiratory systems. In the premature baby both systems are too feeble to stand such depressive action. Obstetricians, consequently, refrain as much as possible from giving painkillers in premature deliveries, and, when they must, cut down the dosage to considerably below that used in full-term births.

A premature baby's temperature immediately after birth fluctuates in response to the new environment, while a full-term baby holds a fairly stable temperature regardless of minor variations in the surrounding air. Therefore, an incubator with regulated temperature, humidity, and oxygen flow, in effect reproducing the conditions of the womb, is a must. The baby is even transported from the delivery room to the nursery in a portable incubator.

Incubator temperature is usually close to what the baby's own temperature should be, which is considerably higher than room temperature. The room may be 70 degrees Fahrenheit, the incubator about 88. A device called a thermistor senses the baby's skin temperature and relays the information to the heat control element.

In the incubator the baby's heart and lungs are electronically monitored. New devices, such as a vinyl-covered "foam" vest, are used to protect the very tender skin and allow monitoring at the same time.

SURVIVAL CHANCES ENHANCED FOR TINY PREMATURE INFANTS

Although premature delivery is the major contributor to infant deaths and health problems, all aspects of care for premature infants have improved dramatically during the past fifteen years. The health and behavioral sciences have gained knowledge on the dangers of either too little or too much oxygen; chilling; malnutrition; acidosis; low blood sugar; and parent-infant separation, along with changes in management of these conditions.

According to Arthur E. Kopelman, M.D., East Carolina University Medical School, Greenville, North Carolina, even the tiniest infants are much more likely to live now than ever before. Writing in the June 1978 issue of the *American Journal of Diseases of Children* (published by the American Medical Association), Dr. Kopelman gave a fairly rosy picture. Babies who weigh 2.3 to 2.8 pounds at birth after only seven months' gestation have a much better chance of surviving and of growing up free of handicaps today than fifteen years ago.

One study, which found that only 5.1 percent of pregnancies terminated in premature delivery, also showed that these infants resulted in 85 percent of all early deaths, excluding those due to fetal malformations. But Dr. Kopelman believes that at least two thirds of infants of 28 weeks gestation can survive. The great majority of these survivors will be normal. Perhaps 10 to 20 percent, though, will have disabilities, some of them handicapping. At present an estimated one billion dollars is expended yearly for intensive care of premature and low-weight infants.

THE BABY'S APPEARANCE

The premature baby looks different from the full-term infant. Here is a medical description—but don't let it frighten you. For the present, just remember that the premature baby does *not* look like the full-term infant. If you need to refer to this description later on, it may ease your concern.

The baby's body is generally small and puny, since the weight of *viable* (capable of living) infants varies from 1 pound, 5 ounces to 5½ pounds.

The baby's skin is soft and pinkish red. Sometimes it hangs in folds. The outermost layer of the skin is thin, and the blood vessels are easily seen.

The baby has little fat, so his/her features tend to be angular.

The baby will have a lot of hair, especially on the arms and legs, the forehead, and the upper part of the back.

The baby's face may look old, and the skull is round or oval. The *fontanels* ("soft spots") in the skull are large and the bony unions are prominent.

The baby born too soon lies in a deep sleep and may have to be aroused for feedings; efforts at sucking may be weak or absent. Also, the baby's cry is feeble, and all movements are slow.

The infant's body temperature tends to be below normal and is inclined to be irregular. This baby needs lot of warmth and nourishment.

SPECIAL PROBLEMS OF PREMATURITY

The premature baby may have problems like:

Apneic spells. These affect the smallest of infants. The baby stops breathing altogether and turns blue. This is more frightening to see than it is in reality. Usually these spells end spontaneously; the baby starts breathing again. But no one waits to find out. Nurses in attendance will instantly try to start up the breathing. Sometimes the flick of a finger on the baby's heel will do it. (Probably the brain centers which regulate respiratory movements are too immature for normal control.)

Hyaline membrane disease. This is a continuation of the circulation pattern of the fetus. When the baby is still unborn, only a small part of the blood pumped from the fetal heart passes through the lungs, because oxygenation of the blood and removal of the carbon dioxide occur in the placenta.

In the womb the baby's lungs are collapsed; the mother is doing the breathing for her baby. After birth the baby's lungs expand to take on all the work of breathing and pumping blood to the rest of the body. To do this, the blood flow must be rerouted within the heart and great blood vessels.

In hyaline membrane disease this rerouting does not take place. Without help from the placenta, not enough blood passes through the newborn's lungs to oxygenate the blood and remove the wastes. At the same time, a glass-smooth material forms on the linings of the smaller air passages which gives the condition its formidable name. The disease rarely lasts longer than three days but it ranges from mild to fatal. (John F. Kennedy's third child, born two months prematurely, succumbed to it.) Victims are given oxygen, antibiotics, and intravenous fluids. Today, babies with hyaline membrane disease usually survive, because of advanced medical technology.

Jaundice. This is a common condition among newborns. But premature babies tend to develop *excessive* jaundice. This is due to the immaturity of their livers, which may be unable to process *bilirubin,* a yellow chemical derived from red blood cells as the latter go through their cycle of forming, disintegrating, and being removed from the bloodstream. In a few days this disability should be overcome sufficiently to take care of current bilirubin production and the backlog.

The significant factor is the rate at which the jaundice decreases or increases. Most babies require no treatment at all. Severe cases may cause brain damage such as cerebral palsy or hearing impairment. They are treated by changing their blood through an exchange transfusion, which is just what it sounds like.

Infection. A premature baby can have a serious infection with only minor symptoms. Constant and careful watchfulness is necessary.

Feeding. This may be a serious difficulty. The smallest infant may not have the strength or energy to suck. An immature swallowing apparatus may cause choking, gagging, or inhaling liquids. Feeding from a nipple won't work. Instead, a tube is passed through the baby's nose and throat into the stomach, which usually works.

Weight loss. Most babies lose *some* weight after they are born in the hospital, but premature babies lose more. It may take a premature baby several weeks to get back the lost weight.

Some parents find it difficult to care for and about this infant who seems to have created problems. These feelings partly result from the lack of bonding and the continued absence of the baby for a time. Parents who feel this way sometimes hide it even from themselves, and as a camouflage become overconcerned. The very best preventive is being with baby a lot and learning to care for your own newborn as much as possible. If hospital personnel try to use the infection-scare technique to keep you out and away, don't believe it! You are no more a germ carrier than any nurse—probably less so! Another point to remember: If this conflict arises, talk out your feelings with your baby's other parent.

THE AFTEREFFECTS OF PREMATURITY

The more premature your baby, the greater the likelihood of handicaps—like lowered intelligence, learning difficulties, impaired hearing, vision problems like myopia and astigmatism, physical clumsiness, cerebral palsy.

If your baby is born before 33 weeks, chances of lasting serious problems are greater. The baby's lungs, for instance, are not fully developed until that time.

On the bright side, if your baby is nearer the 40-week norm than the 33-week dividing line, the chances are that, despite a slow start, the child will catch up. Also, today the inventions of medicine are indeed miraculous—and may be of some help. Further, some of the world's great brains were premature babies. Yours is in good company!

There is often a time lag: a baby who was born before expected—who was premature—usually will have a later development. If your baby was early by a month, add one month to the age that babies usually do things. If s/he was two months early, add two months, and so on. You'll find a chart that will give you a guide to *average* baby development in a later section of this book (on page 298). It is based only on the average, but will spare you unnecessary worrying, time, and energy! Or you can use any other developmental guide. Just remember to add the month or two. Of course, there are some babies who do not fit into averages and still catch up later on. Don't worry—but do check around.

A Grasp Like Iron

When the palm of the infant's hand or sole of his foot is stroked, he will close on the object in a grasp that is strong and determined. The more premature he is, the more determined and unremitting his grasp may be. Seven-month premature babies can be picked up by their hand grasps and held in the air, clinging to the examiner's fingers, as if they were holding on to a tree branch for dear life. (T. Berry Brazelton, M.D., *Infants and Mothers*, 1969)

Cure Not Prevention

The concept of primary prevention of complications of pregnancy and delivery and prevention of neonatal abnormalities through sound prenatal nutrition has been supplanted by secondary prevention, which consists of elaborate intensive care nurseries which electronically monitor premature babies, many of whom would have been normal size at birth. The relatively new specialty of neonatology (or perinatology), with its emphasis on treatment of abnormalities (many of which would have been unnecessary had primary prevention been applied), seems to be an appropriate addition to the medical hierarchy. (Tom Brewer, M.D., and Jay Hodin, "Why Women Must Meet the Nutritional Stress of Pregnancy," *21st Century Obstetrics, Now!*, 1978)

SPECIAL CARE FOR SPECIAL BABIES

Special centers to care for mothers and babies who are considered "high-risk" represent a big development. These are called "regionalized perinatal services" and are now to be found throughout the United States.

Their existence has been aided by the federal government and the Robert Wood Johnson Foundation. The latter is funding (with $2.7 million) a major evaluation of eight of these regional centers. Among the questions that the study is expected to answer is whether saving high-risk infants leads to more damaged babies. According to the foundation's *Special Report No. 2*, of 1978, "Virtually no perinatologist or neonatologist believes this is the case." And the foundation believes that preliminary results apparently support these doctors:

"Intensive care therapy for critically ill neonates has not saved children who are brain-damaged or severely handicapped, but has been responsible for an improved physical and development status for survivors."

There has been, according to one California study, both a 30 percent mortality *decrease* of infants weighing less than 3 pounds 5 ounces (1,500 grams) and also a *decrease* of definitely abnormal infants.

Also, the centers apparently have reduced the mortality rate of premature and other high-risk infants. In nine hospitals in the United States and Canada *decreases* in deaths of infants were from twenty-five to forty-two percent.

But the Johnson Foundation report also raises several basic problems. One is related to transporting a mother-to-be to centers far from home.

In practice, the transport of a mother-to-be presents problems. . . . the transport of a pregnant woman, especially over long distance, disrupts the individual and her family. Alone, in strange surroundings, away from her family, the experience can be stressful. One nurse, who has seen the problem close at hand, explains: "Women who are transported need a great deal of support."

Another problem is the quite incredible cost factor. "Bills for a high risk pregnancy and birth in the $20,000 range are considered normal; more severe cases in the $40,000 to $50,000 range are by no means rare."

As a result, forty-eight states have laws which prevent insurance companies from avoiding coverage for the newborn infant.

It is both marvelous and ironic that we are now developing ways to help sick and very sick newborn babies live free of handicaps. Marvelous because the gift of life is always awesome and usually joyous. Ironic because, in my opinion, many of these babies would not be sick at all if the same intensity of care and services and knowledge were applied at the beginning of their time span—just before or just after conception. Ironic, too, because so many "well" babies need help and care of different kinds—if not an isolette and a specialized regional center. Would that we could continue to help these infants—and begin to help all the others not yet born!

◇ ◇ ◇

When Mothers Must Leave the Baby Behind

Then there comes what I call "the Flower Pot Phase." One mother told me how she felt going home with a Flower Pot in her lap instead of a baby. She felt lonely, unfulfilled, despairing of her child's life and a complete failure. Entering one's home without a baby when everything at home is prepared for the baby is an equally difficult time. Then the social network begins to impinge. Relatives, friends and neighbors need to be informed as to the baby's condition, and the adjustment to life at home without the baby but the baby living in the hospital. . . .

. . . What can happen when immediate separation takes place and the time for the parents to develop these abilities is delayed?

It certainly seems to have an effect on "normal parenting and bonding" as shown by both animal and human studies. . . .

. . . The separated group of mothers had decreased feelings of self-confidence in their ability to perform social tasks, e.g. calming the baby, understanding what the baby wants and showing affection to the baby during the period of separation. . . .

On the follow-up visits at 12 and 15 months post discharge, non-separated mothers continued to touch their babies more than separated mothers.

Observations showed that full-term mothers smiled more at their infants and maintained more ventral contact both at the one-week and one-month post discharge observations than either premature group. . . .

. . . A follow-up study of 160 babies of birth weight less than 1500 grams . . . found in the group . . . 6 months to 6 years after birth that the parents continued to need a lot of reassurance while their children are growing up, and that parents remain overprotective and over-anxious about these children. (Rose Brobstein, chief pediatric social worker, Stanford University, lecture presented at American Psychological Association, 1976)

◇ ◇ ◇

What Can a Parent Do

Parents can have an active participation in the early developmental needs of their premature and high risk infant. Too frequently we see premature infants who have achieved biological survival but who are critically deficient in neurophysiological development due to a deprivation of sensory, social, and emotional involvement with the most powerful force in their lives—a parent. And most usually this is the mother. Parents must no longer accept the "wait and see" regime which is frequently advised them by well-meaning medical personnel at the advent of a high risk infant. The infant has an inborn "stimulus hunger" for such stimulation as gentle touch, body contact, body position, vestibular stimulation and sound. These stimuli are normally made available to the infant through the whole gamut of small acts by which an emotionally healthy mother can consistently show her love for her child. . . .

There is a significantly high number of premature births among the child abused population, and the early and prolonged separation of mother and infant, deprived of early sensory bonding and attachment, may be one of the contributing factors. (Ruth D. Rice, Ph.D. Lecture presented at American Psychological Association, 1976)

◇ ◇ ◇

NURSING WHEN THERE ARE COMPLICATIONS

IF YOUR CHILD IS BORN PREMATURELY

Yes, yes, yes! Breast milk is even more important to the premature infant than it is to the full-term baby. Yet very few hospital premature units are set up to feed these infants with mother's milk. (Albert Einstein College of Medicine in New York City is one that is and does.) At the very least, your milk can be expressed manually or by breast pump and given to your baby in a bottle or through an eyedropper. But you *may* be able to hold and feed the baby yourself, if you and the hospital personnel can arrange for

this. Every ounce of human contact you can provide will be of immeasurable value to a baby who is largely isolated during those crucial first days and weeks.

IF YOUR CHILD IS BORN BY CESAREAN SECTION

Again, yes, you can still breast-feed. In fact, *insist upon it*. This is one good reason to pack some pronursing literature in your suitcase: *if* you have a cesarean unexpectedly and if your doctor or nurses try to discourage you from nursing, you will have the material right there to confirm and support your desire to nurse. And to tell you how to do it and what to do.

IF YOUR BABY IS HOSPITALIZED

The same principle holds true here. Premature infants are often in the hospital for weeks. So are babies born with some correctable defect. If you can manage the rest of your life and time, you can work out the ways to breast-feed your baby under these circumstances—given the willingness of doctor and hospital to cooperate with you. As with everything else, your own advance knowledge about their attitudes can help you at the time.

IF YOU OR THE BABY IS SICK

The nature and seriousness of the sickness is involved here. For all minor ailments (colds and others) breast feeding is still desirable. For anything more serious, check with several doctors and with a La Leche League group before you accept the fact that you cannot nurse. If you are taking a medication for an ailment, you may be able to stop nursing for a short while—but keep up the milk supply—and resume breast feeding when you are well again. Women who must take a regular medication for a long-lasting condition (diabetes, epilepsy) may not be able to nurse. If your baby is jaundiced (a common condition), you may stop nursing for a few days, continuing to express your milk, and then resume it.

The Baby's Birth Position

Just as babies differ in length, weight, and appearance, so too their actual entry into the world may differ. Some babies do *not* come out of the womb head first. Birth position can have large effects. The position of the baby at the time of delivery influences the length of labor, the type of delivery, postpartum aches and pains.

Presentation is the term used to describe which part of the baby is closest to the birth canal as the event approaches—which part of the baby is *presented* first, in other words. There are three major types:

Vertex—head first presentation
Transverse—side presentation
Breech—bottom or legs presentation

You can relax, however! In a good ninety-five percent of all births, the baby is born head first. The shape of the uterus is that of an upside-down pear. Just before birth the baby's head fits into the smaller part. This is fortunate, since the head-first position offers the fewest risks in delivery. The head is the largest part of the infant. As the baby makes its way through the birth canal, its head stretches the passage so the rest of the body slips through with no effort and the head is molded by the walls of the canal to fit through the birth passage, making its emergence into the world smoother.

In about 4 out of 100 births the buttocks or legs come first. Usually the breech position itself does not physically affect the mother to any major degree, but it does pose three times the risk for the baby.

The baby's head in these cases is not gradually squeezed through the birth canal, and therefore is more difficult to deliver. And since the baby's bottom fits less snugly into the pelvis than the head, there is a danger that the umbilical cord will become compressed between the baby's body and the pelvis, cutting off the baby's oxygen supply. Also, since a manual or forceps delivery is more likely in a breech birth, there is a greater possibility of a broken or separated bone or two.

A large pelvis is required for a successful breech birth. If the pelvis is too small, a cesarean is necessary.

Breech presentations are much more common in premature births. Most babies are in the breech position until about the thirty-second week. After that they revolve 180 degrees to the vertex position. If not, the doctor can manipulate the fetus manually in late pregnancy by pressure at different points on the mother's abdomen to turn the baby around. This is *external version*. (There is also *internal version* during labor.)

Some doctors argue against version. They maintain that if it is successful the baby would have turned anyway. They may be right. Sometimes a doctor shifts the baby's presentation and the baby, almost defiantly, shifts right back again in a couple of hours. If the baby remains in a *transverse presentation*, the only answer is a cesarean.*

---

*Doctors in general rather quickly resort to a cesarean in breech-birth situations. But alternative birth centers find that such births can be managed without forceps or cesareans. Breech births occur in three percent of all births.

There are several types of breech presentations:

Frank breech. This is the most common. It is, in effect, a jackknife position with the baby's thighs flexed on his/her abdomen and the legs straight so the feet are up around the ears.

Complete breech. In this presentation the infant is sitting cross-legged in the bottom of the uterus.

Footling breech. This is similar to the complete breech except one or both feet are extended.

Knee breech. In this presentation the baby seems to be kneeling on one knee in the bottom of the uterus, that knee presenting. This is the rarest of the breech presentations.

A breech birth is often felt in the upper back instead of the low back and low abdomen as in vertex births. The baby's skull is pressing against the mother's spine. Usually if you assume a position during labor that gets the pressure off your spine, you will feel better. Semireclining, standing, and forward-leaning positions help. So does pelvic rocking in a hands-and-knees position or leaning against the wall. Back massage and counterpressure at the point of the pain, a hot-water bottle, or a heating pad help, too. The only "don't" is don't lie flat. You can be delivered on your side or on your hands and knees, if necessary. It all depends on (1) which way you are more comfortable and (2) how cooperative your doctor is.

Breech babies sometimes need resuscitation, but most are born without any problems.

In most cases, by the time labor starts, the doctor has a good idea of the relative sizes of the mother's pelvis and the baby's head. If this is a first pregnancy and the baby is in a breech position, an *X-ray pelvimetry* will probably be done for the exact measurement of the pelvis.

A woman who has had a breech birth is more likely to have another one than a woman who hasn't. But even among these mothers, the chances are only one in four.

A WARNING SIGN: MECONIUM

If the birth is to be a breech delivery, there may be an early signal of a problem. It is not at all unusual for *meconium* (the dark tarry substance found in the fetus's large intestine) to be expelled from the mother's vagina after her membranes rupture because the baby's rectum is directly above the cervix. This should be reported *instantly* to the doctor because it can be a sign of fetal distress.

If the baby is *not* in a breech presentation, and meconium appears, it is even more likely that the baby is having trouble.

Lots of women don't realize that the meconium is coming from the baby. In fact, they may not even know what it is. Many women become embarrassed when this substance appears. If this happens to you, don't—for one minute—become embarrassed. If it happens while you are home, put on a sanitary napkin or clean cloth (because there may be more) and head for the hospital. If you're out, get to the hospital right away.

The Cesarean Section

WHAT IS A CESAREAN BIRTH?

A cesarean section is the delivery of an infant through a surgical incision in the mother's abdominal wall, performed under anesthesia.

A woman who has had a cesarean delivery is, in medical parlance, "postoperative and postpartum"—she has had major surgery *and* a baby delivery. Obviously, more problems could develop than in the usual delivery.

Here are the reasons doctors give for believing that a cesarean is necessary:

There is definite disproportion in size between the head of the fetus and the mother's pelvis, which is the reason given for about one third of cesarean births.

There is an extreme narrowing of any part of the pelvis.

The mother-to-be has uterine tumors.

She has toxemia—the generalized symptoms of which are fever, diarrhea, vomiting, quickened or depressed respiration, and shock.

The mother-to-be is hemorrhaging.

There is a difficult presentation of the fetus. (The baby is going to be born feet first or is positioned sideways.)

The mother has diabetes.

She has a history of habitual abortions.

She has a history of operations to repair holes in the bladder or rectum.

In cases of prolonged labor, when the uterus isn't functioning effectively, or the cervix isn't dilating properly, the baby's safety may be involved.

The fetus is well past term, and the placenta shows signs of aging.

The older age (past thirty-five) of a woman having her first baby may (or may not) affect the elasticity of the pelvic organs.

There has been heavy bleeding in the last months, caused by the detachment of the placenta from the uterus wall and/or by the placenta attaching to the wall *below* the baby.

The Rh factor may create a situation of danger to the fetus during the last weeks of pregnancy—if the mother develops antibodies against the fetus, thereby causing brain damage to the infant. A cesarean (or induced labor) can prevent this.

Lengthy labor (or lack of it) after the membranes have ruptured is a condition in which infection can develop.

An earlier C-section is believed by some doctors to guarantee subsequent operations because of the (as yet unproven) possibility that the old scar will split.

Fetal distress is called this because the baby's heartbeat has slowed dramatically, or the umbilical cord has twisted so much that the fetus is not getting enough blood, or the placenta is detached from the uterus wall. There is considerable dispute about just what *is* fetal distress, however.

Evidence from electronic fetal monitoring that the baby is having some problem. The question is how accurate the interpretation of the readings is.

These are only some of the reasons why cesareans are performed. Some reasons are indisputable: baby or mother would die without the operation. Many, however, are questions of medical judgment—and of how much risk a doctor will take on either side, with or without cesareans.

WHAT TO ASK YOUR DOCTOR BEFORE A CESAREAN

Childbirth-preparation classes often give only passing mention to cesarean sections. Yet cesareans have become so frequent that at least one woman in each class is likely to have such a birth. Many women having a baby for the first time in their thirties are more subject to cesareans.

The majority of cesareans are emergencies. In some instances, however, they can be predicted. For example, it's sometimes difficult to diagnose the disproportion between the pelvis and the baby before labor begins. But your doctor may suspect it. In that case he may order a sonogram in your last month of pregnancy or during early labor.

In any event, all sources agree that the number of cesareans is rising. The 1977 *Precis*, published by the American College of Obstetricians and Gynecologists, notes that "in high-risk centers . . . acceptable rates [of cesareans] as high as 18 to 25 percent are extant."

Indeed, for the average hospital, 10 to 15 percent is considered reasonable. This figure would mean there are 300,000 to 450,000 babies born by cesarean section each year in the United States.

These two facts—the last-minute, emergency nature of cesareans, plus their increasing number—mean that your early questions to your doctor should include questions about his or her beliefs concerning cesareans.

- Does s/he perform many cesareans? How many?
- Why? What are the reasons she or he performs the operation?

- Who is consulted, and when?
- If you *must* have the operation, will you and your husband have the opportunity to consult a second doctor yourselves?
- What type of incision does the doctor recommend?
- What type of anesthetic is used?
- Can your husband be present during the cesarean?
- Will all future deliveries be cesarean if your first one is?
- How will you feel the first forty-eight hours after surgery?
- What postoperative restrictions or problems can you expect? Diet? Exercise? Difficulty with bowel movements?
- Can you carry older children before your incision heals?
- If you're scheduled for a cesarean and know that you don't want more children, can you have a tubal ligation performed during the operation?

WHAT HAPPENS WHEN A CESAREAN OCCURS?

The modern cesarean does not necessarily mean that the mother is unconscious. She may be under a general anesthetic; but sometimes, if the operation is not an emergency procedure, it can be done with epidural or spinal anesthesia. As is usually the case with surgery, the mother is given a tranquilizer first to help combat nervousness. She may have some help after the operation from a light anesthetic in the form of nitrous oxide (laughing gas). For the mother who remains awake during the cesarean, there is the tremendous reward of seeing her baby almost immediately after birth. If a cesarean is not done under general anesthetic, in some hospitals the father, too, may be present. Hospitals permitting this have found that fathers are a great help in supporting the mother, and are *not* overwhelmed by the surgical atmosphere. An article in *Medical World News* in 1977 estimated that 15 percent of U.S. hospitals currently encouraged fathers to attend cesareans.

The operation usually lasts about an hour. It only takes about five minutes for the baby to be born and the rest of the time is taken up by repairing the injury to the mother.

Surgeons have devised the so-called bikini cut, an incision just above the pubic bone, which, when healed, may be covered by the pubic hair, and this is used when possible.

The cesarean baby, who has not gone through the normal birth process, is generally much less wrinkled than the vaginally born infant, and is not as stimulated to manage on his or her own. Such an infant has to be watched rather carefully. Then, too, the infant is likely to be affected—perhaps in a long-term way—by the drugs used in the operation. There have been some indications that cesarean babies are quieter, more passive. Leboyer and others believe that the infant needs the achievement of being born to develop an active personality. So, despite the fact that normal birth may cause more discomfort, it still remains the best way for babies and mothers unless there are compelling medical reasons for the operation.

For the cesarean mother there are the risks attending any major surgery, although, according to a 1977 report of the American College of Obstetricians and Gynecologists (ACOG), "the maternal mortality rates are the same for vaginal and cesarean deliveries in many well-run obstetric clinics." (In general, though, the maternal mortality rate has gone up in past years—something that seems to be related to the recent increase in cesareans. The late Dr. Guttmacher said that the risk is two to three times that of normal births. And there are people who dispute the figures of ACOG. The key may be ACOG's use of the phrase "well-run." We just don't know which *are* well-run and how many such clinics there are.)

There are women who think they would prefer to avoid the problems of normal birth by having a "simple" cesarean. There is nothing simple about a cesarean. It is a major operation. It bears a greater risk for the mother, and there are possible problems for the baby. The operation should only be used as a last resort. So don't *elect* to have a cesarean. Make sure your doctor is not going to *elect* a cesarean for you unless it is vital.

◇ ◇ ◇

AFTER A CESAREAN

Following a cesarean most doctors prefer that the mother remains in the hospital for at least a week. How quickly she regains her strength depends on several things. She may sleep for hours if the labor preceding the operation was severe or lasted a long time. But if she went into surgery reasonably rested, she may be fully alert within a fairly short time and be capable of snuggling *and* breast-feeding her baby.

The degree of the mother's discomfort after the operation is also variable. Nevertheless, the classic advice is to move as much as possible or as soon as possible regardless of the pain. Activity speeds a return to normal breathing, eating, and excretion patterns.

Once the uterus is healed, it is usually as strong as before. It is just as possible for a woman to have more children after a cesarean as after a noncesarean birth, and it is possible, too, to have a normal vaginal birth the next time.

The baby is often rushed away from the operating room to the Special Care nursery for close observation. It is standard in some hospitals to treat all cesarean babies as "high risk." Cesarean babies *are* more likely to have respiratory problems, but many cesarean babies go into Special Care unnecessarily merely because it's hospital procedure. Some hospitals even require that the baby remain in the nursery a fixed number of days or hours regardless of the infant's condition.

Should you undergo a cesarean, there are some areas you can still control. If your baby is healthy, yet locked away in this Special Care nursery, *don't accept this as necessary. Fight it.* Insist that your baby be released to the central nursery or directly to you so you can start rooming-in. If this fails, visit and touch your baby in the Special Care nursery until the staff releases the infant.

Having the father present is particularly meaningful to prepared parents who have looked forward so much to sharing the birth experience. Make it clear to the doctor that your preparation *has* included your husband and that you want him there with you! He need not see the operation, but can still hold your hand and comfort you. If a father-to-be really doesn't want to be present, he should not force himself nor should his wife force the issue.

Afterward you may be in pain and need comfort. Yet you also experience a natural desire to cuddle and care for your new baby—not to mention the rest of your family. There are some steps that may help you to cope with this conflict:

Talk about your feelings. Discuss honestly

the very real disappointment you have had as well as all your doubts with your husband, close friends, and your doctor, too.

Get in touch with other women who have had cesarean sections. One group is called Cesarean Sections Education and Concern (CSEC). Contact them at 15 Maynard Road, Dedham, Massachusetts 02026. They'll let you know if there is a chapter of their organization near you. In addition, Appendix C of *Have It Your Way* by Vicki E. Walton (Bantam Books, 1978) contains a three-page list of cesarean-childbirth groups.

Exercise in Bed After a Cesarean

Between walks, and even before you get up for the first time, it is very important to have some exercise right there in bed. Wiggle your toes. Flex your calves. Push your feet against the end of the bed. Place a pillow under your knees and move your feet

around in circles. Bend them up and down at the ankles.

Lie on your back, with one knee bent and the other stretched out straight. Tighten your abdomen slightly. Now, slide the bent leg out straight along the bottom sheet and back up again. Change legs.

Lie on your back with your knees bent and your feet flat on the bed. Now raise your head, hold it there for about thirty seconds, then lower your head.

You can even rock your pelvis from side to side—no more than is tolerably uncomfortable—and, lying propped up a little under your head and shoulders, your knees bent, reach forward with your arms and try to touch your knees. Don't go too far. Just a little stretch will do.

(Richard Hausknecht, M.D., and Joan Rattner Heilman, *Having a Cesarean Baby*, 1978)

How It Used to Be: The Ancient Operation

There are historical hints in the Talmud that some women of two thousand years ago survived a cesarean operation. But the first recorded instance of a specific woman surviving the operation was around A.D. 1500. A Swiss (whose profession was the castration of pigs) operated successfully on his own wife. The operation was not named after Caesar's method of birth, but his name means "to cut," and the operation did refer to someone in his family who was born in this manner.

Another Reason for Cesarean Increase

Doctors at Beth Israel question the argument that monitoring increases Caesarean sections, just as they question the charge of infection rate increases. While there has been an increase in the number of Caesarean births at Beth Israel, as well as throughout the country in recent years, there is no clear evidence that it can be attributed to the monitoring. Dr. [Emmanuel] Friedman [OB-GYN Chief] says, "We have reviewed our data at the hospital and it clearly demon-

strates that fetal monitoring has not increased the Caesarean section rate. The increase in Caesarean sections during the past decade is due to the greater frequency with which a diagnosis of fetopelvic disproportion is being made." There was in fact no increase in the number of Caesarean sections performed in 1978 over the previous year at Beth Israel Hospital. ("Fetal Monitoring Saves Lives," *Wellbeing at Beth Israel Hospital*, 1979)

WHOSE GUILT IS IT?

To avoid unneeded cesarean sections, some hospitals require two separate medical opinions before a cesarean section can be performed.

Other doctors, however, see the increased rate of cesareans as an indication of the intelligent application of technology. It has been found, explains Dr. Allan Charles of Chicago's Michael Reese Hospital, that long and difficult deliveries may lead to neurological problems—minimal brain damage. Should the child reach about four years and develop learning disabilities, the response on the part of some parents has been to sue the delivering physician. Naturally, doctors don't want lawsuits! Nor do parents want impaired children, when the disability *might* have been avoided by a cesarean delivery.

Unfortunately, women who have undergone a cesarean section are frequently burdened with much self-doubt and guilt, and often terribly disappointed.

The reason for a cesarean *should* be clearcut: two lives are in balance—a mother's and her unborn child's—and the doctor should only act to diminish the danger to both of them or to one of them, as the case may be. There *are* unnecessary cesareans. But you as a lay person usually will not know when the operation is not necessary. Therefore, the guilt, if any, should be your doctor's, not yours!

MORE QUESTIONS

Although there is disagreement on the maternal mortality rate, some doctors believe that the usual rate of 2 to 3 deaths in 10,000 may increase with cesareans to 5 in 10,000.

Some doctors are worried about the rising cesarean rates. But during the 1979 annual convention of the American College of Obstetricians and Gynecologists, many obstetricians seemed quite in favor of the operation. There seemed to be little thinking through of what this major operation might be, mean, or do to mother, child, and father, and to the family unit, perhaps.

The author of this book is concerned about this point of view. Especially when it is expressed by those who have a large stake to protect. There is, to my mind, a possible conflict of interest in doctors promoting a serious operation—for which they are paid a substantial fee.

There are questions to be asked. Among the possible reasons for cesareans, there are points made largely by the nonmedical profession about the management of pregnancy and labor. Do the practices of hospitals and doctors increase the likelihood of cesareans? How many cesareans might be iatrogenic in nature? Is the legal question the major one weighing on the medical mind? Why don't preparation-for-childbirth classes educate parents-to-be on the cesarean and the many factors which surround it? Why don't doctors tell their patients—especially older or high-risk ones—about cesareans? What evaluation procedures are there on the need for the operation?

Without years of direct medical experience, it is hard to condemn medical results in a very technical area. But a rise in the rate of operations is a serious matter. And I do feel it is long past time for questions to be raised.

THE LEGAL REASONS

The major reason for the rise in cesareans may well be the lawsuits that are claiming damage to the baby or child from a forceps delivery. It is so easy to avoid this kind of suit in a difficult-birth situation through the use of a cesarean. Of course, there may be another kind of lawsuit down the road—those claiming impairment to child and mother *and* family unit *as a result of* a cesarean!

ADVICE FROM DR. LEBOYER: HOW TO HANDLE A CESAREAN BABY

"If you understand that being born through a cesarean section is even more traumatic for the child, all you have to do, immediately afterward, is to talk to this child; make the child understand, [whispering] 'Yes, yes, it's been very difficult, but it's all right now. It's all right.' And although there is no language in a newborn baby, and the child is not going to understand the words of course, it will fully take and understand what you say.

"It's a rupture of a sort of rhythmic, continuous process. It's going to leave a mark. [But] it is clear that at times we have to do a cesarean section. I don't mean to say that all women should have a natural childbirth. We never know what to expect, but whenever a cesarean section is necessary, or forceps or anything, whenever there have been greater difficulties in birth, it is *all* the more necessary to understand that there is even more fear, and when I say fear, of course, it's an understatement. And what do we do usually with newborn babies born through cesarean section? We put them in incubators, [where they are] terrified by their solitude. So keep the baby with somebody, anybody. If the father is there or in the next room, that's the best one. Because he knows the voice of the father."

IF YOURS IS A SPECIAL BABY

If you become the parent of a special child, you might want to keep several thoughts in mind. First of all, don't bother to look for a source of guilt, a place to lay blame. It's *not* your fault. It's *not* your husband's fault. Birth defects do happen without known cause or reason.

But let's say you believe that the defect *can* be traced to something you did or didn't do during your pregnancy. Shouldn't you then shoulder your justifiable burden of guilt? Actually, no—even if it's true. Guilt immobilizes. It prevents you from accepting yourself with all your quite human deficiencies. And if you can't accept yourself, it will be harder to accept your baby—and that baby's deficiencies. What your special child needs most of all is loving, supportive parents, who can get over and forget about the past—and move on positively from here.

Further, with the advances in medical knowledge and technology, your child has more of a chance at a better life than he or she would have had even a generation ago. Just ten years ago, for example, children who acquired diabetes in their infancy were likely to go blind. Today, painless laser treatments have all but eliminated the problem.

In addition to medical advances, we have progressed greatly in our understanding of psychological factors. The first, second, or twentieth sight of a child born with a birth defect—a cleft palate, for example—can give any parent a large-scale heartache. Knowing this, talking about the feelings involved, perhaps crying to each other and to others about it, certainly seeking professional help, are progressive steps that help diminish the ache, the rage, the sorrow. And, as these feelings become less dominant, it becomes easier to love that baby regardless of his or her appearance.

Taking action to help your child is one of the most productive things you can do. There is a vast network of specialized experts and organizations just waiting for your call, ready to provide advice and assistance. If you need help finding out where to go and how to make that first contact, ask your doctor for literature and guidance. The National Library of Medicine in Bethesda, Maryland, can provide a computer printout listing all sources of information on the subject of your child's disability.

Seek out other parents of children with similar disabilities. You're not alone in the world. And you and your child need some good friends who will understand your predicament. Others who have experienced your situation will be able to offer a strong shoulder, solid advice, and solutions to problems of daily living, such as transportation and baby-sitting services. You can pool your time and abilities to keep up on the latest medical research and fight for legislation that would be in your interest.

The best information about forming a self-help community group is from people who have already founded one. Ask them how they did it. Two such organizations are: Juvenile Diabetes Society, 23 East 26th St., N.Y., N.Y. 10010; and Spina Bifida Association of America, 300 Madison Avenue, N.Y., N.Y. 10017.

If you're old enough to be a parent, then you're old enough already to know from experience that life will always be dishing out some new trial or tribulation for you to handle.* Keep your perspective and sense of humor—and don't let your child's birth defect limit your life any more than it has to! Give him or her the greatest possible shot at

---

*Life, after all, is quite fair. Sooner or later it breaks everybody's heart.

high self-esteem and happiness by (1) taking care of the problem as much as you can, then (2) minimizing its importance.

As many specialists in the child-care field have pointed out, the key factors for any child are that child's parents and their ability to enjoy and love and approve of their offspring, "warts and all"—plus a community which makes that ability more possible. A fussing or critical approach is even more important to avoid with a special child. The ability to consider a child a child first and foremost with the same needs for fun and play and caring as all children—and with an incidental defect which requires some arrangements—helps parents to live with such a child in a more ordinary way.

For those of you whose babies are born with defects—physical or mental—that cannot be fixed, you too need to accept the present and your own feelings about the baby and yourself and your partner. But the future matters even more to you. A baby born with hemophilia or Down's syndrome or cerebral palsy is at our present state of knowledge never going to recover to normalcy. But the enormous strides that have been made in helping such children learn to live with enjoyment and *up* to their potential have come about because some parents have looked to and worked very hard for the future. Not just for the sake of their own children, but for all the others to come. And that, of course, is the gift of the child born with a severe uncorrectable handicap or defect. He or she brings into the world the ability to *help a parent* learn and see and love and grow and do—to become a person with infinitely more dimension, far beyond what that parent ever envisioned for himself or herself in the past.

Not everyone can accept and use that gift. In fact, very few of us can at present. But those few will help the others to find better ways to live with and do for such a special child. They have found and will find ways to move society toward better conditions for

parents and children, so that pressures on parents will be far less in the future.

For those of you who cannot move the world, however, and who need just to keep body and soul together in the face of a family crisis, there are a few things you need to be particularly aware of:

It is vital to face the fact that both your lives (and your pictures of life with a child) have been blighted and will continue to include severe overwhelming problems. These will range from your own death wishes against the child to friends and relatives turning away from you. Facing facts can help deal with them.

There are national organizations for practically every defect you can think of. Tie in to one. Get their literature.

Give *yourselves* (and I emphasize the plurals for a good reason) plenty of time off. Get good substitute care, if you have to beg for it, or exchange for it.

Be very watchful and accepting of each other's emotions; marriages that include a handicapped child are at more risk. Also, try not to neglect other children you may have because of your special child.

Pester the various governments, their agencies, and *your* representatives to learn about whatever benefits you might be entitled to—and also to push for any others.

Believe that there *is* a benefit to having a special child, and you will find at least one.

Make use of religious organizations and groups, even if you are not religious. Such organizations often have a lot to offer people who need comfort and other kinds of help.

Explore and use whatever community resources you can, including personal one-to-one therapy.

Become friends with other parents in the same situation.

Expectations and Depressions

You Should Prepare As Actively for Postpartum As for Childbirth

The few studies that psychologists have done on adjusting to motherhood reveal that women who received information about how to cope with the postbirth physical and emotional changes experienced fewer disturbances than did those who did not receive information. Moreover, women whose husbands participated in the birth process experienced even fewer postbirth difficulties. (Lyn DelliQuadri and Kati Breckenridge, *Mother Care,* 1978)

YOUR BABY IS HERE, AND HOW DO YOU FEEL?

The answer to that question may seem obvious. Of course, you feel great. You both have achieved one of the major landmarks of life—having your very own baby. Why shouldn't you feel great? You are eager to start life off anew with this marvelous creature you have produced.

Actually, there is a very large range of reactions to parenthood, both immediately and later on. Ambivalent feelings about having a baby are fairly common. Prebaby excitement and fantasies may turn to postbaby disappointment and feelings of being burdened. Lots of parents-to-be build up beautiful images that no reality can meet. There is a strong letdown, a pervasive feeling that is negative and unhappy. This type of letdown is known as the "postbaby blues."

Some authorities, particularly in the medical profession, believe that the change in hormonal balances, as the result of the birth of the baby, is primarily responsible for women feeling low and dispirited for some days after the birth of the baby. Others lean much more toward a social-emotional explanation, that is, the new mother (or father) is not ready for a baby yet; s/he does not have sufficient help; s/he has not understood the process and what will be required—thus, s/he is afraid of the requirements that are descending. Since adoptive mothers (and fathers) experience these feelings, too, the latter explanation seems to make more sense. In any event, the range of reactions to parenthood should all be considered within the "normal" sphere, and should all be accepted and understood.

If you don't like your baby's looks, this is not a dreadful feeling. If you wish that you didn't have the baby, you're still part of the human race. If you are jealous of the attention that a baby brings, and wish that you could have some of that attention, you should know that you share such feelings with many, many others. The ability to realize that not all of your feelings about the new baby are going to be happy ones—and the ability to accept such feelings in yourself—will go a long way toward helping you deal with them.

Let me mention some possibilities:

- You may not like your baby.
- You may not like being a parent.
- You may feel left out.
- You are very likely to feel let down at some point.
- You may resent the responsibility.

- You may feel that what you've gone through is not worth it.
- You may believe that you are a pariah, as a result of such feelings.
- You may be unable to tell anyone about the fact that you are unhappy about the birth of the new baby.

If these feelings occur, try to realize that we are all extremely complex individuals. To be able to accept yourself despite such negative and unhappy emotions during this supposedly joyous time is an ability that some of us do not have. But not liking yourself for the way you feel can lead to more problems later, unless *that* feeling is examined and looked at.

There have been many studies over the years which indicate that the birth of a baby brings crisis into the lives of the young couple—a crisis which marks a total change of life-style for mother and father. Your rate and stage of reaction may be quite different from your wife's or husband's. The ways in which you handle the crisis are the key to what happens next in your life.

There is an absolutely marvelous book called *Mother Care* by Lyn DelliQuadri and Kati Breckenridge. Both authors bear rather famous family names in the history of the helping professions. They themselves have great credentials. Lyn DelliQuadri is a psychiatric social worker and Kati Breckenridge is a clinical psychologist. Their book, which you will find quoted in this section, is the best one I have read on ways to deal with the emotional transitions of becoming a parent. The key element that these authors (and anyone who deals with people going through crisis situations) recommend is: recognition and expression, and then an attempt to deal with the problems that the new situation creates in the way you feel and act.

What can or should be done about the "baby blues"? How does one prevent such a situation from occurring, or continuing? What can you, or those who are close to you, do to make it easier?

Here is my own list of steps that can help prevent or ameliorate that postbaby let-down feeling:

Without suppressing negative feelings, try to view having a baby in a positive light. Think of advantages and pleasures as much as you can.

Realize that you may well feel let down for a few days after your baby is born.

Acknowledge the fact that men as well as women go through such feelings.

Decide in advance, if possible, what you will do to help yourself during this period—rehearse a little, in other words.

Plan to talk about it to someone with whom you feel comfortable.

Let your partner know what you are feeling, without expecting him or her to be able to do anything about it.

Do try to arrange for a family-centered birth, for rooming-in, and for a lot of togetherness with your spouse during the entire birth and postbirth process. This will probably help to prevent the "baby blues." (Some women may feel too much responsibility for the baby with rooming-in, and no one should force herself to accept an uncomfortable situation.)

Talk to new mothers and fathers and others about to have a baby before yours is born. Bring along their telephone numbers to the hospital. If possible, form a little group, so that you will have people to consult who have gone through a similar experience.

If your parents can be helpful, talk to them.

Be sure you have planned as much physical help with the baby in the first week or two or three after the birth as you can get.

Arrange in advance, as much as you can, for relatives and friends to give you a hand with (1) time off, (2) time to talk, (3) direct help with the baby, (4) direct help with household or personal chores, (5) visits to doctor or stores, and (6) any problem situations which occur. In other words, arrange for a "relative/friend alert" in advance.

Plan a way of getting out and away from the baby for very brief periods during the first days and weeks after childbirth. Even a ten-minute evening walk outside the house may bring you immediate relief. In hospital or home you may need more time alone than is expected. All of us at times need to be individuals, to be by ourselves, to feel that we have control over small segments of our time and our lives. And if you are prone to the "baby blues," such a need may be more extensive.

Try to bring reading material to the hospital concerning work that you have been involved in. Do try to spend a little time—five minutes here, ten minutes there—to read.

There are specialized journals in every field which will help you feel you have a continuing life outside of your baby and your home. Keep up as much as you can. Your own sense of self-identity will diminish the "baby blues."

Try the varieties of exercises and massages available. The *Mother Care* book gives explicit instructions in a number of exercises.

Body care and self-care can help alleviate down feelings.

List on a piece of paper your expectations of what having a baby will be like. Ask other new parents whether these are realistic.

If you're in the midst of the "baby blues" right now, try to write down what your expectations were. Compare how realistic or unrealistic these were with the reality of the baby here. Do the same thing with your fears and possible resentments. If you know what your fears and angers for the present and for the future are, you will be more able to deal with them.

Talk to your doctor in advance about what, if anything, he or she prescribes for the "baby blues." If your doctor gives medications, you should be aware of this. It may be, especially if you're not nursing, that medication is the best thing for you, but you need to know in advance what various experts advise.

Try to line up one or more trained specialists in this area—educators, social workers, psychologists, psychiatrists—used to working with new mothers and fathers. You may find that a consultation by telephone, or a visit or two, will help you over those rough feelings.

Think of those things which you most like to do. Pleasant and happy things, with or without a baby. If you love great views, or just like to see the pattern of lace that the trees make against a darkening sky, why not look ahead to it? Whatever one, two or three activities or sights you most enjoy in life can be planned so that you will be able to enjoy doing them during the baby's first days or weeks.

If your penchant is for strenuous physical activity which is not possible in the immediate postbaby period, plan a later-in-the-year excursion that will give you something to look forward to. Also, if you can, try to engage in the smaller and easier-to-do-with-a-baby pleasures in life which you can indulge yourself in. Do you like to bake bread? Or collect stamps? Try to select several activities which are just for you alone, and which are enjoyable in their own right.

In all likelihood, you will get past the "baby blues" with flying colors. The majority of people do not experience this low feeling for more than a few days or weeks at a time. But suppose that you are one who is not quite that lucky? You enter what is clinically described as postpartum depression. The next section of this book will give you some indications of what you might be able to expect and do should this condition come to you.

REAL DEPRESSION?

Many of the suggestions that were made in the preceding section on the "baby blues" will be of value to help prevent a full-grown postpartum depression. Be sure to read *Mother Care,* and to keep a copy with you. If you feel that you might be particularly vulnerable, try to do whatever you can in advance to prevent such a low feeling from taking over your life.

Just what is a postpartum depression? Basically, this is a clinical term which refers to a state of feelings that seems inappropriate to the situation and that continues. The feelings have extraordinary depth and last quite a considerable length of time. Like the "baby blues," the reasons may be hormonal, hereditary, environmental, or a combination of causes. The environmental factors are the ones over which you have most control.

The most important thing you can do before your baby comes is to try to assess your own vulnerability to a postpartum depression.

In a 1965 study called "Factors in Post-Partum Emotional Adjustment" reported on in *General Obstetrics and Gynecology,* Dr. Richard Gordon and his associates listed fourteen stress factors that could be used as a checklist to determine whether you are more or less likely to develop a postpartum depression. (The checklist is reprinted in *Mother Care*.) But the majority of women studied with high scores did not come down with the depression. The response of this study shows that one's tendency toward postpartum depression cannot always be predicted.

Yet from my own experience and the accumulated experiences and wisdom of others, I have recognized various factors which do make for higher vulnerability. To help you plan ahead, I have organized my own list of potential danger signals. Read it over but don't consider it a foolproof guide to your behavior—the reason for my including it is simply to alert women and men who have had particularly stressful lives to the fact that they may need *extra help* and should keep this in mind when making all post-baby plans.

Here is my own list:

• Does your family history include a fair amount of serious depression?
• Are you having the baby quite reluctantly?
• Did your mother or father or any much-loved significant relative have a hard time—or difficult feelings—about having a baby?
• Were you frequently treated harshly as a small child by either or both parents, or by a caretaker?
• How do you like your parents? Do they seem very difficult to you at the present time?
• Is your relationship with your spouse primarily a loving and caring one, or are there serious problems?
• Is your husband/wife going to be very resentful about the extra responsibility of a new baby, and not directly helpful in caring for the baby?
• Have you recently moved to a community where there are no close friends or relatives?
• Does your partner's job take him or her away on frequent trips or evening meetings?
• Is your wife's work such that she is going to be unable to pay very much attention to the baby?
• Is your financial situation precarious or very worrisome?
• Are either of you in very bad health? Or is one of your parents in very bad health?

• Are you having the baby without outside assistance in the home or from the community?
• Are you a very closemouthed person who finds it extremely hard to talk about negative feelings?
• Do you tend to be very ashamed of yourself for not doing or feeling "the right thing"?
• Have you had no experience whatsoever with new babies?
• Is your husband's or wife's employer totally uninterested in or totally opposed to providing extra time off for baby care?

Factors such as these are among those which could bring a greater possibility of a postpartum depression in your life. But even if all of these factors apply to you, one overriding element, such as your total joy with babies even when they are bothersome, could be stronger in your life than the combined list. Or, if postpartum depression is primarily hormonal, none of these factors might apply to you and you could still come down with the disease.

Those of you who feel you might be susceptible can take various steps toward prevention or cure. Consider the suggestions below.

SUGGESTIONS ABOUT WHAT TO DO IF YOU THINK YOU'RE SUSCEPTIBLE

The suggestions listed here are stronger than those given in the "baby blues" list above; and very important.

Get in touch with your feelings (that was the reason for the list that precedes this section). Get in touch with your life situation.

Be sure to plan on needing *a lot* of help. Let your relatives and friends know that you really are going to need them. (Even if you're not that close, or don't much care for them, the help may be more important in the long run.)

Let your spouse know (husbands, too, have postpartum depressions) that this is a potential problem for you.

Whatever else you do, make certain that you are not alone in the house with the baby for three or four weeks after the baby comes, and after that period, be sure to try to have someone with you for two or three hours of the daytime, if possible.

Reach out. Join a club; go to the local YWCA or YMCA. Try to make friends with others in a similar situation.

If you can postpone a career and location change during the pregnancy, by all means do so, especially if the change will bring you into a more socially isolated area.

In advance, find the specialist who can give you help should you need it. If you feel particularly shaky, interview one or two people in the helping professions, in private practice, or in an agency—just to see what they are like, and whom you can call upon if the occasion arises. *It is a sign of strength to go for help.*

Plan as much as possible to make things easy on yourself. Don't believe that you can keep an immaculate house, an immaculate baby, cook gourmet meals, go to work, and attend to all of the other chores of living without creating considerable strain.

Take as many preparation-for-childbirth courses as you can.

Try to practice as many positive attitudes of thinking and feeling as you can. It *is* quite possible to psych oneself into a condition close to euphoria *or* depression. You should recognize a potential problem, and do what you can to prevent it. After that try to think about happy things. If you cannot, then be sure to get help immediately.

There are fine distinctions to be made between the extent to which you can genuinely help yourself recover, and to which relying on self-help may simply ignore an essential need for outside counseling-therapy. If you are in doubt, you should talk to a professional who can tell the difference, and who can help you learn the difference yourself.

In addition to professional help, self-help groups are extremely useful. There is nothing quite like sharing and discussing and learning with others in a similar situation.

Still, there are times when one simply must say, There is nothing I can do about this. If you should happen to land in a postpartum depression, and feel that nothing can be done about it—and after all of the at-tempts have been made, continue to feel that there is nothing you can do about it—then there is *still* something left. What is left is a phrase: It is perhaps the most helpful phrase that I have learned in my lifetime. The phrase is "This too shall pass."

It is not possible for the same level of intense feeling to be sustained day-in, day-out, year-in, year-out. Feelings do change in quality and intensity. That's why this phrase may give you the hope that there is a chink of light at the end of the tunnel for you, too.

Generally speaking, most postpartum depressions do not last more than a few months. While it may, during the course of it, feel like the end of life, it is without question *not* the end of life.

POSTPARTUM DEPRESSIONS ARE SOMETIMES TRICKY

A clinical depression is usually easily recognized, if not by the persons or their families themselves, then certainly by professionals. Wide mood swings, major changes in ordinary habits, and intense negative feelings that occur constantly or frequently are among the symptoms. Others may be sleeplessness (or too much sleep), crying without provocation, feelings of hopelessness and helplessness, anxiety attacks, unusual fears, isolating oneself, neglecting one's cleanliness, not eating, a breakdown of one's regular routine, or difficulty with ordinary chores of self-care, home care, or job care.

These are recognizable signs of a problem, particularly if more than one symptom occurs simultaneously, or one or another is especially severe, such as total exhaustion. One strong symptom alone invariably means postpartum depression. A lot of crying for no particular reason, for example; or consistently feeling very bad.

Sometimes, however, postpartum depression is disguised behind a facade. And since the depression is ostensibly not interfering with functioning, it is not recognized for what it is.

The symptoms of this kind of postpartum depression can vary. For example, a woman might be able to take care of her baby, but have a lot of "physical complaints" herself.

She has upset stomachs, her breasts are feeling very tender, her back is aching, she falls and skins her knee. Her complaints are spread over a period of some days, but there seems to be a fairly heavy proportion of physical complaints and minor accidents. Look at the behavior patterns before and after the baby is born. Do these problems total up after a week or two to more than would usually be the case?

Some experts would argue that these kinds of symptoms represent a subconscious cry for attention, and for mothering, and not actual symptoms of a postpartum depression. However, the emotional roots of a postpartum depression are, in part, a need for mothering attention, plus difficulty in accepting responsibility for the baby, and accepting a change of life-style which is limiting for the woman involved. (Not that everyone who has a group of physical symptoms within a week or two is in the midst of a full-blown postpartum depression!) The mother in question is unconsciously using a signaling device indicative of a deeper, underlying feeling that can trigger a full-blown and obvious depression.

Another symptom of depressed feelings is a tremendous amount of busyness. After a baby is born, the woman who never has time to sit down and be calm and do nothing is finding a way of reacting to a life situation, and is avoiding (1) thinking about it, (2) confronting it, or (3) doing anything about its causes. Although there may be a large increase in the work load of the new mother, a tendency to avoid calm and peacefulness may be a way of saying, "I don't really want to deal with being a mother; I want to deal with anything that keeps me busy and keeps me going."

A third symptom of a depressed feeling about parenthood is a considerable amount of disagreement with one's partner concerning the ways of caring for the baby, and ways of being together. This may or may not break out into open quarreling. However, if you find that you are unable to agree with your spouse in large areas, such as what to do about a crying baby, when and whether and how to have sex, how much time to spend together, whether to leave the baby with a baby-sitter for an evening out, or how often to play with the baby, then there is a fair possibility that one or the other of you is inwardly quite depressed about the parental role.

Sharp divisions between a new parent and her or his own parents concerning baby care and times to get together can also be symptomatic of a depressed feeling. Most of the time, despite the fact that they themselves may be quite busy, new grandparents want to be somewhat involved with the new baby. They may express themselves in judgmental or critical ways, which is hard for a new parent to accept. Nonetheless, an inability to deal calmly with this conflict may indicate an underlying depressed feeling about the baby or about parenting.

A dislike or hatred of one's own child is another very strong symptom of trouble. That may be the feeling some people develop because they believe they cannot function well as parents, and particularly, cannot function emotionally as parents.

Interestingly enough, another possible symptom is a parent who is totally absorbed in the baby, to the exclusion of the outside world. While it is true that new mothers, and probably fathers, need the baby almost as much as the baby needs the parent, a total dependence upon the baby for all sources of entertainment and interest can signal a very confused emotional state—probably one of fairly extensive underlying depression.

Of course, it's easy to call anything a depression, and it's possible that many of these symptoms represent other states of being, such as an inadequate sense of identity, or an inability to love—but these are components that can make up a depression as well.

If you or your partner notice one or another of these symptoms, it becomes important to try to take action before the situation gets severe.

HUSBANDS, TOO, CAN GET POSTPARTUM DEPRESSION

In most of the literature, until recently, postpartum depression has been attributed to mothers. This has been an oversight on the part of the professional community, because fathers too suffer from the same feelings of terror and fearfulness at parenthood and of an inability to function as a father. Since the generally accepted role of a new father is still to go out and work during the day and not to assume primary and direct baby care—and since men are taught not to cry—a man's depression is often less noticeable and less noticed. Further, with new fathers, the symptomatology of the depression may take indirect forms.

One of the reasons I earlier included the discussion of less obvious symptoms is because men tend to have these. They get extraordinarily busy in their jobs, and supposedly are unable to give much substitute care to the baby. The question, of course, is: Is this realistic, or essential? Or is it because the father doesn't feel adequate to the fathering role?

Most young men have not had any direct experience with infants and children. Often they have been quite separate from any intimate contact with babies and youngsters. This affects their feelings about their capacity to handle situations, their feelings about themselves as fathers, and about being the husband of a woman who is a mother. Even the simple area of breast feeding can create enormous problems for some new fathers who have traditionally, in our society, viewed the breast as a sex object. Suddenly it becomes a nurturing organ for another human being, albeit his own son or daughter. This situation can place a young man into a panic beneath the cool. That panic can take forms that are not the traditional easy-to-notice forms of depression. They can propel a new father into much more of a separation syndrome than becomes apparent on the surface.

New fathers who are in an unrecognized depression are also particularly subject to extramarital sex experiences. Through the use of sex with another presumably attractive woman, they can at least reaffirm the one function of manhood which brought them to the fathering role. Even if I can't be a father—a particularly good father—I can still be a man, is the way that the subconscious, or even conscious thinking, may develop.

Problems on the job seem to be quite common among new fathers. Employers will have their own versions of why this is the case, that is, the employee was up late at night, took too much time off, is not concentrating on his work.

Too much alcohol (or drugs) sometimes begins with the birth of a baby, and this is also a symptom of depression. In extreme cases abandonment of mother and child, divorce, or whatever can take place.

If the problem is a practical one—not enough sleep, for instance—some arrangement with employers may be possible for the temporary period of time while the baby is up at night. But the likelihood is that a new father is having difficulty in interpersonal relationships, both at home and on the job, because his role as father is causing him problems.

Some of the literature concerning postpartum depression speaks very strongly to the need for fathers-to-be to be supportive and helpful to their wives—in other words, to perform a mothering-fathering function toward the woman who has borne the baby. There is no question that a father who is able to be supportive, considerate, and helpful is minimizing the possibilities of postpartum difficulties for his wife. But a man who is himself having such difficulties is not able to give the basic support to his wife that he might under other circumstances.

The best thing to do in that case is to turn outward to the community for resources to help both mother and father. The fact is that new parents (even those who have *not* experienced depression after the baby was born) simply need a lot of loving care and attention themselves.

◇ ◇ ◇

There's More to the "Baby Blues"

Eight out of ten women experience easy crying, mood swings, and helpless feelings following childbirth, according to Dr. James Hamilton, author of *Postpartum Psychiatric Illness*. . . .

Physicians have traditionally minimized postpartum distress as a "common" and "normal" reaction which may occur three to five days after delivery as a result of the abrupt decrease in hormonal activity. "Normal" women quickly recover and get on with the business of motherhood, many physicians feel; those who do not are often led to believe that they have deep-seated emotional problems and are directed to specialists for psychotherapy or tranquilizers. Dr. John G. Howells sums up the conventional view in *Principles of Family Psychiatry* (1975): "Childbearing is normally an unstressful experience."

Current evidence demands a reevaluation. In November 1977, psychologist Dr. Bertram Cohler told a conference of science writers what women have known for a long time—the birth of a child is a *stressful* event. Basing his conclusion on fifteen years of clinical experience with mothers of all ages, he estimated that one-sixth of all new mothers suffer serious depression requiring professional care, and a much greater percentage struggle alone with their stresses with varying degrees of success. (Lyn DelliQuadri and Kati Breckenridge, *Mother Care*, 1978)

Depressed Feelings Leave Scars

Even a mild post-partum depression, lasting a few weeks, can leave such deep scars that the foundation of the early mother-child relationship is weakened.

It is not uncommon for women, later in life, to have total recall of those early, miserable days. Many trace later feelings of bitterness and disappointment in their roles as wives and mothers back to the first days at home with the new baby, when they felt overwhelmed, isolated, and unsupported. (Dr. Silvia Feldman, *Choices in Childbirth*, 1978)

You Are Not Sick

There are lots of myths about how "natural" and therefore easy it is to be a mother. Being unable to express that you are tired, afraid, or imposed upon, believing that to do so would be cruel or selfish, may intensify feelings of inadequacy, helplessness, and frustration that many women feel as they attempt to cope with the new responsibility and demands of a newborn baby. You may experience thoughts of dropping the baby, smothering it, or starving it. It may be comforting to know that you are not a freak or a sick woman if you have some of these feelings. Many women do.

It is important to understand that this is a period of intense change for you as a woman, and that you are not "sick" for responding to what you feel. There is often the feeling: Women have always had babies and never had problems, so why am I feeling such conflict? In fact, conflict goes along with any major change (leaving home, getting married, menopause). (Beverly Gudanowski, "Pregnancy, Childbirth and After," *The Women's Yellow Pages*, 1978)

Part Seven

AFTERWARD AND BEGINNINGS

The family has been to me like the big bosom of my grandmother. She was a very heavyset woman and she had a rocking chair in the kitchen and all the grandchildren used to go and sit on her lap and being enveloped in that kind of warmth and feeling—it's a wonderful analogy to how I feel about the rest of the family. And that's with all the problems, with all the fights, with all the arguments, with all the differences, with all the fallings out and fallings in. That's with everything. It's still there.

NENA O'NEILL

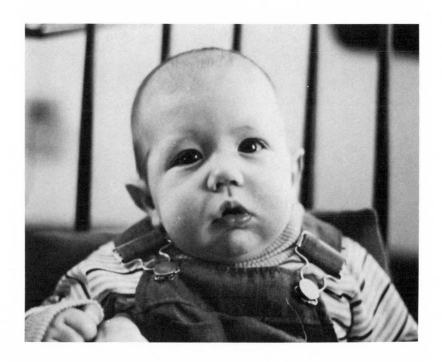

Celebrations and Rituals

After the baby arrives, lots of things will be taking place in your life—some annoying, some routine, some very exciting. You'll be taking care of the baby. You'll be taking care of you. And the other you. You'll be greeting relatives and friends. You'll be experimenting with new and unaccustomed ways of living—like trying to finish a still-warm meal while nursing, or finding that you can let the phone *and* doorbell ring on and on without anxiety because your slippery eel of an infant is in the midst of the daily bath.

Your daily living will at times seem crammed with new experiences—a continuing series of discovery situations summarized under the heading Finding Out What Babies, and Your Baby Especially, Are Like. But first, let's talk about the onetime events of celebrating your baby's birth time.

TELLING THE WORLD

When the big day comes, how will you tell the world? With a baby announcement card, probably. Before deciding upon the card you will use, stop and think. A card should reflect *you* and your life-style. But a birth announcement also tells in subtle ways how you feel about the baby's arrival. Are you inspired to poetry, art, music? Are you feeling pensive, anticipating the life ahead for your newborn?

The card you buy, or the one you create yourself, should express your feeling at this special time. You—and your child—will look at it often in later years and remember.

CHRISTENINGS AND GODPARENTS

Rituals and ceremonies, traditional and conventional though they may be, have great meaning for many people during the change periods of life. Such ceremonies hook into the historical process; they bring a feeling of rootedness in past and future. For children rituals often mean a sense of group identity later in life. That's why the ceremonies of welcoming a baby into the new world make sense for young families. If you do not want to participate in any religious ceremony, you can design your own—or an adaptation of some kind. There are many different styles of wedding ceremonies, so why not another type of "christening"?

For those of you who *do* want a traditional christening, you'll find that there are variations among different faiths. For example, among Roman Catholics christening occurs as soon after the birth as possible, and the child has one set of godparents. Some Protestant denominations permit two godfathers for a boy or two godmothers for a girl. But among Orthodox Jews only male babies have godparents. Some faiths—Baptists and Mormons—wait until the child is old enough to understand the baptismal ceremony.

The words *baptism* and *christening* often are used interchangeably. Actually baptism refers to the sacrament proclaiming a child (or adult) a Christian and admitting that individual to the Church. Christening is the ceremony of naming a child which often includes festivities.

If your religion requires godparents they

should be selected before setting the day for the christening. Your oldest and closest friends are probably best: they will take a lifelong interest in your child. Emotional ties are the basis for the relationship. Godparents are considered to be almost relatives—and have often performed the parental role when necessary.

The traditional present that godparents give at christening time is a piece of engraved silver—a bowl or cup—that the child can hand down to his or her own children. If your first choice of godparents live too far away to travel to the christening, or for some other reason can't attend, they may be represented by proxies!

At church or home the ceremony is often followed by a luncheon or a tea. There are two traditional elements:

The christening cake. This is a white cake with white icing and can be resplendent with sugar roses and an inscription, or can be a simple cake you've made yourself.

The caudle or drink for toasting. Fifty years ago the beverage to serve was hot eggnog in punch cups—or caudle. Today the choice is champagne or champagne punch, or, if you prefer, cocktails or sherry.

Guests eat the cake as a sign that they partake of the baby's hospitality and, therefore, are friends. They join in a toast, proposed by the godfather, to the child's health and prosperity.

JEWISH CEREMONIES FOR THE NEWBORN

When a Jewish male child is eight days old, he is initiated into the faith in a ceremony known as the *B'rith,* or circumcision, ceremony. This is performed in the hospital or at home. Orthodox and Conservative Jews engage a *mohel,* or circumciser; Reform Jews may use a doctor and have a rabbi present. After the operation the child is named. The baby's name is that of a close relative who has died; the name may not always be the same, but the first letter always is. (My cousin Nadine was named after her great-grandfather Nuchum.) The reception following, though not essential, is traditionally a real feast with one empty plate laid at the table into which guests drop coins for charity.

Girls are named in the synagogue the first sabbath after birth, when the father is called up during the reading of the Torah. Sometimes, the service is postponed so that the mother also can be present. Although this ceremony is concerned with naming the girls, some congregations name both boys and girls in the synagogue.

How It Used to Be

We are asked by many young mammas as to the meaning of the phrase "caudle parties."

Formerly the persons who called to congratulate the happy possessor of a new boy or girl were offered mulled wine and plum-cake. Some early chronicler thinks that the two got mixed, and that caudle was the result.

Certain it is that a most delicious beverage, a kind of oatmeal gruel, boiled "two days," with raisins and spices, and fine old Madeira (some say rum) added, makes a dish fit to set before a king, and is offered now to the callers on a young mamma. The caudle-cups, preserved in many an old family, are now eagerly sought after as curiosities; they have two handles, so they could be passed from one to another.

Mary E. W. (Mrs. John) Sherwood,
Manners and Social Usages, 1887

CIRCUMCISION

Circumcision has been practiced for centuries for historical, religious, health, and ritual reasons. Jesus and his apostles were all circumcised.

Circumcision is the surgical removal of the protective flap of skin (foreskin) from the penis. The procedure is performed in a few minutes without an anesthetic, usually on the third or fourth day after birth, unless rituals require waiting. The wound generally heals in seven to eight days.

Though it has come to be especially associated with Judaism, circumcision is used by Muslims. It is an ancient practice, early examples of which can be found among the Egyptians. Originally it seems to have been some kind of initiation rite symbolizing a young boy's entry into manhood. In certain Middle Eastern tribes, as described in the Bible, the newborn son was a threat to the father's prominence in the family hierarchy and circumcision became a jealous act, a "taking away."

Although its routine performance has been dropped from rational medical practice in many countries, circumcision is supported by many on medical and other grounds in North America and Australia. The case for or against circumcision often is more of an emotional-psychological issue than a medical or social one. And among the scientists there is to date no irrefutable evidence on who is right. If you do decide *for* it, then, be certain that electrical equipment is *not* used. This equipment has produced problems.

THE PSYCHOLOGICAL ARGUMENT

Insecurity about "being different" is often a major factor in circumcision. An uncircumcised boy may be in for some teasing the first time he walks into a shower and confronts a group of his circumcised peers—and vice versa.

Women in general don't seem to care if their man is circumcised. One survey showed that most women weren't even aware whether or not a man was circumcised!

Perhaps the most significant psychological factor is sexual identification with family members. In deciding whether or not to circumcise consider if the father (or a brother) is circumcised. Looking the same way as family members can be important to a child's psychological development. This identification with other men in the family seems to be even more important to a child than reactions from his friends and schoolmates.

In general, I am opposed to circumcision, which is routinely practiced all over the United States by non-Jews and non-Muslims. It seems to me that anything that hurts an infant can and does lead to psychological problems, if only temporary. There *is* evidence to back me up. Be sure to make your doctor give you a significant *medical* reason why she or he favors circumcising your baby boy.

ANOTHER SLANT ON CIRCUMCISION

Be careful not to have it done by a cross-eyed *mohel* . . . otherwise the child will urinate on the slant for the rest of his life.

Old Jewish joke

What Are Babies Like?

When babies are described, the usual picture is that of a *picture*. A still. Captured for all time. But unmoving. A picture.

My own view of babies is different. The very word *baby* carries with it, in my head, a turning kaleidoscope, a perpetual-motion machine, a constant stream of happenings. Movement. Events. Almost minute-by-minute change.

There are people who are bored by babies. Some who scorn babies may like children because they can "communicate." To me, babies are communicators. They look, they watch. They hold and clench and taste. They listen and absorb. They feel. And most of all, babies move. Eyes, head, legs, arms, mouth, body—there is always movement, often growing movement, developing motion as with a flower . . . the toes going into the mouth . . . the tiny fist grabbing a sunbeam . . . the expressive face showing the surprise and joy of ice cream . . . the constant push to lift head and body from the belly-down position.

Some babies make a lot of noise (this is movement, too). The noise may be crying—of different kinds. Or it may be happy, burbling sounds. Some babies are great composers—experimenting with sounds unbelievable and evocative, ingenious and hilarious. Some are artists of the dance—flat-on-the-back untutored dance, but dance with grace and fluidity and synchronization.

Some babies, in fact almost all babies, are explorers who surpass the combined efforts of Marco Polo, Christopher Columbus, and Neil Armstrong. For babies are exploring many, many worlds simultaneously with every bit of sensory perception and physical ability they have. They look at their working parts, the working parts of the whole baby—and test their capacity to do this and that, to understand this and that. They explore the whole world of *you*—what your parts are, what you can or will or won't do. They look at their immediate environment, and a prism or a pan becomes a world in itself—as does almost every object with which there is contact.

And then, babies—all babies—are producers. They "put on a show"—not consciously, not planned. But they do produce a continuing series of events—each a mini-show in itself—and all adding up to one of the most amazing productions any of us ever can witness—the growth of a human child.

What are babies like? They are a smile and a sigh, a song and a poem, a photograph, yes, and a never-ending, ever-fascinating, always vivid motion picture come to life.

A BABY'S FIVE SENSES— AND OTHER VITAL SIGNALS

Newborns, seemingly so helpless and uncomprehending, actually perceive a great deal.

Sight

In the past it was thought that newborns couldn't focus their eyes, and didn't really look at anything. But investigators have observed that newborns will "track" with their gaze a bright object moved across their field of vision. One group of scientists has found that newborn babies have surprisingly good visual acuity—20/150 vision. Some studies indicate that they are able to discriminate among degrees of brightness, and prefer to look at medium-bright panels rather than very bright or dim ones.

Other studies of the way newborns move their eyes when looking at geometric figures have shown that they seem to select certain features for attention, such as edges and angles. They also tend to scan the environment in a horizontal rather than a vertical direction.

The binocular vision needed for depth perception does not seem to be possible until the second month, but by the third month babies can perceive—and they seem to prefer to look at—three-dimensional objects rather than two-dimensional representations of objects.

Hearing

Scientists once thought that newborns could not yet hear. We now know that although a baby's hearing is poor at birth (since the middle-ear structures do not yet function adequately), newborns do hear. Although their hearing is less sensitive than that of older children, sounds of medium intensity are audible to them, and they are able to distinguish between different pitches. In fact, babies still in the uterus respond in a variety of ways to sound. By about three months of age babies can differentiate tones about one and a half octaves apart. However, the ability to discover where a sound is coming from—called sound localization—is usually thought to take longer to develop, perhaps not until six months of age or even later. Other studies have suggested that the ability to locate sounds, although hard to detect, is not uncommon in newborn babies.

Smell

Studies by a group of investigators at Brown University have shown that newborn babies will respond to a disagreeably odorous gum resin. During the first few days of life infants quickly become sensitive to odors, requiring less intense odors to elicit responses.

Taste

The newborn's sense of taste has also been found to be far more acute than scientists

had previously believed. Babies show through their sucking behavior that they can taste the differences between water, acidic liquids, sugar, salt solutions of various concentrations, and milk.

Touch

Newborns and fetuses, too, are sensitive to both pressure and touch, responding, however, to stimulation in a more general way than they will later on. For example, if a very young infant's hand is touched, he or she will not only move that hand, but also his or her other limbs. Characteristically babies respond to touching by sneezing, sucking, and swallowing.

Stimulation

Babies are quieter and more relaxed . . . when there is a constant stimulus present, such as the ongoing recorded sound of a heartbeat or music played softly and constantly. Does that mean they are happy and they like the sound? It's impossible to be certain; but it's probable that this is the case.

Social Development

The social aspect is an important part of an infant's perceptual environment, from very early in his life. Almost from birth, babies prefer looking at people rather than at animals or inanimate objects. It is reasonable to assume from this that very young babies possess a sense of their humanness—an unarticulated awareness that they are people.

The infant's fascination with other people seems to develop very soon after birth. As the infant matures beyond the first few weeks, faces and figures gain steadily in attractiveness over objects, especially if they are moving. According to investigators at Boston University, as the length of the infant's attention span increases steadily during the first eight weeks, interest in the mother's face increases as well. Overall, during the first eight weeks, babies may look less at their mothers' faces than at the human form in general, but they do show their greatest amounts of mouth and bodily movements when looking at their mothers.

Eye-to-eye contact between mothers and their infants is an important factor in the babies' development.

A major landmark in an infant's social development is the beginning of true smiling, an event usually occurring around the third month. The social smile in response to a face emerges after a period in which infants irregularly smile at a wide variety of stimuli. Social stimulation, even if it isn't visual, can set off smiling once infants are sufficiently mature. Blind babies smile when their senses are stimulated, and sighted infants smile in response to touch. One scientist found that young babies smile more to a nodding, talking person than to one who only nods or talks. (Bertram S. Brown, M.D., *New Clues to Your Baby's Secret World.* Department of Health, Education and Welfare, 1975)

◇ ◇ ◇

The Vital Beat

The tactual sensitivity with which the baby is born has already undergone much preparatory development in the womb. We know that the fetus is capable of responding both to pressure and to sound, and that the beating of its own heart at about 140 beats per minute and the beating of its mother's heart, with a frequency of 70, provides it with something of a syncopated world of sound. Given the knowledge that the baby is laved by the amniotic fluid to the symphonic beat of two hearts, it is not surprising to learn that the soothing effect of rhythmical sounds has been connected, in the hypotheses of some researchers, with the feeling of well-being assumed to exist *in utero* in relation to the mother's heartbeat. (Ashley Montagu, *Touching: The Human Significance of the Skin,* 1971)

◇ ◇ ◇

YOUR BABY'S BRAIN POWER

Until fairly recently, most scientists believed that a baby's brain was practically complete at birth. But two University of Manchester researchers, Dr. John Dobbing and Dr. Jean Sands, have demonstrated that there is a large and very significant spurt in the growth of the brain after birth, lasting for two years. Undernourishment of babies at this time leaves lasting brain damage.

During this time stimulation is vital to this growth. The brain itself is adversely affected physiologically by *a lack* of handling, touching, playing.

When you respond to your baby—by picking your infant up, talking to or feeding her or him—you are stimulating the growth and development of the sensory organs and the brain structures that make them work. Just as important, you are teaching your baby that someone cares, that the world can be a rewarding place, and that s/he has some control over that world.

There are even more fantastic possibilities concerning the stimulation infants need. A neuropsychologist of the National Institute of Child Health and Human Development, Dr. James Prescott, believes the experimental evidence points to a strong connection between violent behavior in later life and *lack* of sufficient touching and handling as a baby. He suggests a possible permanent defect in the pleasure centers of the brain when a baby is deprived of movement and sensory caring. Does human violence begin when a mother does *not* pat or stroke her baby? Dr. Prescott would vote yes.

The interrelationship between touching, body contact, the sense of pleasure, physical play, and the development of normal sexuality is summed up by Dr. Mary Calderone, president of the Sex Information and Education Council of the United States, in an address for a national seminar, sponsored by the Girls Clubs of America in June 1978. She said:

"At birth, babies are already sexually functional: male fetuses have been having erections in the uterus, as determined by sonograms; infant girls begin a periodic cycle of lubrication of the vagina with the same sweating mechanism described by Masters and Johnson for adult women. . . .

"Before birth, sensitization by the sex hormones occurs in the sex centers of the brain, thus probably assuring that the child eventually will be responsive to certain sex-related socialization and learning processes. After birth, maternal or pleasuring body contact is essential for learning adult reproductive behavior. Experiments show that infant monkeys separated from their mothers at birth and never having contact with other monkeys will not know how to mate in adult life. So normal mating does not happen just by instinct. Babies need parents who are nurturing, part of which should consist of close and warm body contact . . . one researcher [Dr. Prescott] relates sensory and stimulus deprivation of babies, either human or animal, with later disturbances in sexual and social behavior . . .

"There is general agreement among researchers that sexual behavior is learned, with gender identity of the child programmed by cues from parents and irreversibly formed by the first two years of life at the latest. . . ."

Early Language Development

	RECOGNITION	ATTENTION	PRODUCTION
2 months		Attends to voice and face.	Cooing and other non-crying sounds.
3 months	Anticipates bottle.		Chuckles, vocal-social reaction, i.e. produces sounds on seeing or being spoken to.
4 months	Activity increases at sight of toy.	Turns to voice sitting.	Shakes rattle, spontaneous social smile, laughs out loud.
5 months	Smiles at mirror image.	Turns to sound sitting.	Squeals.
6 months	Discriminates strangers.		Spontaneous vocal-social production, including vocalizing to toys, etc., and mirror image. Grunts, growls.
7–8 months	Pats mirror image.		Likes to produce sounds by banging objects, polysyllabic vowel sounds, single syllables, i.e. da, ba, ka, etc.

Real language begins at 8 to 9 months with specific activity based on understanding and memory—reacting therefore to symbols. Verbal symbolic production begins.

	ATTENTION	PRODUCTION
8–9 months	Looks for object just put out of sight—short visual memory is emerging. Adjusts to gesture, "bye-bye," "peek-a-boo." Responds to name, "no-no" or disapproving tone of what is said.	Double syllables—dada or equivalent. Imitates sounds within repertoire, lip-smacking for good taste. Meaningful use of "mama" and "dada." One word like "hi," "baba" (bye-bye), etc.

By one year separation from the environment is emerging in terms of being a "self" which makes response possible which could not occur earlier because of lack of separation.

12 months	Gives an object to mirror image, gives a held object in response to verbal request and gesture, or either alone.	Two real words, not "mama" and "dada."

Ursula Jacobs, Marin Montessori School, Corte Madera, California, 1970

A Baby's Temperament

We reject both the "nurture" and the "nature" concepts. Either by itself is too simplistic to account for the intricate play of forces that form the human character. It is our hypothesis that the personality is shaped by the constant play of temperament and environment. . . .

Children do show distinct individuality in temperament in the first weeks of life, independently of their parents' handling or personality style. Our long-term study has

I. HEAD CONTROL

    1. Prone: lifts head
       (begins 1 month)

    2. Head and shoulder development
      a. On elbows
        (3 months)

      b. Arms straight
        (5 months)

    3. Head held steady while being pulled to a sitting
       position (begins at 3 months, completed at 5 months)

II. LOCOMOTION

    1. Rolling
      a. Back to stomach
        (5 and 6 months)

b. Stomach to back
   (5 and 6 months)

2. Creeping: stomach on ground
   (7 months)

3. On all fours: lower-trunk development

4. Creeps reciprocally
   (10 months)

Using reciprocal pattern

III. SITTING BALANCE

1. Equilibrium reactions: balance
   (6 months)

2. Beginning sitting

    a. Push of center; upper-trunk development

    b. Leans forward on hands
       (7 months)

3. Completed: also going from sitting to prone
   (10 months)

IV. STANDING BALANCE

  1. Bounces: takes fraction of own weight
     (7 months)

2. Pulls to feet
   (10 months)

3. Stands momentarily
   (14 months)

V. WALKING

   1. Walks while two hands are held
      (12 months)

   2. Walks while holding one hand
      (13 months)

   3. Walks alone
      (15 months)

Adapted from Infant Kit, Marin Montessori School, Corte Madera, CA.

CHARACTERISTIC BEHAVIOR CHART

Characteristic	Most Babies First Do This Between
How she or he behaves with other people	
Looks at your face	Birth–1 month
Smiles when you smile or play with him/her	Birth–2 months
Smiles on own	6 weeks–5 months
Pulls back when you pull a toy in hand	4–10 months
Tries to get a toy that is out of reach	5–9 months
Feeds self crackers	5–8 months
Drinks from a cup by self	10–16 months
Plays peekaboo	6–10 months
Plays pat-a-cake	7–13 months
Plays with a ball on the floor	10–16 months
How she or he uses hands and eyes	
Follows an object with eyes for a short distance	Birth–6 weeks
Follows with eyes from one side all the way to the other side	2–4 months
Brings hands together in front of him/her	6 weeks–3½ months
Grasps a rattle placed in fingers	2½–4½ months
Passes a toy from one hand to the other	5–7½ months
Grasps a small object (like a raisin) off a flat surface	5–8 months
Picks up a small object using thumb and finger	7–10 months
Brings together two toys held in hands	7–12 months
How she or he uses ears and voice	
Pays attention to sounds	Birth–6 weeks
Makes vocal sounds other than crying	Birth–6 weeks
Laughs	6 weeks–3½ months
Squeals	6 weeks–4½ months
How she or he handles whole body	
Holds head off of bed for a few moments while lying on stomach	Birth–4 weeks
Holds head upright lying on stomach	5 weeks–3 months
Holds head steady when you hold him/her in sitting position	6 weeks–4 months
Rolls over from front to back, or from back to front	2–5 months
Sits without support when placed in a sitting position	5–8 months
Gets self into sitting position in crib or on floor	6–11 months
Takes part of weight on own legs when held steady	3–8 months
Stands holding on	5–10 months
Stands for a moment alone	9–13 months
Walks holding on to furniture	7½–13 months
Walks alone across a room	11–15 months

Adapted from U.S. Department
of Health, Education and Welfare, *Infant Care*, 1973

now established that original characteristics of temperament tend to persist in most children over the years. . . .

. . . A child's temperament is not immutable. In the course of his development the environmental circumstances may heighten, diminish or otherwise modify his reactions and behavior. For example, behavior may become routinized in various areas so that the basic temperamental characteristics are no longer evident in these situations. Most children come to accept and even take pleasure in the bath, whatever their initial reactions may have been. The characteristics usually remain present, however, and may assert themselves in new situations even in form of an unexpected and mystifying reaction. (Alexander Thomas, Stella Chess, and Herbert G. Birch, "The Origin of Personality," *Scientific American*, August 1970)

The Love That Produces a Genius

[The] learning of the first eighteen months is a prodigious intellectual feat. No wonder every parent thinks his baby is a genius. He is!

And like all geniuses this baby works indefatigably at his discoveries. He is intoxicated with his new-found world; he devours it with every sense organ. He marvels at the bit of dust he picks up in his fingers. A piece of cellophane, a scrap of foil, a satin ribbon will fill him with rapture. He revels in the kitchen cupboards, pursues the hidden treasures of drawers, waste-baskets and garbage cans. This urge for discovery is like an insatiable hunger that drives him on and on relentlessly. He is drunk with fatigue, but he cannot stop. The hunger for sensory experience is as intense and all-consuming as the belly hunger of the first months of life. . . .

. . . The hunger that once was exclusively body hunger has been transformed into a voracious appetite for the world. Love that centered first in the mother who satisfied body needs has expanded and ramified to embrace the ever-widening horizons of his world. The baby is in love with the world he has discovered through his mother's love, and he behaves like those intoxicated lovers in songs and verse who find that the whole world has been transformed through love and the most common objects are infused with beauty. (Selma H. Fraiberg, *The Magic Years: Understanding and Handling the Problems of Early Childhood*, 1968)

If your baby does not conform to this timetable, do not worry. Some of the world's great geniuses did not speak until age 3, did not crawl at all. However, a major variation from the pattern should be looked into. There may be a problem that is hard to see at first.

What Do Babies Need?

SOME BASIC BABY NEEDS

A sense of warmth and love for a baby—no matter what s/he does, no matter how s/he interferes—is the greatest asset any parent can have. Next in importance is a fairly constant expression of these warm feelings. How can s/he tell how you feel? Through *a lot* of physical contact—gentle and secure. Through the tone of your voice. Through the quality of your care. Through play and games. Through the way you respond to his or her cries.

Your baby also needs the sense of a warm family and a warm home. How you get along with your husband may seem like a remote question in baby care. But a furious argument is heard by a baby (remember, s/he *listens* and s/he is afraid of loud noises), and though s/he cannot understand what it is all about, a baby's body responds to unhappy sounds. On the other hand, fun and sharing between parents make for happy sounds and faces, and an almost palpable atmosphere of pleasure and warmth—even for an infant.

Your baby's ability to hear is a key to one of the most important things s/he needs: lots of sweet talk and singing. Don't be afraid of baby talk, unless you *never* speak regular adult English. But what more natural thing for a new parent to do than to cuddle and baby-talk a tiny infant? A fairly steady stream of any talk (adult or baby) while you're giving your baby a bath, dressing her, playing with him, will start your child off with a sense of language as communication with you. Singing is, of course, something that all children love and respond to, whatever their age or stage. And the lovely thing about a baby is that s/he doesn't care about the quality of your singing!

Because s/he has recently come from a rolling, rocking situation, your baby feels comforted when you rock him/her—slowly and evenly, not jerkily. Use that boon of all mothers and babies—a straight-backed rocking chair. S/he needs to be securely held so that s/he won't feel as though s/he is falling (s/he is afraid of falling, remember?). Supporting the head is essential in the early months. Be careful of the soft spot, too.

Visitors are also *needed* by an infant—they

How It Used to Be

Ancient Egyptian remedy to stop child's crying:
"Pods-of-the-Poppy-plant, Fly-dirt-which-is-on-the Wall,
Make it into one, strain, and take for four days.
It acts at once!"

Cyril P. Bryan, ed. *The Papyrus Ebers*, 1931

are fun and help the baby get accustomed to other people. Unless your visitors are all children with colds and sharp pencils to poke, you can let them come and look and coo when your baby is awake.

Many people believe that babies comprehend little in the first few months. They also feel that s/he's pretty unaware of who and what's around and what's happening. This is not true. Even from the first days, a baby senses quite a bit. Through skin, ears, stomach, even eyes, s/he is stimulated and responds. A sense of curiosity, a drive to find and develop, the ability to communicate—these are present in all babies to a high degree. How much these qualities are expanded, how much your baby's potentialities are realized, rests in large measure on what happens in the early months.

Don't expect your baby to sleep, sleep, sleep—to give *you* lots of time and peace. If s/he's sleeping so much, it means s/he won't have much time for sociability with you.

Get into the habit, even from the beginning, of moving your baby around to be near you. Show off things you're using, explain what you're doing. You'll be helping your young student *want* to understand you.

Have toys around—lots of them. Don't just hand him or her a bunch of them all at once. But continue substituting one or another while s/he's awake. This includes bath toys, sleep toys, just ordinary objects to hold. Keep all *sharp, hard,* or *tiny* objects away, however. Never give toys with wheels or small parts which can come off and be put into a tiny mouth. Keep soft children's picture books on hand; play children's records now and then.

Change the baby's position and perspective on the world frequently. Even in the first months a baby will get a new view of things around if s/he's placed in a playpen for a while, then a bassinet or crib, then a carriage, then on your bed. *Be sure* to stay right there even if you think s/he can't roll off.

When s/he goes visiting or shopping, give your baby the explorer's perspective by showing him or her all you can about new places. In the park or backyard put your own explorer on the grass for a few minutes, then hold him or her up to bushes and trees and flowers.

In other words, consider what *you* would want to see and learn about everything around *you*—and give your baby the opportunity to start to see and learn, too. You are certain to develop a child with more curiosity and a livelier interest in people and things.

Some parents think that a baby should fit into the family and carry on with great amounts of noise while their offspring is sleeping. Other parents keep everything very hushed. Actually, neither is the "right" way.

Of course, babies will sleep through anything—but this is often the sleep of exhaustion and means *less rest.* On the other hand, a certain amount of pleasant background noise won't hurt a baby at all, and gradually s/he will get over this great "delicacy" and learn to sleep easily. Of course, babies—as people—vary in terms of being light and heavy sleepers, and you might adjust your home circumstances toward more or less noise depending upon your own little sleeper's needs. Dry diapers, comfortable clothing, some fresh air, a darkened room, a good mattress, fitted crib sheets, or the motion of a carriage are aids to good sleeping.

One other great aid to better snoozing for small snoozers is the kind of sleeping position. Many parents, fearful of smothering their babies, lay them only on their backs. But your baby, on the belly, will be able to lift and turn the head, if his or her arms are placed above the head. (Take a test first.) The value of the belly position is that it allows a baby to bring up that often present but not apparent last burp. A burp stuck inside is likely to wake an infant up crying in an hour.

But your baby's sleeping position should be changed frequently. Constant sleeping on the abdomen may be bad for the hips; constant sleeping on the back may flatten the head. Therefore, put your baby down in different positions to sleep. Then s/he won't become dependent upon just one sleeping position.

One last caution: Avoid the kind of restrainers that will keep your child in a vise-like grip while she or he sleeps. Also avoid fuzzy blankets, wool blankets, blanket holders, stuffed toys in the crib (until the baby's much older), and pillows.

All babies vomit occasionally for no known reason, and all babies spit up. Some do it many times daily. Vomiting can have various causes: juggling the baby around too much, not burping, or a lot of gulping. Unless the vomiting is severe, or the spitting up is constant, you can ignore either provided that your baby is otherwise fine. To prevent spitting up and vomiting, see that you hold your baby straight up for some minutes after feeding. Also, lying on the right side may help. This particular problem usually disappears when solid foods are introduced or by six months of age. However, don't feel pressured into starting your baby on solids too quickly.

Introducing solid foods to your infant before five months of age may interfere with establishing sound eating habits and contribute to overfeeding and consequent obesity in later life, according to a group of researchers from the Department of Pediatrics, University of Iowa, Iowa City. Their recommendation appeared in the January 1979 issue of *Pediatrics*, the monthly scientific journal of the American Academy of Pediatrics.

"From the time of the first feeding, the infant should be permitted to stop eating at the earliest indication of willingness to stop," said the researchers. "If this is to be encouraged, it must be possible for him to communicate in some way with the individual who is feeding him."

Most infants in the United States are fed some solid foods by the age of two months, largely because of social pressures, aggressive marketing by the infant-food industry, and by the belief that feeding of solid food will help an infant sleep through the night.

Most of all, after all is said, your baby needs to be appreciated, to be enjoyed by both of you as much as possible, just for what she or he is—a baby, yours.

◇ ◇ ◇

The First Few Weeks: You and Your Baby

Newborn Management
A. The infant needs stimulation
   1. touch and motion
   2. sound—human voices especially
B. A newborn often needs help in quieting. Parents may try
   1. bundling
   2. rocking
   3. firm touch
C. Allow demand feeding within reason
D. Give the infant experience in the prone position when awake in order to maintain its ability to lift its head

E. Respond to its cries—he has no other way to communicate

Problems
A. Crying
   1. some babies are fussy near your dinner time
   2. family members may be tense or tired
   3. keep him near you in basket or use baby carrier
B. Bathing and grooming
   1. not necessary to bathe infant daily
   2. infants dislike the bath at first
   3. avoid powder with talc, which is dangerous for infant to inhale
   4. avoid oils unless there is a rash, when lanolin is best
   5. soap is not needed at first, except possibly for the scalp
   6. use the tub bath only after the navel is healed
   7. cut the baby's nails when he is asleep
C. Colic
   1. may be the result of over-filling the small stomach
      a. feed the infant more frequently, but less each time
      b. cuddle the baby with each feeding
   2. do not prop the baby in a sitting position
   3. when there is abdominal discomfort, place the baby over a small hot water bottle in the prone position with diaper covering the bottle*
   4. drinking a little warm water may help
   5. bubbling once more may help
   6. colic may occur in connection with teething
   7. if there is a great sucking need, using a pacifier may be indicated so that the baby does not overfeed
D. Bowel movements
   1. at first the meconium stool is like tar
   2. next the stools contain mucus
   3. the breast-fed baby has thin stool for many weeks
   4. the infant may appear to strain with the passage of feces, but still not be constipated
   5. green color indicates bile, but is not dangerous
   6. illness may be indicated by foul-smelling stool in breast-fed babies
   7. formula may cause unpleasant odor of stool in healthy babies

*Be *very* careful of any hot water bottle. Stay right there. Use only very briefly.

8. some diarrhea may occur when a tooth is about to erupt

E. Cord
  1. a disinfectant is put on the stump, which usually prevents infection
  2. if a foul odor and/or inflammation appear, you may need to see an MD
  3. the stump will drop off by itself after 2 weeks or so
  4. wipe around the base of the stump daily with alcohol to speed drying
  5. protect the cord stump from urine

F. Birth marks
  1. these rarely last
  2. sometimes no treatment is required

G. Some infants have a strong preference for one breast
  1. this may be related to a desire to turn the head one way; i.e. a right-sided dominance will cause the baby to prefer the left breast so that he can turn his head to the right
  2. sometimes milk may flow more easily from one breast

Development

A. Sleep
  1. the baby sometimes sleeps through the night after reaching the weight of about 11 pounds, which may be after 6 to 8 weeks
  2. early in the second month, there are periods of wakefulness up to an hour or more several times a day
  3. by the end of the second month, the baby may be awake 8 or 10 hours out of twenty-four
  4. sleeping patterns of babies vary widely. Your baby may be more wakeful than average or may not sleep through the night until later

B. Activity
  1. a smile may appear by the fourth or fifth week, or earlier
  2. if put on the abdomen, the baby will do push-ups
  3. enjoys a period of playing with toys such as rattle
  4. urine is held longer and the diaper is more wet when baby voids
  5. a feeding may last a full hour at times
  6. stools may be larger and not always regular
  7. arms whirl when infant is supine
    a. leave baby's hands free
    b. the little scratches which may be caused by his waving arms heal

readily and he benefi able to explore his worl
fingers

8. he begins making throat sou the second month
9. his eyes focus and he can follow jects better and more readily
10. the baby recognizes and responds special persons by the third month or before

American Institute of Family Relations

◇ ◇ ◇

More Pointers for Parents

Sleeping, Bathing, and Fever

Most babies prefer sleeping on their abdomen. This is a somewhat safer position than on the back since the baby is less likely to gag or choke if he spits up milk, food, or mucus. But if the infant who prefers sleeping on his back is forced to sleep on his abdomen, he will reward your efforts with irritability, crying, and sleeplessness. So it is best to let *him* decide. . . .

A baby's sleeping habits are usually erratic for the first three months. At times he may be motionless in a deep sleep. This period may be followed by sleep with groaning, irregular breathing, thrashing about, sighing, sneezing, gurgling, and occasionally crying. All this is normal. . . .

Support the baby's back and head with one forearm while you use the other for bathing him. A soapy, wet, wiggly baby can be difficult to hold until you find a grip that suits you both.

Never let go of the baby—not for an instant. *Never leave any baby or toddler alone in the bath even for a second!* A baby can drown in an inch of water. Let the phone or the doorbell ring. . . .

Feeling the baby will not give you an accurate estimate of how high his temperature is. Many times the baby who feels overly warm to the touch may have a normal temperature. When in doubt, use a thermometer. . . .

Any fever in a newborn is abnormal. A rectal temperature above 100.5 degrees means you need medical advice. (Glenn R. Stoutt, Jr., M.D., *The First Month of Life: A Parents' Guide to Care of the Newborn,* ed. Marvyn Womack, 1978)

◇ ◇ ◇

...by being
...with his
...nds in
...ob-

...icates that a
...ght hours
...oate and
...or this
...home
...rtant
...u field.
...t his room
...uld be moved
...oe hung at the foot
...es mounted around the
...e for the baby to observe,
...stomach. Visual stimulation is
...ed more important than exercise. An

illustration of this point is taken from the Hopi Indians who still bind the babies and carry them on their backs. The babies suffer no impairment of motor coordination because, it is believed, their visual field, enhanced and enriched, is more crucial at a very early age. After forty-eight hours a baby, just as an adult, will block out something that has been sitting in his visual field. Constant change is necessary for adequate visual, as well as auditory, stimulation. (Notes from lecture delivered by Mary Ann Newcomb at the Marin Montessori School, October 1970)

How It Used to Be

There is no part of a women's duty to her child that a young mother should so soon make it her business to study, as the voice of her infant, and the language conveyed in its cry. The study is neither hard nor difficult; a close attention to its tone, and the expression of the baby's features, are the two most important points demanding attention. The key to both the mother will find in her own heart, and the knowledge of her success in the comfort and smile of her infant.

Mrs. Isabella Beeton, *Beeton's Book of Household Management*, 1861

Spoiling Babies?

Those infants who are conspicuous for fussing and drying after the first few months of life, and who fit the stereotype of the "spoiled child," are those whose mothers have ignored their cries or delayed long in responding to them. . . .

. . . Maternal responsiveness promotes desirable behavior rather than spoiling a child. Infants whose mothers have given them relatively much tender and affectionate holding in the earliest months of life are content with surprisingly little physical contact by the end of the first year. Although they enjoy being held, when put down they are happy to move off into independent exploratory play. In contrast, those held for relatively brief periods during the early months tend to be ambivalent about

contact by the end of the first year; they do not respond positively when held, but yet protest when put down and do not turn readily to independent activity. (Silvia M. Bell and Mary D. Salter Ainsworth, "Infant Crying and Maternal Responsiveness," *Child Development*, December 1972)

AN INTERFERING PERSON

The dark-haired baby of six months was screaming his head off in the Northampton, Massachusetts, restaurant. His mother and father were having dinner with friends, and the baby was expected to stay quietly penned in a small baby seat on top of the table. Instead, he became a huge embarrassment. His mother scolded him, then carried him out of the room for a few moments. As soon as he was back, his cries began afresh. Then his father tried a strong authoritarian tone which only increased the volume of the screams. Then the father took him out of the room. Finally, at a fifth go-round, when the mother began to shake her baby to keep him quiet, I stepped in. I always am an interfering person when babies or children are crying.

The baby came to my arms as though he had found safety in a sea of threatening monsters. His cries stopped immediately. I rocked and sang and gurgled a bit. His parents ate their dinner, completely happy to be relieved of their "problem." "The lady with the magic arms," the waitress labeled me to my husband.

But it was not my arms particularly. Not even me. It was what I knew about crying babies. They need attention, as a plant needs water. And they need quality, caring attention—no quarter or half measures will do. They need to know that *their* need is considered very important, if not basic, to their parents. And then, after these facts are recognized, the baby can leave lap and arms, play quietly for a while (not too long) with rattle or toy.

Actually, even the most seriously neglected babies I have met still are able to respond to emotional and physical attention, to caring. And when you must leave them, their basic life situation unchanged, there is nothing but anguish to feel—because it is so easy with these, or almost *any* baby, to give and get love. This is obvious when you answer a baby's cries.

A BASIC CHECKLIST

What do babies need? Here is my own list. Babies need:

To be fed when hungry.
To sleep when sleepy.
To be washed when needed.
To be warm.
To have sunlight (head covered) and air.
To be examined by a doctor regularly.
To be held a great deal.
To be snuggled.
To be rocked and swayed.
To have freedom of movement.
To be sung and talked to.
To be comforted.
To be played with.
To be laughed with.
To be stroked and massaged.
To hear music often (not too loud).
To have visitors and to go visiting.
To feel a pleasant, calm atmosphere.
To live in a clean and safe environment.
To see a lot of interesting, colorful things.
To be enjoyed.
To have a family.

Family Matters

The Whole World Was Right There

When I held that baby in my arms for the first time, I felt as though the whole world was right there. It was as though God had entrusted to my wife and me heaven and earth all wrapped up in one tiny infant. (former U.S. Senator Birch Bayh)

WHAT THE STUDIES SHOW: HOW FATHERS AND MARRIAGES AFFECT BABIES

How well your baby grows and develops is greatly affected by the baby's *father*, and by your marriage. This is the startling conclusion of the recent research in a number of studies on fathers, mothers, infants, and the ways they behave toward and relate to each other.

Ross D. Parke, a psychologist at the University of Illinois, described and summarized the studies (his own and others) in a special seminar on child development sponsored by the Council for the Advancement of Science Writing at the New York Academy of Sciences in November of 1978. (His work is also presented in a chapter in a *Handbook of Infant Development*, Wiley, 1979.)

There are numerous chainlike effects and reactions between parents and their babies.

For example, how much and how well the man of the family helps his wife (or partner) can affect the progress of the pregnancy and birth—and how she cares for the baby. Parke

sums it up: "The extent to which the father has been supportive of his wife during pregnancy, labor and delivery and in the immediate postpartum hospital period will probably determine the ease with which women adjust to their new mothering role."

Both the emotional and physical support (sharing house and baby care) a man gives may be a crucial factor in the quality of a mother's care for her baby.

And the quality of the marriage relationship itself can be a vital factor for the infant's responsiveness, alertness, and even more ability. As one researcher said: "A good baby and a good marriage go together."

The converse is true: Negative feelings toward each other on the part of husband and wife resulted in more and stronger negative feelings toward the baby.

One of the findings of the research suggests that single parenthood, or very absent fathers, means less smiling and touching of babies. When either mother or father is present, the other partner smiles more at the baby—and explores the baby's body more.

Fathers tended to play with babies more, while mothers tended to take care of them more—although fathers of middle- and upper-class background were likely to participate in caretaking more often than fathers of other classes. And in two studies, fathers tended to hold and rock newborn infants *more* than mothers. Lamaze classes may have had an effect here since over half of these men had attended the classes. Bonding at birth may be even more significant since all but one of these fathers were present during the actual birth.

But fathers also have a direct as well as an indirect impact on the ways babies behave.

Parke declares that "evidence from a variety of settings . . . as well as a range of cultures indicates that quality of father-infant interaction has a clear impact on the infant's developing social responsiveness." Intellectual development is also very much affected. "Paternal involvement and nurturance, in particular, are associated with cognitive competence, but boys are more generally affected than girls," according to Parke's summary of the research. Further, the father's role is important in this development from the earliest days and weeks. (Unfortunately, both parents, and especially fathers, seem to react more positively to boy babies than to girl babies. Clearly, the sex stereotypes which are so harmful to children persist as strongly as that other child-harming stereotype—racial and ethnic discriminations.)

Many couples shift toward the more traditional roles after a baby is born and there are many families in which the father's greater involvement causes much conflict. It is seen as a threat rather than a help.

(Of course, you need to know how both you and your husband do and *will* react to his baby caring or housecleaning.)

On the whole, fathers are simply not able to spend much time with their babies. The amount of time is surprisingly limited, according to many different reports.

In view of the strong patterns that emerge from the research, this fact is particularly alarming and discouraging.

Since fathers can have many clear-cut beneficial effects on both mothering and on baby development, it stands to reason that they should have the time *and* the ability to give to their families.

Instead, our society, unlike those of some other countries (Sweden and Denmark among them), almost programs fathers out of the picture through work arrangements and demands—and through insufficient learning opportunities.

Ross Parke, and every other expert I know, pleads for changes in the way we do things for new parents. Training for fathering (and mothering) at early school age is even more vital than training for reading, writing, and arithmetic—and for jobs and careers.

All the negative statistical rates (postpartum depression, child abuse, retardation, family breakup) will, in all likelihood, be reduced considerably by universal and excellent training for parenting. And all the positive statistical rates—brighter, more capable babies and children, happier parenting and families, better physical and mental health—are likely to go up with such a program.

But training alone, without substantial shifts in the ways we do or don't do things for new families, will not have as much influence as it could. We need substantial changes in our family living patterns and in our work patterns.

The research indicates that the support and involvement of other family members has strong effects upon new babies as well.

And leaves for fathering and more flexible working hours can make a crucial difference for new parents. The coming shorter work week will aid both our economy and the babies of our society as well. Changing work times and places—so that baby making and baby having takes priority—is one of the most basic ways we can help produce a healthier and happier generation than our own.

◇ ◇ ◇

DHEW

Who Should a Father Love?

Answer me quick! What's your number one job as a father?

To provide food and shelter? Protect? To build an image? Educate? Be a good example? Discipline?

To which comes the loud, clear answer—none of these! As I see it *my number one job as father is to love my children's mother well.*

. . . One day, in a symposium on child development, I heard a new thing. The lecturer was a famous pre-adolescent psychiatrist. His subject was: "Importance of Parental Harmony as the Primary Source of Emotional Stability in the Growing Child."

Of course I applied what was said to my children. And this is how it came through: the greatest thing I could do for them was to show them a good thing going between a male and a female.

So we decided to get specific. We worked out a simple two-point program, like this:

1. Once a week out together for dinner alone! No guests. No entertaining. This is our dinner date for each other only. . . .

Fifty-two times a year. No exceptions.

2. Fifteen minutes a day visiting in-depth. . . . This is no small talk about bills, the kids, planning the weekend. The subject now is what's going on inside.

By watching their folks, children learn how to relate; they're more secure. . . . But maybe the greatest thing going on inside is that they can get with their sexuality at the right time in the right way. They are getting the best sex education possible—a mother and father who love each other.

From somewhere, if we are to survive, we must produce a generation which knows how to love. (Charlie W. Shedd, *The Best Dad Is a Good Lover,* 1977)

◇ ◇ ◇

The Nuclear Family: Here to Stay?

The overwhelming majority of American people (87 percent) still live in nuclear families that include a married couple and/or a parent and one or more children. This assertion is not meant to minimize the extent of recent changes but to imply that the American people have been showing a great degree of resilience in coping with pressures that affect their family life and are likely to continue to do so. (Statement of Paul C.

Glick, senior demographer, Bureau of the Census, May 23, 1978)

◇ ◇ ◇

The Family Heart

A man remarked quietly, "Of course, my grandmother was the heart of our family. As long as she lived we were all to some degree tied together, because we were all tied to her. As long as she lived, we lived as a family." Rather sadly he added, "Families need a heart—that one person who provides the home base for everyone, who knows where everyone is and how everyone is getting along. Now families don't have a heart and that is a great loss, even though most of them don't know it." (Leontine Young, *The Fractured Family,* 1973)

◇ ◇ ◇

HOW PARENTS CAN LEARN

Most new parents—from time immemorial—have learned about babies from their own first and second babies. Oh, yes, they have in other times and other places received a *lot* of basic parenting education just from living in close, easy contact with other people's tots and toddlers. People grew up with babies visible in home and community. Our society—rigidly structured and individualistic in architectural, economic, and generational ways—has precluded this method of learning.

Now, parents are largely on their own with their first baby—and the literature. But when there is a palpable need, often after a time lag, something happens to fill that need. And that is what has started to happen today. In addition to courses in childbearing and childbirth there are other nonacademic courses and seminars and workshops and parent gatherings and exchanges all centered on the area of *child rearing.*

Some, like the Mother-Infant Workshops, led by a very warm nurse, June Barlow, R.N., and social worker Jammy Weintraub, ACSW, in New York, begin during pregnancy—and later include the infants themselves. They hold intimate low-fee sessions in their own homes, as well as at the Parents' Center of the YWCA. The sessions included forty-five women during 1978.

Others have different kinds of programs. Mothers Matter, run by Kay Willis in Rutherford, New Jersey, handles 14 to 18 people in five sessions. Also in New York, at the Feminist Center for Human Growth and Development, there are small groups of mothers, fathers, single parents. A course is offered called Assertiveness Training for Mothers.

The Brookline (Massachusetts) Early Education Project (BEEP) is an example of a unique experiment. Here new parents volunteer for BEEP and a public school teacher consultant goes into the homes of just-born babies to help the parents raise competent, emotionally healthy children. This person works with the parents until the child is five years old. Parents also drop into the center to borrow books and toys, to chat with other parents, and to seek advice.

In Seattle, Washington, Parenthood Education Programs presents an Infant Series and a Preschool Series for parents called a Parenting Sampler. In five sessions the Infant Sampler covers Child-Guidance Techniques (for preventing and reducing conflict and changing behavior); Safety and First Aid (creating a safe environment, equipment, first-aid techniques); Food and Nutrition (introduction, baby food, food problems); Child Development (developmental sequence, individual differences, fostering development); Activities (understanding the importance of play, and the appropriate toys and experiences).

The Parents' Center on New York's Upper West Side, founded by a group of social workers and psychologists, has a number of services with a varied schedule of rates. The Living Room is an informal, drop-in aid to forming friendships and creating a mutually supportive "extended family." The Self-Help Desk gives practical answers, plus contacts and information for baby-sitting, day trips, and weekend vacations and a means of sharing special holiday dinners or other events. The Library provides written materials useful to parents. The Parents' Forum is an informal rap group three evenings a month. Parents' Panels take place once a month with guest speakers on a wide variety of topics. The list goes on and on: Free Legal Clinic, Free Money Management Clinic, Parents' Workshops, Individual Consultation, The Warm Line, and more.

That marvelous innovation, The Warm Line, is also a feature of another group across the country. This is PIPS Thalians Community Mental Health Center at the Cedars-

Sinai Medical Center in Los Angeles. PIPS stands for Pre-School and Infant Parenting Service and employs clinical social workers and child-development specialists to help parents of children just born through five years. Call-backs on The Warm Line are within twenty-four hours and guidance is given about problems of "sleeping, eating, crying, toileting and tantruming." PIPS has a Parents' House as a clubhouse where mothers and fathers and their infants and toddlers can gather, share experiences, and receive guidance in parenting from trained professionals on the spot. All sorts of groups and combinations (mothers and infants, single mothers, couples, both parents and infants) meet weekly. A Mother's Morning Out program offers young mothers a way to leave their children in the care of other mothers while the staff supervises. A toy-lending library, a baby-equipment exchange, and a resource library for parents are other features of PIPS. This organization is nonprofit, conducts fund-raising events and uses volunteers.

Of course, there are a growing number of organizations which train professionals as they work with new parents. These include the Center for the Study of Parent Involvement in Oakland, California, and the Center for Parent Education in Newton, Massachusetts.

PARENTS AND BABIES TOGETHER

In a 1980 interview with June Barlow, co-founder of New York City's Mother-Infant Workshops, she described some of the happenings of the sessions:

SCS: How do you manage to get any time at all with the mothers when the babies are there?

JB: The babies stay on the floor, in the front. The mothers take care of them, if necessary, and if they cry, we talk loud! As they begin to really move around, it can get a little hectic.

SCS: How do the babies get on together?

JB: As they get to know each other we have seen such interaction. The books say, "Oh, babies don't interact, there's only parallel play." But we really get a sense that they know each other. First they might be a little hesitant. But you see the change as they spend time together. We were surprised.

SCS: I've seen babies even a few weeks old respond to another person.

JB: I think babies like babies. They like somebody down there at their level, their own size, and something that's moving.

SCS: What do mothers seem to get out of the sessions?

JB: The mothers ask questions like: "Why don't I feel instant love for the baby? Why do I feel like throwing her out, throwing in the towel, disappearing?" And another mother will say, "Gee, I felt that same way too." There's nothing like it when another mother recognizes that her feelings are normal. Many times another mother has the answer before we do. It's really great the way they support each other.

SCS: Do you ever get grandparents in?

JB: We had one who visited. It happened to be after a session when our mothers talked about their own mothers, because they realize how that relationship changes during pregnancy and after the baby is born and how important it is in their being parents. They learn so much from their own mothers.

SCS: What do they say about the effect of the baby on the family?

JB: They just weren't prepared for how tired they would be . . . how it changes their sex life because you lose your spontaneity. It is a tremendous adjustment becoming a family. The husbands, for the most part, do get into taking care of the baby. But sometimes they have to be asked more than the mother would like. I love the husbands to come because often the men are quite open. They discuss their feelings, and our generation's husbands never did that.

SCS: Are most of the women working?

JB: Most are not. We have some who do take off time from work. All have had careers. Eventually, they plan to go back, but many thought they would go back right away and found they didn't want to at all. They're really hooked. They love taking care of that baby.

SCS: What do you try to convey to them?

JB: We try to say to our parents: "You have an effect on the baby. But not everything. They're going to be coming in contact with so much. Don't feel guilty. There are just too many other things that affect the baby." I

want to get them off the hook that everything they do is crucial.

Some Signs That Parent-Infant Unity Is Satisfactory

1. Parents find pleasure in the infant and in tasks for or with him/her.
2. Parents understand baby's moods and can offer comfort, thereby relieving the infant's tension.
3. Parents can read the baby's cues for new experiences; they can also sense the child's fatigue level and do not over-stimulate him/her for their own pleasure. (Sam Bittman and Sue Rosenberg Zalk, Ph.D., *Expectant Fathers*, 1978)

PROBLEMS AS A PARENT?

If you are not comfortable with your baby, you are probably having a problem getting used to parenthood. There are other signs which indicate that you should seek professional help. For example: if you find your baby's drooling, body odor, fluids, or vomiting disgusting; if you feel your baby is quite ugly; if you cannot hold your baby close or find yourself letting the head dangle or avoiding eye contact and conversation with your infant. In addition, as *Expectant Fathers* points out, sudden and rough handling is a sign of parental stress, as is extreme worry about the baby's health or convictions that the baby has some physical defect. The perception of an infant as an adult—such as the belief that the baby does not love or is judging the parent—is a serious symptom and of grave concern. Do not hesitate to get outside help from a counselor or therapist.

Super Mom

Today we are all taught many things in school, but learning how to parent is not one of them. Society expects a woman to be an "instant mother" just because she can have a baby. The pressure to be a "super Mom" pushes on one side and the pressure to be a "liberated" and "fulfilled" person by working outside the home pushes on the other.

Our workshop mothers feel the crunch. We try to help the mothers look at these conflicts, talk about them with others in the same position and come to grips with them in order to enjoy being a mother. (June Williams Barlow, R.N., *Alumnae in Action*, Fall/Winter 1977)

Parents' Unique Experience

We are becoming a society of dependent parents on the advice and instruction of psychologists, parent counselors, and pediatricians. We must understand that no professional or textbook on parenting or child care will give the answer. It is the unique and trial-by-error experience we all go through as parents that makes our role rewarding, interesting, on-going and intellectually stimulating. (Jerry Cammarata, first father to win a paternity leave, at Governor's Conference on Families, 1980)

What Does Family Life Mean to Me?

Not quite everything. Adult love is first in my lexicon. But after that . . . Family means an entire vocabulary. Reciprocity. Togetherness. Sharing. Caring. Concern. Fun. Learning. Trust. Family means an endless kaleidoscope of scenes. The everyday dinner table with shining faces and tumbling talk. The morning sleepy rush with big round eyes, crumpled hair, and that expectant sense of getting ready. The tears and trouble times with soft patting hands and soft soothing words. The times of shouting arguments—and of making up. The vacations and holidays and parties with that special "just us" feeling and festive accoutrements or that equally special time of relatives and friends joining together with us to celebrate.

Family means a series of abstractions with a concrete base like home and food and noise and clean-ups and mess-ups and being with someone and laughter and times for doing things and arrivals—and departures.

Family. What does it mean? It means a place to be a baby, a place to be a child—or childish. It means a place to grow up—and out—with. It means a place to return to and to renew from. It means the people in the place, wherever that place is, however that place changes or shifts.

And for me, at my present stage of life—and for millions and millions of other people, including each of you—whatever your present age, Family means something even more. It means a place to grow old. With arms to cushion the steps and voices to fill the silences and smiles and kisses to lighten the days and comfort the nights. (Shirley Camper Soman)

Family Rights

ARE THERE RIGHTS IN CHILDBIRTH?

There are many bills of rights for children, one of which is included in this volume. There are also several bills of rights for hospital patients, and a bill of rights for pregnant women conceived by Doris Haire. This book also includes a bill of rights for parents. There may be others in existence.

One area which does seem to represent a large gap in the history of Bills of Rights is that of *childbirth*. My own attempt to meet that lack follows. Some may wonder how such provisions can be made for everyone. This is a realistic concern. However, we need and should have, in the many complicated areas of life, an ideal to strive toward. Our Constitution's Bill of Rights is such an ideal, and even today does not ensure the full exercise of all of those rights for everyone in our society.

By providing what I believe is a different kind of Bill of Childbirth Rights—and what may be a first—I hope to provoke thoughtful examination of the present state of this crucial time in almost everyone's life. I hope also to provide a basis for a different view of childbirth for future families. For the sake of our children let's hope that others will help to refine and bring this (or another) Bill of Childbirth Rights into full legality.

A BILL OF CHILDBIRTH RIGHTS

1. *The right to knowledge.* All young people have a right to know the basic principles of having a baby. These shall include the physiological processes, their socioeconomic and emotional concomitants, and the health and/or medical procedures involved.

2. *The right to be trained.* All people expecting future parenthood have the right to be trained for their roles. They have the right to adequate preparation *before, during* and *after* pregnancy and childbirth in order to prepare their bodies and their lives for the future.

3. *The right to choose.* All parents-to-be have the right to know in advance and actually to see, if possible, the alternatives for baby carrying and for baby having.

4. *The right to be treated as an adult.* All parents-to-be have the right to be treated as responsible human beings, capable of making choices, when presented with sufficient information.

5. *The right to preventive health care.* All parents-to-be have the right to every health aid in advance, to prevent complications as much as possible. This shall include anything needed to ensure a pressure-free pregnancy and childbirth but not be limited to free or low-fee prenatal care; full nutritional aid; exercise guidance; economic and social aids.

6. *The right to family participation in advance.* All families have the right to training-for-grandparenting, the involvement of relatives during the pregnancy, including training-for-grandparenting. Courses for relatives in having a baby can make a crucial difference to the new baby and the parents.

7. *The right to be together.* Parents/relatives—all people having a baby have the right to be together during labor, birth, and after the baby is born. Parents have the

312

right to be physically together with their new baby for the entire postbirth period.

8. *The right to decide upon other birth-time factors.* All parents-to-be have the right to *informed choices* concerning the details of birthing practices, such as position.

9. *The right to after-the-baby help.* Parents have the right to trained family or household assistance during the first weeks after the baby arrives.

10. *The right to the best conditions for baby raising.* All new parents have the right to expect society's provisions for the best aids for baby care and raising. These include good, safe neighborhoods; decent, safe housing; a clean environment; information and services to help families over tough spots; economic opportunties; peaceful ways of settling problems.

A NEW BILL OF RIGHTS FOR CHILDREN

I am also including my own version of a Bill of Rights for Children. There are many such attemps at definitions. Mine, first published in my book, *Let's Stop Destroying Our Children*, was distilled from many of these and is, I hope, the clearest and most comprehensive.

1. Any and every child has a right to a family who wants him/her—the child's own family, if possible.
2. Any child has a right to the kind of physical safety and health care that ensures the best growth and development before and after birth.
3. Any child has a right to the basics of life itself: enough *good* food and water, clothing, shelter, and love.
4. Any child has a *right to learn* (to be educated) about him/herself, the human race, the world—in order to find ways for self-protection, self-support, and ways to live with others.
5. Any child has a right to enjoyment, a right to play, a right to laugh.
6. Any child has a right to a community that cares for him/her and his/her family in ways that help his/her life and growth.
7. Any child has a right to professional help for him/herself and for his/her

family to enable the family to stay (and grow) together.
8. Any child has a right to a government that protects him/her from neglect, cruelty, and exploitation of any kind and yet recognizes a child's need for independence, as well as dependence.
9. Any child has a right to the same constitutional protections (federal or state or local) that anyone else is entitled to.
10. Any child, whatever his or her condition, has a right to understanding, tolerance, acceptance on the part of all adults.
11. Any child has a right to adult models who demonstrate consideration for others, integrity in living, a desire to work out problems, a sense of ethical values, and, most especially, compassion and empathy.
12. Any child has a right to a peaceful, nonracist world where violence and massacres and wars are considered obsolete.
13. Any child has a right to his and her own identity as an individual.
14. Any baby, any child born alive has the right to live.

PARENTS' RIGHTS: WHAT ARE THEY?

Honor thy father and thy mother. This commandment, given to Moses on Mount Sinai with the others, has been ringing in the ears of parents and children through three thousand years of history. Is it valid today? Should you expect your new baby to grow up with this perspective? And aside from validity, does it even happen in our world?

The fact is that, like it or not, you probably can't expect this kind of relationship with your child. No longer are respect and honor automatically conferred on age and parenthood, a situation which is greatly lamented by many older people.

Do parents have *any* rights at all? The answer, of course, is yes, many. But since everyone is focused on the rights of children to be, to do, to grow, to feel as they like, it might *seem* as though you as a parent are simply an appendage without any rights at all. Actually, the two sets of rights should not be separated. Parents' rights are largely tied in with children's rights.

There are various ways of looking at it. For example, you might question whether parents have the right to govern the mind and body and behavior of their child. Or taking another tack, do parents have rights concerning their state of parenthood? Some people believe that parents have clear-cut rights versus government agencies. Do they also have rights in relation to other organizations of society—nonprofit agencies, industry, labor? Finally, what kind of rights does a parent have just as a person?

Since the legal profession and the judiciary have *not* clearly defined the rights of parents or even the rights of children as yet, the definitions in this book are based to some extent upon opinion rather than a body of law. What is really needed is a presidential commission to probe both sets of rights on all levels—historically, legally, sociologically, and in terms of actual practice. Such a commission could propose the adoption of a rights code for children and parents. A code would define the specific areas of potential or actual conflict of rights between children and parents, and of family rights versus the government and other organizations. A code could lead to an amendment to the U.S. Constitution on behalf of children and their parents.

One problem is always definition. But I do think that this complex area of discovery can be simplified by looking at it in parts. My own idea of the rights of parents covers (1) parents' rights in terms of society on both legal and ethical-moral grounds, (2) parents' rights in direct situations with children, and (3) parents' rights in terms of institutions. What follows is my view of some of those rights.

A BILL OF PARENTS' RIGHTS

1. *Parents have a right to be parents,* to care for and guide their children in the basic areas of life. At the same time, they have a right to be people themselves, not just parents.

2. *Parents have a universal right to be informed and educated about children. Before parenting,* as well as after, they need to know what babies and children are like, what the varieties of development can be.

3. *Parents have a right to a safe and healthy environment in which to grow and raise their children.* They should be informed if the activities of industry or government are increasing health risks for their children, or for themselves.

4. *Parents have a right to good economic and social conditions.* Children whose fathers or mothers are suddenly without work are subjected to far graver risks than children whose parents work.

5. *Parents have a right to stability as a family,* to not be displaced or moved around through military or industrial needs, unless their very lives are threatened.

6. *Parents have a right to every opportunity and resource to help avoid arbitrary or precipitous child removal by agents of the government, or by anyone else.*

7. *Parents have a right to safe, healthy, alternative sources of care for their children at any age and for whatever reason.* Parents have a right to expect that the society will provide a network of low-cost, high-quality childcare services of various kinds.

8. *Parents have a right to special considerations by their employers, including the right to reasonable work time off for childbearing and child rearing without penalty,* and at least matching the circumstances provided by the most comparable advanced society.

9. *Parents have a right to the equal involvement of both parents in their child's birth and care;* the ability of fathers to contribute as much to their children's care as mothers.

10. *Parents have a right to universal, skilled counseling services to ease trouble spots.*

11. *Parents have a right to enjoy their children.* They have a right not to be so hassled by the problems and difficulties of living in our society that children are a burden rather than a pleasure.

12. *Parents have a right to regular adult time alone,* provided that it is not harmful to their children.

13. *Parents have a right to their own opinions and values and to attempt to guide their children in such directions,* provided that the guidance is not harsh and harmful.

14. *Parents have a right to be treated with consideration by their children under reasonable circumstances and to prevent behavior which offends them or their own rights as a person,* provided that they do not invade their children's right to privacy, or trample on other basic rights of all children.

15. *Parents have a right to protect their substance and sustenance against unreasonable demands.*

16. *Parents have a right to know (from the*

institutions of society) what the status of their child is at any given time, including the right to see and control their child's records (with the child's permission) from hospitals, schools, centers.

17. *Parents have a right to decide upon the medical treatment* or lack of medical treatment of their child unless it is a case of life or death or serious damage, or unless the child requests privacy from medical personnel.

18. *Parents have a right to be advocates for their children,* to request needed services, and to get better services, *including deciding who shall care for their child in school or hospital (or wherever)* and to remove the child from persons who seem actually or potentially harmful.

19. *Parents have a right to form a lobby, to organize for a better life for their child/children.*

20. *Parents have the right to prevent their children's involvement with any institution in which there is a threat to their health and safety.*

21. *Parents have the right to all the basic legal benefits of the society:* public welfare funds, preventive and emergency health care, Social Security support when death or injury has cut off self-support, protection against abuse from a spouse or anyone else.

WHY CHILDREN'S RIGHTS?

Having a baby may seem to be a completely personal and individual matter. It may seem to be far removed from the children's rights issue—which somehow has strong overtones of courts and judges and juvenile delinquents and institutions for children. And you're not involved in any of that stuff; you're in the midst of the lovely process of baby making and family building.

Without affecting the wonder and creativity of that process, I must, however, let you know that you are right smack in the middle of the children's rights issue.

Your baby's basic health can be largely determined by the principle that every infant *has the right* to a healthy start in life, if possible. Your nutrition, the number of your prenatal examinations, the extent of your knowledge about good prenatal conditions, the availability of genetic and other counseling—all can be greatly affected by this idea. If this "right" were a legal right, universal free or low-cost health aids would be routinely available to all pregnant women

and their partners. There would be no question about quality prenatal care. Your baby would have the right to be born healthy, short of "acts of God" or factors beyond human control.

As another example, there is strong evidence that the separation of mother from infant right after birth is harmful to babies. Why then would anyone be permitted to create this separation? If your baby had *the right* to the best care available, no one would be able to separate the two of you.

Not all babies are equally vulnerable, of course. Specific conditions can affect children differently. Some people/babies are stronger, more immune, or whatever it takes to survive without harmful effects.

An absolutely marvelous man I knew, Sidney Hollander, lived to age 90 smoking and drinking his way through life. His wife lived to 88 on the same route. My father, also a smoker, died of lung and esophagus cancer at 70. Other smokers die at 35 or 40 years.

The human organism is not monolithic. It varies in its capabilities from person to person.

But if there are no rights or very uneven rights for babies/children, the possibility of more harm to more infants is greater. And yours may be one of the babies more affected.

The fight for rights for children has been having some effects and there will be other long-range effects. Here's why:

- Our population has become and will remain better educated.
- Women have become active in seeking better life conditions.
- Men, too, are joining women in trying for improved circumstances for childbirth and child care.
- There have been multiple revolutions in the area of childbirth and child care.
- The humanistic movement has influenced vast areas of life and the way that we think about people.
- The old-style thinking about children has been demonstrably hurtful, and change has been necessary.

There are other important reasons why you should be concerned with children's rights. How you are able to respond to, handle, treat your own infant, can be strongly influenced by what the society in general *allows* you to be and do.

It is much easier to be carefree and joyful during a childbirth and in caring for an infant if:

- You are in good health and well cared for.
- You are economically secure.
- You had a reasonably good childhood yourself or the ability to get professional help to recast your own early experiences.
- You have family supports or other supportive services nearby.
- You had the educational background to search for the best for yourself and your baby-to-be.

If your baby is born with some physical or mental problem, there are now some sources of help—but only because other parents believed that *their* children *had the right* to such help.

The self-help group, Parents Anonymous, for parents who think they may have child-neglect or -abuse problems, has received large government funds. This has happened only because our society recognized that children *have the right not to be abused* by their parents (or anyone else), and that parents *have the right* to seek and get preventive help.

We don't provide enough preventive help. We still don't recognize that right in all of its ramifications. But we are a society on the move to better our children's lives. And whatever retrogressive forces exist—and they are strong and many—they will fade. The force of the need, the force of humanity's move forward, the force of the media—all of these forces are too strong for retrogressing, backward, know-nothing instincts at work to keep children subjected and demeaned.

Yes, we will have children with full rights—sooner or later. And, yes, your role as parent will be much easier and better if you are able to consider your new child as someone with specific rights now, and with increasing rights as that child develops. Your baby, from those first marvelous moments, will be much more than your baby. He or she will be a person.

THE REVOLUTION

In the course of doing this book, I have discovered the revolution in childbirth that has been taking place for some decades now, but most sharply during the 1970s. What shall I call it? The Consumer's Revolution? The Parents' Revolution? Ah, yes . . . it can only be the Babies' Revolution. For this is a movement all about babies—how they are grown, how they are born, how their most intimate and immediate environment reacts to them, how the larger world perceives and receives them.

From this, there is a revolution? as any one of my forebears would ask, in disbelief. Yes, a revolution!

What else can I call the extensive revolt against traditional birthing methods? Isn't it a revolution, albeit a small one, when parents reject the hospital as the only place to have a baby? When they oppose the universal application of anesthesia? When they insist upon being together as a family during and after childbirth? When they try to find doctors and midwives who will help make their baby's entry into our world pleasant and easier? When some nurse in public? Isn't it a revolution when every standard practice of the traditional medical approach of the last fifty or seventy years is being questioned?

As a result of my research and reading, I recognize an unusual mix of the new and the different. Some of the new goes back to ancient ways: a different position during delivery from the flat table-cum-stirrups method, for instance, or having a baby at home with a woman attendant.

Today's way of having a baby is ancient, but new. Ancient, because centuries of women had their babies without benefit of sophisticated technology and scientific research, but only with the enormous physical sensation of two bodies at work together. New, because women are becoming informed about choices and alternatives, have become prepared, and have consciously made their choices for childbirth which increases the possibilities for better feelings.

Some aspects of the Babies' Revolution *are* new. Even the concept of prepared childbirth, for example. The idea of pregnancy-into-labor exercises to ease the birth. The idea of husbands sharing in the birth itself, or even of children being present. The notion that some medical techniques of handling pregnancy and delivery can be positively harmful to normal women and babies.

But, new or old, or a blend of both, the Babies' Revolution means a different perception about having a baby—and different ways of doing so. Not that all of the subscribers to this revolution agree with each other. There is controversy about almost every method.

And where do I stand: recognizing and understanding this revolution but still an observer on the sidelines? You, the reader, have a right to know. I am in the midst of my own personal revolution. I wish I could go back and do it all over again. Obviously, I can't go back in actuality. However, the history of childbirth practices in itself is very interesting. Further, many people still do not understand that birth practices and baby care have been changing radically. For these reasons, I decided to include a brief list comparing my own beliefs before and after doing this book.

These are only some of my opinions and biases, past and present. As you can see, I have been "shook up"—and am very grateful for it. I hope that my own personal revolution in thinking will help you to have your baby in the very best way for all of you.

And if you can, don't mourn about it. Don't feel fated or unhappy. You're doing what you do *your way* (and it's *your* childbirth!) or because there is, for your situation, no other way. And don't worry

about it. Not everyone can have a revolution—or even want one!

As for me, my two childbirths were great but, because of hospital/doctor practices, a lot was missing. And now, in my own revolution, I wish that I could be reincarnated in the future as a young woman, pregnant again for the first time, ready and waiting and knowing that I would have the most total and joyous experience of childbirth that it was possible to have. With feeling, and knowledge, all the way from the Babies' Revolution.

THE POLITICS
OF CHILDBIRTH

"Having a baby is a political affair!" my young cousin, Paula, a new mother, declared. Her baby had been born in Boston's Women's Hospital in 1980. Among all the women there at the time, she had been the only one who was not anesthetized, who had gone through a natural childbirth preparation. Of course, I agreed with her. Having a baby *is* a matter of politics.

For those of you who do not see politics mixing into your very personal, very inti-

The Issues of Politics

1) *Who's in Charge?*
   Authority or authoritarianism?
   Power or excessive control?
2) *Who's Making Money?*
   Fairly or unfairly?
   Reasonably or excessively?

3) *Who's Deciding Your Rights?*
   To know or be ignorant?
   To do as you wish or as others wish?
4) *What Are Your Rights?*
   To be let alone or not?
   To be helped or not?
   To be treated fairly or not?

5) *What Is Good for the Society?*
   For the present generation?
   For the future generation?

The Issues of Childbirth

1) *Who Decides on Your Childbirth?*
   How and where it will be?
   How much control you will have?
2) *What Must You Pay?*
   What are you getting for the dollar?
   Why so much?
   Is it all necessary?
3) *How Can You Know Your Rights*
   if you don't know that you have them?

4) *What Rights Are Basic in Childbirth?*
   The right to
   –know the options
   –compare the results
   –understand the process
   –decide what to do, and
     what should be done
5) *What Kind of Society Do You Want for Your Child?*
   How can this be possible if other children don't have the same right to a safe and fair and peaceful world—which all starts with how your baby is born and grows before and after birth?

mate life, let me give you a little chart. I do so in the high hopes that raising everyone's consciousness about baby-having may help to change common attitudes and practices for many other parents-to-be and their babies. Politics and legislation (or its lack) affect everybody's pregnancy, childbirth, and child raising.

THE BABIES' REVOLUTION AND ME

My Prior Beliefs

The natural environment has some problems, and we should be fairly careful—but having a baby is not particularly related to the environment.

What you eat during pregnancy is important—but you should limit your intake. You are not eating for two.

Some drugs during pregnancy and delivery may be necessary, even for healthy women.

Learning exercises and breathing techniques are overly praised, and don't work for many women.

Fathers can be wonderful and helpful during pregnancy and labor, but their participation must be very limited.

Babies are bound to cry at birth, and to be disoriented. Naturally, you can't touch the baby for hours. The baby is too fragile.

Nursing is marvelous for both mother and baby, but if you can't nurse—or don't feel like it, that's fine.

Complications of childbirth are unpredictable and cannot be prevented, only ameliorated by top medical care using the latest equipment.

One should never have a home birth—unless it can't be avoided. And hospitals are the *only* place to have a baby, just in case. . . .

You must have an obstetrician for complete safety at delivery. Midwives are nice as an additional aid.

My Present Beliefs

Everything about the environment can have direct effects on the process of having a baby, and on babies themselves.

What you eat during pregnancy is crucial and your intake of good foods should not be limited, unless there is a major health problem. Further—you *are* eating for two.

No drugs are ever necessary for healthy women—and we don't know the long-term effects of many.

Learning exercises and breathing techniques are not praised enough, and *do* work for most women.

Fathers should be totally involved at all times if couples so desire it . . . and they should be helped *to* desire it through preparation.

Babies usually can be joyous or peaceful right after birth. And it should be considered medical malpractice for mothers and fathers *not* to be able to touch and hold their infant right away.

Nursing is essential and is possible for almost all women; physical problems can usually be prevented or cured.

Many complications can be prevented by top prenatal and childbirth care. Medical technology *does* save lives in difficult cases, but most births are not high-risk.

Home births are too wonderful to deny to most families; they may be safer for normal births than hospitals, and they can be made even safer. Hospitals provoke some of the complications they supposedly avoid.

Trained midwives should be available throughout the country for parents in most normal births. Obstetricians and others can be present or called upon as needed.

My Prior Beliefs	My Present Beliefs
It's better for a baby if the mother doesn't work outside the home for the first few years, but if she has to, it's not so crucial.	It's crucial. People (mothers *or* fathers) should get paid to stay home for a child's first two years of life.*
Childbirth is a highly individual and very private matter.	Childbirth, while individual and private, is not only that; it is a large and overriding public concern. And our laws and practices need to be examined and our priorities changed.

*While the quality of time matters more in childcaring than the quantity, there can be *no* quality if there's not *enough* time spent by parents with their child.

Resource List *

Action for Child Transportation Safety
P.O. Box 266
Bothell, Washington 98011
(206) 623-0387 *524-7235*   *842-3277*

ACTS is a national organization with five chapters, formed in 1972 by three young mothers concerned about the safety of infants and children riding in automobiles and buses. Members include concerned parents, and health and safety professionals. ACTS is affiliated with Physicians for Automotive Safety—PAS. Together, both work to regulate child-restraint systems in cars and to establish national standards for safety and performance. A newsletter and educational materials are available (please send self-addressed, stamped envelope): *This Is the Way the Baby Rides*, a pamphlet for parents shopping for car carriers, and other pamphlets and kits, films, and displays are available at individual and group prices. Some areas have a loan service for infant carriers.

Administration for Children, Youth and Families
U.S. Department of Health and Human Services
400 6th Street SW
Washington, D.C. 20201
(202) 755-7762

ACYF was formed in 1977 from a number of government offices (The Children's Bureau, Headstart, Child Welfare Services, Child Development, Youth Development), to assist parents and children from infancy through adolescence. It coordinates publicly and privately operated programs for children throughout the fifty states and the U.S. territories, developing model legislation and standards for them to follow. Finally, it assumes a continuing responsibility for focusing attention on the needs of children and their families. Help for families in crisis is offered at local levels through twenty-four-hour emergency services. The newly created Information Exchange for Child Welfare Resources gives Information on programs and materials. Single copies of publications on a wide variety of child-care subjects are available free from: Publications, Administration for Children, Youth and Families, P.O. Box 1182, Washington, D.C. 20013. This agency has published the famous *Prenatal Care*, *Infant Care*, *Your Baby's First Year*, and *Your Child From One to Six*.

*There are many, many other helpful organizations apart from those included here. Some (ACOG and AAFP, for example) are referred to in the text of the book. Others—well, one can't mention *everything*.

American Academy of Husband-Coached Childbirth
P.O. Box 5224
Sherman Oaks, California 91413
(213) 788-6662

Founded in 1950 by Robert A. Bradley, M.D., the academy offers instruction in the Bradley method in thirty states: in-depth natural childbirth training without medication, with husbands very actively involved. Free information includes names and telephone numbers of local teachers, classes, speakers, and book and film lists.

American Academy of Pediatrics
1801 Hinman Avenue
Evanston, Illinois 60204
Central office (Evanston) (312) 869-4255
Washington, D.C., (202) 525-9560

The Academy has fifty-four local affiliates with fifteen thousand members (board-certified pediatricians) in every state and in Canada (directory available). Publications include manuals, pamphlets, reprints, supplements (150 titles), price reduction for quantity orders. *Sample subjects covered:* infectious diseases, accidents, child abuse, day care, drugs, nutrition, handicaps, genetic screening.

American Association for Maternal and Child Health
P.O. Box 965
Los Altos, California 94022
(415) 321-2825

This organization was founded almost sixty years ago to coordinate all factors of maternal and child health and infant mortality. The four thousand members include doctors, nurses, hospital administrators, dieticians, social workers, paramedics. It holds annual congresses, sponsors *American Baby* (monthly), free to members and expectant and new parents, and has a reprint list of many pamphlets, some in Spanish.

American College of Nurse-Midwives
1522 K Street NW
Washington, D.C. 20005
(202) 347-5445

The college has forty chapters with sixteen hundred members—all certified nurse-midwives licensed to practice by local and state authorities on a post-R.N. or -master's degree level. It publishes *Journal of Nurse-Midwifery.* Accredited nursing schools at many universities throughout the United States teach midwifery; a list is available from the college, as well as a reference list of materials.

American Foundation for Maternal and Child Health, Inc.
30 Beekman Place
New York, New York 10022
(212) 759-5510

The foundation conducts interdisciplinary research in maternal and child health. It acts as a clearinghouse on birth practices throughout the United States and many other countries. The annual conference disseminates research findings of interest to doctors, midwives, and other specialists who work with mothers or newborns. Pamphlets—*The Pregnant Patient's*

Bill of Rights; How to Get What You Want from Your Birth Experience; How the FDA Determines the Safety of Drugs: Just How "Safe" is Safe?—are available on request if you send a stamped business-size self-addressed envelope for each one.

American Health Foundation
240 East 43rd Street
New York, New York 10017
(212) 953-1900

This institute was established in 1968 for research into disease and disability prevention, with particular reference to the hazards of the workplace, the effects of personal health habits—particularly smoking—and the role of nutrition in disease prevention. The AHF is committed to promoting preventive medicine on a national level and has sponsored clinics and outreach programs for schools and working people. There is a professional journal available, *Preventive Medicine,* and other publications.

The American Institute of Family Relations
5287 Sunset Boulevard
Los Angeles, California 90027
(213) 465-5131

The institute has six branch offices in Southern California. These offer marital and family counseling and courses leading to degrees in childbirth education and family therapy. The institute supervises childbirth classes throughout Southern California. A list of publications on sex, marriage, childbirth, and other topics is available from the institute's main office.

American National Red Cross
Nursing Services
2025 E Street NW
Washington, D.C. 20006
Main office (202) 857-3800

The American Red Cross has 3,108 chapters nationwide run by volunteers and staff members. Almost all area chapters give classes in Preparation for Parenthood. Each class has about seven sessions with no fee. There are now Parenting classes for families with children under two, in which the emotional and physical health, safety, development, and other aspects of early childhood are covered. Publications are available.

American Society for Psychoprophylaxis in Obstetrics
1411 K Street NW
Washington, D.C. 20005
(202) 783-7050

This organization trains and certifies teachers of the psychoprophylactic (Lamaze) method of childbirth preparation and encourages the setting up of childbirth education groups. There are fifty affiliated groups in twenty-five states with a membership of seven thousand physicians, childbirth educators, other professionals, and parents. A directory is available. Paperback books and leaflets on childbirth topics can be ordered through the society, and a film on prepared childbirth is available for rent or sale. ASPO publishes *Conceptions* and the *Professional Bulletin* for its members.

Association for Childbirth at Home International
P.O. Box 1219
Cerritos, California 90701
(714) 994-5880
(National headquarters) (213) 802-1020

Founded in 1972, this association has 425 leaders and trainees in the United States and Canada teaching ACHI series for parents (six sessions). Three thousand members (professional and lay) include doctors, nurses, certified nurse-midwives, lay midwives, and parents. It conducts intensive leader-training series, with certificates to teach, on East and West coasts and by arrangement for a fee. One hundred fifty titles on childbearing, including *Giving Birth at Home*, *Birth Notes*, a quarterly journal, the ACHI bookstore list, birth supplies, and general information, are available by mail.

Cesarean Sections Education and Concern
15 Maynard Road
Dedham, Massachusetts 02026
(617) 326-2534

CSEC has eleven national affiliates, fifteen hundred members. Membership includes parents of cesarean-delivered babies; medical, paramedical, and other professionals. Descriptive brochure, newsletter, slides and tapes, and other material available. Cesarean-childbirth classes and both personal and telephone discussions are given.

Child Welfare League of America
67 Irving Place
New York, New York 10003
(212) 254-7410

The league is over sixty years old, a privately supported organization devoted to improvement of care—and services—for children, youth, and family. Almost four hundred affiliated local agencies (in the United States and Canada) provide services, including counseling, that support, supplement, or substitute for parental care and supervision. Main focus is on adoption and foster care, but day-care and homemaker services are also among the programs of aid to young parents. An extensive publications list has books of interest to new parents with particular problems. The League publishes a directory and a monthly journal, *Child Welfare*, as well as many other publications and publication lists on a variety of subjects.

Family Service Association of America
44 East 23rd Street
New York, New York 10010
(212) 674-6100

Founded in 1911, this national accrediting organization has 275 member agencies all over the United States and Canada, as well as individual members. The local agencies provide casework and family counseling services and various other programs for help with parent-child, marital, mental health, and everyday problems of living. The association holds regional meetings, as well as national biennial conferences, publishes *Social Casework: The Journal of Contemporary Social Work*, monthly; *Highlights*, bimonthly, and other publications. It provides information on family life, encourages courses in Family Life Education, as well as Homemaker Service programs and other helpful aids for families.

Food and Drug Administration
5600 Fishers Lane
Rockville, Maryland 20852
(301) 443-3170

The FDA exists to protect the public from hazards to health and well-being in the area of drugs and food. It sets standards of performance for manufacturers, evaluates products prior to marketing, conducts inspections, and initiates legal enforcement actions. It publishes various free guides: *When Baby's Life Is So Much Our Own, Drugs and Pregnancy, Alcohol and Birth Defects, Advice on Breast Feeding and Drugs, Listening As a Fetus Becomes a Baby, Consideration for the Evaluation of Drugs Used for Infants and Children.* They can be obtained by contacting the office listed above.

Food and Nutrition Board
2101 Constitution Avenue NW
Washington, D.C. 20418
(202) 389-6366

Founded in 1940, this advisory body in the field of food and nutrition is part of the National Research Council. In 1948 it began studies of toxic substances and in 1950 established a committee on food protection. Specifications on food standards were used by the United Nations Food/Agriculture and World Health organizations. Publications on *Recommended Dietary Allowances, Maternal Nutrition and the Course of Pregnancy, Nutritional Supplementation and the Outcome of Pregnancy,* and *Fetal and Infant Nutrition and Susceptibility to Obesity* are among titles available. (Books for sale; reprints of reports, no charge.)

Home Oriented Maternity Experience
511 New York Avenue
Takoma Park, Maryland 20012
(202) 726-4664

HOME has a national resource list of twelve hundred lay and professional people interested in providing for prepared and safe home births. There are a medical advisory board and two thousand active members. Parents desiring a home birth may write for names of local resources from HOME's national list. HOME's comprehensive guide to home birth, *Home Oriented Maternity Experience,* is a modest price. Series of meetings, pamphlets, and recommended reading list are available.

Human Lactation Center
666 Sturges Highway
Westport, Connecticut 06880
(203) 259-5995

HLC is a nonprofit organization committed to worldwide research and education on lactation. Its periodical, *The Lactation Review,* is free to members. The center endeavors to give mothers and health professionals firsthand, in-depth information on all infant-feeding practices worldwide, with attention to realistic life situations. Booklets and pamphlets available.

International Childbirth Education Association
8060 26th Avenue S
Minneapolis, Minnesota 55420
(612) 881-9194, 854-8660

An international federation interested in family-centered maternity and infant care, ICEA
has twelve thousand members. A network of local services is independently run by three
hundred volunteer groups of professionals and parents. Includes childbirth education classes;
publications centers; regional conferences; health-care referrals, on request; and special
needs/interests resource committees. Members' fee includes membership directory (annual), discounts at publication/distribution/supplies center, and subscription to ICEA news
(available for a small fee to nonmembers). ICEA Distribution Center, P.O. Box 9316, Midtown Plaza, Rochester, New York 14604, will send free catalog of books and audiovisual
materials (with price list) and low-cost pamphlets on breast feeding and related information.

La Leche League International
9616 Minneapolis Avenue
Franklin Park, Illinois 60131
(312) 455-7730

The league, founded in 1956, has over sixty thousand members worldwide. This organization has been a major factor in reviving breast feeding. Through more than four thousand
chapters, it encourages mothers on breast feeding, and gives them specific instructions on
how to do so. In local communities, mothers—and babies—meet weekly to discuss problems with a La Leche leader in charge of each session. Area meetings are addressed by
members of the Medical Advisory Board (thirty-seven specialists in breast feeding and
related fields). Membership in the league includes the LLL *News*. A manual, *The Womanly
Art of Breastfeeding*, is available. Publications are one hundred titles on feeding and child-
care.

March of Dimes Birth Defects Foundation
1275 Mamaroneck Avenue
White Plains, New York 10605
(914) 428-7100

The March of Dimes, with 1,125 chapters, in every state, estimates that 250,000 children
each year are born with congenital birth defects, including low birth-weight. The organization sponsors research and preventive medical service programs to combat this serious
problem. There are March of Dimes-supported programs at medical centers, hospitals, and
clinics to help give pregnant women preventive care. The organization has sponsored vaccination drives against rubella and the Rh factor. It funds genetic-counseling services. It
helps fund and develop special intensive-care units for newborns in medical centers
throughout the United States and has educational materials and programs in schools for
parents-to-be. A publication list is available.

Maternity Center Association
48 East 92nd Street
New York, New York 10028
(212) 369-7300

MCA operates an out-of-hospital maternity service and childbirth center for low-risk families. A membership of three hundred supports the association by contributions. MCA has
pioneered Self-Help Education Initiated in Childbirth (SHEIC), a part of its ongoing pro-

gram of information service to expectant families. Three obstetricians and attendant midwives staff the center, which publishes many booklets and a monthly magazine newsletter (*Briefs*) of the latest maternity and child-care developments. Information on this and other center publications available on request. MCA also has established a new program of helping to replicate such centers. With the aid of a grant from the John H. Hartford Foundation, MCA now sponsors the Cooperative Birth Center Network.

National Association for the Advancement of Leboyer's Birth Without Violence, Inc.
P.O. Box 248455
Coral Gables, Florida 33124
(305) 665-9506

This is the national membership organization supporting Leboyer techniques of childbirth. It publishes a newsletter and other printed matter free for members, and sponsors film showings, discussions, and printed material on gentle birthing. A list of Leboyer doctors is available through the NAALBWV.

National Association of Parents and Professionals for Safe Alternatives in Childbirth
P.O. Box 267
Marble Hill, Missouri 63764
(314) 238-2010

Founded in 1975, this organization has 2,500 lay and professional (fifty percent each) members interested in alternative methods of maternity care—family-centered childbirth programs—including home-birth and birth centers. Choice is the key concept. Annual conferences draw participants from every state in the United States and from Canada. Publications of conference proceedings on childbirth practices are available for modest sums. NAPSAC acts as a referral service for expectant parents and consultant for professionals. It publishes a quarterly, tapes, and books. NAPSAC *Directory of Alternative Birth Services* and consumer guides contain names and addresses of training programs, physicians, midwives, and centers, and tips for evaluation of services.

National Genetics Foundation, Inc.
555 West 57th Street
New York, New York 10019
(212) 586-5800

The foundation arranges referrals to medical genetics centers for persons with genetic disorders or the possibility of genetic disorder. It provides and evaluates family health history questionnaires. A publications list of relevant pamphlets is available on request.

National HomeCaring Council
67 Irving Place
New York, New York 10003
(212) 674-4990

This organization was incorporated in 1962, and has six hundred members in every state who provide homemaker and home-health-aide services in their communities. This organization sets standards. Such aides are trained and supervised by their local agencies and work with a wide variety of people, young and old, sick and disabled. A homemaker or aide may be available in specific childbirth and infant-care situations, where there may be a social or a health problem. The council publishes a newsletter and other materials.

National Institute of Child Health and Human Development
Department of Health, Education and Welfare
9000 Rockville Pike
Rockville, Maryland 20814
(301) 496-4000

The institute, constituted in 1962, concentrates on disease prevention and the health of American children. Research areas include pregnancy, congenital abnormalities, childhood origins of adult disease, learning disorders, mental retardation, fertility and infertility, population dynamics. NICH publishes findings of its activities and conducts seminars and workshops. Information on publications and research interests is available from headquarters.

National Institute of Mental Health
5600 Fishers Lane
Parklawn Building, Room 17099
Rockville, Maryland 20859
(301) 443-4515 (public inquiries)

This federal agency is now supporting, among its many other programs, mental health programs in prenatal clinics. Children and adults with mental problems may be assisted at a local community mental health center. NIMH will answer requests for mental health information from the public; and pamphlets, brochures, and fliers are available. Upon request, NIMH will supply single free copies of publications on such subjects as the mental health of children, autism, and depression. It publishes a directory on facilities and programs for children with mental illness.

National Organization of Mothers of Twins Clubs
5402 Amberwood Lane
Rockville, Maryland 20853
(301) 460-9108

This group numbers 233 clubs and 8,625 members in the United States and Canada. Any parents of "multiples" (and sometimes adoptive mothers) may join. Promotes research and increased awareness. Quarterly newsletter (MOTC's *Notebook*) gives advice and support. *How to Organize a MOTC* (one dollar) and a leaflet *Your Twins and You* (no charge) are available from headquarters.

National Safety Council
444 North Michigan Avenue
Chicago, Illinois 60611
(312) 527-4800

The council has more than eleven thousand members and eighty-one accredited chapters nationwide. It is a national clearinghouse for information on accidents and ways to prevent them, and maintains a huge library of accident-prevention data. Publications include ten nationally distributed magazines and an extensive range of books and pamphlets. A publications list is available.

National Sudden Infant Death Syndrome Foundation
310 South Michigan Avenue
Chicago, Illinois 60604
(312) 663-0650

There are chapters of this organization in thirty-nine states. Members are parents and family of SIDS victims and those considered "high risks," and related professionals. Parent to parent contacts are available from all chapters. The newsletter *The Tree of Hope* is published twice yearly. A publications list of pamphlets and fliers about SIDS and educational programs on SIDS and related issues are available on request.

National Women's Health Network
224 Seventh Street SE
Washington, D.C. 20003
(202) 543-9222

This organization represents more than 1,000 local women's-health groups, projects, centers, clinics, health professionals, and consumers. It publishes *Network News* bimonthly and Newsalerts to announce hearings, legislation, meetings, and more. You can get up-to-date health and medical information from this group, as well as local and national contacts.

Parents Without Partners, Inc.
7910 Woodmont Avenue
Bethesda, Maryland 20014
(301) 654-8850

Any single parent (some grandparents attend meetings) of a living child is eligible to join this 170,000-member organization with one thousand chapters in fifty states and Canada. Local volunteer groups help member-parents and children through programs of family, educational, and adult activities. Information on community workshops, seminars, support groups, legal research, and publications are available on request, as well as location of nearest chapter. Publications lists of inexpensive material directed to single parents are available from the international office.

Resources in Human Nurturing, International
3885 Forest Street
Denver, Colorado 80207
(303) 388-4608

RHNI's membership (ninety-five percent professionals in maternal and child health) enables it to schedule seminars and classes in breast feeding in several cities; provides reference and referral services to help those who may have problems with breast feeding. It also provides consultation and aids in human lactation studies. It publishes *Journal of Human Nurturing* four times a year, containing commentary and articles on human nurturing, and a quarterly newsletter, *RHNI Bulletin*. Schedule of meetings on breast feeding and other areas of mother and infant health is available. Distributes Lact-Aid nursing supplementer.

The Salvation Army
National Headquarters
50 West 23rd Street
New York, New York 10010
(212) 255-9400

Since its founding in 1865 the Salvation Army has given emergency aid to the sick, needy, and homeless. Its efforts to provide care for young mothers without family or other resources have been expanded to include pregnancy testing, prenatal and postpartum care, and vocational and job-training guidance. There are twenty-six Salvation Army maternity homes. Child care is offered in Salvation Army and foster homes supervised by the Army's foster home and adoption service. There are almost ten thousand local SA centers throughout the United States, within reach of the telephone.

Society for Protection of the Unborn Through Nutrition
17 North Wabash Avenue
Chicago, Illinois 60602
(312) 332-2334

SPUN is a national organization whose goal is to educate expectant mothers and health-care professionals on the importance of prenatal nutrition. The organization acts as a clearinghouse to provide information on the adverse effects of restrictive dietary practices and is a source of referral for lawyers in relevant legal cases. SPUN members receive the newsletter, *The Pregnant Issue: Medicate or Educate?* Upon request, a list of members in specific areas (yours) will be mailed. SPUN will provide speakers for classes and workshops. Publications are available.

U.S. Consumer Product Safety Commission
Washington, D.C. 20207
(800) 638-8326 (toll-free)

This agency has been active since 1974. It performs research into the safety and effectiveness of various products, including furniture and toys, and operates the National Electronic Injury Surveillance System (NEISS). This system reports all product-related injuries in 119 hospital emergency rooms nationwide on a daily basis and has led to products being repaired or removed. A free *Catalog of Publications, Films and Slides* can be requested from the agency. This lists materials available to the public, including pamphlets on products and all kinds of safety issues inside and outside the home. The toll-free hotline can take orders for publications and complaints about product hazards or injuries. The numbers are:
Continental United States (800) 638-8326
Maryland only (800) 492-8363
Alaska, Hawaii, Puerto Rico, Virgin Islands (800) 638-8333

Bibliography

WOMEN

Boston Women's Health Book Collective. *Our Bodies, Ourselves: A Book By and For Women*. 2nd rev. ed. New York: Simon & Schuster, 1971.

Edry, Carol. Edited in cooperation with the Women's Action Alliance. *The Women's Yellow Pages: Original Sourcebook for Women*. New York: St. Martin's Press, 1978.

Grimstad, Kirsten, and Susan Rennie, eds. *The New Woman's Survival Catalog*. New York: Coward, McCann & Geoghegan, 1973.

Linde, Shirley. *The Whole Health Catalog: How to Stay Well Cheaper*. New York: Rawson Associates Publishers, 1977.

Paulsen, Kathryn, and Ryan A. Kuh, eds. and comps. *Woman's Almanac: Twelve How-to Handbooks in One*. Philadelphia: J.B. Lippincott Co., 1976.

Steiner, Shari. *The Female Factor: A Report on Women in Western Europe*. New York: G.P. Putnam's Sons, 1977.

PREGNANCY AND PRENATAL CARE—GENERAL

Brewer, Gail Sforza, ed. *The Pregnancy After Thirty Workbook*. Emmaus, Pa.: Rodale Press, 1978.

Flanagan, Geraldine Lux. *The First Nine Months of Life*. New York: Simon & Schuster, 1962.

Fleming, Alice. *Nine Months: An Intelligent Woman's Guide to Pregnancy*. New York: Stein & Day, 1972.

Hall, Robert E. *Nine Months' Reading: A Medical Guide for Pregnant Women*, rev. ed. Garden City, N.Y.: Doubleday & Co., 1963.

Hotchner, Tracy, *Pregnancy and Childbirth*. New York: Avon Books, 1979.

Marzollo, Jean, comp. *Nine Months, One Day, One Year: A Guide to Pregnancy, Birth, and Baby Care*. New York: Harper & Row, 1975.

Maternity Center Association. *A Baby is Born*. New York: Grosset & Dunlap, 1974.

Morton, Marcia Colman. *Pregnancy Notebook*. New York: Workman Publishing Co., 1972.

Nilsson, Lennart. *A Child is Born*, rev. ed. London: Faber & Faber, 1977.

Queenan, John T., ed. *A New Life: Pregnancy, Birth and Your Child's First Year*. New York: Van Nostrand Reinhold Co., 1979.

U.S. Department of Health, Education and Welfare, Office of Child Development, Children's Bureau. *Prenatal Care*, Bureau Publication No. 4. Washington, D.C.: U.S. Government Printing Office, 1973.

Wachstein, Alison Ehrlich. *Pregnant Moments: The Experience of Pregnancy and Childbirth*. Dobbs Ferry, N.Y.: Morgan & Morgan, 1979.

PREGNANCY AND PRENATAL CARE: BODY AND HEALTH

Abse, D. Wilfred, Ethel M. Nash, and Lois M.R. Louden. *Marital and Sexual Counseling in Medical Practice*, 2nd ed. New York: Harper & Row, 1974.

Bing, Elisabeth. *Making Love During Pregnancy*. New York: Bantam Books, 1977.

———. *Moving Through Pregnancy*. New York: Bantam Books, 1975.

Brewer, Gail Sforza, with Tom Brewer, *What Every Pregnant Woman Should Know: The Truth About Drugs in Pregnancy*. New York: Random House, 1977.

Cooke, Cynthia W., and Susan Dworkin. *The Ms. Guide to a Woman's Health*. Garden City, N.Y.: Doubleday & Co., Anchor Press, 1979.

Dilfer, Carol Stahmann. *Your Baby, Your Body: Fitness During Pregnancy*. New York: Crown Publishers, 1977.

Hartman, Rhondda Evans. *Exercises for True Natural Childbirth*. New York: Harper & Row, 1975.

Lauersen, Niels, and Steven Whitney. *It's Your Body: A Woman's Guide to Gynecology*. New York: Grosset & Dunlap, 1977.

Levin, Arthur. *Talk Back to Your Doctor: How to Demand (and Recognize) High-Quality Health Care*. Garden City, N.Y.: Doubleday & Co., 1975.

Mayer, Jean. *Health*. New York: D. Van Nostrand Co., 1974.

Noble, Elizabeth. *Essential Exercises for the Childbearing Years*. Boston: Houghton Mifflin Co., 1976.

Williams, Phyllis. *Nourishing Your Unborn Child*. New York: Avon Books, 1974.

Woods, Nancy Fugate. *Human Sexuality in Health and Illness*. St. Louis: C.V. Mosby Co., 1975.

PREPARING FOR PARENTHOOD

Bittman, Sam and Sue Rosenberg Zalk. *Expectant Fathers*. New York: Hawthorn Books, 1978.

Boston Children's Hospital Medical Center. *Pregnancy, Birth and the Newborn Baby: A Publication for Parents*. Delacorte Press, Seymour Lawrence Books, 1971.

Boston Women's Health Book Collective. *Ourselves and Our Children: A Book By and For Parents*. New York: Random House, 1979.

Cole, K.C. *What Only a Mother Can Tell You About Having a Baby*. New York: Doubleday & Co., Anchor Press, 1980.

DelliQuadri, Lyn, and Kati Breckenridge. *Mother Care: Helping Yourself Through the Emotional and Physical Transitions of New Motherhood*. Los Angeles: J.P. Tarcher, 1978.

Fabe, Marilyn, and Norma Wikler. *Up Against the Clock: Career Women Speak on the Choice to Have Children*. New York: Random House, 1979.

Guttmacher, Alan F. *Pregnancy and Birth: A Book for Expectant Parents*. New York: The Viking Press, 1956.

———. *Pregnancy, Birth, and Family Planning: A Guide for Expectant Parents in the 1970s*. New York: New American Library, 1973.

Kelly, Marguerite, and Elta Parsons. *The Mother's Almanac*. Garden City, N.Y.: Doubleday & Co., 1975.

Montagu, Ashley. *Touching: The Human Significance of the Skin*. New York: Columbia University Press, 1971.

Princeton Center for Infancy. *Parents' Yellow Pages*, ed. Frank Caplan. New York: Doubleday & Co., Anchor Books, 1978.

Salk, Dr. Lee. *Preparing for Parenthood: Understanding Your Feelings About Pregnancy, Childbirth, and Your Baby*. New York: David McKay Co., 1974.

Schultz, Terri. *Women Can Wait: The Pleasures of Motherhood After Thirty*. Garden City, N.Y.: Doubleday & Co., Dolphin Books, 1979.

CHILDBIRTH

American Journal of Nursing Co. *Maternal and Newborn Care: Nursing Interventions.* Continuing Nursing Series. New York, 1973.

American Society for Psychoprophylaxis in Obstetrics. *The Psychoprophylactic Method of Childbirth: An Introduction.* Washington, D.C., 1977.

Arms, Suzanne. *Immaculate Deception: A New Look at Women and Childbirth in America.* Boston: Houghton Mifflin Co., 1975.

Bean, Constance. *Labor and Delivery: An Observer's Diary: What You Should Know About Today's Childbirth.* New York: Doubleday & Co., 1977.

————. *Methods of Childbirth: A Complete Guide to Childbirth Classes and Maternity Care.* Garden City, N.Y.: Doubleday & Co., Dolphin Books, 1974.

Berezin, Nancy. *The Gentle Birth Book: A Practical Guide to Leboyer Family-Centered Delivery.* New York: Simon & Schuster, 1980.

Brennan, Barbara, and Joan Rattner Heilman. *The Complete Book of Midwifery.* New York: E.P. Dutton & Co., 1977.

Chock, Judy and Margaret Miner. *Birth.* New York: Thomas Y. Crowell Co., 1978.

Ewy, Donna, and Rodger Ewy. *Preparation for Childbirth: A Lamaze Guide,* rev. ed. New York: New American Library, Signet Books, 1976.

Feldman, Silvia. *Choices in Childbirth.* New York: Grosset & Dunlap, 1978.

Haire, Doris. *The Cultural Warping of Childbirth.* Seattle: International Childbirth Education Association, 1972.

Klaus, Marshall, and John Kennell. *Maternal-Infant Bonding.* St. Louis: C.V. Mosby Co., 1976.

Klaus, Marshall H., Treville Leger, and Mary Anne Trause, eds. *Maternal Attachment and Mothering Disorders: A Round Table.* Sausalito, Calif.: Johnson & Johnson Baby Products Co., 1975.

McCleary, Elliott H. *New Miracles of Childbirth: What Medicine Is Doing to Make Childbearing Safer and Easier.* New York: David McKay Co., 1974.

Obstetrical Practices in the United States. Washington: U.S. Government Printing Office, 1978.

Stewart, David, and Lee Stewart, eds. *Safe Alternatives in Childbirth.* Chapel Hill, N.C.: National Association of Parents and Professionals for Safe Alternatives in Childbirth (hereafter cited as NAPSAC), 1976.

————., eds. *21st Century Obstetrics, Now!,* Vols. 1 and 2. Chapel Hill, N.C.: NAPSAC, 1977.

Walker, Morton, Bernice Yoffe, and Parke H. Gray. *The Complete Book of Birth.* New York: Simon & Schuster, 1979.

Wright, Erna. *The New Childbirth.* New York: Simon & Schuster, Pocket Books, 1971.

CESAREAN BIRTH

Donovan, Bonnie, and Ruth Allen. *The Cesarean Birth Experience.* New York: Beacon Press, 1977.

Hausknecht, Richard, and Joan Rattner Heilman. *Having a Cesarean Baby.* New York: E.P. Dutton & Co., 1978.

Wilson, Christine Coleman, and Wendy Roe Hovey. *Cesarean Childbirth.* New York: Doubleday & Co., Dolphin Books, 1977.

HOME BIRTH

Brooks, Tony, and Linda Bennet. *Giving Birth at Home.* Cerritos, Calif.: Association for Childbirth at Home International, 1976.

Hazell, Lester Dessez. *Birth Goes Home*. Chapel Hill, N.C.: NAPSAC, 1978.
Home Oriented Maternity Experience: A Comprehensive Guide to Home Birth. Washington, D.C.: HOME, 1976.
Sousa, Marion. *Childbirth at Home*. New York: Bantam Books, 1977.
Ward, Charlotte, and Fred Ward. *The Home Birth Book*. Garden City, N.Y.: Doubleday & Co., 1977.

NATURAL BIRTH

Bradley, Robert A. *Husband-Coached Childbirth*, rev. ed. New York: Harper & Row, 1974.
Bing, Elisabeth. *The Adventure of Birth: Experiences in the Lamaze Method of Prepared Childbirth*. New York: Ace Books, 1970.
————. *Six Practical Lessons for an Easier Childbirth*, rev. ed. New York: Bantam Books, 1977.
Dick-Read, Grantly. *Childbirth Without Fear: The Original Approach to Natural Childbirth*, 4th ed. rev. by Helen Wessel and Harlan F. Ellis. New York: Harper & Row, 1978.
————. *Childbirth Without Fear: The Principles and Practice of Natural Childbirth*, 2nd ed. rev. New York: Harper & Bros., 1959.
Kitzinger, Sheila. *The Experience of Childbirth*, 4th ed. New York: Penguin Books, 1978.
————. *Giving Birth: The Parents' Emotions in Childbirth*. New York: Taplinger Publishing Co., 1971.
Lamaze, Fernand. *Painless Childbirth: Psychoprophylactic Method*, trans. L.R. Celectin. New York: Simon & Schuster, Pocket Books, 1977.
Leboyer, Frederick. *Birth Without Violence*. New York: Alfred A. Knopf, 1975.
Tanzer, Deborah, with Jean Libman Block. *Why Natural Childbirth: A Psychologist's Report on the Benefits to Mothers, Fathers and Babies*. New York: Schocken Books, 1972.
Walton, Vicki E. *Have It Your Way: An Overview of Pregnancy, Labor and Postpartum, Including Alternatives Available in the Hospital Childbirth Experience*. New York: Bantam Books, 1978.
Wolberg, Lewis R. *Hypnosis: Is It For You?* New York: Harcourt Brace Jovanovich, 1972.

BREAST FEEDING

American College of Obstetricians and Gynecologists. *Guidelines on Pregnancy and Work*. Chicago, 1977.
Eiger, Marvin S., and Sally Wendkos Olds. *The Complete Book of Breastfeeding*. New York: Workman Publishing Co., 1972.
Gerard, Alice. *Please Breast-Feed Your Baby*. New York: New American Library, 1970.
Harris, Stephanie G., and Joseph H. Highland. *Birthright Denied: The Risks and Benefits of Breast Feeding*. Washington, D.C.: Environmental Defense Fund, 1977.
Raphael, Dana. *The Tender Gift: Breastfeeding*. New York: Schocken Books, 1976.
La Leche League International. *The Womanly Art of Breastfeeding*, 2nd ed. Franklin Park, Ill., 1963.
Richardson, Frank Howard. *The Nursing Mother: A Guide to Successful Breast Feeding*. New York: Prentice-Hall, 1953.

THE WORKING MOTHER

Cotton, Dorothy Whyte. *The Case for the Working Mother*. New York: Stein & Day, 1965.
Fraiberg, Selma. *The Magic Years: Understanding and Handling the Problems of Early Childhood*. New York: Charles Scribner's Sons, 1968.
Skelsey, Alice. *The Working Mother's Guide to Her Home, Her Family and Herself*. New York: Random House, 1970.

Stellman, Jeanne Mager. *Women's Work, Women's Health: Myths and Realities*. New York: Pantheon Books, 1977.

U.S. Senate, Ninety-fifth Congress. *Discrimination on the Basis of Pregnancy, 1977, Hearings before the Subcommittee on Labor of the Committee on Human Resources*. Washington, D.C.: U.S. Government Printing Office, 1977.

NAMING THE BABY

Browder, Sue. *The New Age Baby Name Book*. New York: Workman Publishing Co., 1974.

Rule, Lareina. *Name Your Baby*. New York: Bantam Books, 1963.

Smith, Elsdon C. *Naming Your Baby*. New York: Greenberg Publishers, 1943.

Wells, Evelyn. *What to Name the Baby*. New York: Doubleday & Co., 1953.

INFANT AND CHILD CARE

Baumgartner, Leona, Susan Aukema, and Marilyn Kostick. *The Parents' Guide to Baby Care*. New York: Grosset & Dunlap, 1977.

Brazelton, T. Berry. *Infants and Mothers*. New York: Delacorte Press, 1969.

Comer, James P., and Alvin F. Poussaint. *Black Child Care: How to Bring Up a Healthy Black Child in America*. New York: Simon & Schuster, Pocket Books, 1976.

Consumer Guide editorial staff. *The Complete Baby Book*. New York: Simon & Schuster, Fireside Books, n.d.

Levy, Janine. *The Baby Exercise Book: For the First Fifteen Months,* trans. from French by Eva Gleasure. New York: Pantheon Books, 1973.

Pomeranz, Virginia, and Dodi Schultz. *Mothers' and Fathers' Medical Encyclopedia*. New York: New American Library, 1977.

Prudden, Bonnie. *How to Keep Your Child Fit from Birth to Six*. New York: Harper & Row, 1964.

Rivers, Peg, ed. *My Baby's Book of Child Health: The Infant and Toddler Years*. New York: Crane Publishing Co., 1971.

Samson, Joan. *Watching the New Baby*. New York: Atheneum Publishers, 1974.

Smith, Lendon. *Feed Your Kids Right*. New York: Delta Books, 1980.

Spock, Benjamin. *Baby and Child Care*, rev. ed. New York: Hawthorn Books, 1976.

Stoppard, Miriam. *Book of Baby Care*. New York: Atheneum Publishers, 1977.

Stoutt, Glenn, Jr. *The First Month of Life: A Parents' Guide to Care of the Newborn*, ed. Marvyn Womack. Oradell, N.J.: Medical Economics Co., 1978.

U.S. Department of Health, Education and Welfare, Office of Human Development, Office of Child Development, Children's Bureau. *Infant Care*. Washington, D.C.: U.S. Government Printing Office, 1974.

The U.S. Government Book of Infant Care. New York: Award Books, 1968.

INFANT AND CHILD GROWTH AND BEHAVIOR

Camper, Shirley. *How to Get Along With Your Child*. New York: Belmont Books, 1962.

Caplan, Frank, ed. *The First Twelve Months of Life: Your Baby's Growth Month by Month*. New York: Grosset & Dunlap, 1973.

Church, Joseph. *Understanding Your Child From Birth to Three: A Guide to Your Child's Psychological Development*. New York: Random House, 1973.

Fraiberg, Selma H. *The Magic Years*. New York: Charles Scribner's Sons, Lyceum Edition, 1968.

Gordon, Ira. J. *The Infant Experience*. Columbus, Ohio: Charles E. Merrill Publishing Co., 1975.

Howe, Michael. *Learning in Infants and Young Children*. Stanford, Calif.: Stanford University Press, 1975.

Hymes, James L. *The Child Under Six*. Englewood Cliffs, N.J.: Prentice-Hall, 1963.

Ilg, Frances L., and Louise Bates Ames. *Child Behavior from Birth to Teen*. New York: Harper & Row, 1955.

Jackson, Jane Flannery, and Joseph H. Jackson. *Infant Culture*. New York: Thomas Crowell Co., 1978.

Leach, Penelope. *Babyhood: Stage by Stage, From Birth to Age Two: How Your Baby Develops Physically, Emotionally, Mentally*. New York: Alfred A. Knopf, 1976.

Mahler, Margaret S., Fred Pine, and Anni Bergman. *The Psychological Birth of the Human Infant: Symbiosis and Individuation*. New York: Basic Books, 1975.

Marzollo, Jean, and Janice Lloyd. *Learning Through Play*. New York: Harper & Row, 1972.

———. *Supertot: Creative Learning Activities for Children from One to Three and Sympathetic Advice for Their Parents*. New York: Harper & Row, 1977.

Soman, Shirley Camper. *Let's Stop Destroying Our Children*. New York: Hawthorn Books, 1974.

———. *You and Your Baby*. Boston: John Hancock Society, 1965.

Stone, L. Joseph, Henrietta T. Smith, and Lois B. Murphy, eds. The Competent Infant Series. Vol. 1, *Behavior of the Newborn: Prenatal and Perinatal Influences*. Vol. 2, *The Infant's First Year: Learning and Development;* Vol. 3, *The Social Infant*. New York: Basic Books, 1978.

White, Burton L. *The First Three Years of Life*. Englewood Cliffs, N.J.: Prentice-Hall, 1975.

Yahraes, Herbert. *Developing a Sense of Competence in Young Children*, U.S. Department of Health, Education and Welfare Publication No. ADM 78-643. Washington, D.C.: U.S. Government Printing Office, 1978.

COMPLICATIONS—BIRTH DEFECTS

Apgar, Virginia, and Joan Beck. *Is My Baby All Right? A Guide to Birth Defects*. New York: Simon & Schuster, Pocket Books, 1972.

Greenblatt, Augusta and I.J. *Your Genes and Your Destiny*. New York: Bobbs-Merrill, 1979.

Wicka, Donna Konkel, and Mervyn L. Falk. *Advice to Parents of a Cleft Palate Child*. Springfield, Ill.: Charles C. Thomas, Publisher, 1970.

CHILDREN AT HOME

Arena, Jay M., and Miriam Bacher. *Child Safety Is No Accident: A Parents' Handbook of Emergencies*. Durham, N.C.: Duke University Press, 1978.

———. *Dangers to Children and Youth*. Durham, N.C.: Moore Publishing Co., 1971.

Clopper, Irene. *Growing Up With Toys*. Minneapolis: Augsburg Publishing House, 1974.

Cohen, Maurice. *Making Children's Furniture With Hand Tools*. New York: Drake Publishers, 1978.

Consumer Guide. *Whole House Catalog*. New York: Simon & Schuster, 1976.

Consumers Union of the United States. *Guide to Buying for Babies*. Mount Vernon, N.Y., 1975.

Fontana, Vincent J. *A Parents' Guide to Child Safety*. New York: Thomas Y. Crowell Co., 1973.

German, Don, and Joan German. *Make Your Own Convenience Foods*. New York: Macmillan Publishing Co., 1979.

Gilson, Hilary. *Children About the House*. London: Design Council, 1976.

Green, Martin I., producer. *A Sigh of Relief: The First-Aid Handbook for Childhood Emergencies*. New York: Bantam Books, 1977.

Harmon, Murl. *A New Vaccine for Child Safety*. Jenkintown, Pa.: Safety Now Co., 1976.

Jones, Sandy. *Good Things for Babies*. Boston: Houghton Mifflin Co., 1976.

Lawson, Donna, and Jean Conlon. *Superbaby Cookbook*. New York: Macmillan Publishing Co., 1974.

McDonald, Linda. *Baby's Recipe Book*. New York: A.S. Barnes & Co., 1972.

Mandell, Mel. *Being Safe*. New York: Saturday Review Press, 1972.

Palmer, Bruce. *Making Children's Furniture and Play Structures*. New York: Workman Publishing Co., 1974.

Sunset Books. *Children's Rooms and Play Yards,* 2nd ed. Menlo Park, Calif.: Lane Publishing Co., 1977.

Turner, Mary Dustan, and James S. Turner. *Making Your Own Baby Food,* rev., updated, expanded ed. New York: Workman Publishing Co., 1976.

Weiss, Mark. *Free for Baby and Mother: An Encyclopedia of Things Available to Parent and Child at No Cost*. New York: A.S. Barnes and Co., 1972.

NUTRITION

Bieler, Henry G. *Food Is Your Best Medicine*. New York: Random House, Vintage Books, 1973.

Clark, Linda A. *Know Your Nutrition*. New Canaan, Conn.: Keats Publishing, 1973.

Davis, Adelle. *Let's Have Healthy Children,* rev. expanded ed. New York: Harcourt Brace Jovanovich, 1972.

Lappe, Frances Moore. *Diet for a Small Planet,* rev. ed. New York: Random House, Ballantine Books, 1975.

Wade, Carlson. *Vitamins and Other Food Supplements and Your Health*. New Canaan, Conn.: Keats Publishing, 1974.

Watson, George. *Nutrition and Your Mind*. New York: Bantam Books, 1974.

Williams, Roger J. *Nutrition Against Disease*. New York: Bantam Books, 1973.

HISTORY AND MYTH

Aries, Philippe. *Centuries of Childhood: A Social History of Family Life,* trans. Robert Baldick. New York: Vintage Books, 1962.

Beeton, Isabella. *Beeton's Book of Household Management*. London, 1861. Reprint. New York: Farrar, Straus & Giroux, 1969.

Bel Geddes, Joan. *Small World: A History of Baby Care from the Stone Age to the Spock Age*. New York: Macmillan Publishing Co., 1964.

Buchan, William. *Domestic Medicine*. Philadelphia, 1809.

Bull, Thomas, M.D. *Hints to Mothers*. New York, 1853.

Bundesen, Herman N. *Our Babies: Their Feeding, Care and Training*. Chicago: Bowman Dairy Co., 1946.

deMause, Lloyd, ed. *The History of Childhood*. New York: Psychohistory Press, 1974.

Drake, Mrs. Emma Angell. *What a Young Wife Ought to Know*. Philadelphia: Vir Publishing Co., 1901.

Eastman, Nicholson J. *Expectant Motherhood,* 2nd ed. rev. Boston: Little, Brown & Co., 1947.

The Female Instructor or Young Woman's Companion. Liverpool, 1811.

Findley, Dr. Palmer. *The Story of Childbirth*. Garden City, N.Y.: Doubleday, Doran & Co., 1933.

Grotberg, Edith H., ed. *Two Hundred Years of Child Health in America,* U.S. Department of Health, Education and Welfare Publication No. OHD 77-30103. Washington, D.C.: U.S. Government Printing Office, 1977.

Harland, Marion. *Eve's Daughters: or, Common Sense for Maid, Wife and Mother*. New York: Charles Scribner's Sons, 1885.

Haskell, Arnold, and Min Lewis. *Infantilia*. London: Dobson Books, 1971.

Hunt, David. *Parents and Children in History: The Psychology of Family Life in Early Modern France*. New York: Bantam Books, 1970.

Leach, Maria, ed. *Dictionary of Folklore Mythology and Legend*. New York: Funk & Wagnalls, 1949.

Litoff, Lucy Barrett. *American Midwives: 1860 to the Present*. Westport, Conn.: Greenwood Press, 1977.

Lowry, Edith B. *Your Baby: A Guide for Young Mothers*. Chicago: Forbes & Co., 1915.

Napheys, George H. *The Physical Life of Women: Advice to the Maiden, Wife and Mother*. Philadelphia, 1889.

Pliny. *Natural History*. Cambridge, Mass.: Harvard University Press, 1942.

Read, Mary L. *The Mothercraft Manual*. Boston: Little, Brown and Co., 1921.

Rongy, A.J., M.D. *Childbirth Yesterday and Today*. New York: Emerson Books, 1937.

Sherwood, Mary E.W. (Mrs. John). *Manners and Social Usages*. New York: Harper & Bros., 1887.

Speert, Harold. *Iconographia Gyniatrica: A Pictorial History of Gynecology and Obstetrics*. Philadelphia: F.A. Davis Co., 1973.

Strassfeld, Sharon, and Michael Strassfeld, eds. *Second Jewish Catalog*. Philadelphia: Jewish Publications Society of America, 1976.

U.S. Department of Labor, Children's Bureau. *Infant Care*, Bureau Publication No. 8. Washington, D.C.: U.S. Government Printing Office, 1914.

U.S. Department of Labor, Children's Bureau. *Prenatal Care*, Bureau Publication No. 4. Washington, D.C.: U.S. Government Printing Office, 1913.

Weiser, Francis X. *Handbook of Christian Feasts and Customs*. New York: Harcourt, Brace & Co., 1952.

Wertz, Richard W., and Dorothy C. Wertz. *Lying-In: A History of Childbirth in America*. New York: The Free Press, 1977.

Wood-Allen, Mrs. Mary. *What a Young Woman Ought to Know*. Philadelphia: Vir Publishing Co., 1913.

Woolfolk, William, and Joanna Woolfolk. *The Great American Birth Rite*. New York: The Dial Press, 1975.

BIOLOGICAL

Price, Jane. *You're Not Too Old to Have a Baby*. New York: Farrar, Straus & Giroux, 1977.

Rorvik, David M., and Landrum B. Shettles. *Choose Your Baby's Sex: The One Sex-Solution Method that Works*. New York: Dodd, Mead & Co., 1977.

———. *Your Baby's Sex: Now You Can Choose*. New York: Dodd, Mead & Co., 1970.

Tanner, James M., and Gordon Rattray Taylor, and the editors of *Life*. *Growth*. New York: Time Inc., 1965.

FURTHER READING FOR PARENTS

Atkin, Edith, and Estelle Rubin. *Part-Time Father*. New York: New American Library, 1976.

Babcock, Dorothy E., and Terry D. Keepers. *Raising Kids O.K.: Transactional Analysis in Human Growth Development*. New York: Avon Books, 1977.

Bettelheim, Bruno. *Dialogues with Mothers*. New York: The Free Press, 1962.

Brazelton, T. Berry. *Infants and Mothers: Differences in Development*. New York: Delacorte Press, 1969.

Biller, Henry B. *Father, Child and Sex Role: Paternal Determinants of Personality Development*. Lexington, Mass.: Heath Lexington Books, 1971.

Brekelbaum, Barbara, et al. *Your Guide to Services for Handicapped Children*. Chicago: Coordinating Council for Handicapped Children, n.d.

Callahan, Sidney Cornelia. *Parenting: Principles and Politics of Parenthood.* Garden City, N.Y.: Doubleday & Co., 1973.

De Rosis, Helen. *Parent Power/Child Power.* Indianapolis: The Bobbs-Merrill Co., 1974.

Dodson, Fitzhugh. *How to Father.* New York: Nash Publishing Corp., 1974.

———. *How to Parent.* New York: New American Library, 1971.

Egleson, Jim, and Janet Frank Egleson. *Parents Without Partners.* New York: Ace Books, 1961.

Faber, Adele, and Elaine Mazlish. *Liberated Parents—Liberated Children.* New York: Avon Books, 1974.

Gatley, Richard H., and David Koulack. *Single Fathers: A Guide for Separated and Divorced Fathers.* New York: Doubleday & Co., Anchor Press, 1979.

Ginott, Haim G. *Between Parent and Child: New Solutions to Old Problems.* New York: Avon Books, 1965.

Gilbert, Sara D. *What's a Father For?* New York: Parents' Magazine Press, 1975.

Goode, Ruth. *A Book for Grandmothers.* New York: Macmillan Publishing Co., 1976.

Honan, William E. *Child Sense: A Guide to Loving, Level-Headed Parenthood,* rev. ed. New York: Basic Books, 1977.

Ilg, Frances L., and Louise Bates Ames. *Parents Ask.* New York: Harper & Bros., 1962.

Klein, Carole. *The Single Parent Experience.* New York: Avon Books, 1973.

Levine, James A. *Who Will Raise the Children: New Options for Fathers (and Mothers).* Philadelphia: J.B. Lippincott Co., 1976.

Liedloff, Jean. *The Continuum Concept.* New York: Alfred A. Knopf, 1975.

McBride, Angela Barron. *The Growth and Development of Mothers.* New York: Harper & Row, 1973.

McFadden, Michael. *Bachelor Fatherhood: How to Raise and Enjoy Your Children as a Single Parent.* New York: Walker & Co., 1974.

Salk, Dr. Lee. *What Every Child Would Like His Parents to Know.* New York: David McKay Co., 1972.

Scharlatt, Elisabeth L., ed. *Kids Day In and Day Out: A Parents' Manual.* New York: Simon & Schuster, 1979.

Shedd, Charlie W. *The Best Dad Is a Good Lover.* New York: Avon Books, 1977.

———. *Smart Dads I Know.* New York: Avon Books, 1975.

Sullivan, S. Adams. *The Father's Almanac.* New York: Doubleday & Co., Dolphin Books, 1980.

Weinstein, Grace. *Children and Money: A Guide For Parents.* New York: Schocken Books, 1975.

The Woman's Almanac. Philadelphia: J.B. Lippincott, 1976.

Young, Hope. *MOMMA: The Sourcebook for Single Mothers,* eds. Carol Young and Nancy Young. New York: New American Library, 1976.

Young, Leontine. *The Fractured Family.* New York: McGraw-Hill Book Co., 1973.

Index

Infant seats, 183
Infections and diseases, 50, 241,
        263. *See also* specific
        problems
    and breast feeding, 266
Insurance, 85–87
Intelligence (intellectual de-
        velopment), 12, 42. *See
        also* Brain; Mental retar-
        dation
Intercom, 204
Internal examinations, 14–15
International Childbirth Edu-
        cation Association, 325
Intravenous feeding, 137
Inverted nipples, 157
Italians, 67–68

Jaundice, 241, 263
Jewish ceremonies, 288–89
Jobs. *See* Working

Karyotyping, 18
Kibbutzim, 72–73

Labor. *See* Birth; Premature
        babies
Ladders, emergency, 205
La Leche League, 156, 247, 325
Lamaze, Fernand (Lamaze
        Method), 100, 101, 126,
        322
Language development, 293
Lanugo, xv, 241
Late births, 259
Laxatives, 50
Lead poisoning, 195, 198–99
Learning, 298, 299
    disabilities, 144
Leboyer, Frederick, 102–4, 238,
        273–74, 326
Leg problems, 40
Leukemia, 52
"Lightening," 219
Liquids, 44

March of Dimes Birth Defects
        Foundation, 325
Marijuana, 50
Maternity Center Association,
        115–16, 325–26

Maternity leave. *See* Working
Meats, 43
Meconium, 268
Medications. *See* Drugs
Medicine chests, 204
    babies', 201
Megavitamins, 50
Menstruation, 250
    and arrival date, 11
Mental retardation, 12, 48, 144,
        148
Midwives, 91, 97, 232. *See also*
        Nurse-midwives
Milk and milk products, 43. *See
        also* Feeding
Minerals, 43
Miscarriage. *See also* Genetics
    aspirin and, 50
    and job hazards, 68–69
Money, 82–87
    costs of parenthood, 83–84,
        85, 94
    costs of premature care, 265
    dollar-wise pregnancy, 84–85
    insurance, 85–88
    new family budget, 82–83
    and working. *See* Working
Mongolism (Down's syn-
        drome), 17, 19
Morning sickness (nausea), 12,
        38–40, 44
Mothers-in-law, and the deliv-
        ery, 223
Moving, 192–96
Multiple births, 254–58, 327
    and complications, 257
    and nursing, 257–58

Names, 214–18
    around the world, 215–16
    Jewish naming rite, 288
    most popular, 218
Narcotics, 50
National Association for the
        Advancement of
        Leboyer's Birth Without
        Violence, Inc., 104, 326
National Association of Parents
        and Professionals for
        Safe Alternatives in
        Childbirth, 92, 106–107,
        121–22, 326
National Commission on
        Working Women, 71
National Genetics Foundation,
        Inc., 326

National HomeCaring Council,
        326
National Institute of Child
        Health and Human De-
        velopment, 327
National Institute of Mental
        Health, 327
National Institute of Occupa-
        tional Safety and Health,
        69
National Organization for
        Women (NOW), 72
National Organization of
        Mothers of Twins Clubs,
        327
National Safety Council, 327
National Sudden Infant Death
        Foundation, 328
National Women's Health Net-
        work, 328
Natural childbirth. *See* Pre-
        pared Childbirth
Nausea. *See* Morning sickness
Neighborhoods. *See* Moving;
        Environment
Nitrous oxide, 68–69
Nurse-midwives, 91, 92, 96–97,
        111 ff., 321
Nursery, 197–201. *See also*
        specific equipment
    all about, 197–99
    elements for, 197
    for growing up, 200
    kitchen equipment to or-
        ganize, 200–1
    things for medicine chest, 201
Nurses, baby, 209–10
Nursing. *See* Breast feeding
Nutrition (diet; eating; food),
        12, 25, 42–48, 324, 325
    babies and. *See* Breast feed-
        ing; Bottle feeding;
        Feeding
    dos and don'ts for food, 46
    intravenous feeding, 137
    need for iron, 43
    need for supplements, 44
    need for vitamins A and C
        and folic acid, 44–45
    and prematures, 260–61
    and sex of baby, 7
    watching weight, 45–48
    what to eat, 43–44

Obstetricians, 91 ff. *See also*
        Birth

Sleeping pills, 50
Smell, sense of, 291
Smoke alarm, 204
Smoking, 50, 51
Social development, 291–92
Society for Protection of the
   Unborn Through Nutri-
   tion, 329
Sodium bicarbonate, 50
Sonography. *See* Ultrasonic
   scanning
Sound, 292. *See also* Hearing
Sound waves. *See* Ultrasonic
   scanning
Space, need for, 191
Special children. *See* Birth de-
   fects
Speculum, 14
Speech. *See* Talking
Sperm. *See* Conception
Spinal anesthetic, 130
Spoiling babies, 304
Stairs, and safety, 205
Stillbirth. *See also* Genetics;
   Premature babies
   aspirin and, 50
Stimulation, 291. *See also*
   Senses
Stools, birthing, 143
Strawberry marks, 241
Stretch marks, 49
Stroking, 243
Strollers, 183
Suctioning, 140, 234
Supplements, vitamin, 44
Swedes, and birth, 104–5
Swimming childbirth, 104

Talking (speech), 243, 300
   language development, 293
Taste, 291
Tax savings, 85
Tea, 50
Teen-age pregnancy, 260–61

Teeth, care of, 25
Telephone and numbers list,
   205
Temperament, 293–99
Temperature, 303. *See also* Pre-
   mature babies
Thyroid, 148
Tiredness. *See* Fatigue; Rest;
   Sleep and sleeping
Touch, sense of, 291
Toxoplasmosis, 50
Toys, 186–90, 301
Training for parenting, 308–309
Tranquilizers, 50, 53
Transverse presentation, 267
Travel, 74–76. *See also* Moving
   equipment for babies,
   175–76, 182–85
Triplets, 254
Twins, 254–58, 327

Ultrasonic scanning, 18, 20–21
Ultrasound. *See* Fetal monitor-
   ing; Ultrasonic scanning
Umbilical cord, 5, 8, 232 ff., 302
   in breech birth, 267
   clamping, cutting, 140, 234
Underwear, maternity, 78–79
U.S. Consumer Product Safety
   Commission, 329
Uterus. *See also* Birth; Concep-
   tion
   after delivery, 235

Vacations, 74–76
Vagina. *See also* Episiotomies;
   Sex
   in delivery, 227–32
Varicose veins, 40
Vegetables, 43–44, 46
Vegetarians, 46

Venereal disease, 12
Vernix, xv, 241
Visitors, infants' need, 300–11
Vitamins, 43–45, 150
   megavitamins, 50
Vomiting, 301–2. *See also*
   Morning sickness

Walkers, baby, 188
Walls, nursery, 198, 199
Waterproof pads, sheets, 180
Weight, 45–48
   babies', 263
   how it breaks down, 47
   how much to weigh, 47–48
   and salt, 47
Well-being, sense of, 12–13
Windows, 199, 205, 206
Women's Economic Round
   Table, 71
Working, 31, 64–73, 167
   author's opinion, 72–73
   baby now, work later, 70–71
   checklist, 67
   hidden job hazards, 68–69
   job rights, 70
   no need to stagnate, 72
   and nursing, 65, 152–53 ff.
   should you keep on, 64–66
   support for mothers, 71–72

X chromosomes, 16, 17, 18
X rays, 51–52
Xylocaine, 131

Y chromosomes, 16, 17

Zygote, xiii, 8